THE AUTHORS

Former record producer Andrew Calcutt is a lecturer, journalist and broadcaster whose previous publications include *Arrested Development: pop culture and the erosion of adulthood*, *Beat: the iconography of victim culture from the Beat Generation to Princess Diana*, and *White Noise: an A-Z of the contradictions in cyberculture*.

He fronts a 'free and easy listening trio', The Smokers, and never spends enough time with his family.

Richard Shephard was born into a literary family; his mother worked as a researcher in the London Library and then at Foyles bookshop.

He co-edited the *Waterstone's Guide to Crime Fiction* and is currently managing editor of the Waterstone's website.

CULT FICTION

a reader's guide

Library of Congress Cataloging-in-Publication Data
is available from the United States Library of Congress.

Cover design by Andy Martin

This edition of *Cult Fiction* is published under license from Prion Books Limited, London, UK

First published in the United States in 1999 by Contemporary Books
A division of NTC/Contemporary Publishing Group, Inc.
4255 West Touhy Avenue, Lincolnwood (Chicago), Illinois 60646-1975 U.S.A.
Copyright © 1998 by Andrew Calcutt and Richard Shephard
Printed in Singapore
International Standard Book Number: 0-8092-2506-9
99 00 01 02 03 04   19 18 17 16 15 14 13 12 11 10 9 8 7 6 5 4 3 2 1

CULT
FICTION

a reader's guide

Andrew Calcutt
& Richard Shephard

CB
CONTEMPORARY BOOKS

CULT CONTENTS

Jean Genet	Herbert Huncke	Ted Lewis
Sylvie Germain	Aldous Huxley	Mark Leyner
William Gibson	Joris Karl Huysmans	Jack London
André Gide	John Irving	H P Lovecraft
Donald Goines	Tama Janowitz	Malcolm Lowry
William Golding	Sebastien Japrisot	Colin MacInnes
David Goodis	Alfred Jarry	Norman Mailer
Alasdair Gray	Jerome K Jerome	Dan Mannix
Radclyffe Hall	B S Johnson	William March
Patrick Hamilton	Erica Jong	Cormac McCarthy
Dashiell Hammett	James Joyce	Horace McCoy
Knut Hamsun	Franz Kafka	Carson McCullers
Jim Harrison	Anna Kavan	Ian McEwan
John Hawkes	James Kelman	Patrick McGrath
Nathan Heard	William Kennedy	Thomas McGuane
Richard Hell	Jack Kerouac	Jay McInerney
Joseph Heller	Gerald Kersh	Gustav Meyrink
Gil Scott Heron	Ken Kesey	Martin Millar
Hermann Hesse	Stephen King	Henry Miller
Carl Hiaasen	Jerzy Kosinski	Yukio Mishima
Chester Himes	Milan Kundera	Michael Moorcock
S E Hinton	Hanif Kureishi	Seth Morgan
John Clellon Holmes	Gavin Lambert	Walter Mosley
Stewart Home	Ring Lardner	Ryu Murakami
Nick Hornby	Sheridan Le Fanu	Robert Musil
Robert E Howard	Elmore Leonard	Vladimir Nabokov
Dorothy B Hughes	Doris Lessing	Anaïs Nin

< vii >

CULT FICTION

Jeff Noon
Flann O'Brien
Flannery O'Connor
Joyce Carol Oates
George Orwell
Dorothy Parker
Pier Paolo Pasolini
Mervyn Peake
Georges Perec
Robert M Pirsig
Sylvia Plath
Edgar Allan Poe
Richard Price
Thomas Pynchon
Raymond Queneau
Thomas de Quincey
Raymond Radiguet
Ayn Rand
Simon Raven
Derek Raymond
John Rechy
Ishmael Reed
Luke Rhinehart
Anne Rice
Rainer Maria Rilke
Tom Robbins
Henry Rollins

Damon Runyon
Leopold von Sacher-Masoch
J D Salinger
James Salter
Jean-Paul Sartre
Budd Schulberg
Bruno Schulz
Delmore Schwartz
Hubert Selby Jr
Will Self
Samuel Selvon
Mary Shelley
Alan Sillitoe
Herbert Simmons
Iain Sinclair
Iceberg Slim
Susan Sontag
Terry Southern
Gertrude Stein
Bruce Sterling
Robert Louis Stevenson
Bram Stoker
Robert Stone
D M Thomas
Jim Thompson
Hunter S Thompson

Newton Thornburg
John Kennedy Toole
Alexander Trocchi
Dalton Trumbo
Boris Vian
Gore Vidal
Kurt Vonnegut Jr
Keith Waterhouse
Denton Welch
Irvine Welsh
Nathanael West
Oscar Wilde
Charles Willeford
John A Williams
Colin Wilson
Jeanette Winterson
Thomas Wolfe
Tom Wolfe
Tobias Wolff
Cornell Woolrich
Richard Wright
Rudolph Wurlitzer

< viii >

Just what is cult fiction?

Back in the early seventies, popular culture began to be something that could be talked about with the reverence traditionally reserved for all things classical, and rock journalists started writing about bands who enjoyed a 'cult following'. This meant that while they were usually too 'difficult' for mainstream tastes and prejudices, they nevertheless occupied a central position in the lives of a devoted fanbase. There were quasi-religious overtones in the use of the phrase: these performers had been selected by a disparate community of people and held up as icons. Their work was interpreted as something like a sacred text, which carried within it an integral attitude to life, an alternative existential world-view. They were not just novel entertainers, they were auteurs whose canon of work built up a stylised outsider perspective from which to watch the modern world go by. While few people – Deadheads excepted – would admit to being part of a cult following, everyone more or less agreed that the phenomenon existed.

In tandem with the pop revolution and the rise of the counter-culture which helped collapse the distinctions between highbrow and lowbrow culture, there developed a similar notion of the cult author – read, admired and believed in the same way as their rock counterparts. Just as rock and pop offer an alternative world view to classical music so cult fiction offers an alternative and radical path to the recognised canon of high literature.

Cult fiction is a shaky concept at best and in no way finally quantifiable. It is a 'catholic church' and takes its authors from every denomination. Some, in fact, are arch-modernists culled from the aforementioned Literary Canon; avant-gardists whose narrative strategies break the rules and cross boundaries to question the very nature of reality. Yet the majority operate outside the traditional literary *conservatoire*. Cult fiction in its first instance came from (although it didn't know it at the time) the rise of the great cities which produced the mythical bohemian enclaves: the Left Bank in Paris, Greenwich Village in Manhattan and Soho in London, areas where artists lived shoulder to shoulder with the immigrant communities and the criminal fringe. They were places where the young and disaffected could find life with a raw edge and experiment with new lifestyles. As places of creative cross-pollination they continue as a subject and source of cult writing today. Other cult authors first operated in the pulp and popular margins and have only recently had their popular arts reappraised. Others are representatives of excluded minorities, whether black, gay or the politically extreme.

To attempt a definition, cult fiction is literature from the margins and extremes. It is usually a work that is written by or about, or gives voice to or imagines a section of society that is different (deviates/ transgresses) from the mainstream, and therefore offering a different angle on social reality. Deviance, as many criminologists have pointed out, is anything that is labelled as such. Likewise the deviant behaviour at the core of cult fiction can be anything that is seen as socially undesirable or unacceptable that unites a hidden community in recognition of a truth. This carries through from the benign (trainspotting or an unhealthy obsession with record collecting) to the truly malignant (satanic murder rituals). Of course the deviance need not involve any action at all and can be transgressive in thought alone, just so long as it dislocates the book, its protagonist(s) and its readers from the generally accepted world view of society at large. The targeting of a 'mainstream' is always a necessary simplification and, in a way, the definition of cult fiction we've described could be said to include all fiction – by nature an authorial consciousness is always outsider. Yet some views of the world are more skewed than others. In some cases the cult view is not from the margins at all but from other worlds altogether. Sci-fi and the fantastic imagine new worlds and spaces that both harbour the reader from our own world and cast a critical glance back.

By reading such books and identifying with their protagonists, readers of cult fiction then are identifying themselves as dislocated too. Readers seek to share the experience of alienation which cult fiction investigates. This is one view. But not every guy in a suit on the rush hour train reading a battered copy of *American Psycho* need necessarily be as unlovable as Patrick Bateman. Not every Bukowski fan need be an alcoholic. It is equally likely that in reading these works we are enjoying the experience of extremes vicariously without ever having to leave our mundane mainstream existence. Pure escapism. 'Reading the book' can cynically be seen as only a couple of notches up from 'buying the T-shirt' – literature as another 'lifestyle' decision. Others may read their cult fiction ironically or blankly taking the buzz and thrill but none of the philosophical intention. As we all know, there are as many ways to read as there are to write. Yet what is certain is we are all fascinated by life at its extremes, whether it be pushing sexual limits or understanding the mind of a mass murderer, because it is in this rarefied, uncoded atmosphere that human truths are to be found.

What, then, represents the social margins (or a transgression of the mainstream) in cult fiction? Essentially anyone who is not towing the line and has to pull against social norms in order to force themselves into being. The list of transgressives would have to include in no particular order: those perceived as sexual deviants (gay, lesbian, S&M, fetishists), gamblers, hustlers, grifters, drug users, drug dealers, political radicals, philosophical radicals, drifters, hobos, hippies, punks, new agers, soldiers, prisoners, black and ethnic minorities, pornographers, prostitutes, pimps, alcoholics, fighters, gangs, criminals, the immoral, the amoral, killers, psychopaths, occultists, religious extremists, anarchists, bohemians, the insane, cynics. Some of these are loners, like those celebrated in Colin Wilson's *The Outsider* while others are what cultural critic Dick Hebdige has defined as subcultures. Most of the people in the list have *chosen* their lifestyle. As usual the black and gay communities get a bad deal by being appropriated by the white middle-class readership for their outsider qualities or otherness. Throughout the 40 years since Norman Mailer wrote his seminal essay 'The White Negro' about whites who want to be black (more precisely, whites who want to be what they think of as being black), there has always been a 'tyranny of expectancy' in which whites expect an idea of 'black', and blacks are in no position not to give it to them. Thankfully for some time now the diaspora of black literature and the gay and lesbian canons have had a rich enough diversity to dispel the mythology of them being solely ghetto pimps and bathhouse binrakers respectively. Yet, however much they are an un-PC stereotype black pulp writers of ghetto life still offer an essential taste of life on the margins with everything stacked against you.

Accordingly, we drew up a list of authors, then set about writing fairly short entries on each of them, summarising their lives and listing their themes and preoccupations, interspersed with anecdotes and criticisms. The result of our efforts is *Cult Fiction: a reader's guide.* It is intended to serve as a concise and entertaining introduction to those writers you've vaguely heard of and always wanted to find out more about, and also as a standard work of reference for a milieu that is not accustomed to reference books. We realise that our list is by no means exhaustive and that some omissions, and probably some inclusions, will be the cause of grave offence: that is part of the fun as far as we are concerned. We also recognise that exposing our authors to this kind of treatment may even endanger their cult status. That too is all in the game.

In the pecking order of cult fiction, pride of place is reserved for those authors whose walk is as transgressive as their talk. Writers (with a capital 'W') are expected to be as dislocated from the mainstream as their characters. The most charismatic cult writers are those who seem to have lived as saints, seers or pioneers of consciousness at its extremes. In some instances, the colourful lives of cult authors are revered more than their books. That is why writers such as Kathy Acker, Bill Burroughs, Charles Bukowski and Donald Goines rank so highly. Their art does not survive, vampiric, off the life blood and experiences of others; they dip their pens in their own blood.

Other writers are seen as gatekeepers and holy dealers of particular fictional worlds with readers craving their next literary fix like a sacramental drug. The most cultish of cult authors live far from the madding crowd and the celebrity trail, and their distance from the world of chatshows and book launches is taken as further indication of their virtuous estrangement from the mainstream. There is a reverse etiquette at work here which demands that the most sought-after cult writers should be monkish, modern reclusives. If they happen to have died before being discovered as writers, their separation from the mainstream and the baubles of commercial success is guaranteed for all eternity, and their cult kudos tends to rise even higher.

Still, defining 'cult' is a risky business. In the end, cult status is given and taken away by the audience. Just as deviance is that which is labelled as such, so 'cult' is what people think it is. Currently, cyber-space seems to be the place to ascertain what readers think of writers and whether they qualify as 'cult'. While some authors turn up next to nothing on the Net, others generate pages and pages and site after site of worship, biographical rumour and exchanged opinion. Some authors are transformed in the hands of their fans. There are even occasions when the cult writer, as created by his following, bears little or no resemblance to the real-life author and the original purpose of his published work. Thomas De Quincey is a case in point. He was a man of the Enlightenment; in other words, he believed that the human capacity for rational understanding was as infinite as reality itself; and it was in this light that he chronicled his experiments with opium. Towards the end of the twentieth century, however, De Quincey's experiments have been re-interpreted according to the mood of our times, as a drug-fuelled retreat from reality and as a turn against rationality. Now regarded as a precursor to the drug-addict and 'sexistentialist' Alexander Trocchi, the new De Quincey is a contingent fiction invented by his modern-day following. His status as a cult writer has everything to do with the mindset of today's readership and comparatively little to do with his own mentality as originally expressed in his published work. His is an extreme case, but it shows how readers not writers can put the cult into cult fiction, in the light of or sometimes despite the life and times of the author and his text. Similarly authors like Hermann Hesse and Lewis Carroll were adapted and read against the grain in the 60s to suit the purposes of that particular generation.

The feminists among you will have concluded by now that we are 'linguistically challenged'. We are referring, of course, to our own use of the masculine pronoun and possessive: 'he' and 'his' rather than 'she/he' and 'hers/his'. The usage is deliberate. Essentially cult fiction is a boy thing. Cult followings and the cult canon tend to be made up largely of males, possibly because women simply do not have the time for such nonsense. The small number of women writers who have been allowed to enter into the canon suffer the same homogenised fate as the black and gay writers – they are either martyred victims like Anna Kavan and Sylvia Plath or extreme Amazons like Kathy Acker.

When men were men who went to war and brought home the bacon, on their days off they read novels peopled by heroes. But one of the characteristics of cult fiction is that heroes are noticeable by their absence. The protagonists of cult fiction tend to be hanging around in the waiting room of history, bored, often dissipated or perhaps trying desperately to maintain their integrity. Modern man no longer looks to brave horizons, his view is introspective. Identity is fractured and uncertain. The best our anti-heroes can offer is assertion of the self, at worst angst-ridden dismemberment. Cult fiction is what young men read at a time when they can no longer harbour great expectations or offer grand actions.

If you go along with the view that cult fiction is separate and somehow hidden from the mainstream, then by defining it and by exposing some of its shadowy luminaries to a wider audience we are killing cult fiction. But this is the elitist's take on cult fiction: the angle of the tired, been there, done that, well-read individual who has been pursuing such fiction and refining his opinions for many years and wants to keep his quarry to himself. One of the readers this book is designed for is the type that does not read, who is handed a copy of *Fear and Loathing in Las Vegas* or *Naked Lunch*, falls instantly in love and wants to know where to go to get some more. Hopefully this book offers a partial guide to what would otherwise be a journey by hit and miss deduction, relying only on dodgy word of mouth.

In any case, conglomerate publishing had driven the knife into cult fiction before we got there. In the wake of Irvine Welsh's *Trainspotting* and its runaway success, the selling machines set out to capture this newly discovered, non-traditional literary market. How many books are now aimed squarely and cynically at club culture, with jacket-designers taking their brief from DJ flyers and other 'yoof' accessories? In 1997 Welsh's *Ecstasy* was even tied in with a dance CD. And while mainstream publishers are pumping out new cult fiction, all kinds of advertisers are keying in to the cult fiction tradition as a way of connecting with young consumers. Just as old, beyond-the-pale rock'n' rollers are now drafted in to sell everything from sports wear to computers and credit cards, so those from the literary margins and their 'special' aura are being recruited to sell whatever needs selling. The first sighting of this was a number of years ago when Levi's ran a series of magazine advertisements based around original excerpts from Raymond Chandler, Jack Kerouac and Hunter S Thompson which mentioned the Levi's brand name.

Of course, hardselling of books is nothing new. In fact many a cult fiction author was born out of exploitation culture. In the seventies New English Library did exploitation novels on everything from bikers to bovver boys. In the forties and fifties the Pocket Book pulp stands wrapped everything from Faulkner to Somerset Maugham up as lurid tales for the wayward. Yet they also gave us true originals in the likes of Jim Thompson and David Goodis. When the Beat and Hippie cultures were riding high every book going that could be vaguely considered leftfield was dressed up as hip to the times with jackets showing a goateed hep cat here and a paisley swirl there.

In a sense, our guide is an attempt to canonise the true saints and sinners of cult fiction before the latest marketing department-inspired wannabes flood the bookshop shelves, and before the idea of deviance becomes just another marketing tool. (By the way, this is not to say that the door to the cult canon is necessarily closed. There are still plenty of real writers just beginning out there – Brady Udall, Jeffrey Eugenides, George Saunders and Chuck Palahniuk – who may, given time, qualify.) But in one respect, we are already too late. In a decade when the spin doctors have their political front men rub shoulders with pop star rebels it seems that transgression is no longer as transgressive as it once was. Instead of it being a form of disconnection from society at large, society is now trying to sell itself back to us through shared notions of transgressive activity. What was the counterculture is now over-the-counter culture, the deviant behaviour at the core of cult fiction has reached the middle of the marketplace, and there is nothing anyone can do about it.

Perhaps by setting out to identify real cult fiction we too are charlatans cashing in on the fact that authentic outsider status is much sought-after nowadays. We'll leave that for you to decide. Look out for *Cult Fiction Vol II*, sponsored by American Express.

< xvi >

Kathy Acker

1944/48?–1997
The pirate punk princess

Born of German-Jewish stock, Kathy Acker was brought up by her mother and stepfather (her natural father left her mother before Kathy was born) in a prosperous district of New York. At 18, she left home and worked as a stripper. Her involvement in the sex industry helped to make her a hit on the New York art scene, and she was photographed by the newly fashionable Robert Mapplethorpe. Preferring to be known simply as 'Acker' (the name she took from her first husband Robert, and which she continued to use even after a short-lived second marriage to composer Peter Gordon), she moved to London in the mid-eighties and stayed in Britain for five years. In the nineties, when breast cancer was diagnosed, Acker refused orthodox medicine in favour of alternative therapies and a concerted attempt to heal herself. 'I will make myself well or at least I will die in control of my own body,' she declared. She died of cancer in November 1997.

For Acker, the assertion of control over her own body was synonymous with being in control of her life. In her last years, the cancer inside her was the focus of her attempted self-control. Previously she had focused on sexuality as the prime site of self-creation. Acker wrote as she lived: her first novel *The Childlike Life of the Black Tarantula: some lives of murderesses* (1975) is suffused with sexual imagery and experimentation, in preference to plot and character development, as is the book which brought her fame and notoriety in Britain, *Blood and Guts in High School* (1984).

The uncertainty over Kathy Acker's age is indicative of a contrary writer committed to both the destruction and the creation of identity – a contradiction encapsulated in *In Memoriam to Identity* (1995). While Acker mocked the artificial conventions of literary language, she nevertheless created an authoritative, authentic voice of her own. Iconoclast and deconstructionist, she inspired a cult following of Ackerites. Although she railed against the literary establishment and followed in the footsteps of those like William Burroughs who set out to destroy rational thought and the literary forms associated with it (she once said that she did not expect readers to go from the beginning to the end of her books, but rather to dip into them at will; she also said that in the end it all comes down to baby talk and nonsense: 'goo goo'), Acker the leather-jacketed teacher at the San Francisco Art Institute and body-piercing guru was a proper schoolmistress in matters of timekeeping and class discipline. In her online tribute to Acker, Diamanda Galas recalled 'a conversation with her late at night in Switzerland, and I was astonished to discover not only a provocateur but an extremely rigorous thinker with an encyclopedic knowledge of her craft'. Perhaps Acker never got shot of the reverence for high *Kultur* imparted to her by her grandmother.

Acker's paradoxical character is matched by the contradictory responses that she prompted. Shortly before her death, *Time Out* books editor Brian Case condemned her as 'a major bore', and dismissed her *Bodies of Work: Essays* (1997) as 'a windy collection' of 'the worst sort of American avant-garde rambling'. For Case, Acker's questioning of literature (why write?) was trite, and her focus on sexuality left him equally unaroused ('"How exactly does my body feel pleasure…There's a definite difference in my physical being or body between when I'm being fucked and I'm not being fucked." That's sorted out, then. Avoid.') In the opposite camp, when the *Independent's* Suzanne Moore learnt of her death she wrote a paean to Acker as 'a pirate, a pioneer, a punk princess'. Moore contrasted the awesome Acker persona ('She was a literary outlaw and she would take no prisoners') with the intensely likeable person underneath: 'I soon found myself chatting to this tiny woman about jewellery and shopping and her motorbike and how much she fancied Moira Stuart, the news reader…She was funny and sharp and immensely vulnerable.' She paid homage to Acker as the woman writer by whom 'the word was made flesh – female flesh'.

In the canon of cult fiction, there are few writers who have proved so controversial that their death has prompted a sheaf of for and against letters in a national newspaper, as occurred in the *Guardian* after Acker's untimely demise.

MUST READ *Blood and Guts in High School, Don Quixote, The Childlike Life of the Black Tarantula: Some Lives of Murderesses, Eurydice in the Underworld*
READ ON **Georges Bataille**, **William Burroughs**, **Gertrude Stein**, Tank Girl

Nelson Algren
1909–1981
Wanderer of the wild side

Born of Swedish-immigrant parents, Nelson Ahlgren Abraham moved at an early age from Detroit to Chicago. At Illinois University he studied journalism. His experiences as a migrant worker during the Depression provided the material for his first novel *Somebody in Boots* (1935). Throughout his life Algren identified with the American underdog: poet and critic Kenneth Rexroth summed up his attitude as 'it is better to be out than in…better to be on the lam than on the cover of *Time* magazine'. From 1936 to 1940 (the highpoint of left-wing ideas on the US literary scene) he was editor of the Illinois Writers' Project. In 1942, after putting the finishing touches to his second novel, he joined the war as an enlisted man. *Never Come Morning* (1942) received universal acclaim, and eventually sold over a million copies. Algren's

Machine, who feels he is a victim of 'the great, secret and special American guilt of owning nothing, nothing at all, in the one land where ownership and virtue are one'. Algren reworked some of these themes in *A Walk on the Wild Side* (1956, filmed in 1962 with Laurence Harvey; the title was borrowed 16 years later by Lou Reed). But this was in the middle of the postwar boom and poverty row was out of fashion. Critic Leslie Fiedler dismissed Algren as 'a museum-piece – the last of the Proletarian Writers'.

Algren's style is a dark naturalism that passionately records the details of trapped urban existence with flashes of melancholy poetry. His characters are the lowlife drifters, whores, junkies and barflies of poverty row (the place that James Cagney came from in *Angels with Dirty Faces*). He records the bravado of their colloquial language and lays their predicament bare. Of bar-room brawlers he writes: 'They fought, not because the liquor was in them, but because it did not fill them enough.'

Algren's critics see his work as artless, shambolic and long-winded, while his champions believe he is a grimly compelling and compassionate writer who forged a direct line between Céline and Dostoevsky, through the hard-boiled school, all the way to the Beats. As with many US Depression-era novelists, he was feted in France and claimed by the existentialists as one of their own. Jean-Paul Sartre translated his work, despite the fact that Algren had an affair

Nelson Algren

story collection *The Neon Wilderness* (1947), was also well received. His star continued to rise until the onset of McCarthyism (the witch-hunts against communists and leftists in the USA in the early 1950s).

Filmed in 1955 with Frank Sinatra and Kim Novak, Algren's best-known book is *The Man with the Golden Arm* (1949). Published in 1949 it won the first National Book Award. Set in the underbelly of Chicago, it is the tale of ex-soldier, card dealer and morphine addict Frankie with his lover, writer Simone de Beauvoir. Algren is lovingly portrayed by de Beauvoir in her novel *The Mandarins* (1954) and in her autobiography. He was rather less generous about her writing. Of her philosophical treatise *Ethics of Ambiguity* (1986) he said 'It's like eating cardboard', and he once told a journalist that de Beauvoir 'couldn't write a scene in a restaurant without telling you everything on the menu'.

MUST READ *A Life on the Wild Side* by Bettina Drew*, Neon Wilderness, The Man with the Golden Arm, A Walk on the Wild Side*
READ ON Edward Anderson, Sherwood Anderson, **Charles Bukowski**, Céline, **Jack Kerouac**, John O'Hara

Richard Allen

1920–1993

No more like a skinhead than Greta Garbo

'Richard Allen' is the name on the front cover of the million-selling *Skinhead* books. The name was thought of by the editors at the London publishing firm New English Library and given by them to Jim Moffatt, one of a number of hack writers who churned out their books to order.

Born in Canada of Irish extraction, Jim Moffatt came to Britain and learnt his trade writing up to six stories a week (thrillers, spies,

Westerns) for pulp fiction magazines. He moved on to writing books, and by the mid-seventies reckoned he had produced 250 in the previous 20 years, at a rate of 10,000 words a day when deadlines were approaching. Meanwhile, the managing director of the ailing New English Library imprint was desperate to make inroads into a new audience of younger readers; his editorial board came up with the idea of commis-

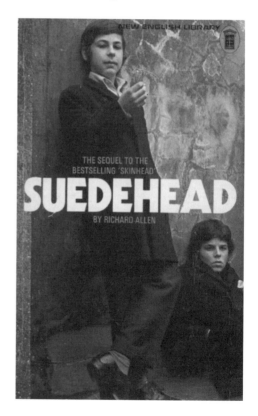

sioning a novel set in the emerging skinhead subculture. Ignoring his agent's advice that 'he was no more like a skinhead than Greta Garbo', Jim Moffatt insisted he could do the job. In six days he wrote *Skinhead* (1970), featuring Joe Hawkins, the hippie-bashing bovver boy from London's East End. The book was an immediate hit, and many of its youthful readers were convinced that the author was a real soccer hooligan, not a 55-year-old Canadian who always wore a jacket and tie and whose lurid tales of sex and street violence were written from the same seafront cottage in Sidmouth in which he also penned a column for the local paper.

Moffatt/Allen wrote another 17 books for New English Library. He never did rewrites and claimed that he hardly read his own material after having written it: any decent writer, he said, 'should have the story in his head'. In *Suedehead* (1971) Joe Hawkins grew his hair (slightly), donned an (Aber)Crombie overcoat, and landed a job in a City law firm (temporarily) – all in the interests of pulling a better class of bird. In *Skinhead Farewell*, Moffatt/Allen killed off Joe. 'Cop-killer Hawkins' died in a plane crash while being escorted back from Australia. Moffatt's real-life relationship with NEL came to an end soon afterwards. As is customary, Moffatt was paid an advance to write his books; and he had started to 'drink away his earnings'. He wrote his last title for NEL while confined to the office next to that of the managing director. Moffatt tried to keep up with the times: he wrote books on glam and punk for another publisher, but these were not a great success. Perhaps the demon drink had made him lose his bottle as a writer.

Moffatt died of cancer in the early nineties, just at the time when the skinhead style was coming back into fashion. In the two years before he died Moffatt negotiated an agreement which allowed George Marshall, editor of the *Skinhead Times*, to republish what he had written under the name of Richard Allen. The *Skinhead* series had already caught the attention of Stewart Home, who in the mid-eighties used to sit in the British Library reading NEL titles at the rate of six a day, and who decided to incorporate the style of Allen et al. into his own experimental fiction.

In the nineties the Allen books became fashion accessories in the lifestyle known as 'New Lad'. The Lad was essentially an ironic (but not so funny?) retake on endangered masculinity; given that skinheads first emerged in the late sixties as an exaggerated response to the erosion of traditional working-class districts, it seems appropriate that Allen's *Skinhead* series should have been temporarily taken over by another cult that was equally nostalgic about masculine values.

MUST READ *Skinhead, Skinhead Farewell, Suedehead*
READ ON **James Hadley Chase, Nik Cohn, Stewart Home**, Colin MacInnes, Tony Parsons

A IS FOR ALCOHOL

5 authors who sought solace in the bottle and their chosen poisons

ERNEST HEMINGWAY

double daiquiris when at home in Cuba, a Tusker lager before bagging big game in Kenya

WILLIAM FAULKNER

'Civilisation begins with distillation' was his maxim. Once dedicated a book to 'Mr Courvoisier, without whom...'

F SCOTT FITZGERALD

king of the Prohibition cocktail, so preferably anything made in a bathtub

MALCOLM LOWRY

mezcal – drink of the desert – the only tipple fit for a weary human sacrifice

CHARLES BUKOWSKI

anything he could get his hands on, before being weaned on to wine later in life

Martin Amis

1949–

Greying enfant terrible of British letters

The younger son of novelist Kingsley, Amis was educated at schools in Britain, Spain and America. At 14, he appeared in the film of Richard Hughes's novel *A High Wind in Jamaica* ('It was my only experience of motion pictures – and one so traumatically embarrassing that it can still make me gasp with shame...I was a plump and bewildered pubescent with no theatrical talent whatever').

After achieving a first-class degree in English from Oxford, Amis worked for the *Times Literary Supplement* and the *New Statesman*. His first novel, *The Rachel Papers* (1973), which won the Somerset Maugham Award, was praised for its scathing wit and precocious intelligence and was made into a rather anaemic film in 1989. *Dead Babies* (1975), a surreal black comedy, was temporarily renamed *Dark Secrets* because of the negative response to its title, which it resumed in the eighties.

Like his father, he is interested in character and identity, how it expresses itself and what lies hidden. *Success* (1978) is a comedy of revenge between two mismatched foster brothers: one is rich, handsome and happy; the other, unattractive, dull and frustrated, while *Other People* (1981), which J G Ballard called 'a metaphysical thriller, Kafka reshot in the style of *Psycho*', is the disorientating tale of an amnesiac woman trying to reconstruct her selfhood.

There have been nods to sci-fi with *Einstein's Monsters* (1987), a collection of stories dealing with the menace of nuclear Armageddon; the Booker Prize nominated *Time's Arrow* (1991), with its structural borrowing from Kurt Vonnegut (time goes backwards), and its controversial Nazi narrator blandly noting the experiments at Auschwitz; not to mention the apocalyptic background for *London Fields* (1989).

His most accomplished novels are *Money* (1984) and *London Fields*, which both capture their milieu and its language perfectly (the transatlantic film business and lowlife London respectively). *Money*, subtitled '*a suicide note*', is a tale of greed and excess in an age of hyper-capitalism; as such it is a quintessential eighties novel. It is the story of John Self, a grotesque film director who is 'addicted to the twentieth century', absorbed by its pace, its gadgets and its moral bankruptcy. *London Fields* – 'Not a whodunit. More a whydoit' – draws parallels between the self-orchestrated murder of Nicola Six and the imminent extinction of the earth.

Along with *The Information* (1995), these two novels form a loose 'London' trilogy. *The Information*, which concerns an envious relationship between a successful and a failed writer, is most notable for the sum of the advance (around £500,000) that Amis's American agent, Andrew Wiley, managed to extract for it. In recent years, Amis notoriously spent £20,000 on a new set of teeth, but only £106 on his marriage in July 1998 to American heiress, Isabel Fonseca. He blamed it on experiencing a 'cataclysmic mid-life crisis' prompted partly by the death of his father, novelist Kingsley Amis.

His 1997 novel, *Night Train,* is a miniaturist philosophical exploration of the noir genre and its idiom, following a female detective, Mike O'Hoolihan, to a dark conclusion.

Amis's forte is his ability to contort language and speech to make it fizz like the very environment it addresses. His gymnastic touch with language is often masterly. Yet the superstructure of his novels lacks the fine crafting that he offers line by line in his prose, and overall his novels suffer as a result. For his literary gameplaying Amis is deeply indebted to Nabokov, whom he admits was 'a man who I have always idolised'. Iain Sinclair described Amis as 'Granta Man': entertaining in small bursts, but more of an arranger of clever set pieces than a substantial author.

MUST READ *London Fields, Money, Night Train*
READ ON Saul Bellow, **Vladimir Nabokov**, **Will Self**, **Kurt Vonnegut**

A

CULT FICTION

Guillaume Apollinaire

1880–1918

The man who invented surréalisme

Though born in Rome, Apollinaris Kostrowitzky came from Polish stock. As a 20-year-old he moved to Paris and took on the identity of Guillaume Apollinaire, futurist poet, dramatist and essayist. His work is an essential part of the dynamic that begins in the 1890s with Alfred Jarry shouting '*merde*' at bourgeois culture and culminates with Marcel Duchamp exhibiting a lavatory pan as a work of art.

Apollinaire strove to create a new poetry that rejected traditional metre and vocabulary. Even in the depths of war he was committed to this cause, as demonstrated in his manifesto *L'Esprit Nouveau et les Poètes* (*The New Spirit and the Poets*). He was equally antagonistic to the positivist outlook that underpinned most European thought and literature in the latter half of the 19th century. Like many futurists in other countries at the time, Apollinaire became intensely patriotic at the outbreak of the First World War and volunteered for frontline service. He was wounded, and while recovering wrote the verse-drama for which he is best remembered: *Les Mamelles de Tirésias* (*The Tits of Tirésias*; 1918). At its première, a young man caused a disturbance by brandishing a revolver.

The young man was Jacques Vache, who dedicated his life to humour and making fun of conventions until he committed suicide in 1919. Vache was a profound influence on the surrealists (André Breton, Louis Aragon, Paul Eluard et al.), as was Apollinaire, who coined the term *surréalisme* in reference to *The Tits of Tirésias*. Only by chance, however. Apollinaire had been using the term *surnaturalisme* to describe his work. Given the pride of place allotted by the surrealists to chance and the arbitrary, it seems pertinent to ask whether Apollinaire would be revered as an important influence if he had kept on using his original term and had not, by chance, decided to swap it for the one word that can be said to sum up the artistic endeavour of the interwar period: *surréalisme*.

Apollinaire also wrote erotic fiction, notably *Amorous Exploits of a Young Rakehell*, *Flesh Unlimited* and *Onze Mille Vierges* (*Eleven Thousand Virgins*, 1989).

MUST READ Much of Apollinaire's original verse now seems almost unreadable. The spirit of iconoclasm was his main contribution to the development of the 20th-century sensibility.
READ ON Louis Aragon, *The Bacchae* by Euripides, **André Breton**, **Jean Cocteau**

<8>

Antonin Artaud

1896–1948

Madness as enlightenment

Actor, director, playwright, essayist, theoretician, lunatic: the multifaceted work of Antonin Marie Joseph Artaud is inextricable from his traumatic life. Indeed, he was probably one of the first individuals to have his whole life interpreted as an artistic statement.

Born and brought up in Marseilles, Artaud published a literary review while still at school at the Collège du Sacré Coeur. In 1915 he destroyed all his writing and was sent to a nearby sanatorium. He was conscripted in 1916 (during the First World War), but was discharged nine months later on medical grounds. He sat out the rest of the war in various sanatoria and health resorts. Arriving in Paris in 1920, he found work on the magazine *Demain*. In 1922 Artaud played Tiresias in Jean Cocteau's *Antigone*, with sets by Picasso and costumes by Coco Chanel. In 1923 he published his own literary periodical and a book of poems, *Tric-Trac du Ciel*. He joined the surrealists in 1924 and the following year became director of their research bureau. Also in 1925, he directed a play by Aragon and published two stories, 'L'Ombilic des Limbes' and 'Le Pèse-Nerfs'. In 1926, Artaud co-founded the Théâtre Alfred Jarry; in 1927 he appeared in Abel Gance's film *Napoleon*, in which he played Marat. He was sub-

sequently offered the part of the young monk in Carl Dreyer's film *La Passion de Jeanne d'Arc*.

Artaud broke with the surrealists when many of them became communists. He objected to revolutionary Marxism on the grounds that it was a form of rationalism – and rationalism, according to Artaud, had ruptured the emotional fabric of mankind. For the same reason, he strove to create a form of theatre that was less reliant on language. In 1930 he visited Berlin to work on a number of (silent) films, including Pabst's version of Bertolt Brecht's *Threepenny Opera*. In 1931 he published a very free translation of *The Monk*, Matthew Lewis's Gothic novel. This was a precursor to Artaud's visionary idea of the Theatre of Cruelty, in which drama would swoop down on the audience like a medieval plague, causing havoc and psychological disturbance.

By this time (the early thirties) he was going into hospital for detoxification treatment. In 1936, after the failure of his play *The Cenci* the previous year, Artaud went on a long trip to Cuba and Mexico. On his return, he underwent repeated detox treatments. In August he left France for Ireland, but on 30 September he arrived back in Le Havre, under arrest and in a straitjacket. In 1938 his famous essay, *The Theatre and its Double*, was published, but Artaud spent most of the year – and the following nine years – in various asylums. On 4 March 1948 he was found dead in his room at the Ivry asylum.

Artaud was not a great success in any of his

chosen professions. But just as he was coming to the end of his life, a number of people – among them Beat poet Allen Ginsberg and his close friend Carl Solomon – started to pick up on his extraordinary intensity, which is reflected in the writing and in his appearances on film. Artaud became an icon of the early counterculture, and has remained influential ever since. The director Peter Brook tried to implement some of his ideas on theatre in the famous Royal Shakespeare Company production of the *Marat/Sade*. In Paris, the radical students of May 1968 looked upon Artaud as a role model. The anti-psychiatrist R D Laing was impressed by Artaud's belief that 'madness' was a label imposed upon visionaries by a bureaucratic society; he has been a major influence on the great French theorists Gilles Deleuze and Félix Guattari, and on Michel Foucault. The idea of Artaud as an outsider who rejected rationality and the comparative safety of bourgeois civilisation seems to have been more important than what he actually wrote. In addition, the music critic and Lenny Bruce biographer, Albert Goldman, has suggested that the whole of rock music can be seen as an enactment of Artaud's idea of *The Theatre and its Double*.

MUST READ *Artaud* by Martin Esslin, *The Theatre and its Double*
READ ON **William Burroughs**, **Alfred Jarry**, R D Laing, **Ken Kesey**

Paul Auster
1947–
Metaphysical detective

Auster was born in Newark, New Jersey, and his parents divorced when he was a young man. After a year spent travelling in Europe, he enrolled at Columbia University and spent a year in Paris on an exchange. Returning to Columbia in 1968, he wrote articles and reviews

Paul Auster

while anti-Vietnam protests and student riots raged around him: 'In the summer of 1969, I walked into a post office…I studied the posters of the FBI's ten most wanted men pinned to the wall. It turned out that I knew seven of them.'

After publishing a crime novel pastiche, *Squeeze Play* (1982), written under the pseudonym Paul Benjamin (who would later appear as a blocked writer in his screenplay for the film *Smoke*), Auster wrote his most celebrated work, *The New York Trilogy* (1987), a series of linked metaphysical mysteries concerned with the fragile relationship between words and meaning. In many ways, these three playful deconstructions of the detective genre form a meeting point between the hard-boiled novelists of the thirties and the postwar European existential writers.

Auster can be seen as postmodern incarnation of the well-established tradition of New York Jewish writers, yet his painstakingly crafted reflexive fictions also have a deeply European sensibility. As in the works of his friend and fellow novelist Don DeLillo, Auster's books are latent with symbols and significance which never fully reveal themselves to make a unified meaningful whole. Identity and meaning are always condemned to be in search of themselves.

More novels followed: *Moon Palace* (1989), *The Music of Chance* (1990) and *Leviathan* (1992). *The Music of Chance* was filmed in 1992, and featured a cameo by Auster himself. *Mr Vertigo*, appeared in 1994, the story of a young boy who is taught to magically fly by a strange Svengali figure. Taking in the sweep of American culture from the early years of the century, it was something of a departure for Auster and reminiscent at times of E L Doctorow. It had a less tortured mood that his earlier fiction but some Auster fans found it disappointingly light-weight. Since then he has scripted and co-directed *Smoke* and its companion film *Blue in the Face* with Wayne Wang, about life surrounding a Brooklyn cigar shop and he sees film as the way forward. Yet he finally returned to the novel in 1999 with *Timbuktu*, the story of a maniac drunk who lost it in the 60s and has wandered ever since. The book is narrated by his dog Mr Bones.

MUST READ *The New York Trilogy, The Country of Last Things, Leviathan*
READ ON **Samuel Beckett**, **Jorge Luis Borges**, **Albert Camus**, Jerome Charyn, **Don DeLillo**, Peter Handke

J G Ballard

1930–

The apocalyptic British Burroughs

James Graham Ballard is the son of an English businessman who ran a textile firm in Shanghai. After the bombing of Pearl Harbor in 1941 and the invasion of China by Japan, Ballard and his family were interned in a civilian prison camp for nearly three years. Their incarceration is not only the central experience in Ballard's hugely successful autobiographical novel *Empire of the Sun* (1984, filmed by Stephen Spielberg); it also underpins much of his other writing.

After the war, Ballard and his family moved to England. He read medicine at Cambridge University but did not graduate. In 1956 he started writing sci-fi stories and publishing them in *New Worlds* magazine, edited by Michael Moorcock. His first novel, *The Drowned World*, appeared in 1962, and although set in a flooded London of the future, the vision of Shanghai ('a cross between ancient Babylon and Las Vegas') looms large: compare the passage in the essay collection *A User's Guide to the Millennium* (1995) in which Ballard recalls that 'my own earliest memories are of Shanghai …when the streets of the city were two or three feet deep in brown silt-laden water'. Two further novels, *The Drought* (1964) and *The Crystal World* (1966), complete a loose trilogy of disaster novels told by unreliable and increasingly demented narrators who are steadily drawn down into the alien, post-apocalyptic swamp that they set out to describe.

In the late sixties Ballard began to experiment with sex and violence. He produced *The Atrocity Exhibition* (later the subject of a Joy Division song) and the controversial *Crash* (1973), involving perverse sexual fantasies about car crashes and bringing new meaning to the term auto-erotic. When David Cronenberg released a film of *Crash* in 1997, it caused even more controversy. *High-Rise* (1975, shortly after the huge Barbican Centre complex was built in London) is a savage satire on the breakdown of social order in a high-rise technological paradise.

Ballard's main characteristic as a writer is his deployment of what J B Priestley called 'inner space', a kind of Freudian cosmos where the most terrifying alien landscapes are to be found within the author's mind. Ballard himself noted: 'The dream worlds invented by the writer of fantasy are external equivalents of the inner world of the psyche.' By connecting fantasy with psychology Ballard took sci-fi out of the genre ghetto. He invested it with a wider range of cultural and scientific references and used its fantastic universe as an instrument to explore the modern human condition. As with all great sci-fi writers Ballard's works are not meditations on a distant future but fantastic realisations of the here and now. He once said

< 12 >

that 'the future in my fiction has never been more than five minutes away'.

In 1992, Ballard listed among his ten favourite books, Nathanael West's *Day of the Locust*, William Burroughs's *Naked Lunch*, *The Secret Life of Salvador Dali* (the surrealists have been a major influence on Ballard's fictional landscapes) and the Los Angeles *Yellow Pages*, which he 'stole from the Beverley Hilton' and which he claimed was 'as surrealist in its way as the Dali autobiography'.

MUST READ *Crash, The Drowned World, Empire of the Sun, High-Rise*
READ ON **William Burroughs, Samuel R Delaney, Philip K Dick, Michael Moorcock,** Robert Silverberg, **Kurt Vonnegut**

Iain (M) Banks

1954–
Eamonn with a feersum imadjinayshun

Iain Banks (mainstream novelist) and Iain M Banks (sci-fi writer) are one and the same person. Born in the Scottish town of Dunfermline, Banks read English at Stirling University. He dallied with rock music, writing a number of songs that remained unperformed until 1998 when they were featured in the radio version of his novel *Espedair Street*, which was adapted in the style of a radio rockumentary, but he always wanted to write.

Banks without the 'M' hit paydirt with his first novel, *The Wasp Factory* (1984), featuring a sexually ambiguous child called Frank who murders other children and then retires to his 'factory' to torture animals. Published shortly after a moral panic in Britain about the effects of screen violence and in the same year as the censorial Video Recordings Act, *The Wasp Factory* was accused of being the literary equivalent of a video nasty. *Walking on Glass* (1985) dealt with incest in an upfront manner and prompted questions as to whether any of it was autobiographical. 'Being an only child I didn't have much opportunity for it', Banks replied, 'and I didn't fancy my mother or father.' *The Crow Road* (1992), critically acclaimed when televised on BBC2, is also a family melodrama laced with murder. The central plotline of *Complicity* (1993) centres on a serial murderer with a penchant for knocking off establishment figures. 'I'm against the death penalty,' Banks explained, 'but at the same time it was very cathartic for me to write about somebody doing all these horrible things to these, you know, bastards.'

The combination of high fantasy and low realism is a hallmark of Banks's writing. He has pointed out that *Espedair Street*, set in the seventies but not conceived as a book until 1985, 'is a fantasy novel set in reality, at a time when people who are young enough to still have outrageous fantasies get their hands on enough money to fulfil them'. *A Song of Stone* (1997) has been described as 'a *Mad Max* set in the

< 13 >

B IS FOR BLACK

10 African–Americans who fuelled their rage with ink

CHESTER HIMES
jailbird turned king of crime on the page

RICHARD WRIGHT
the black existentialist

DONALD GOINES
writing pulp in the am, doing junk in the pm

ISHMAEL REED
inspired comicbook avant–garde antics

CLARENCE COOPER JR
the black William Burroughs

RALPH ELLISON
Invisible Man who came alive on the page

ICEBERG SLIM
turned from pimping flesh to pushing words

WALTER MOSLEY
bringing race and politics to Chandler's LA

JAMES BALDWIN
black, gay, bug–eyed and brilliant

MALCOLM X
from crime and despair to salvation

Scottish Highlands – a post-apocalyptic novel [which] uses incest as a subtext'.

The output of sci-fi writer Iain M Banks includes *Consider Phlebas* (1987), *The State of the Art* (1989) and *Against a Dark Background* (1993). In 1994, Banks produced the most extravagant sci-fi story of the decade, using overlapping multi-narratives (another hallmark: he says it 'keeps people interested') and phonetically written narrative. The title – *Feersum Endjinn* – was also spelt phonetically; once again, this surreal mix of fantasy and banality was driven by the fearsome imagination of its prolific author.

MUST READ *Consider Phlebas, The Crow Road, Feersum Endjinn, The Wasp Factory*
READ ON **Angela Carter**, **J G Ballard**, John Webster

Georges Bataille

1897–1962
sex, death and surrealism

Born in Billion, Puy-de-Dome in central France, Bataille's mother was of dubious sanity and his syphilitic father died mad and blind when Bataille was just 18 – his father's deathbed ravings and refusal to see a priest having a profound effect on the young man.

Converting to Catholicism on the eve of World War One, Bataille joined a seminary in

1917 with the intention of becoming a priest, but experienced a loss of faith in 1920 when he began to encounter the works of Nietzsche. During the twenties he became involved with the surrealist movement and began writing after undergoing a liberating period of psychoanalysis. During this time he married his first wife (he was married twice), Sylvia Makles – later to be the wife of Jacques Lacan. Arguments ensued during the late twenties between Bataille and André Breton who accused him of splintering the Surrealist movement. The two later joined forces to fight against Fascism in the thirties.

Much of Bataille's time was dedicated to his academic and philosophical writings. He founded and edited several journals and was the first to publish, among others, Barthes, Foucault and Derrida (all of whom owe him a philosophical debt). He was frequently in financial difficulties and his only real trade was that of librarianship. He was finally freed of financial constraints when an auction of paintings arranged by Miro, Picasso and others set him up for his few remaining years. Bataille's own philosophy (he was one of the first modern theorists to be truly interdisciplinary) offers a kind of spiritual transcendence for a Godless world based on notions of bodily transgression and excess.

His fictions which include *The Story of the Eye, Blue of Noon, L'Abbé C* are sublime works of surrealism whose plots are almost wholly concerned with the transgressive relationship between sex, death and degradation, which has had him dubbed the 'metaphysician of evil'. *The Story of the Eye*, the dreamlike tale of a young couple whose carnal odyssey explores the boundaries of sexual taboo, is packed with endless horrific and unsettling violations (culminating in orgasmic murder) which Bataille renders strangely sensuous and deeply affecting.

MUST READ *The Story of the Eye, Eroticism: Death and Sensuality*
READ ON **André Breton, William Burroughs, Marquis De Sade, Jean Genet**

John Barth

1930–
Lost in the funhouse of literary invention

When John Barth was born in Cambridge, Maryland, along with his twin sister, his three-year-old brother remarked: 'Now we have a Jack and a Jill.' The names stuck, and (Jack) Barth spends a few pages of his non-fiction collection, *The Friday Book* (1984), bemoaning that the nursery rhyme names perpetuated his twinness, and influenced his writing, ' My books tend to come in pairs; my sentences in twin members.'

His first two books, *The Floating Opera* (written in 1956 when Barth was only 24) and *The End of the Road* (1958) are absurdist, nihilistic comedies about the search for existential meaning. By the time he was on to the second pair, *The Sot-Weed Factor* (1960) and *Giles Goat-Boy* (1966), his preference was for hugely ambitious and inventive, deconstructive metafictions. The gargantuan *The Sot-Weed Factor* is an epic pastiche of 17th-century English prose – described by its author as a 'moral allegory cloaked in terms of a colonial history'. Widely praised, it was described by the critic (and Barth's friend) Leslie Fiedler as: 'Something closer to the great American novel than any other book of the last decade.' In *Giles Goat-Boy* he refashioned the world as a huge university, divided into twin campuses, 'East' and 'West', each controlled by a powerful computer – a metaphor for a society gone insane with logic.

Barth's fiction is a heady mixture of the humorous and the cerebral; an endless display of verbal fecundity, where the reader is constantly reminded that not just the novel but reality itself is a fictional construct. Barth has been known (like Kurt Vonnegut) to step into his own fictions and also to bring fictional characters from different books together (*Letters*, 1979). Commenting on his own love of complexity Barth once said, 'I admire writers who can make complicated things simple, but my own talent has been to make simple things complicated.'

As a teenager Barth moved to New York where he attended the prestigious Juilliard School of Music. Finally eschewing music, he attended Johns Hopkins University, receiving a Masters degree in Literature before pursuing his academic career. During his brief stay at Juilliard, Barth was more interested in arranging music than composing it, and this is evident in his writing, as he himself attests: 'At heart I'm an arranger still, whose chiefest literary pleasure is to take a received melody – an old narrative poem, a classical myth, a shopworn literary convention, a shard of my experience…and, improvising like a jazzman within its constraints, reorchestrate it to present purpose.'

MUST READ *The Floating Opera, Giles Goat-Boy, The Sot-Weed Factor*
READ ON **Donald Barthelme**, **Jorge Luis Borges**, Robertson Davies, **Thomas Pynchon**

Donald Barthelme
1931–1989
Comic king of collage

Born in Philadelphia and raised in Houston, Texas, Barthelme was the son of a professor of architecture, and trained as an art historian. He moved to New York, and started writing short fiction for various magazines, including *Contact*, *Harper's Bazaar* and the *New Yorker*. His first collection, *Come Back Dr Caligari*, was published in 1964 and featured Barthelme's trademark: short fictions that took ancient and modern myths apart, putting them in unusual

< 16 >

surroundings, creating ironic, funny, and occasionally, macabre collages. As Barthelme put it: 'Unlike things are stuck together to make, in the best case, a new reality.' For Barthelme the modern universe is absurd, our old unified culture is dead and its language poorly equipped to deal with the chaos of a postmodern environment. Barthelme's fictions mimic the changing channels of a TV set, mixing genres and registers in guerrilla raids on the language of our popular culture in a radical attempt to say something fresh.

Barthelme's first novel, *Snow White* (1967), based on the anodyne Walt Disney film, demonstrated his deconstructionist techniques brilliantly and consolidated his growing reputation. It also contained a key phrase that illustrated his devotion to minimalism: 'Fragments are the only forms I trust.'

He once noted that parody was 'a disreputable activity, ranking only a little higher on the scale of literary activity than plagiarism', but, in fact, virtually everything he wrote was parodic and he used every facet of the written word for his own unique ends. As critic Morris Dickstein observed: 'The trash of inert language is his meat and drink', and Barthelme's stories were 'a collage of styles bleached and truncated into one pure and rigorous style of its own'.

He was part of a growing body of American writers in the sixties and seventies, including Richard Brautigan, John Hawkes, William Gass and Robert Coover, who were trying to develop something new for literature, and Barthelme was, as Coover said, 'one of the great citizens of contemporary world letters'.

Author and peer Thomas Pynchon summed him up perfectly: 'Barthelme…happens to be one of a handful of American authors, here to make the rest of us look bad, who know instinctively how to stash the merchandise, bamboozle the inspectors, and smuggle their nocturnal contraband right on past the checkpoints of daylight "reality".'

MUST READ *The Dead Father, Sixty Stories, Snow White*
READ ON Woody Allen, **John Barth**, **Richard Brautigan**, **Robert Coover**, **Kurt Vonnegut**

Simone de Beauvoir
1909—1986
Not the wife of Jean-Paul Sartre

Born in Paris at a time when the car and the telephone were still largely absent from the French capital, Simone de Beauvoir went on to become an icon who represents the unencumbered lifestyle of the modern woman in the second half of the twentieth century. This is largely a result of her relationship with the philosopher and novelist Jean-Paul Sartre. In 1929 she and Sartre made a pact which distinguished between their 'essential life' together and

< 17 >

'contingent' affairs: theirs was a permanent commitment to each other, but without the burden of marriage or even of living together. Such an arrangement might be considered trendy nowadays, but in the 1920s it was unheard of. Cynics have suggested that this was merely a convenient formula which allowed Sartre to enjoy the favours of philosophy-groupies while roping de Beauvoir into a permanent relationship. Judging by her affair with the American writer Nelson Algren, however, she too seems to have enjoyed the measure of independence which their arrangement allowed for.

De Beauvoir wrote six semi-autobiographical novels focusing on female protagonists and their struggle for independence and self-fulfilment in the intellectual milieu of postwar Paris. *The Mandarins* (1954, dedicated to Nelson Algren) was described by the *New Statesman* as 'a dazzling panorama of the giants of the Left Bank'. The *Guardian* noted that 'the characters, especially the women, are uninhibited and sometimes predatory. The dialogues are salty, frank and realistic. The characters' amorous adventures are set down with microscopic exactitude.' Equally precise is de Beauvoir's account of the political controversies of the day, as they impinged upon her social circle. The overall effect is what Hollywood copywriters used to describe as 'life-enhancing'. As the novel ends, its protagonist decides not to commit suicide but to jump 'feet first into life' by publishing a new weekly magazine.

The Second Sex (1949–1953) is probably de Beauvoir's best-known work. Starting from the existential notion that people define themselves through their opposition to others, she argues that men have exploited an accident of biology to define women as the ultimate 'Other', thereby projecting all their alienation and frustration on to the female; meanwhile women have been socialised into accepting this state of affairs and their secondary role within it. The book was fairly influential at the time of its publication, but became even more so when it was adopted as a seminal text by the burgeoning feminist movement of the late sixties and seventies.

Those who dismiss de Beauvoir as no more than Sartre's sidekick have obviously paid insufficient attention to her own writing. However, de Beauvoir's account of her last days with Sartre before his death in 1980 tend to confirm the suggestion that there was something obsessive about her feelings for him.

MUST READ *The Mandarins, The Second Sex*
READ ON Marilyn French, **Erica Jong, Doris Lessing,** Anita Loos, Martha Gellhorn, Mary Wollstonecraft

< 18 >

Samuel Beckett

Samuel Beckett

1906–1989
Not three dots, but two

Born in Foxrock, a middle-class suburb of Dublin, Samuel Barclay Beckett received the best education that Protestant ascendancy in Ireland could provide, culminating in the top first-class degree of his year in Italian and French at Trinity College, Dublin, and a reputation as a golfer, swimmer and cricketer (the future Nobel Prize winner for literature was even mentioned in Wisden, the cricketing bible). After graduation he left Dublin for Paris (on the run from Irish parochialism and British influence). He lectured in English at the Ecole Normale Supérieure before returning to Dublin as a lecturer in English, then going back to Paris in 1932 as secretary to his fellow Irish writer James Joyce. Beckett spent the Second World War in the French Resistance and was awarded the Croix de Guerre. In 1947 he was diagnosed as suffering from a malignant throat cancer.

Beckett's early poems and fiction (*More Pricks than Kicks*, 1934, *Murphy*, 1938, and *Watt*, 1943, published 1953) had been written in English. But in the five years after cancer was diagnosed he made prolific use of the French language, writing the major prose trilogy *Molloy* (1951), *Malone Dies* (1951) and *The Unnameable* (1953), four novellas, the play *Waiting for Godot* (premièred in 1952) and *Texts for Nothing* (1955) – all in French. Beckett's later plays include *Endgame* (1957), *Krapp's Last Tape* (1959), *Happy Days* (1961), *Not I* (1973) and *Ill Seen Ill Said* (1981). He also wrote a script for the silent-film star Buster Keaton, simply entitled *Film* (1967).

In later years Beckett was as brief as he had previously been prolific. *Breath* (1970) consists of a mound of rubbish on stage and the prerecorded sound of one single breath. Beckett developed a close working relationship with the actress Billie Whitelaw and while rehearsing with her one day, he interrupted to show her three dots between two phrases in the script. 'Would you make those three dots, two dots?' he asked. Then he took out a pen and crossed out the third dot. His last publication, *Stirrings Still* (1988), comprised little more than 1,500 words and the limited, first edition went on sale at £1,000 a copy – 66p a word. They are now priced at £2,000 a copy.

Beckett was awarded the Nobel Prize in 1969 with a citation which read: 'He has transmuted the destitution of modern man into his exaltation.' Would that this were so. For although Beckett clothes the failure of modern man in some sort of poetic dignity (which, paradoxically, sometimes includes black farce and undignified humour), he is by no means exaltant about the human condition. Instead, like Sophocles' *Oedipus at Colonus*, he has learnt to live with his/our fate and come to recognise both the futility and the inevitability of our trying to escape it.

According to the obituary in the *Independent*, 'critical writing about Beckett now exceeds that of all past or present human beings written during their lifetime' (this was long before the death of Princess Diana). The same obituarist described Beckett as 'almost certainly the greatest prose stylist of the century…encapsulating the human condition in words that rediscover and change the chemistry of language'. *The Times* dubbed him the 'unassuming genius who probed the quandary of human

< 20 >

existence'. British newspapers were not always as fulsome in their praise. When *Waiting for Godot* was first performed in Britain in 1955, the drama critic of the *Daily Mail* observed: 'This play comes to us with a great reputation among the intelligenstia of Paris. And so as far as I am concerned, the intelligentsia of Paris may have it back as soon as they wish.'

MUST READ *Malone Dies, Molloy, The Unnameable, Watt*
READ ON **Albert Camus, Fyodor Dostoevsky, James Joyce, Flann O'Brien, Derek Raymond**

Brendan Behan
1923–1964
Borstal boy

Brendan Behan was born in a working-class district of Dublin when the Irish civil war (between those who accepted the 1921 treaty with Britain and the ensuing partition of Ireland, and those who did not) was still raging. Leaving school at 14, Behan was apprenticed to a house painter. Soon afterwards he joined the IRA and was sent on a mission to England. After attempting to blow up part of Liverpool docks, he was sentenced to 14 years and packed off to a British borstal (prison for juvenile offenders). In 1946 there was an amnesty for Irish Republican prisoners and Behan was released. But the following year he was imprisoned again and in 1952 was deported from Britain to Ireland.

At this time Irish Republicanism was split between a vigorous, modernising and sometimes Marxist wing, and a side to the movement that was more concerned with tradition and what would now be called Irish ethnicity. Both of these currents are discernible in Behan's writing. His is a young man's prose: the autobiographical *Borstal Boy* (1958) is a vigorously fictionalised account of his own exploits which puts Behan in roughly the same mould as 'ginger man' J P Donleavy and other literary heroes of the sixties. On the other hand, while in prison Behan took the trouble to learn Gaelic from fellow Irish detainees, and his second play was premièred in Gaelic under the title *An Giall* (subsequently produced in English as *The Hostage*, 1958).

Behan was acutely conscious of the close connections between folk music and the Irish literary tradition. There is an element of balladry in his writing, and plenty of the bawdy also. Caricature was another of Behan's talents – with mixed blessings, perhaps. Towards the end of his life, sitting at the back of the auditorium nursing a crate of stout while Joan Littlewood's Theatre Workshop got on with the job of rehearsing *The Hostage* for its London opening, Behan came close to paddywhackery, Irishness overplayed to the point of self-caricature. (After the play's opening he was embraced by Princess Margaret. Asked how this accorded with his Republicanism, he replied: 'Ah, we must always leave room for a little humbug.') He once said he was nearly born in a glass, describing himself as a drinker with a writing problem. His brother Brian (also a writer) has suggested that if Brendan came back from the dead he would have to bless every child in the parish, just in case he was the father. Brendan Behan died in 1964, before the Irish question became explosive again.

MUST READ *Borstal Boy*, *Brendan Behan: a life* by Michael O'Sullivan, *The Hostage*, *The Sayings of Brendan Behan* edited by Aubrey Dillon-Malone.
READ ON James Connolly, **J P Donleavy**, **James Joyce**, **Alan Sillitoe**

Thomas Berger

1924–
Bawdy comic of the American Dream

Following military service, Cincinatti-born Thomas Berger worked as an editor and academic librarian. His acclaimed cycle of black comedy novels took three decades to write. In *Crazy in Berlin* (1958), protagonist Carlos Reinhart surveys the end of the Second World War and sees through the American Dream. In

B

CULT FICTION

Reinhart in Love he goes to college under the GI Bill. *Vital Parts* (1970) shows Reinhart becoming even more alienated from the American Way of Life, before achieving some form of personal redemption in *Reinhart's Women* (1981). Throughout the series, Reinhart is an innocent, stumbling through a cynical society.

Although it is by no means a comic novel, the untruth behind the American Dream is also at the core of Berger's most famous book, *Little Big Man* (1964), the story of Jack Crabb, a 111-year-old white man who survived the Battle of the Little Big Horn and was adopted by the Cheyenne. It demythologised the West, exposing the cynical truth behind the 'heroic' façade (but as Jack Crabb himself says: 'The truth is always made up of little particles, which sound ridiculous when repeated.'). *Little Big Man* is an imaginative feat based on meticulous research. Berger recalled that 'After reading some 70 books about the Old West I went into a creative trance, in which it seemed as though I were listening to Jack Crabb's narrative.' The *New York Times* hailed it as 'the best novel ever about the American West'. The film version was released in 1970, starring Dustin Hoffman as Crabb. 1999 saw the publication of the long-awaited sequel *The Return of Little Big Man*.

MUST READ *Crazy in Berlin, Little Big Man*
READ ON **E L Doctorow**, Dee Brown, Ron Hansen, **Joseph Heller**, Shelby Foote

B IS FOR BOOGIE NIGHTS

5 books from the club culture

DANCER FROM THE DANCE
Andrew Holleran
love and death amid the NY 70s gay disco scene

MORVERN CALLAR
Alan Warner
heroine with a corpse who is lured by Balearic beats

HEAVEN'S PROMISE
Paulo Hewitt
living through acid house's first summer of love at the Shoom

THE MARABOU STORK NIGHTMARE
Irvine Welsh
a bit of ecstasy and dance in between the violence and horror

DISCO BISCUITS
Sarah Champion ed.
hit-and-miss dance scene fiction sampler

< 22 >

Ambrose Bierce

1842–1914?
The old cynic

Raised in Indiana, Bierce fought for the Union in the Civil War, and was wounded twice, once in the head. Some of his best stories (anthologised in *Tales of Soldiers and Civilians*) were based on his wartime experiences.

After the war, undecided whether to continue his army career or to take up journalism, he tossed a coin – and became a writer. From 1872 to 1875 he lived in England, where he wrote amusing tales for *Fun* and similar periodicals. During this period he published two collections, *Nuggets and Dust Panned Out* (1873) in California and *Cobwebs from an Empty Skull* (1874), both under the pseudonym Dod Grile. Bierce returned to America in 1877. In San Francisco, he worked for William Randolph Hearst's paper, the *Examiner*. His vitriolic columns earnt him the nickname 'Bitter Bierce' ('I sell abuse,' he wrote). Astonishingly prolific, between 1868 and 1909 he wrote 34 million words in various forms (verse, stories, journalism), all of them handwritten with a goosequill.

Bierce's most notable achievement is his unique lexicon, which he worked on for 25 years before publication in 1906. Originally entitled *The Cynic's Word Book*, in 1911 it was republished as *The Devil's Dictionary*. It is an epic monument to cynicism, as shown by Bierce's definitions of love: 'The folly of thinking much of another before one knows anything of oneself', or 'A temporary insanity curable by marriage'. Or his definition of certainty as 'being mistaken at the top of one's voice'. Bierce's *Collected Works* (12 volumes 1909–12) received mixed reviews, prompting him to write: 'Mark how my fame rings out in every zone, A thousand critics shouting: "He's unknown!" '

His friend and mentor the journalist James T Watkins knew otherwise, and told him: 'You are to become a classic and…the test of a critic's acumen…will be his attitude to Ambrose Bierce.' In 1913, Bierce went to Mexico to report on the rebellion led by Pancho Villa. He was never seen again.

MUST READ *The Devil's Dictionary, Tales of Soldiers and Civilians*
READ ON **Ring Lardner**, P J O'Rourke, **Oscar Wilde**, H L Mencken, I F Stone

Jorge Luis Borges

1899–1986
The father of magic realism

Born in Argentina, educated in Switzerland and at Cambridge, and subsequently a member of a post-First World War avant-garde movement in Spain, the Ultraists, Jorge Luis Borges created a distinctive literary voice by drawing from a wide variety of sources throughout world literature. Although he may have thought that the contours of literature were already too definite to allow a relatively young country like Argentina to make a unique contribution, Borges's creative manipulation of literary traditions produced the combination of the magical and the realistic which became magic realism – the unmistakable voice of Latin American writing in the late 20th century.

Borges returned to Argentina from Europe in 1921. In 1923 he published his first book of poems. Although he is best known for his short stories, Borges did not start publishing these until 1941. A selection from various collections was translated into English and published as *Labyrinths* in 1962. This is the collection which made Borges famous in the English-speaking world. Its collage of the abstract and the everyday is full of paradoxes, which in turn express both the contradictions and the connections between the world of literature and the real world beyond it – all this meshed together in a brand of cultural pessimism which became more popular as the Anglo-American hopes of the sixties turned into the fears of the seventies. The critic Malcolm Bradbury has said of Borges: 'He is both a highly modern and a peculiarly timeless writer, setting his stories in many ages and places and writing symbolist fables about the task of writing itself.' Some critics, of course, believe that writing about

writing is little more than pretentious self-indulgence.

Borges went blind in the mid-fifties. He was made director of the Argentinian National Library in 1955 but was subsequently demoted by Peron (husband of Eva) and put in charge of chickens instead of books. Borges's cynicism towards politics is encapsulated in his telling analysis of the Falklands War between Britain and Argentina in 1982: 'two bald men fighting over a comb'. His fiction continues to exert a strong influence over the brand of literary and social theory known as structuralism, as in John Sturrock's *The Ideal Fictions of Jorge Luis Borges* (1977).

MUST READ *Labyrinths, The Literature of Exhaustion* by John Barth
READ ON **Samuel Beckett**, Gabriel García Márquez, G K Chesterton, **Vladimir Nabokov**

Jane Bowles

1917–1973
writing is 'hell'

Jane Auer spent her first 14 years in either Manhattan or Long Island. Six months after being sent away to school in Massachusetts, she broke her leg in a riding accident and subsequently contracted tuberculosis of the knee. Eventually an operation was performed which

< 24 >

permanently fused the knee joint. She was no longer in pain but was left with a permanent limp.

Three years later she met Paul Bowles, a young composer (he later gave up music to become a writer) who was to become her husband. She had already embarked on a series of lesbian affairs. This series did not come to an end after their wedding, but the Bowles's marriage was by no means an empty shell; it was certainly unconventional (they maintained separate finances for 30 years), but the two writers lived together in the North African city of Tangier and retained an intense affection for each other until Bowles's death in 1973 following a stroke.

For Jane Auer Bowles, life was often as fraught and complicated as the protracted knee injury of her youth. She suffered deep depressions, once attempted suicide by slashing her wrists, and underwent electric shock treatment. In drink and drugs she found temporary solace, but seems to have spent many years agonising over life and what – if anything – it is for.

The protagonists of Jane Bowles's best-known work, the novel *Two Serious Ladies* (1942), are as angst-ridden as their creator and lead lives that are just as fraught as hers. When Mrs Copperfield travels to Panama, she finds she prefers the company of the prostitute Pacifica to that of her husband, who is himself captivated by the primitive exoticism of the place. Meanwhile, in Manhattan Christina Goering is dissatisfied by a series of companions and partners. The two women eventually meet but are too self-obsessed to comfort each other. One commentator described the novel as a 'chronicle of despair'.

If personal relationships were often a source of pain to Jane Bowles and her fictional protagonists, so too was the act of writing itself. Paul Bowles observed that his wife might agonise for the best part of a week over a single page. Meanwhile Jane Bowles admired the relative ease with which Paul was able to write, although she is said not to have been jealous of his ability.

Jane Bowles's personal agonies over her own writing meant that her output was minimal. She left behind a handful of short stories, a stage play, a puppet play and the recently republished novel, *Two Serious Ladies*. In the early nineties she was tipped for bigtime rediscovery. But maybe there was just not enough of Jane Bowles to warrant it.

MUST READ *Two Serious Ladies*
READ ON **Kathy Acker**, Katherine Mansfield, Virginia Woolf

< 25 >

B

Paul Bowles

1910–
Swami of the dark side

The son of a dentist, Paul Frederick Bowles was born into prosperous American East Coast suburbia. Aged 11, he experimented with his own responses to pain by attempting to circumcise himself with a needle. As a young man in New York he experimented with music, poetry and painting – and the Communist Party. He was a contributor to the avant-garde magazine *transition*, companion to composer Aaron Copland and a friend of modernist author Gertrude Stein. But in July 1947 Bowles turned his back on politics, modernism and the USA. He sailed out of Brooklyn harbour bound for Morocco, where he has lived for half a century. Around the same time, he also changed from being primarily a man of music into a novelist and short-story writer. Bowles's first novel, *The Sheltering Sky* (1949), was filmed by Bernardo Bertolucci in 1990, with John Malkovich in the leading role of Port Moresby.

Although cruel and macabre incidents occur frequently in his fiction (he has been a lifelong fan of Edgar Allan Poe), Bowles's writing style always remains deadpan. The mismatch is deliberate, for the key theme in Bowles's work is alienation. His protagonists are alienated from Western civilisation. In retreat from the 'mechanised age', they tend to wander through exotic cultures (Central American, North African) from which they are equally alienated; throughout these personal odysseys, the internal life of the Bowles protagonist is almost always alienated from his activity in the outside world.

Bowles's sense of being an invisible spectator in his own life is a precursor to Andy Warhol's feelings of separation from his own existence: compare Bowles's autobiography *Without Stopping* (1972) to Warhol's *From A to B and Back Again*. His detached style and his near-celebration of alienation, might be described as the literary equivalent of the 'birth of the cool'. (Published in 1949, Bowles's first novel is almost exactly contemporaneous with the Miles Davis album *Birth of the Cool*.)

When biographer Christopher Sawyer-Laucanno invited Norman Mailer to comment on Bowles's work, the writer–pugilist replied:

'Paul Bowles opened the world of Hip. He let in the murder, the drugs, the incest, the death of the Square (Port Moresby), the call of the orgy, the end of civilization: he invited all of us to these themes a few years ago, and he wrote one short story, "Pages From Cold Point", a seduction of a father by a son, which is one of the best short stories written by anyone.'

Bowles's critics, on the other hand, accuse him of being cold, morbid and fatalistic.

MUST READ *Collected Short Stories, An Invisible Spectator: a biography of Paul Bowles* by Christopher Sawyer-Lauçanno, *Let it Come*

< 26 >

*Down, The Sheltering Sky, You Are Not I:
a portrait of Paul Bowles* by Millicent Dillon
READ ON **William Burroughs**, **Albert Camus**,
Graham Greene, **Jim Thompson**

Kay Boyle

1902–
Expat writer turned activist

Born in St Paul's, Minnesota, and educated at
the Cincinnati conservatory of music, Boyle
published her first poem while in her teens. In
1922 she moved to Paris, where she befriended
many of the 'Lost Generation' of writers and
artists as they lingered on the Continent in a
state of post-First World War disillusion.

Boyle became acquainted with the suicidal
poet–publisher Harry Crosby. She left her husband for Ernest Walsh, publisher of *This
Quarter* magazine. But Walsh died in 1927, five
months before their child was born. Boyle went
to Neuilly to live in a commune run by
Raymond Duncan, brother of the dancer
Isadora, but when Duncan used the funds from
lecturing on the joys of simple living to buy a
luxurious American car, she left and returned to
Paris, later satirising the commune in her short
story 'Art Colony'.

Boyle's first collection appeared in 1929,
comprising experimental stories that were often
written in what she called the 'language of hallucination'. Poet William Carlos Williams
praised it: 'Her short stories assault our sleep.
They are of a high degree of excellence; for that
reason they will not succeed in America, they're
lost, damned.' Two further collections followed:
The First Lover (1933) and *The White Horses of
Vienna* (1936). Boyle's novels generally draw
on the experience of being an American expatriate in Left Bank Paris (*Plagued by the
Nightingale*, 1931 and *Generation without
Farewell*, 1960).

The novel *Avalanche* (1944) is set among the
French Resistance and shows Boyle becoming
more politically conscious. After the liberation
of Paris she became a foreign correspondent for
the *New Yorker*. Meanwhile, back in McCarthy-
ite (red-baiting) America, she came to be seen as
a dangerous radical. In 1953 she was blacklisted
and sacked from the *New Yorker*.

In 1963 Boyle settled in San Francisco and
started teaching at the university. She became a
prominent protester against the Vietnam War.
During a demonstration which blocked the
entrance to the Oakland (military) Induction
Centre, Boyle was arrested and jailed alongside
protest singer Joan Baez. When she supported
the student strike in 1968, she was fired but
promptly reinstated.

The FBI had a file on her that ran to 2,000
pages, including reports that she had an affair
with pro-fascist poet Ezra Pound before the
First World War ('I would have been no more
than ten,' she noted drily).

In over 35 books, Boyle wrote (as she said of Harry Crosby), 'with an alertness sharp as a blade and as relentless'.

MUST READ *The First Lover, Plagued by the Nightingale*
READ ON Margaret Atwood, Harry Crosby, Katherine Mansfield

Michael Bracewell

1957–
A very English Bret Easton Ellis

The five novels of Michael Bracewell investigate the stirrings of life in the dead soul of modern British society. In this respect Bracewell is not unlike Bret Easton Ellis (*Less Than Zero*,1985; *American Psycho*,1991), though his subject matter and style are generally more restrained, perhaps in keeping with the English location of his fiction. Stand-outs are *The Conclave*, which has been described as the best novel about yuppies ever written, and *Saint Rachael* (1996), which describes the search for redemption on the part of a 30-year-old man who is just getting by on Prozac after his wife has walked out. Bracewell's other novels are *The Crypto-Amnesia Club* (1988), *Divine Concepts of Physical Beauty* (1989) and *Missing Margate* (1988). He cut his critical teeth writing for *frieze*, the magazine associated with up and coming BritArtists in

< 28 >

the late eighties and early nineties. Articles on pop music by Bracewell sometimes appear in broadsheet newspapers, and in 1997 he published an historical investigation into Anglo-pop culture, *England Is Mine: pop life in Albion from Wilde to Goldie*. This should have put him on the cultural map alongside Jon Savage (*England's Dreaming*, 1992) and Greil Marcus (*Lipstick Traces*, 1989) but has so far failed to do so.

MUST READ *The Conclave, Saint Rachael*
READ ON **Bret Easton Ellis**, F Scott Fitzgerald, **Jay McInerney, Oscar Wilde**

Leigh Brackett

1915–1978
The original genre–splicer

A Los Angeleño, Leigh Brackett was a childhood fan of Edgar Rice Burroughs (creator of Tarzan) and the John Carter Martian stories. Her first short story 'Martian Quest' was published in *Astounding Science Fiction* magazine; but her first novel was the hard-boiled *No Good From A Corpse* (1944). She made a career in both genres – science fiction and crime, as well as writing the occasional Western and script-writing for Hollywood. Brackett also tried splicing together the different conventions from the various literary fields in which she worked.

As a regular contributor to *Planet Stories* alongisde Ray Bradbury and her husband Edmond Hamilton, who earnt his nickname 'world saver' by churning out stories in which an imperilled Earth was always saved from destruction in the final chapter, Leigh Brackett specialised in sword and sorcery yarns such as *The Sword of Rhiannon* (1953). This experience stood her in good stead when, shortly before her death, she scripted *The Empire Strikes Back* for director (and pulp fiction fan) George Lucas.

Brackett's crime books are *The Tiger Among Us* (1957; citizen-turns-vigilante and seeks to revenge himself on a gang of juvenile delinquents; it was filmed as *13 West Street* starring Alan Ladd, whom Chandler once described as 'a small boy's idea of a tough guy') and *Silent Partner* (1969). In 1946 she ghost-wrote *Stranger At Home* for film actor George Sanders. *No Good From a Corpse* (so hard-boiled that nobody realised it was written by a woman) attracted the attention of Howard Hawks, who drafted Brackett to work with William Faulkner and Jules Furthman on the screenplay for Raymond Chandler's *The Big Sleep*. Brackett's ending (for censorship reasons the original was not allowed to stand) met with Chandler's approval. Hawks must have liked it too, for Brackett became one his favourite screenwriters with credits on *Rio Bravo, Hatari!, El Dorado* and *Rio Lobo* – all films about male bonding that were written by a woman. After working on the remake of *The Long Goodbye* (1974), Brackett judged that Chandler himself 'might even have liked' what Robert Altman did to Philip Marlowe.

Brackett sometimes wrote sci-fi stories in a hard-boiled style: 'Starke wasn't sure where he was anymore. Venus was a frontier planet, and still mostly a big X.' Thirty years before William Gibson's *Neuromancer*, she was attempting to put Chandler out in (cyber)space.

MUST READ *The Big Jump, The Sword of Rhiannon, The Tiger Among Us*
READ ON Ray Bradbury, **Raymond Chandler, William Gibson, Dorothy B Hughes**

Scott Bradfield

1955–
Genre-bending Californian satirist

Bradfield was born and raised in California and educated at the University of California, Irvine, where he received a PhD in American literature. He stayed on to teach there for five years.

His early stories were in the sci-fi vein and were published in magazines such as *The Twilight Zone, Ambit, Other Edens, Interzone and Omni*. His first collection, *The Secret Life of Houses*, appeared in 1988. The author Brian Moore called him 'the most original voice of the new generation of Californian writers', describing his stories as being 'filled with a haunting tension between the ordinary lives we lead and the darker dreams that lurk at the edge of our minds'.

His first novel, *The History of Luminous Motion* (1989), is a stunning horror story for the millennium. It is narrated by Phillip, a precocious yet severely displaced seven-year-old who spends his life driving down the freeways with his mother, 'moving together into the lights of cities and stars'. Phillip's already fragile world starts to unravel when the re-emergence of his father brings the threat of stability; combined with the appearance of his new friend Rodney (an inspired cross between Holden Caulfield and Charles Manson) it results in a mind-boggling climax.

What's Wrong with America (1994) is an hilarious satire of modern America, chronicling the picaresque adventures of Emma O'Hallahan, a Californian grandmother who shoots her overbearing husband, buries him in the garden and enters widowhood fuelled on TV dinners, chocolate and cheap brandy, meeting cult leaders and serial killers along the way. *Animal Planet* (1995), an updated Orwellian satire featuring a crow who leads an animal revolution and becomes a media celebrity, was even funnier.

MUST READ *The History of Luminous Motion*
READ ON **Martin Amis**, Gordon Lish, **Kurt Vonnegut**

< 30 >

Richard Brautigan
1935–1984
The court jester of the counter-culture

Born in Tacoma, Washington, Brautigan was influenced by the Beat writers and specifically the San Francisco renaissance poets (Michael McClure, Kenneth Rexroth, Gregory Corso, Lawrence Ferlinghetti and Allen Ginsberg). His first publications were poetry volumes including *The Galilee Hitchhiker* (1958) and *The Octopus Frontier* (1960).

Brautigan's first novel, *A Confederate General in Big Sur* (1964), won critical acclaim. His next, *Trout Fishing in America* (1967), was a commercial success, selling over 2 million copies worldwide. Detailing the search for the perfect fishing spot, the book took in San Francisco city parks, Oregon woodlands, Idaho campsites and a Filipino laundry. The failure to find the spot symbolised the cultural aridity of mainstream American life. Both books exhibit Brautigan's inimitable style: imaginative fantasy where the normal laws of reality and the traditional logic of fiction are cast aside in favour of brilliant free-thinking bejewelled with a charmingly whimsical poetic innocence. They are the embodiment of hippiedom.

Around the time of *Trout Fishing*, Brautigan became involved with the San Francisco Mime Troup and the Diggers – radical activists who

Revenge of the Lawn
Stories 1962-1970 by Richard Brautigan

$1.95

only two sentences long) but each one was darker than its predecessor. The change in Brautigan's mood, from psychedelic optimism to Nixon-era paranoia, is discernible in the contrasting titles of his stories and prose/poems: *Please Plant this Book* (1968), combining verse and packets of seeds, and *Loading Mercury with a Pitchfork* (1976), expressing his increasingly pessimistic sense of absurdity.

For some critics, Brautigan's early naivety is now as embarrassing as love beads. Modern ears are more tuned to his darker, later voice, as heard in *Sombrero Fallout* (1931) and *The Tokyo–Montana Express* (1980).

His final book, *So the Wind Won't Blow it Away*, appeared in 1982. Rather than go the way of his old Mime Troup/Digger colleague Peter Cohon, aka *Jagged Edge* film star Peter Coyote, who also does voiceovers for car adverts, a depressed Brautigan shot himself. It was several weeks before his body was discovered.

MUST READ *Revenge of the Lawn, Sombrero Fallout, The Tokyo–Montana Express, Trout Fishing in America*
READ ON **Ken Kesey, Terry Southern, Robert Stone, Kurt Vonnegut**

donated free food to itinerants, scoffed at the meaningless psychedelic rituals enacted in Haight–Ashbury, and distributed leaflets to drug-addled hippies, saying : 'How long will you tolerate people transforming your trip into cash?' and 'Your style is being sold back to you.'

As the summer of love went sour, so Brautigan's books lost their naivety. They retained their quirky style (some chapters were

< 31 >

André Breton

1896–1966
Surrealist and non-novelist

Born in Normandy, the young André Breton became a Dadaist during the First World War and immediately afterwards published an experiment in 'automatic writing' (*Magnetic Fields*, 1920) in collaboration with Philippe Soupault. Like Soupault, Breton went on to join the surrealists; but whereas his one-time collaborator only stayed for three years, Breton became one of the senior figures in the group (especially as editor of the journal *La Révolution Surréaliste*). He continued to explore the relationship between the unconscious, the coincidental and the arbitrary throughout his creative life.

In his book, *Interviews*, Breton declared that chance (which he defines as 'nothing else than the geometric locus of these coincidences') is 'the problem of problems' in that it stands for the relationship between necessity and freedom. Here Breton is using the terminology of Marxism. When he joined the Communist Party in 1930 it had the effect of splitting the surrealists between those who shared his idea of surrealism as a revolutionary art (in a highly politicised sense) and those, like Salvador Dali, who were set against it.

In his *History of Surrealism*, Maurice Nadeau likens Breton's *Nadja* (1928) to Louis Aragon's *Paysan de Paris* (*The Peasant of Paris*;

1924). These narratives are not novels, says Nadeau, but 'direct personal accounts of a short period spent in pursuit of "surreality", plus lengthy reflections on the very meagre events reported'. *Nadja* is the 'unretouched' account of Breton's 'chance encounter' with an attractive woman of Russian origin who lives in something approaching a state of clairvoyance. Chance intervenes to bring Nadja and Breton together on a number of occasions, and also to pull them apart. Breton seems to suggest that Nadja is his familiar spirit or alter ego, but just at the point when he comes to identify with her fully, she is pronounced insane and enters an asylum. Nadeau insists that 'The facts related seemed, indeed, so hard to believe that the public has preferred to assume that they were invented. Yet nothing is imagined in *Nadja*, everything is utterly, rigorously true.'

Nadja is testament to the surrealists' preoccupation with real-life coincidences. As a piece of writing, it would work better if Breton had allotted a larger role to his own imagination and used real-life events as the mere basis for a straightforward novel. But to the surrealists, that would have been to remove the whole point of the exercise.

MUST READ *Nadja*
READ ON Louis Aragon, **Jean Genet**, Arthur Koestler, **Alexander Trocchi**

< 32 >

Poppy Z Brite

1967–
Post-punk Poe

Born in the same year as the original 'summer of love', Poppy Z Brite's fiction is imbued with the spirit of the counterculture, mixed in with the Gothic style associated with the place of her birth, New Orleans, and her literary antecedent Edgar Allan Poe.

Like many of her contemporaries, Brite came into writing almost by accident, as a way of staying out of the career structure and the values associated with the American way of life. She has held down a variety of offbeat jobs: exotic dancer, artist's model and 'mouse caretaker'. Brite enrolled at the University of California but dropped out to write her first and best horror novel, *Lost Souls*. Bringing vampirism into the era of rock'n'roll, it is the tale of white trash drug-crazed vampires with a habit of storing their victims' blood in whiskey bottles, who hit the road to New Orleans in search of blood and good times. It was followed by *Drawing Blood*, about a cartoonist, the only survivor of his family's murder at the hands of his father, who returns years later to the house where it happened; *Wormwood* (originally called *Swamp Foetus*), a collection of early short stories; and *Exquisite Corpse*, the story of two gay cannibal serial killer lovers who hang out and cause mayhem in a moody Gothic New Orleans.

Her most recent ventures have been a controversial biography of Courtney Love and another novel *The Crow*, which once again features a serial killer.

Brite shares with Poe a wilful concentration on death and decay. But she bears the marks of other influences besides literary ones. She takes a passionate interest in underground comics and zombie films (especially if they are made in Italy), and is a keen listener to seventies glam metal and contemporary 'death rock'. The self-

Poppy Z Brite

conscious overkill of these musical genres is evident in her writing. Her story, *His Mouth Will Taste Of Wormwood*, about two absinthe drinkers who rob a grave and don't even live to regret it, may become an important part of the new literature associated with the rehabilitation of this appropriately decadent drink.

Brite was born in the same city as Anne Rice, and their names have been linked as leading lights in New Gothic literature. But whereas Rice seems to be looking for redemption, Brite's characters, although just as well drawn, are more on the look-out for sex and drugs (or maybe redemption-through-sex-and-drugs), and in this respect her brand of Goth tends more towards the pornographic than the existential.

MUST READ *Drawing Blood, Lost Souls*
READ ON **Truman Capote**, **Edgar Allan Poe**, **Anne Rice**, Tennessee Williams

Charles Bukowski

1920–1994
The dirty old man of American letters

Charles Bukowski was born in Germany but brought up (from the age of four) in Los Angeles. His father abused him, and Charles later described him as 'a cruel, shiny bastard with bad breath'. To shield himself from his father, he began drinking at the age of 13.

Alcohol was probably the most important element in the remaining 60 years of his life.

Bukowski had an early ambition to be a writer, but after receiving a drawerful of editors' rejection slips in his twenties, he decided 'just to concentrate on drinking' and embarked on a ten-year binge across America. He took on a variety of menial jobs in order to pay his drink bills: petrol station attendant, lift operator, lorry driver, and ovenman in a dog biscuit factory. All of these jobs, he recalled, involved working for foremen with 'rodent eyes and small foreheads'.

In 1955 Bukowksi was hospitalised with an alcohol-induced bleeding ulcer and came close to death. As soon as he got out of hospital he hit the nearest bar, but he also took up writing again. As he put it, 'I was supposed to die, and didn't, so I started writing again. But instead of short stories it came out as poetry.' Published in 1959, Bukowski's first book of poems was 30 pages long and the print run was only 200. The second volume (1963) received some critical acclaim. During his lifetime, Bukowski published a total of 32 books of poetry and was described by Jean Genet and Jean-Paul Sartre as America's 'greatest poet'. But Bukowski refused to receive Sartre, who was anxious to meet him: 'No way baby! I wasn't into Sartre one little bit, I just had my bottle to take care of.'

While drink fuelled the activity of writing, Bukowski's drink-fuelled lowlife lifestyle was also the subject matter of his prose, which often features his alter ego Henry Chinaski.

< 34 >

Describing his restless existence as 'this mad river, this gouging, plundering madness that I would wish upon nobody but myself', Bukowski also recognised that this is what gave him something to say. 'If you're going to write,' he added, 'you have to have something to write about. The gods were good. They kept me on the street.'

Bukowski published five books of short stories, including *Notes of a Dirty Old Man*

(1969) and *Life and Death in a Charity Ward* (1974). His first novel, *Post Office* (1971), based on his experience of working in a sorting room, was commissioned by John Martin of the radical Black Sparrow Press, who promised Bukowski 100 dollars a month for life. The story is that Bukowski wrote the novel in 20 nights, and consumed 20 bottles of whiskey in the process. He went on to produce five more novels, including *Factotum* (1975), *Women* (1978), *Hollywood* (1989), *Septuagenarian Stew* (1991), and the detective story *Pulp* (1994) – published posthumously, but before he died Bukowski described it as 'easily the dirtiest, weirdest thing I've ever written'.

In the seventies Bukowski's second wife Linda (in 1956 he had married Barbara Frye, the rich publisher of a small poetry magazine, but the marriage did not last) fed him vitamins and weaned him off spirits and on to wine. Towards the end of his days, Bukwoski the ex-street bum lived in a house with a swimming pool, drove a black BMW and wrote on a computer (he still enjoyed listening to the same recorded music that he used to play in seedy hotel rooms – Sibelius, Mahler, Rossini). His routine consisted of waking up 'around noon. Linda and I'll have some breakfast, then I'll go to the track and play the horses. Then I'll come back and I'll swim and I'll sit at the computer and I'll crack me a bottle.' The various phases of his life are documented in his autobiography, *Ham on Rye* (1982).

Bukowski's life and writing inspired two films, *Tales of Ordinary Madness* (1983) and *Crazy Love* (1989). He also wrote the script for *Barfly* (1987), in which his experiences as a young man were portrayed by Mickey Rourke. Sean Penn was originally cast in the lead role, and Bukowski said he would have preferred him because Penn could both take a drink and take jokes made at the expense of his (then) partner Madonna.

A longstanding friend of Raymond Carver, Bukowski is also numbered among the original dirty realists of American letters. Politically correct critics point out that he is also 'dirty' in an undesirable sense: the sexism in his writing is legendary and by his own admission he was once accused of rape. Some of his work is little more than bar-room braggadocio, but there is also veritas in his vino. 'The worst of it', said one critic, 'has the edge of coughed-up whimsy and barroom bragging, but the best has the shock of truth.' Bukowski's assessment of his own literary performance was almost as even-handed: 'I got my act up. I wrote vile but interesting stuff that made people hate me, but made them curious about this Bukowski.'

MUST READ *Factotum, Ham on Rye, Post Office, Pulp*
READ ON **Patrick Hamilton**, Ernest Hemingway, **Malcolm Lowry**, Mickey Spillane

Mikhail Bulgakov
1891–1940
Satirist of the Stalinist era

The eldest of six children, Bulgakov studied at Kiev Theological Academy (where his father was Professor of Divinity) and Kiev University from where he graduated as a doctor in 1916. For 18 months, he practised in the north-western province of Smolensk. In his written accounts from this period (some appeared in a literary magazine, others in a medical journal), he writes movingly of the rigours of his work: being stranded '32 miles from the nearest electric light', or keeping wolf packs at bay with a pistol. Worse still was his despair, prompted by the ignorance and suspicion with which the peasants greeted his medicine.

Bulgakov abandoned medicine in 1920. He worked as a journalist until the immediate successs of his first novel, *The White Guard* (1925). Adapted into a play and retitled *The Days of the Turbins*, it was performed triumphantly at the Moscow Arts Theatre. Stalin himself saw it 15 times and considered Bulgakov Russia's most gifted playwright. In 1929 however, the play was taken off and Bulgakov was blacklisted. This was the start of the campaign of official harassment (recorded in a diary he called 'Under the Heel') that would haunt him until his death.

Bulgakov's masterpiece, *The Master and*

Margarita, was completed in 1939, a year before he died. It is a multilevel fantasy featuring the Devil and a sharpshooting cat. There is also a novel within the novel, concerning Pontius Pilate (the Roman governor in the story of Christ's crucifixion) and his fateful encounter with a wise beggar. As a fantasy, *The Master and Margarita* is ambitious and surreal; as a satire on Stalin's regime, it was daring and delightful. First published in the West in 1967, it did not appear in Russia until 1973.

The Master and Margarita inspired some of Mick Jagger's lyrics to 'Sympathy for the Devil'. The novel contains the line 'Manuscripts don't burn', a reference to Bulgakov's papers, including his diary, which the secret police confiscated and kept for years. When Bulgakov eventually got his papers back, he promptly burnt them. Afterwards he wrote: 'Familiar words flickered before my eyes…They only disappeared when the paper turned black and I furiously finished them off with the poker.' Ironically, if the authorities had not kept copies, none of Bulgakov's writing would exist today.

MUST READ *Manuscripts Don't Burn: the diaries of Bulgakov, The Master and Margarita*
READ ON Nikolai Gogol, Yevgeny Zamyatin

Anthony Burgess
1917—1993
The clockwork man

Born in north-west England into an Irish family (John) Anthony Burgess (Wilson) studied linguistics and literature at Manchester University (which later awarded him an honorary doctorate). His first love, though, was music, and he had composed a number of works before enlisting in the Royal Army Medical Corps during the Second World War. After the war Burgess entered the British colonial service (as an education officer he trained local teachers in Malaya and Borneo), but in 1959 a doctor diagnosed that he was suffering from a brain tumour and he was retired on medical grounds. By that time Burgess had already written *A Vision of Battlements* (1953, published in 1965) and what became known as his Malayan trilogy: *Time for a Tiger* (1956), *The Enemy in the Blanket* (1958) and *Beds in the East* (1959). When the medic announced that he had only a year to live, Burgess proceeded to write five more novels in 12 months in the hope of providing for his first wife who was, as he believed, soon to be widowed. But the doctor's diagnosis was wrong and Burgess enjoyed another 33 years of rude health; unlike his first wife, who died fairly soon after this episode. In 1968 Burgess married an Italian countess, and they spent much of their time on the Continent

< 37 >

– although Burgess managed to appear frequently on TV chat shows and as a columnist in British newspapers.

Burgess's output amounts to more than 50 books (besides operas and symphonies), including two volumes of autobiography. His many novels sometimes appear to have been written by rote: the stories and the characters are often mechanical. Nevertheless, there is a coherent if cynical worldview which underlies them all. God is a joker or a fool, and humanity is smart at a day-to-day level but stupid in the end. Any kind of politics that promises progress is to be distrusted, as is the postwar world of consumerism and mass marketing. But if Burgess despairs of his fellow men, he is consistently in love with language and the games a writer can play with it. The linguist and the man of letters are closely connected in his oeuvre.

The linguistic game that brought Burgess to a younger audience was his invention of 'nadsat', the argot or street slang that he put into the mouths of Alex and his 'droogs', the protagonists of *A Clockwork Orange* (1962), which chronicles the rise of a new and violent generation whose cynicism is surpassed only by that of the state. Although Burgess intended the novel to be a meditation on free will and psychological behaviourism (popular at the time, and exerting an influence on public policy), teenagers seized the novel, with its unique language and the thoroughly modern persona of Alex, and read it as a sort of *Tom Jones* of juvenile violence. This effect was compounded when *A Clockwork Orange* was filmed by Stanley Kubrick (1972), and later withdrawn by him following a moral panic about 'copycat killings' allegedly perpetrated by youths wearing the costume of Alex and his droogs.

Burgess's fans underline his satirical take on power and its apparently inevitable abuse (*Earthly Powers*, 1980; *Kingdom of the Wicked*, 1985). Critics suggest that Burgess could sometimes be self-obsessed: appearing on BBC's *Newsnight* immediately after the death of author Graham Greene, he could not help talking about himself; even his 'tribute' to Mozart on the bicentennial of the composer's birth, *Mozart and the Wolf Gang* (1991), was partly motivated by the difficulty which the young Burgess had experienced in 'fit[ting]' Mozart into my sonic universe'.

MUST READ *A Clockwork Orange,*
Earthly Powers
READ ON Graham Greene, **Ian McEwan**,
Anthony Powell, **Simon Raven**

< 38 >

William (Seward) Burroughs Jr

1914–1997
El hombre invisible

Dressed in collar and tie, three-piece suit and a fedora, William Burroughs always looked like the straight man among the Beat Generation. But his writing – violent, satirical, scatological, pornographic – makes the others look like Enid Blyton (see Ginsberg, Allen; Clellon Holmes, John; Kerouac, Jack). Burroughs was born into Midwestern, middle-class respectability, which he despised. After studying English at Harvard and medicine in Vienna, he trained as a glider pilot with the American military but was discharged as unfit for service in September 1942. While working in the shipyards of New York he became addicted to what he called Opium Jones, or G[od's] O[wn] [Medicine], i.e. heroin. According to the critic and avant-garde publisher John Calder, the 'subculture of the junkie' was to become Burroughs's 'metaphor for modern life' – a life in which humanity, says Burroughs, is victimised by addiction to power, money and sex. (Interestingly, Burroughs produced the bulk of his writing *after* he came to London and took an apomorphine cure under the direction of Dr John Dent.)

Published under the pseudonym William Lee, his first book (*Junkie: confessions of an unre-deemed drug addict*, 1953) was written in the deadpan style of Dashiell Hammett and Paul Bowles; unlike *Naked Lunch* (1959, title supplied by Jack Kerouac; edited by Allen Ginsberg), an orgiastic torrent of words which set the pace (ultra-fast) and the tone (low moral) for most of the Burroughs's oeuvre.

Naked Lunch features cartoonish characters such as Dr Benway, a mad scientist dedicated to Automatic Obedience Processing, and the Lobotomy Kid, who manufactures the Complete

William Burroughs

All-American Male, an 'all-purpose' blob of jelly with a black centipede at its centre. The resulting text is as in-yer-face as *Loaded*, but with dollops of 'spurting jissom' and orgasmic asphyxiation from the homosexual Burroughs where the tame lads' mag has to make do with straightforward tits'n'arse.

There is no traditional narrative in *Naked Lunch*. The book was built around short episodes and made ground-breaking use of the fold-in or cut-up technique originally developed by the surrealist painter Brion Gysin, whereby, according to Calder, 'the random putting-together of lines by the author with lines from selected texts by others and chance newspaper cuttings would bring a totally new text into existence'. In Burroughs's hands this technique produced not literature about drugs, but literature on drugs.

Intitially banned in the USA, *Naked Lunch* was first published by the pornographer Maurice Girodias in Paris. Its publication prompted American novelist and critic Mary McCarthy to compare Burroughs to the Anglo-Irish satirist Jonathan Swift (author of *Gulliver's Travels* and *A Modest Proposal*). She found 'many points of comparison…not only the obsession with excrement and horror of female genitals, but disgust with body politics and the whole body politic'.

Naked Lunch eventually came out in Britain in 1964, as part of *Dead Fingers Talk*, an amalgam which also included *The Soft Machine* and *The Ticket that Exploded*. 'Ugh,' responded the grande dame of English letters, Edith Sitwell, 'I

do not wish to spend the rest of my life with my nose nailed to other people's lavatories. I prefer Chanel No 5.' The ensuing correspondence continued in the *Times Literary Supplement* for a further 13 weeks. Burroughs retained his notoriety for at least another four decades.

Burroughs's later work was somewhat less outlandish, however. In 1983 he went as writer in residence to the University of Kansas, where he became devoted to his vegetable garden.

Influences on Burroughs include heroin, gangster movies, science fiction and Samuel Beckett. Thousands of creative people have been influenced by his work. Apart from the bands (*Soft Machine*, *Dead Fingers Talk*) which took their names directly from his work, the numerous rock icons who have paid homage to Burroughs directly include David Bowie, Debbie Harry, REM, and Nirvana. In 1992 *Naked Lunch* was filmed by David Cronenberg (*Videodrome, Crash*). Burroughs even appeared in a recent advert for Nike. More broadly, his intention of setting words free from the restraining discipline of grammar and rational thought has been taken up by scores of songwriters and musicians, while his habit of doing satirical violence to his subjects was replicated by cartoonists such as Robert Crumb, as well as by the punks of the seventies and the 'alternative' comedians of the eighties.

As well as harsh criticism, Burroughs's work has attracted many accolades: 'The only American writer who may conceivably be pos-

< 40 >

sessed by genius' (Norman Mailer); 'He's a writer' (Samuel Beckett); 'Ultimately he may become one of the few writers of our time who have helped to change the world by changing our perception of it' (John Calder). He has also been dismissed as 'A Giacometti sculpture in a demob suit' and 'a dirty old man', to which Burroughs replied: 'I wish I was a DIRTIER old man. I'm ashamed to go 24 hours without thinking about sex.' He was 81 at the time.

Given Burroughs's influence on contemporary culture, it is interesting to note that he got into writing by accident. It was 1951. A September afternoon in Mexico City. Burroughs and his common-law wife Joan Vollmer were partying in a room above a bar when he announced to the assembled company that the duo would perform their 'William Tell act'. Vollmer placed a glass on top of her head, and Burroughs shot at it with the gun he carried. Except that this time he missed, and Vollmer fell dead. Burroughs jumped bail and was never tried for her death, but he subsequently explained his work as an attempt to come to terms with what he had done:

'I am forced to the appalling conclusion that I would never have become a writer but for Joan's death, and to a realisation of the extent to which this event has motivated and formulated my writing…the death of Joan brought me in contact with the invader, the Ugly Spirit, and manoeuvred me into a lifelong struggle, in which I had no choice except to write my way out.'

If Burroughs got into writing because of this tragic accident, his literary success was not of his own making either. Naked Lunch is in fact Allen Ginsberg's compilation of the scraps of paper and lurid rants that he found scattered around Burroughs's room. If not for Ginsberg, Burroughs might have spent the rest of his life skulking in alleyways waiting to score. Furthermore, the celebrated 'cut-up' technique is a virtue made necessary by Burroughs's chronic inability to hold down a storyline.

Burroughs is often trumpeted for putting into effect Friedrich Nietzsche's commandment to 'destroy all rational thought'. But as literary critic Macolm Bradbury and counterculturist Jeff Nuttall have observed, this also implies the destruction of the author and the reader too. Burroughs's writing may be mind-blowing, but it is also cynical and corrosive. In railing against stale literary forms and a stagnant, hypocritical society, it simultaneously expands the mind and shrinks the self. Burroughs seems to want all our lives to be as arbitrary and accidental as his own.

Incidentally, he was still playing with guns 40 years later. In the eighties he exhibited 'action paintings' produced by taking potshots at tins of paint.

MUST READ *Cities of the Red Night, Junkie, Naked Lunch*
READ ON **Kathy Acker**, **Paul Bowles**, Robert Crumb, **Herbert Huncke**, **Will Self**

James M Cain

1892–1977
Poet laureate of the hard—boiled
school

Having graduated from Washington College in Chestertown, Maryland, James M Cain spent some years searching for something worthwhile to do. He was a clerk, a meat-packer, an unhappy teacher, a so-so singer (he gave up music after a year's training) and a failed writer. Somehow he managed to talk himself into a job as a journalist, and that's how he learnt to write in the economical but highly effective style that became his trademark.

Cain was a frequent contributor to H L Mencken's *American Mercury* before moving to Hollywood in 1931 to write film scripts. There he produced his first novel, *The Postman Always Rings Twice* (1933, originally entitled *Bar-B-Que*), about an adulterous and murderous affair (steamy enough to be banned in Boston), followed in quick succession by *Double Indemnity* (1936), *Serenade* (1937; utilising his training as a singer), *The Embezzler* (1940) and *Mildred Pierce* (1941). In 1947 Cain got married for the third time and the following year he moved to Hyattsville, Maryland, where he remained until his death in 1977. He was much happier during these 30 years, but it is generally reckoned that his writing went off the (hard-)boil.

< 42 >

In the Depression years between 1931 and 1941 Cain became the poet laureate of the first-person male confessional novel. According to critic Paul Skenazy these are tales of economic and emotional woe, in which guilt and imprisonment are always just around the corner. His protagonists have done wrong; they know it but they could not help it. They are like moths who, after a flashpoint of desire (money, a woman or

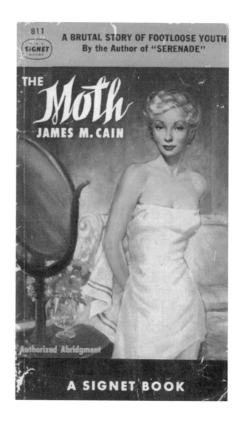

811 SIGNET

A BRUTAL STORY OF FOOTLOOSE YOUTH
By the Author of "SERENADE"

THE *Moth*
JAMES M. CAIN

Authorized Abridgment

A SIGNET BOOK

both), are lured helplessly to their self-inflicted doom. Critic Geoffrey O'Brien suggested that 'if the Cain hero ultimately embraces his own catastrophe, it is because it is the most interesting thing that has ever happened to him'.

Set in the urban wilderness of diners, bars and pool rooms, Cain's stories are written in a terse vernacular with never a word wasted; sentences last only as long as it would take for the action they describe to occur in real time. This is the epitome of pulp writing (Edmund Wilson noted that it was 'always in danger of being unintentionally funny'). But Cain claimed that 'hard-boiled' only existed in the minds of the critics; he also claimed never to have read Dashiell Hammett, the crime writer to whom he is often compared.

The journalist and novelist Tom Wolfe reckons that Cain is incomparable: 'Nobody else has ever pulled it off the way that Cain does, not Hemingway, not even Chandler.' The latter felt differently, dismissing Cain as 'a Proust in greasy overalls, a dirty little boy with a piece of chalk and a board fence and nobody watching'. Ross MacDonald, whose Lew Archer is nearly as memorable as Chandler's Philip Marlowe, believed that Cain had produced 'a pair of American masterpieces, back to back'. In France, Cain was regarded as the essence of American cool. *The Postman Always Rings Twice* was the inspiration for *The Outsider* by Albert Camus, who described it as the first existential novel from the USA. Many of Cain's novels were filmed in Hollywood; the film versions became prime examples of the core text of American existentalism, aka film noir.

MUST READ *Double Indemnity, Mildred Pierce, The Postman Always Rings Twice, Serenade*
READ ON **Albert Camus**, **Dashiell Hammett**, Ernest Hemingway, **Horace McCoy**

Paul Cain

1902—1966
Hardest of the hard—boiled

'Paul Cain', the pseudonym of Chicagoan George Sims, saw 'life in its toughest phases' before moving to Los Angeles aged 18. Three years later he was writing Hollywood scripts under the name Peter Ruric.

From the mid-twenties to the early thirties, Sims/Ruric travelled around the world. He subsequently claimed to have been a bosun's mate, a Dadaist painter and a professional gambler. In 1931 he called himself Paul Cain and wrote his first story for the premier pulp fiction magazine *Black Mask*. Four more stories for *Black Mask* were subsequently put together and published as Cain's one and only novel, *Fast One* (1933), which Raymond Chandler described as 'some kind of high point in the ultra hard-boiled manner'. Chandler also praised the book's bleak conclusion, saying it was 'as murderous and at the same time poignant as anything in that manner that has ever been written'. The *New York Times* was not so favourable, describing it as 'a ceaseless welter of bloodshed and frenzy, a sustained bedlam of killing and fiendishness'.

Cain wrote a few more stories for *Detective Fiction Weekly* and *Star Detective Magazine* before switching to screenplays for films such as *The Black Cat*, starring Boris Karloff and Bela Lugosi, and *Mademoiselle Fifi*, adapted from two Guy de Maupassant stories and produced by the king of B-movie chillers, Val '*Cat People*' Lewton. He retired from scriptwriting owing to ill health, but in 1946 published a crime story collection, *Seven Slayers*. In the early fifties he wrote culinary articles for *Gourmet* magazine, and in the sixties he wrote some fairly tasteless TV scripts. Cain died of cancer in 1966, leaving behind possibly the hardest-boiled crime novel ever, with its 'short staccato sentences that jet from the pages like black sparks'.

MUST READ *Fast One*
READ ON **Dashiell Hammett**, Richard Stark, Raoul Whitfield

Italo Calvino
1923–1985
Surreal satirist

Born in Cuba, Italo Calvino grew up in San Remo, Italy, and was educated at the University of Turin. At 18 he was forced to join the Young Fascists (this was the era of Mussolini), but in 1943 he joined the Resistance and fought the Nazis with the partisan forces in Liguria. During the forties he wrote for the Communist newspaper *L'Unità*. When he subsequently left the Communist Party he felt deeply distressed. In his collection of essays, *The Literature Machine* (1944), Calvino recalls: 'Having grown up in times of dictatorship, and being overtaken by total war when of military age, I still have the notion that to live in peace and freedom is a frail kind of good fortune that might be taken away from me in an instant.'

Following in the footsteps of Cesar Pavese, Calvino signed up with the Turin-based publishers Einaudi. In 1947 he published his first novel, *The Path to the Nest of Spiders*. This was essentially a Neo-realist work, contemporaneous with the Italian Neo-realist cinema of Roberto Rossellini and Vittorio de Sica, which gives little indication of Calvino's future use of fantasy and folk tales. During the Cold War years, with freedom once again at risk, Calvino published a trilogy which combined fantasy and history with satire and surrealism – a combina-

< 44 >

tion that was to become his hallmark. These three novels were collected together as *Our Ancestors* (1960). *Invisible Cities* (1972), another surreal fantasy in which Marco Polo invents dream-cities to amuse Kubla Khan, won the prestigious Premio Felrinelli Award in 1973. Of Calvino's *If on a Winter's Night a Traveller* (1979), Salman Rushdie declared: 'He is writing down what you have always known except that you've never thought of it before.'

Calvino died while working on *Under a Jaguar Sun* (1991), a collection of stories on the five senses. 'Sight' and 'Touch' were never completed.

MUST READ *If on a Winter's Night a Traveller, Our Ancestors*
READ ON **Jorge Luis Borges**, John Gardner, **Franz Kafka**

Albert Camus

1913—1960
The Rebel

Albert Camus was born in the (then) French colony of Algeria. A year later, his father died fighting for France in the trenches of the First World War. His youth was characterised by poverty (he regarded his intellect as a means of escape), a passion for football and the onset of tuberculosis. In 1934 Camus joined the Communist Party, but left it the following year. He worked in the theatre and as a journalist. In 1939 he produced a series of articles about social conditions in the Algerian town of Oran.

In 1940, Camus moved to Paris to work on the evening paper *Paris Soir*, but when the French capital was occupied by German troops he decamped to Lyons where, in 1942, he joined the Resistance group Combat. As a clandestine contributor to the underground newspaper of the same name, Camus returned to Paris. In the years 1944 to 1946, following the liberation of the capital, two of his plays were premièred and his second novel, *The Plague* (1947), won the coveted Prix des Critiques. He lived the life of a Left Bank *intello* until he was ostracised for refusing to support the terrorist tactics of the Algerian FLN. In 1957, Camus was awarded the Nobel Prize for his work as a dramatist, essayist and novelist. Less than three years later, on 4 January 1960, he was killed in a car accident.

'There is no love of life without despair of life.' In this one sentence, Camus summed up the contradictory elements in his own work. His first essays, written in Algeria, are concerned with the powerlessness and loneliness of human beings in the face of death and nature. In 1938, looking back at his early work and the Mediterranean life which informed it, Camus wrote:

'What struck me then was not a world made after the measure of man but one closing up over man. No, if the language of these lands was in harmony with what reverberated deep within me, the reason is not that it answered my questions but that it made them superfluous. It was not thanksgiving that could rise to my lips but the *nada* which could not have been borne but in the sight of lands which are crushed by the sun.'

His early emphasis was on despair rather than love of life.

Camus later described Meursault, the protagonist of his first novel, *L'Etranger* (*The Outsider*, 1942), as a man 'who loves the sun that casts no shadows'. He is a seeker of absolute truth who finds it sadly lacking in the absurd rituals of society, including the convention that a son ought to cry at the funeral of his mother. Meursault is subsequently condemned to death after killing an Arab in a fight on the beach (the fictional incident that 40 years later inspired the song 'Killing An Arab' by The Cure). Camus later explained that his anti-hero was really condemned because 'he does not play along…In our society anyone who does not cry at the burial of his mother runs the risk of being condemned to death.' In the philosophical essay *Le Mythe de Sisyphe* (*The Myth of Sisyphus*; 1942, named after the character in Greek mythology condemned to spend eternity pushing a rock up a hill and then watching it roll down again), Camus further developed the idea of human society as an exercise in absurdity.

Informed by his own experience in the French Resistance, the later work of Camus asks how we can retain our humanity in opposition to crushing, 'totalitarian' social systems such as Fascism. His answer is that we can preserve our humanity as long as we give up on grandiose schemes for making history and content ourselves with surviving it instead. In this notion of a reduced sphere of responsible activity on the part of human beings, Camus went beyond his earlier nihilism and achieved something like a state of grace. Although associated with alienation and angst (which is surely what prompted Mancunian Mark E Smith to name his band The Fall after a novel by Camus), he once said that he saw in himself an 'invincible summer'.

By rejecting both left- and right-wing political ideologies and challenging the hitherto unquestioned notion of 'progress' as the accumulation of human mastery over the world, Camus set the tone for today's widespread scepticism towards politics and politicians. He also anticipated some aspects of the Green ethos in its concern with the risks involved in the attempted human domination of nature. The *Sunday Times* recently described him as 'the last great French thinker'.

MUST READ *The Fall, The Outsider, The Plague, The Rebel*
READ ON Søren Kierkegaard, **Jean-Paul Sartre**, **Richard Wright**, any of the American hard-boiled school

Truman Capote

1924—1984
Shooting Southern star

Truman Streckfuss Persons Capote made his debut in 1948 with *Other Voices, Other Rooms*, a rites-of-passage Gothic novel which both reflects and exaggerates the American South in which he grew up (a 10-year-old Truman appears as a character in *To Kill a Mockingbird*, the novel about race and the South written by Capote's neighbour Harper Lee). In the fifties, Capote made his name as a 'new journalist' writing intimate psychological profiles of the rich and famous for upmarket magazines such as *Vogue*, *Harper's Bazaar* and the *New Yorker*. As a journalist, he always boasted that he never needed to take notes, but some of his interviewees complained that his work was riddled with inaccuracies as a result. Capote's style was new in that he brought the imaginative techniques of a novelist to the previously staid routine of celebrity interviews: pop writers of the seventies such as Mick Farren and Nick Kent were largely retreading the ground that Capote had carved out nearly a quarter of a century earlier.

Capote used his keen observation of the New York social scene to write *Breakfast at Tiffany's* (1958), which was bowdlerised and filmed with winsome Audrey Hepburn in the lead role of Holly Golightly. His powers of

Breakfast at Tiffany's
Truman Capote

The story on which the Paramount Picture was based,
starring Audrey Hepburn and George Peppard

PENGUIN BOOKS 2/6

observation were also deployed in a series of barbed witticisms directed at his literary rivals. Lillian Hellmann he described as looking like 'George Washington in drag'. The English theatre critic Kenneth Tynan was dismissed as a hack writer with 'the morals of a baboon and the guts of a butterfly'.

As a socialite himself, Capote's greatest moment was the Black and White Ball that he threw at the New York Plaza Hotel's grand ballroom on 28 November 1966. Attended by the greatest celebrities of that era, from Frank Sinatra to Elizabeth Taylor and the Duke and Duchess of Windsor, the event was duly reported in *Vanity Fair*, *Esquire* and all the glossies; it went down in the annals of New York as the swingingest moment of the sixties. But Capote the party animal became something of a self-caricature. One millionaire host said to his wife: 'Let's keep him. We can put him on the mantel.' In the eyes of others he became known as 'the little monster'.

Short, increasingly rotund, speaking with a Southern twang and a nasal lisp, effeminate, homosexual, a drug user (he is said to have once lost 4,000 dollars' worth of cocaine between alighting from a car and getting inside his apartment), and an alcoholic, Capote was not always the belle of the ball. What began as a valuable gift for self-publicity later turned into a gross form of self-obsession. After he divulged some ugly secrets (or manufactured some ugly rumours?) in an instalment of his never-to-be-finished work *Answered Prayers* which was published in *Esquire*, Capote was embroiled in a series of rancorous feuds, notably with essayist and novelist Gore Vidal. In his later years Capote was so desperate for compliments, and so jealous of anyone else in the limelight, that he is rumoured to have bared the breasts of a Hollywood starlet whose *décolletage* was attracting the attention of partygoers – attention that

Capote wanted for himself, and himself alone. After visiting Capote in 1978, Martin Amis depicted him as a burnt-out case, exhausted by years of playing the socialite game and eventually coming off the worse for it.

As a writer, Capote is most famous for *In Cold Blood* (1965), the true but fictionalised story of the apparently motiveless murder of a wholesome Midwestern farming family by a pair of alienated drifters. Derived from Capote's long interviews with the convicted killers, Richard Eugene Hickock and Perry Edward Smith, *In Cold Blood* is a riveting combination of journalism and fiction which was immediately hailed as the first example of a new literary form, the 'non-fiction novel'. Capote's detractors pointed out that 19th-century novelists had done plenty of first-hand research – Dickens went on police raids, for example. Kenneth Tynan complained that Capote had not tried to stop the execution of Hickock and Smith because a reprieve for them would have lessened the dramatic effect of his 'factoid' novel. Meanwhile journalist (and subsequently novelist) Tom Wolfe praised Capote for destroying the traditional literary hierarchy which had novelists at the top, 'men of letters' (essayists and reviewers) in the middle, and hack journalists at the bottom.

Capote certainly helped to blur the distinction between fact and fiction in literature, but only history will judge whether this has been a blessing or a curse.

MUST READ *Breakfast at Tiffany's, In Cold Blood, Other Voices Other Rooms, Truman Capote: in which various friends, enemies, acquaintances, and detractors recall his turbulent career* by George Plimpton
READ ON Harper Lee, Tennessee Williams, **Tom Wolfe**

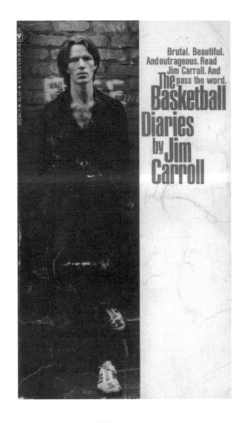

Jim Carroll

1951–
Shooting hoops and heroin

Raised a Catholic, Carroll was a precocious teenager who excelled at basketball, writing, doing drugs and lying. He won a scholarship to Trinity High School in Manhattan and became an All-City basketball star, as described in his first book *The Basketball Diaries* (1969; filmed in 1995 with the miscast Leonardo DiCaprio in the lead role). Eschewing the life of a sports star for that of writer, junkie, and demi-monde celebrity, Carroll started contributing verse and prose pieces to *Rolling Stone* magazine, *Poetry*, and the *Paris Review*. His poetry collection, *Living at the Movies*, was published in 1973.

Carroll was hanging out with the luminaries of the New York arts scene, many of whom appeared in his second volume of diaries *Forced Entries* (1987) – Allen Ginsberg, Bob Dylan, Andy Warhol (Carroll 'worked' briefly at the Factory), Terry Southern, William Burroughs (who wrote that '*Forced Entries* captures the early-seventies period in New York better than anything I've read in a long time'), even Salvador Dali. When not playing the social butterfly, Carroll was injecting heroin and/or amphetamines, swallowing barbiturates by the handful and finally, fleeing to a California retreat to clean up.

Towards the end of *Forced Entries*, Carroll

admitted: 'I have been considering lately writing lyrics for some rock-and-roll bands. Certain friends have prompted me towards this idea for years. Some…have even made the ridiculous proposition that I sing these songs…that I actually front a band!' As frontman for the imaginatively named Jim Carroll Band he made three albums: *Catholic Boy*, *Dry Dreams*, and *I Write Your Name*. In 1991, he did what he probably should have done all along, and released *Praying Mantis*, a spoken-word recording.

MUST READ *The Basketball Diaries, Forced Entries*
READ ON **William Burroughs**, Allen Ginsberg, Patti Smith, **Hunter S Thompson**

Lewis Carroll

1832–1898
Children's stories for adults

Lewis Carroll, the pseudonym of Charles Lutwidge Dodgson, was the Oxford don who created Alice, sometimes described as the most popular female character in fiction. Eldest son of the rector of Daresbury, Cheshire, in northwest England, Dodgson was himself ordained in 1861. A fastidious and exacting man who always wore gloves, even in the hottest weather, he never became a parish priest, but lived his entire adult life within the rarefied precincts of Oxford University, where he lectured in logic and mathematics. Dodgson was also an expert practitioner in the (then) novel techniques of photography. In the mid-19th century dons were expected to remain celibate, and it is likely that Dodgson never had a full sexual relationship. He displayed a keen interest in pre-pubescent girls, but critics are divided as to whether his interest was of a sexual nature.

The character of Alice was based on Mary, the second daughter of Henry George Liddell, dean of Dodgson's college (and co-author of the standard Greek–English lexicon). The stories which later became *Alice's Adventures in Wonderland* (1865) were devised at least in part during boating trips on the Thames in which Dodgson was accompanied by Mary Liddell. But the friendship with the Liddell family came to an end which remains as mysterious as it was abrupt, and Dodgson turned his attention to other young girls. Each year he would holiday in Eastbourne on the south coast of England, and subsequently record in his diary the various acquaintanceships he had struck up with successive pre-pubescent females.

Carroll is often praised for rendering childhood into prose which is as sublime as childhood itself. Dr Jonathan Miller, who directed a version of the Alice stories for television in 1966, has suggested that they are about a girl on the cusp of puberty who is perturbed by the looming absurdities of adulthood. Carroll himself seems to have been ill at ease in his rela-

< 50 >

tionships with grown-ups. Perhaps he sought solace in the presumed perfection of childhood. Judging by the darker tone of *Through the Looking Glass* (1871), Carroll was by no means certain that his notion of childhood would survive the assault of the adult world.

At the time of their publication, Alice's adventures were regarded as children's stories and Carroll was revered as the 'saint of the children'. In today's climate of concern about child sexual abuse, his fascination with young girls tends to be seen as far from saintly. His stories too are generally viewed in a different light. In the mid- to late sixties, when the hippies expressed a preference for drug-induced dreams over mundane reality, they seized upon Alice's adventures as an early parable of their own sensibility. The new-found popularity of Lewis Carroll among late teenagers and twentysomethings was demonstrated by the appearance of his characters in the song lyrics of the counterculture, such as Jefferson Airplane's 'White Rabbit' and The Beatles's 'I am a Walrus'.

Since the sixties, many aspects of the hippie sensibility have gone mainstream, and millions of grown-ups have rediscovered Alice as part of a growing disaffection with the absurdity of the adult world. In the nineties, Alice continues to be a fashionable character, as indicated by Jeff Noon's 'third book' of her adventures (*Automated Alice*) in which she is transported to the modern world. Lewis Carroll also wrote sur-

real and humorous verse such as 'Jabberwocky' and *The Hunting of the Snark*.

MUST READ *Alice's Adventures in Wonderland, Through the Looking Glass*
READ ON **Angela Carter**, Edward Lear, **Jeff Noon**

Angela Carter

1940–1992
Fierce feminist fairy tales

Born in Sussex in 1940, Angela Carter read English at Bristol University, lived for two years in Japan, and was fellow in creative writing at Sheffield University from 1976 to 1978. From 1980 to 1981 she was visiting professor on the writing course at Brown University, Providence, Rhode Island; in 1984 she was writer in residence at the University of Adelaide in south Australia. Carter's poetry has been published in the *London Magazine* and the *Listener* (a literary magazine run by the BBC; now defunct); for 20 years she was a major contributor to *New Society*, the current affairs and culture weekly which is now part of the *New Statesman*. With director Neil Jordan, she wrote the script for the film *The Company of Wolves*. She translated the fairy stories of Charles Perrault; her first book-length non-fiction work, *The Sadeian Woman: an exercise in cultural history*, was published by the feminist publishing house Virago in 1979.

Carter's fiction has been described as 'entertainment for boys and girls who like their De Sade mixed with Suchard chocolate'. She combines sex, violence and fairy tales in what one critic dubbed 'everyday life among the mythic classes', and is widely known as the godmother of a magic realist sensibility that is both Gothic and British. After making her debut with *Shadow Dance* (1965) her second book, *The Magic Toyshop* (1967), was a modern myth of an orphaned girl who has the horrors when she goes to live with her uncle. It won the John Llewellyn Rhys Prize in 1967. Carter's novel *Several Perceptions* was another award winner (Somerset Maugham Prize, 1968). *Heroes and Villains* (1969) is a post-apocalyptic romance combining magic, religion and adventure. After *Love* (1971), Carter wrote *The Infernal Desire Machines of Doctor Hoffman* (1973), the story of a war fought against a diabolic doctor and his attempt to demolish the structures of reason and so liberate mankind from the chains of the reality principle. Novelist Ian McEwan said it 'combined exquisite craft with an apparently boundless reach'.

The Times recommended *Nights at the Circus* (1985) on account of Carter's invention of 'a new raunchy, raucous, Cockney voice for her heroine Fevvers, taking us back into a rich, turn of the nineteenth-century world, which reeks of human and animal variety, and has produced her most flamboyant novel to date'. The *Observer* commented: 'Ms Carter's new novel is a mistress-piece of sustained and weirdly wonderful Gothic that's both intensely amusing and provocatively serious.' *The Passion of New Eve* (1977) is set in a futuristic New York which has become the City of Dreadful Night where dissolute Leilah performs a dance of chaos for Evelyn, a young Englishman who is fated, post-castration, to become the new Eve. Baroque in style, apocalyptic in vision, black in humour, it is a pilgrim's progress through a world of disintegration and shifting sexuality.

Carter also published four volumes of short stories, including *Fireworks* (1974), *The Bloody Chamber* (1979; winner of the Cheltenham Festival Award) and *Black Venus* (1985), featuring her fictionalisation of historical characters such as Lizzie Borden and Baudelaire's syphilitic mistress. For some, Carter's heady mix of fact and fantasy, real life and mythology, is nothing short of magical. Others find her witchy brew too lurid and even poisonous.

MUST READ *Black Venus, Heroes and Villains, The Magic Toyshop, Nights at the Circus, Several Perceptions, The Passion of New Eve*
READ ON **Nick Cave, Patrick McGrath, Jeanette Winterson**

< 52 >

Raymond Carver

1938–1988
The American Chekov

Ray Carver was born into a poverty-stricken family in Clatskanie, Oregon at the tail-end of the Depression. The son of a violent alcoholic, he married at 19, started a series of menial jobs and his own career of 'full-time drinking as a serious pursuit'. A career that would eventually kill him. Constantly struggling to support his wife and family Carver enrolled in a writing programme under author John Gardner in 1958 and he saw this as a turning point.

Rejecting the more experimental fiction of the sixties and seventies, Carver pioneered a precisionist realism reinventing the American short story during the eighties, heading the line of so-called 'dirty realists' or 'K-mart realists' – Richard Ford, Tobias Wolff, Ann Beattie, Jayne Anne Phillips who wrote in sensitive detail of ordinary lives of quiet desperation in small-town blue-collar America. Set in trailer parks and shopping malls they are stories of banal lives that turn on a seemingly insignificant detail. Carver writes with meticulous economy suddenly bringing a life into focus in a similar way to the paintings of Edward Hopper. His characters lead unheroic lives where things are frequently left unspoken – everything being implied through the minutiae of the story rather than being said. As well as a master of the short story Carver was an accomplished poet publishing several highly acclaimed volumes.

His earlier story collections, *Will you Please Be Quiet, Please?*, are more honed and pessimistic. After the 'line of demarcation' in Carver's life – 2 June 1977, the day he stopped drinking – his stories become increasingly more redemptive and expansive (*Cathedral*, 1983). Alcohol had eventually shattered his health, his work and his family – his first marriage effectively ending in 1978. Ray finally married his long-term partner Tess Gallagher (they met ten years earlier at a writers' conference in Dallas) in Reno less than two months before he eventually lost his fight with cancer.

MUST READ *Where I'm Calling From*
READ ON Anton Chekov, Tess Gallagher, Richard Ford, **Tobias Wolff**

Nick Cave

1960–
The bad seed

Nick Cave is best known as a songwriter and performer who fronted The Birthday Party (named after Harold Pinter's play) before forming his own band (Nick Cave and the Bad Seeds), going on to work with female singers P J Harvey and Kylie Minogue. But he is also a writer of some repute.

Nick Cave's birthplace is the Australian town of Warracknabeal. His mother was a librarian and his father (killed in a car crash in 1976) a troubled English teacher and failed novelist. Brought up in the Anglican church, which accounts for the plentiful biblical references in his writing, Cave attended Caulfield Grammar School in Melbourne, where he played in his first band, The Boys Next Door (also briefly known as Torn Ox Bodies). By the time they moved to London they had changed their name to The Birthday Party, and under that name released two acclaimed LPs in 1981 and 1982 respectively. When The Birthday Party broke up not long after the release of their second album, Cave went to Los Angeles with the intention of writing a film script based on Jack Henry Abbott's *In The Belly of the Beast*. Some of his ideas were later reworked as part of the John Hillcoat prison film *Ghosts of the Civil Dead*. In 1984, in collaboration with post-punk performance artist Lydia Lunch, Cave wrote 50 one-page playlets about pornography and violence, issued under the title *Fresh Cunt in a Can*. In 1988 he appeared in the Wim Wenders film *Wings of Desire* and while in Berlin started writing his first novel *And the Ass Saw the Angel* (1989). The story is told through a series of flashbacks in the life of Euchrid Eucrow, a criminally insane deaf-mute who is sinking into quicksand while on the run from a Southern lynch mob. In its combination of horror and beauty, Cave's fans have compared *And the Ass Saw the Angel* to William Faulkner and Gabriel García Márquez, but some literary critics believe that Cave is unduly flattered by the comparison.

In 1988 Cave published a collection of lyrics and essays, *King Ink*, followed by a second collection, *King Ink II* (1997). His album of cover versions, *Kicking against the Pricks*, recalls the title of an early collection of stories by Samuel Beckett.

MUST READ *And the Ass Saw the Angel*
READ ON **Cormac McCarthy, Carson McCullers, William Faulkner**

Céline

1894–1961
Desperation in the lower depths

Born in Paris to workers who were skilled but still poor (father a clerk, mother a seamstress), Louis Ferdinand Destouches, who subsequently adopted the pseudonym 'Céline', performed a variety of dead-end jobs before enlisting in the French cavalry two years before the outbreak of the First World War in 1914. While serving on the Western Front he was wounded in the head. His wounds caused him physical and mental pain throughout the rest of his life. Released from military service, he studied medicine and emigrated to the USA where he worked as a

< 54 >

staff doctor at the newly built Ford plant in Detroit before returning to France and establishing a medical practice among the Parisian poor. Their experiences are featured prominently in his fiction.

Céline was virulently anti-Semitic (not so exceptional in the 1930s, when one of the slogans at political demonstrations was '*mieux Hitler que Blum*' – we would rather have Hitler than Leon Blum, the Jewish prime minister of France at the time). After the Nazis were driven out of France in 1944, Céline fled to Denmark. He was tried in his absence and sentenced to death, although the sentence was later revoked. Céline returned to France where he lived out his last days in a state of partial paralysis and near-insanity.

Céline's first novel was *Journey to the End of Night* (1932), followed by *Death on the Instalment Plan* (1936). The idea that life is just death on hire purchase gives an indication of the largely pessimistic conclusions that Céline tended to draw from his vision of proletarian existence tinged with madness and violence. His use of lowlife as a metaphor for all our lives seems to have influenced the later generation of writers that includes William Burroughs and Charles Bukowski. Among his own contemporaries, the writer closest to Céline is Henry Miller, although the latter's joyful lust for life is largely missing from his French counterpart.

MUST READ *Death on the Instalment Plan, Journey to the End of Night*

READ ON **Charles Bukowski**, Maxim Gorky, **Henry Miller, George Orwell**

Raymond Chandler

1888–1959
The white knight of LA noir

Chandler's father, a hard-drinking railway employee, abandoned his family when his son was just seven years old. Raymond and his mother moved to England. Educated at Dulwich College, in south London, he worked for the Admiralty and occasionally published verse and reviews in the *Westminster Gazette* and the *Academy* magazine. Of these early efforts Chandler said: 'They are of an intolerable preciousness of style, but already quite nasty in tone…I was an elegant young thing, trying to be brilliant about nothing.'

After serving in the Great War, Chandler returned to America and worked for an oil company in California. He rose to the rank of executive but was sacked for being an alcoholic, and started writing hard-boiled stories for the crime magazine *Black Mask*. This was the beginning of a career in which he created one of the most famous fictional detectives in Philip Marlowe and formulated a literary (and mercilessly accurate) version of California, besides achieving international success through novels and films.

'The swans of our childhood were probably

< 55 >

just pigeons', Chandler wrote in a letter in 1954. His writing is literature dressed down as genre fiction – swans masquerading as pigeons. *Time* magazine described *The Long Goodbye* (1953) as 'awesome' and the *New York Times* said it was 'a masterpiece'. The poet W H Auden observed that Chandler's books are 'works of art' and declared them 'powerful but extremely depressing'. Philip Marlowe is strong

but often verging on the brink of depression. He spends a great deal of time brooding and drinking alone in his shabby office: 'I sat staring at my feet and lapping the whiskey out of the bottle. Just like any common bedroom drunk,' (*The High Window*, 1942) or else getting beaten up, drugged and generally abused by wealthy and sadistic crooks. Sadly, when Marlowe finally meets someone else to drink with (the alluring Linda Loring, whom he first encounters in *The Long Goodbye*), Chandler dries up and the books come to an unconvincing and frustrating conclusion.

Writing did not come as easily to Chandler as it did to Hammett, Cain and other crime writers, perhaps because he knew he was walking the line between pulp and poetry. This tension is visible in the romanticised character of Marlowe and in Chandler's insistence that he must be an honourable man down among the mean streets. Unlike most pulp protagonists, who are driven by forces beyond their control, Marlowe is a rational, reflective figure. Chandler's early writing is an imitation of Hammett's; but alongside the Marlowe character he developed an original voice which, for all the sharp wit and cracking dialogue, speaks primarily of loneliness and the detachment of the human spirit.

As much as Chandler was obsessed (if often disgusted) with Hollywood the place, Hollywood the industry was obsessed with him, and virtually everything he wrote (with the

< 56 >

exception of his voluminous and legendary correspondence) was turned into celluloid. Oscar-winning director/writer Billy Wilder, who collaborated with Chandler on the classic film of James M Cain's *Double Indemnity* said of his work: 'A kind of lightning struck on every page…the dialogue was good …sharp.'

Chandler's critics accuse him of being a misogynist, racist and homophobic. Crime writer George V Higgins, author of *The Friends of Eddie Coyle* (1972), has suggested that Chandler hated his mother and his wife. British critic Russell Davies claimed that he was sexually adrift, 'an unhappy man' who led 'a miserable life'. Mike Davis, author of *City of Quartz*, a cultural and social history of Los Angeles, wrote in 1990 that 'Marlowe, the avenging burgher, totters precariously on the brink of fascist paranoia. Each successive Chandler novel focuses on a new target for Marlowe's dislike: Blacks, Asians, gays, "greasers", and, always, women.' The following year, in a book entitled *In Search of Literary Los Angeles*, Chandler was branded 'a misanthrope, and a bigot', and his unique depiction of the city was cited as being merely a product of 'his own alcoholic disillusionment'.

Loved or loathed, Chandler's influence on crime writers and film-makers remains enormous: Ross Macdonald, Robert B Parker, James Ellroy, Howard Browne, Lawrence Block, and scores of others have acknowledged their debt to him, while directors and scenarists, ranging from Hitchcock to Robert Towne (author of the screenplay for *Chinatown*) to new kids like John Woo and Tarantino, have all either used or plundered his talents.

Two remarkable statements help to illustrate the breadth of this extraordinary writer. Twenty years before his death, Chandler wrote of his life: 'The things by which we live are the distant flashes of insect wings in a clouded sunlight.' At the peak of his fame, when asked by his British publisher to write his autobiography, he replied: 'Who cares how a writer got his first bicycle?'

MUST READ *The Big Sleep, The Letters of Raymond Chandler, The Life of Raymond Chandler* by Frank MacShane, *The Long Goodbye, Raymond Chandler* by Tom Hiney
READ ON **Dashiell Hammett,** Ross Macdonald

James Hadley Chase

1906–1985
'Fascist' thriller

London-born James Hadley Chase (René Raymond) only went to the USA on short visits, yet he wrote around 40 thrillers and gangster stories set there, and in the style of the hard-boiled American pulp writers. Titles such as *There's a Hippy on the Highway* bear witness to the longevity of his literary career, but the book for which he is remembered is the one that made

C

CULT FICTION

C   IS FOR COKE

10 books fuelled by the real thing

STORY OF MY LIFE
Jay McInerney
moneyed Manhattan twenty—nothing
chronicles

LESS THAN ZERO
Bret Easton Ellis
white lines with LA's rich and bored
teens

NOVEL WITH COCAINE
M Ageyev
nasal abuse in 19th century
St Petersburg

POSTCARDS FROM THE EDGE
Carrie Fisher
cokehead rehab California style

SNOWBLIND
Robert Sabbag
memoir of the cocaine smuggling
trade in the 70s and 80s

ICED
Ray Shell
raw confessions of a crackfiend

POWDER BURN
Carl Hiaasen
thriller set amid the Florida drug wars

COCAINE NIGHTS
J G Ballard
murder in a hedonistic community on
the Costa del Sol

COCAINE
Phil Strongman
highs and lows of the London music
scene

POWDER
Kevin Sampson
On—the—road rock'n'roll excess with
everybody's favourite band The Grams

< 58 >

his name back in 1939, *No Orchids for Miss Blandish*, the tale of a wealthy young girl who is kidnapped, held to ransom and raped by a sadistic criminal who lives in awe of his Ma (prefiguring James Cagney's role as Codie in the Raoul Walsh film *White Heat*, 1948).

The popularity of *No Orchids for Miss Blandish* was growing just as British opinion-formers were trying to engender a national spirit to help fight the war against the Nazis, and this seamlessly written story of the cruel and violent use of power seemed to go against all the civilised values that they thought Britain ·was fighting for. In 1944, George Orwell, writing in *Horizon* magazine, reported that 'several people, after reading *No Orchids*, have remarked to me, "It's pure Fascism"'; he went on to concur with their 'correct description'. Orwell had already admitted, however, that 'it is not, as one might expect, the product of an illiterate hack, but a brilliant piece of writing, with hardly a wasted word or a jarring note anywhere'. Other critics described Chase as 'a [William] Faulkner for the masses'.

Written in six weekends during 1938, *No Orchids* was Chase's first novel. It was rejected by Michael Joseph before being taken up by Jarrolds. By the time Orwell wrote his essay of condemnation (he concluded by saying that after witnessing the 'cruelty and corruption' in Chase's book, 'one is driven to feel that snobbishness, like hypocrisy, is a check upon behaviour whose value from a social point of view has

been underrated'), it had sold half a million copies (even during wartime paper shortages), and was read more than any other title by serving members of the British armed forces during the Second World War. The play of the book toured Britain from 1942 until 1949, a year after the release of the first of two film versions (described by the national press as 'nauseating muck…as fragrant as a cesspool'). The Hollywood remake came out in 1971, retitled *The Grissom Gang*.

In 1961 Chase revised *No Orchids*, paying particular attention to the dialogue, which he thought had become outmoded. Republished by Panther, it continued to sell. By 1973, sales had topped 2 million copies.

MUST READ *No Orchids for Miss Blandish*
READ ON **Dashiell Hammett, Stewart Home,** Mickey Spillane, **Jim Thompson**

Jean Cocteau

1889–1963
The poeticisation of everyday life

Born into a rich family that lived in a large house on the outskirts of Paris, Jean Cocteau made a spectacular debut with a slim volume of poems, *Aladdin's Lamp* (1909); soon afterwards he made an equally spectacular conversion to Catholicism. His fashionable exploits were interrupted by the outbreak of the First World War in which he served as an ambulance driver – an experience articulated in his book of poems *Le Cap de Bonne-Espérance* (*The Cape of Good Hope*, 1919). By this time Cocteau had become something of a mentor to other young artists. He wrote sketches for the ballet *Parade* (designed by Picasso, with Diaghilev as impressario) and sponsored the music collective Les Six. In 1918 Cocteau launched his protégé Raymond Radiguet on to the literary scene (Radiguet's *Devil in the Flesh* is the story of the illicit love between a teenage boy and an adult woman whose husband is away at the front). When Radiguet died five years later, Cocteau started using opium. He later recounted his experiences as a drug addict in *Opium* (1930).

Cocteau was a novelist, whose best-known novel (filmed by the author in 1950) is *Les Enfants Terribles* (1929), the story of an intimate relationship between a brother and sister; a playwright, whose most famous drama is *La Machine Infernale* (1934; based on the Oedipus legend it suggests that human activity is pre-scribed rather than the product of free will); a film director, whose greatest film is the retelling of the Beauty and the Beast fairy story (1945); and an essayist who wrote for the newspaper *Le Figaro*. Above all, however, Cocteau thought of himself as a poet. Apart from volumes of poetry and various films which investigate the role of poets, Cocteau described his fiction as '*poésie de roman*', called his plays '*poésie de*

< 60 >

théâtre', and so on. In using such terms, Cocteau is not only referring to poetry as a form of writing; he is also referring to his personal mission to reinstate the poetic sensibility in all the arts, and by implication, in the way we live our lives. In this respect, his work stands in marked contrast to the realist and naturalist styles which had dominated European fiction throughout the previous century.

MUST READ *Les Enfants Terribles, Opium*
READ ON **Lewis Carroll, Jean Genet, Raymond Radiguet**

Leonard Cohen
1934–
Balladeer of love and loneliness

Leonard Norman Cohen was born into a Jewish family living in the largely Catholic, French-speaking city of Montreal. At McGill University he says he learnt to live an unstructured, bohemian life, but nevertheless a 'consecrated' kind of life. As a poet, novelist and singer–songwriter, Cohen has combined elements of both Jewish and Catholic spirituality into an ethos which is equally redolent of bohemian lifestyles and plentiful sex.

In Canada Cohen is known primarily for his poetry and fiction, but the rest of the world got to know him through his recording career,

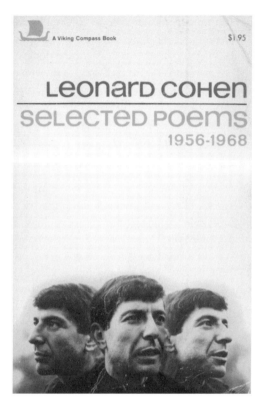

A Viking Compass Book $1.95

Leonard COHen
selected poems
1956-1968

to explore in two subsequent collections, The *Spicebox of Earth* (1961) and *Flowers for Hitler* (1964), albeit in an increasingly eroticised form.

By this time Cohen had published his first novel, *The Favorite Game* (1963), written on the cusp of the sixties in London – which is where he purchased the Burberry overcoat that was subsequently featured in the song 'Famous Blue Raincoat' on his debut album. A second novel, *Beautiful Losers*, followed in 1966. Its British publishers, Panther Books, described it as 'a love story, an orgy, a prayer, a black mass, a shriek, a satire, a joke, an hallucination and a religio-sexual epic of incomparable beauty'. The *New York Times* thought it was 'gorgeously written…overwhelming'. The *Daily Telegraph* reviewer may have been somewhat underwhelmed when he described it as 'the literary counterpart of *Hair* on the stage and *Easy Rider* on the screen'. Cohen's prose, surreal and sometimes overblown, can be interpreted as an added ironic nuance or a sad case of adolescent doggerel being passed off as liberating literature.

In the collection of poems entitled *Book of Mercy*, Cohen used Psalm-like structures and expressed something approaching a personal vision of spiritual redemption. It was published in 1984, about the time that Dylan was also making a return to his religious roots. In the late eighties Cohen's recording career underwent a revival, and although now of pensionable age he is generally regarded as having lots of creative juices left in him.

which took off with *The Songs of Leonard Cohen*, released in 1968 at a time when Bob Dylan had already 'gone electric' and Cohen's haunting voice and sparse acoustic guitar-playing stood out all the more forcefully.

The title of Cohen's first anthology of poems, *Let Us Compare Mythologies* (1956) is a reference to the effect of both Catholic and Jewish identity upon him. It was the latter that he chose

C
a reader's guide

< 61 >

MUST READ *Beautiful Losers, The Favorite Game*
READ ON Allen Ginsberg, D H Lawrence, **Henry Miller**

Nik Cohn

1946–
The speed writer of pop

Born in London, brought up in Ireland, at 15 Cohn moved back to London where he soon became the foremost chronicler of pop with his affectionate but caustic history, *Awopbopaloobop Alopbambaoom* (1969). He also collaborated with artist Guy Peelaert on *Rock Dreams*, a book of portraits and extended captions that set out to sum up the rock sensibility. As a journalist, Cohn wrote for the *Sunday Times*, the *Observer*, and *Queen* – the quintessential Swinging London magazine. Moving to New York in the seventies, he worked for *Esquire* and the *New York Times*. During this period he wrote the piece of factual 'reportage' that became the basis for the film *Saturday Night Fever* – except that, as Cohn himself admitted more than 20 years later, he made the whole thing up.

Cohn's other fiction includes *I Am Still the Greatest Says Johnny Angelo* (1967, republished by Savoy Books in 1980). Johnny Angelo is a fairy-tale figure who embodies the spirit of rock'n'roll; the Savoy edition contains pictures of both trouser-splitting crooner P J Proby and a tongue-wagging Iggy Pop, with captions which suggest that these are two incarnations of the eternal soul of Angelo. Cohn also wrote *Arfur – Teenage Pinball Queen*, said to be the inspiration for Peter Townshend's *Tommy*. Cohn later said of Townshend, '[he] is great at understanding half of an idea'.

Cohn's prose is sometimes crude but always dynamic. He understands the combination of the commercial and the sacramental in the pop/rock experience. As the blurb on the back of *Johnny Angelo* says of Cohn's work, it is 'a bizarre fable for our time, capturing its sickness and horror yet staying true to its grandeur and allure'. Cohn's enemies describe him as a charlatan, and in an otherwise positive introduction to *Awopbopaloobop Alopbambaoom*, Kit Lambert (then manager of The Who) refers to 'accusations of intellectual – even cash – payola' levelled against Cohn during his time as a 'highly partisan' record reviewer at *Queen* magazine. Lambert concluded that Cohn is 'half-martyr to his own myth' who 'sprints across the gilded landscape, although his feet *are* bleeding inside the carefully dirtied down sneakers'. Thirty years later, this mix of spontaneity and calculation is still the essential element in Cohn's literary output.

MUST READ *I Am Still the Greatest Says Johnny Angelo*
READ ON **Richard Allen**, Julie Burchill, **Stewart Home**, Tony Parsons

< 62 >

Colette

1873–1954
'The first woman who wrote as a woman'

Born Sidonie-Gabrielle Collette in rural Burgundy into a home 'overflowing with dogs, cats and children', Colette was educated at the local village school. At 25 she was brought to Paris by her first husband, the writer and critic Henri Gauthier-Villars, who locked his young wife in a room and forced her to write her first novels, the series featuring the heroine Claudine. Gauthier-Villars published these under his own name.

The books were a success but their marriage, whose shortcomings were later featured in *Mes Apprentissages* (*My Apprenticeships*, 1906), was not. After the divorce, Colette kept herself by dancing in music halls for six years, an eventful period which also reappeared in one of her later books (*L'Envers du Music Hall*, 1913; translated as *Music Hall Sidelights*). Her second marriage, which also ended in divorce, subsequently featured in those of her stories which centred on Julie de Carneilhan. In 1935 she married Maurice Goudoket and they lived together until she died, riddled with arthritis, in 1954. Colette was the first woman president of the Académie Goncourt, and was given a state funeral.

In her novels, short stories, essays and auto-biographical pieces, Colette is renowned for her

C IS FOR COUNTER-CULTURE
5 novels to help you free the hippy within

TROUT FISHING IN AMERICA
Richard Brautigan
a surreal search for the perfect fishing spot

STEPPENWOLF
Herman Hesse
self-realisation classic beloved of the Woodstock generation

ANOTHER ROADSIDE ATTRACTION
Tom Robbins
hippy happenings at a highway hotdog hut

ZEN AND THE ART OF MOTORCYCLE MAINTENANCE
Robert Pirsig
on the road in search of spiritual renewal

THE ELECTRIC KOOL-AID ACID TEST
Tom Wolfe
wacked-out antics of the Merry Pranksters

lyricism, her psychological insight, and her lust for life in all its pleasure and pain. Her protagonists, Claudine, Léa, Chéri, Phil and Vinca, Julie de Carneilhan and Gigi embody all these qualities, and prove that she herself followed the advice she gave to a young writer: 'Look for a long time at what pleases you, and longer still at what pains you.' Stories such as *Le Képi*, described as 'the subtle yet ruthless rendering of a woman's belated sexual awakening', appealed to the postwar generation of existentialists who were anxious to live for the moment, just as the prewar generation had been impressed by her lyricism and her poetic rendition of both rural and metropolitan life.

Novelist and essayist André Maurois described Colette as 'the first woman who wrote as a woman' – although fans of Jane Austen may beg to differ. Some critics have also praised Colette for stamping her own personality on everything she wrote, to the point where the author becomes the chief character in all her writing. Others have found this intrusive, and dare to suggest that Colette crowds and even stifles her characters with her own personality.

MUST READ *Chéri, Le Képi*
READ ON **Simone de Beauvoir**, Guy de Maupassant, **Joyce Carol Oates**

Clarence Cooper Jr
1934—1978
The black William Burroughs that never was

Born in Detroit, Clarence Cooper Jr trained as a journalist and became editor of the black newspaper the *Chicago Messenger*. But his journalistic career was disrupted by drug use and abuse, and he spent plenty of time in jail. Cooper wrote a total of seven novels. His work failed to attract the critical attention which it deserved, however, and an embittered Cooper stopped writing in 1967. Poor and unknown, he died 11 years later in New York.

The Syndicate (1960) features hitman Andy Sorrell as he tries to locate the freelancers who pulled off a bank robbery in New Jersey. *Weed* (1961) is a documentary-style account of a community beset by poverty and drugs. Using flashbacks and 'flashforwards' in a genre mix that veers from the highly stylised to the pseudo-documentary, *The Scene* (1960) looks at the lives of cops, pimps, whores and addicts who are all connected by one thing – junk. According to the *New York Tribune*: 'Not even Nelson Algren's *The Man with the Golden Arm* burns with the ferocious intensity you'll find here.' Cooper's last novel was *The Farm* (1967), which examines prison life, love and addiction, and the relationship between all three. In style, it is more experimental than most of his other work.

Harlan Ellison was Cooper's editor at pulp fiction publishers Regency House. He later recalled: 'I knew he was an incredibly talented writer – a lot of people did. But getting readers to listen was another matter.' The *Negro Digest* described Cooper as 'one of the most underrated writers in America, a Richard Wright of the revolutionary era'. The *New York Tribune* highlighted the uncomfortably close relationship between Cooper's life and work in the observation: 'Cooper writes with a personal authority that can only be called shattering, and [with] the searing exactness of one who has lived through the horror.' Cooper's work has recently been revived, first by American publishers W W Norton in their series of Old School cool titles, and then in Britain by Payback Press. Style magazine *GQ* recently declared that Cooper 'should have been the black William Burroughs'.

MUST READ *The Farm, The Scene, Weed*
READ ON James Baldwin, **Donald Goines**, **Chester Himes**, Richard Price

Dennis Cooper

196?–
The last literary outlaw

By 1998 the music critic and gay novelist Dennis Cooper had published four novels in a five-volume cycle of sex, violence and degradation. After *Frisk* (1992), *Closer* (1994) and *Try* (1994), his *Guide* (1998) features a morbid kid and a dwarf who slices him open, a maternal porn director and the pre-teen star of her films whose body is dumped in a vacant lot, a rent boy with Aids and a narrator called…Dennis Cooper, who describes himself as 'an indie rock kinda guy'. *Guide* also features a thinly disguised representation of Alex James from the band Blur ('Alex Johns' from the Britpop band 'Smear'). 'Johns' is drugged and then violently sodomised by a friend of the narrator, who also fantasises about disembowelling him.

Degradation is a recurring theme in Cooper's work. He admitted to the music paper *Melody Maker*:

'My mind is really screwed up. Yes, this book is me. It's my mind. It's not autobiographical, but it's totally my thoughts. Sometimes the perspective is that I'm sick. Sometimes it's how tormented I am. I have to admit that it frightens me because it attracts me…My own interest in sexual violence is really confused…I have so many different reactions, and I'm just trying to get them all in there.'

Bret Easton Ellis has described Cooper as 'the last literary outlaw in mainstream American fiction'. Reviewing *Guide*, the *Los Angeles Times* called it 'the most seductively frightening, best-written novel of contemporary urban life that anyone has attempted in a long time; it's the funniest too, and does for Clinton's America what *The Tin Drum* did for postwar Germany'. Cooper's critics claim that his violent fantasies are simply a self-indulgent, publicity-seeking attempt to shock.

Cooper has also written a graphic novel, *Horror Hospital Unplugged* (1996), in collaboration with artist Keith Mayerson. He has promised that after the final episode in his current cycle of novels, he will write something that is not violent.

MUST READ *Closer, Frisk, Guide, Try*
READ ON **Kathy Acker, Georges Bataille, William Burroughs, James Ellroy, Stewart Home**

Robert Coover

1932–
The all–American parodist

Born in Charles City, Iowa, Robert Coover attended the universities of Southern Illinois, Indiana, and Chicago. *The Origin of the Brunists* (1965), winner of the William Faulkner Award

for best first novel, is a satire on religion in small-town America, chronicling the growth of a cult led by the survivor of a mining disaster. Cooper's next two books were not at all alike. *The Universal Baseball Association, J. Henry Waugh, Prop.* (1968) is an allegorical novel employing America's number-one sport as the main metaphor while, once again, satirising religious beliefs. In 1969, Coover published *Pricksongs and Descants*, a collection of what he described as 'seven exemplary fictions' influenced by the Exemplary Novels written in 1613 by Cervantes, author of *Don Quixote*.

One of Coover's favourite themes, and the subtext of his first two novels, is the distorted relationship between public myth and reality. It re-appears in *Gerald's Party* (1986), a masterfully self-conscious rendition of the English detective novel (the book was dedicated to novelist John Hawkes, a fellow teacher at Brown University, and author of *The Lime Twig*, 1961, itself an inventive exploration of the seedy English thriller), and *A Night at the Movies* or, *You Must Remember This* (1987), a delirious deconstruction of cinema-going that reads as if the punning French poet Raymond Queneau were the projectionist.

Coover's other novels have shown that along with the word-play he is also interested in politics. *The Public Burning* is a fictional account of the showtrial and execution of the Rosenbergs, who were accused of spying for the Soviet Union at the height of the McCarthy witch-

< 66 >

hunts (E L Doctorow did their story first with *The Book of Daniel*, 1971). *A Political Fable* (1968) is a satire on Richard Nixon, originally published as a Dr Seuss spoof entitled *The Cat in the Hat for President*.

Away from politics, Coover has produced a novella, *Spanking the Maid*, (1981; more Queneau-esque romps involving a careless maid, a stern master, and some swollen buttocks), and an earthy reworking of the Pinnochio story, *Pinnochio in Venice* (1991), which prompted the *New York Times Book Review* to label his writing 'work of the purest, unremitting malevolence'. Novelist and critic Angela Carter was more favourable. She described his work as 'unfair, rude, cruel, and murderously funny'.

MUST READ *Gerald's Party, The Origin of the Brunists, Pinnochio in Venice*
READ ON **Donald Barthelme**, William Gass, **John Hawkes, Thomas Pynchon**

C IS FOR CYBERPUNK
5 novels from the digital future

NEUROMANCER
William Gibson
Dashiell Hammett meets Jack Kerouac in cyberspace

SNOW CRASH
Neal Stephenson
living on the edge of Virtual Reality Street

INTERFACE
Stephen Bury
comic capers with virtual politicians

THE ARTIFICIAL KID
Bruce Sterling
on the run with the prince of violent videos

MIND PLAYERS
Pat Cadigan
the only female in the original cadre of cyberpunk

C
a reader's guide

Douglas Coupland

1961–
The cool nerd

Born on the Canadian Nato base in Baden-Sollingen, West Germany, in 1961, at the age of four Douglas Coupland returned to Vancouver where he grew up in a family that was 'unemotional, undemonstrative' and took great pleasure in sleeping. Coupland still does not rise before 11 am. In 1979, he went to art school and learnt to sculpt. He was rewarded with a show at the Vancouver Art Gallery when he was 26. He accepted the commission to write his first book (the publisher had seen some articles Coupland had written for a Vancouver magazine) because he 'needed a new drill' for his work as a sculptor.

The book in question was *Generation X: tales for an accelerated culture* (1991 – not to be confused with Generation X 1977, the band fronted by Billy Idol; or 'Generation X' 1963, the account of young people and their emerging culture written by *Sunday Times* journalists Charles Hamblett and Jane Deverson), which featured a group of detached, white, twenty-something Americans, dispossesed of all but the merest motivation (aka slackers in the eponymous film directed by Richard Linklater, which came out around the same time) and living with a double dose of irony in the soul. This was the book that launched a thousand think-tanks and

commercial strategies (who are Gen X?, how to sell soda pop to Gen X, etc.) – so much so that in July 1995 Coupland wrote a 'death of Gen X' piece in the US magazine *Details* in an attempt to extricate himself from its aftermath.

Coupland's next offering was *Shampoo Planet* (1993), a mainly forgettable story about a 20-year-old and his obsession with hair care which is perhaps meant to be indicative of the younger siblings of *Generation X*. Next up came *Life after God* (1994), a collection of short stories in which Coupland went through the post-religious ironic condition and came out the other side with a kind of DIY spirituality. Coupland returned to top form with *Microserfs* (1995), which follows the fortunes of a group of cool computer nerds who work on a campus that bears a striking resemblance to the Microsoft HQ near Seattle (Coupland lived in the area in order to research the novel). This too closes with a spiritual epiphany. In 1998 Coupland published his most ambitious novel yet: *Girlfriend in a Coma* contains comparatively few brand names and ironic references, but puts a visionary and sometimes apocalyptic gloss on the Couplandish themes of friendship at the end of time (the title seems to suggest that Coupland is turning into Morrissey, the miserabilist from Manchester, but this is not the case). It was written after the author underwent a period of deep depression; he admitted that the girlfriend's coma is possibly a metaphor for his own period of reclusiveness and, ultimately,

< 68 >

recuperation. Coupland's collection of essays, *Polaroids from the Dead* (1996) quickly made its way into the shops that sell only remaindered books.

Coupland has become the doyen of Netizens, but he rarely surfs and does not watch cable TV (aged 20, he resolved never to buy a television set). He was lionised by the London literary scene during his promotional tour for *Microserfs*, but shocked the London literati by appearing at a party given for him by Julie Burchill at the ultra-fashionable Altantic Bar in a get-up that could have been worn by a Canadian farmer out to celebrate his wedding anniversary. Moreover, Coupland does not do drink or drugs (except an occasional puff of pipe tobacco). Instead, he goes hiking twice a week. The man of the postmodern millennium says he has a 19th-century mind. He is cool, he is a nerd: the contradictions in Douglas Coupland make his work especially interesting and particularly appropriate for our paradoxical age.

MUST READ *Generation X, Microserfs*
READ ON **Bret Easton Ellis**, **William Gibson**, Douglas Rushkoff, Brady Udall

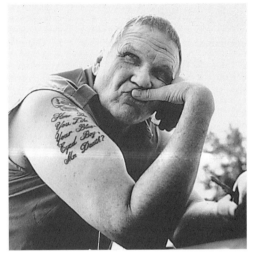

Harry Crews

Harry Crews

1935–
Faulkner in a fright wig

Harry Crews was born into a family of poor white sharecroppers who became even poorer when his father died. Childhood for Crews meant moving each year from one shack to another, while his mother did her damnedest to keep the family together. From his earliest years Crews harboured the ambition to become a writer, although he says he cannot think where he got the idea from. As a young man he enlisted in the Marines and fought in the Korean War, afterwards going to college under the terms of the GI Bill, whereby the state paid for army veterans to finish their education.

< 69 >

As a journalist for *Esquire*, and as a novelist, Harry Crews's writing is almost entirely concerned with the American South. In Crews's fiction (beginning with *The Gospel Singer* in 1968) the South emerges as a country of black humour and grotesque violence, prompting the distinguished critic of cult fiction, John Williams, to describe him as 'Flannery O'Connor on steroids'. Another reviewer suggested the analogy of 'Carson McCullers and Flannery O'Connor strapped side by side on a roller-coaster' as a way to describe Crews's updated Southern Gothic. Tattooed and brawny, Crews himself resembles some of the aggressive characters in his stories. He says of his own white trash life: 'My compulsive need to look for the edge and live on it has marked me in more ways than I would want to know or try to explain.'

A quick glance at some of his scenarios puts you perfectly in the frame of his carnivalesque white trash view of the South: *Car* (1983) is the story of a man who pledges to eat an automobile down to the very last bolt; *The Gypsy Curse* features a man who walks everywhere on his hands – his withered legs strapped to his buttocks; *Feast of Snakes* (1987) is set around an annual rattlesnake hunt; *Body* (1990) is set amid a women's bodybuilding contest; *Where Does One Go When There's No Place Left to Go?* features a writer called Harry Crews who is kidnapped by characters from his own novels; while *Scar Lover* (1992) is dedicated to buddy and movie bad boy Sean Penn.

Although Crews may have an interest in rescuing his beloved land from the prejudices of East Coast liberals (who have often vilified Southerners in an attempt to draw attention away from their own shortcomings), there may also be a 'tyranny of expectancy' at work here. At times, Crews's first-hand depiction of the South, which seems to be populated by the weird and the suicidal, bears an uncanny resemblance to the second-hand caricatures that are so often applied to those living below the Mason–Dixon line.

MUST READ *All We Need of Hell, Body, Classic Crews: a reader, The Gospel Singer*
READ ON **Donald Goines, Cormac McCarthy, Flannery O'Connor**, Mark Twain

Aleister Crowley

1875—1947
The Beast

Aleister Crowley's parents were Plymouth Brethren, and he was educated at a school for sons of this Christian sect, where the main learning aids were the Bible and the birch. The asthmatic Aleister also underwent extracurricular studies in gambling, billiards and women. In 1895 he went to Cambridge University where he developed an interest in poetry and mountaineering. He also met George Jones, a chemist and member of a masonic society, the Hermetic Order of the Golden Dawn (others members included novelist Arthur Machen and Ireland's foremost poet W B Yeats). Crowley joined the Order and rose swiftly through the ranks. He also experimented with hashish, opium, cocaine and black magic, and published three volumes of verse: *Aceldama* (according to the Bible, a field of blood), *Jezebel*, and *White Stains* all printed privately in 1898.

After taking part in the first, if unsuccessful, attempt to climb K2 in the Himalayas, Crowley travelled across Europe. In Paris he met author W Somerset Maugham, who subsequently featured him in his novel *The Magician* (1908). Later, Crowley was immensely flattered by Maugham's book, stating that it was 'an appreciation of my genius such as I had never dreamed of inspiring'. A rumour circulated that

Aleister Crowley

Maugham had sold his soul to Crowley to procure success as a writer and afterwards decorated the walls of his house and the jackets of his books with ancient symbols designed to ward off Crowley's evil spirits.

Crowley spent the rest of his life travelling the world, dragging his wives, mistresses and children with him, painting, writing, occasionally publishing, and always practising magic. His continuous experiments with drugs resulted in chronic heroin addiction. Towards the end of

< 71 >

his life, Crowley was reduced to sponging money and sexual favours off an ever-decreasing number of gullible women. Broke and hopelessly dependent on heroin, he died in miserable cirumstances. 'I'm perplexed,' said the man who for much of his life had been waiting for Death to claim him. His last words were: 'Sometimes I hate myself.'

Although they had little influence on the literary world, Crowley's books, especially his notorious novel *The Diary of a Drug Fiend* (1921), and opiate-enhanced lifestyle found plenty of converts among rock musicians. Led Zeppelin guitarist Jimmy Page bought Crowley's house in Boleskine, near Loch Ness, Scotland, and the band's fourth album included part of the magician's dictum: 'Do What Thou Wilt (Shall Be The Whole Of The Law)'. When the band was plagued by a succession of tragic incidents (singer Robert Plant's near fatal car crash and the death of his son, the death of drummer John Bonham), it was rumoured that a Crowleyesque curse had been placed on them.

MUST READ *The Diary of a Drug Fiend*
READ ON W Somerset Maugham,
Edgar Allen Poe, Montague Summers

James Crumley

James Crumley
1939–
Viet vet turned detective

Crumley grew up mainly in South Texas, later serving three years in Vietnam – an experience he wrote about in his first novel, *One to Count Cadence*. Returning from duty, he studied at the Writer's Workshop at the University of Iowa, and finished his novel, publishing it in 1969 and selling the film rights ('My first but not last experience with Hollywood, the Holy Den of Thieves').

After leaving a teaching position in Colorado, he moved to Seattle and, under the influence of Raymond Chandler and Ross Macdonald, wrote the first of his five crime novels, *The Wrong Case* (1975), featuring Milo Milogradovitch, reluctant investigator with a fondness for peppermint schnapps and cocaine. *The Last Good Kiss* followed three years later, and was critically acclaimed. *Harper's* magazine stated that 'What Raymond Chandler did for the Los Angeles of the thirties, James Crumley does for the roadside West of today.' Crumley saw the book in a somewhat different light: 'The novel would make me enough money to get me into tax trouble, a condition with which I am all too familiar.' It features anti-hero C W Sughrue ('Shoog as in sugar…and rue as in rue the goddamned day').

Dancing Bear (1983), once again featuring Milo Milogradovitch, became Crumley's most successful novel yet: 'All the readers of the earlier novels seemed to come together to buy enough books to keep me from being embarrassed.'

In all Crumley's writing, male friendship is formed through drinking and violence, and the backdrop to the books, usually the evocatively described wilds of Montana, is as integral as whiskey or gunplay, and certainly more so than the 'mystery' element.

After a ten-year gap, during which he put in some time scriptwriting (including a screenplay for James Ellroy's *The Big Nowhere* which was never produced), Crumley returned with *The Mexican Tree Duck* (1993), which again features C W Sughrue. Both he and Milo joined forces in Crumley's latest book, *Bordersnakes* (1997). Both are veterans, Milo from Korea, C W from Vietnam, and both have a volatile predilection for alcohol and drug abuse.

Of his writing Crumley says: 'After all this time since *The Wrong Case*, seven or eight or ten cross-country moves, years of being broke, two more children, two more marriages and divorces, I still don't know why I write detective novels.' Teaching, scriptwriting, having two semi-autobiographical protagonists, alternating them, sticking them in the same book, would all suggest a low boredom threshold – which is probably the answer to Crumley's question.

MUST READ *Dancing Bear, The Last Good Kiss, The Mexican Duck Tree, The Wrong Case*
READ ON **Raymond Chandler, Jim Harrison,** Ross Macdonald

Don DeLillo

1936–
Captain paranoia

The son of Italian immigrants from the Abruzzi mountains, Don DeLillo went to Fordham University in New York. While working in advertising, he cultivated an interest in various aspects of modernism: post-bop jazz, abstract expressionist painting; European arthouse cinema. These elements are discernible throughout his life and work.

DeLillo's first novel, *Americana* appeared in 1971. Its title was prophetic. Each of his 11 novels has dealt with aspects of contemporary American life, deconstructing them through the protagonists' increasing sense of futility and displacement. *End Zone* (1972) plays with an elaborate parallel between American football and nuclear conflict to uncover the violence at the root of US culture. *Great Jones Street* (1973) and *Running Dog* (1978) are both accounts of the greed and hypocrisy at the centre of the music business (for *Running Dog*, read *Rolling Stone* magazine). *Ratner's Star* (1976), an ambitious multilayered work, explores the world of astrophysics and examines the growing sexual awareness of a child prodigy.

Paranoia pervades DeLillo's work: characters are constantly in danger of being pulled out of their depth and plunged into dark activities (such as terrorism and murder) far removed

Don DeLillo

from – but dangerously close to – their everyday world. The random violence of American culture is distilled into a permanent sense of foreboding. DeLillo's protagonists are driven or dragged rather than self-activated; he seems fascinated by the elements of our own making, such as celebrity and the media, which tend to dwarf the human individual.

White Noise (1984) is the story of an academic and his wife who share a fear of death. *Libra* (1988) combines fact and fiction to unravel the

< 74 >

myth-making behind Lee Harvey Oswald and the Kennedy assassination. Reputedly inspired by a rare photograph of legendary author and recluse J D Salinger, *Mao II* (1991) is a reflection on the corrosive power of fame. It has been described by Thomas Pynchon as 'a beauty' which 'takes us on a breathtaking journey, beyond the official versions of our daily history, behind all easy assumptions about who we're supposed to be'. The Salinger-like Bill Gray suggests that the writer's role has been usurped by terrorism: 'I used to think it was possible for a novelist to alter the inner life of the culture. Now bomb-makers and gunmen have taken that territory. They make raids on human consciousness.' Gray's reclusiveness is an attempt to protect his spirit from the destructive demands that society makes on him: 'When a writer doesn't show his face, he becomes a local symptom of God's famous refusal to appear.'

DeLillo's most recent book is *Underworld* (1997), a huge novel which sweeps back from the present day to the detonation of the first Soviet atomic bomb in the fifties. Weaving multilayered fiction around the warp of factual history, it is an exhaustive and highly imaginative chronicle of the American experience of the Cold War. DeLillo has described it as 'the book I'd been writing all my life without knowing it'.

DeLillo used to be grouped with famously reclusive writers such as J D Salinger, Thomas Pynchon and William Gaddis. But when *Underworld* was published he appeared in pub-

lic and gave press interviews. This remarkable writer is reported to be a very ordinary-looking guy. Critic Richard Williams said he is so unremarkable he would be an ideal stakeout man. Some critics still complain that DeLillo 'doesn't like his characters', but it is generally agreed that in his more recent work he has become 'more human'.

MUST READ *Libra, Mao II, Underworld, White Noise*
READ ON **E L Doctorow, William Gaddis, Thomas Pynchon**, William Wharton, **Nathanael West**

Samuel R Delany

1942–
The man who made sci-fi hip

Samuel (Ray) Delany is the Miles Davis of sci-fi. Like Davis, he is black (raised in Harlem) and middle class: while Davis Snr was a prosperous dentist, Delany's dad was a wealthy undertaker, who could afford to send his son to Dalton (an expensive private school), and thence to the upmarket Bronx High School of Science.

In 1960 Delany won a scholarship to spend a few weeks at a prestigious literary summer camp in Vermont, with top-ranking poets like Robert Frost in attendance. When he came

< 75 >

back to New York his father was terminally ill with only a few more weeks to live. By the start of 1961 Delany had distanced himself from his family and embarked upon a bohemian existence in the East Village – at around the same time as a certain Robert Zimmerman (Bob Dylan) was making his debut on the folk-club scene.

Delany married the poet Marilyn Hacker, but also enjoyed casual sex with men, as documented in his memoirs of 'East Village sex and science fiction writing' entitled *The Motion of Light in Water*. In 1973 he published a pornographic novel, *The Tides of Lust*, which includes sado-masochistic imagery. Throughout the seventies Delany was active in the struggle for women's liberation. The protagonist of his novel *Triton* (1976) starts out as a macho man but chooses to become a woman: the book is about sexuality and free choice. Delany, who is professor of comparative literature at the University of Massachusetts at Amherst, has also written extensively as a literary critic. A collected volume of his criticism, *The Jewel-Hinged Jaw: notes on the language of science fiction*, was published in 1977; in 1978 he wrote a structuralist analysis of 'Angouleme', a short story by sci-fi writer Thomas M Disch. Delany's analysis is longer than the original story, which tends to confirm the suggestion that he can sometimes be simultaneouly long-winded and 'word-choked'.

But Delany's reputation rests largely on the work he did in the sixties, as one of a relatively small band of 'New Wave' writers who introduced a new 'cool' sensibility into sci-fi. Instead of a gee-whizz preoccupation with technology and gadgetry in the manner of traditional science fiction (a tradition which came to be known as 'hard sf'), Delany was more concerned with 'cultural speculation, the soft sciences, psychology and mythology' (*The Encyclopaedia of Science Fiction* edited by Peter Nicholls, 1979). His protagonists are equally New Wave: they tend to be outsiders and artists, musicians and criminals, more like pop stars than white-coated scientists or all-American astronauts. The general effect given by Delany's canvas is of a counterculture in space; in this respect his 'speculative fiction' of the sixties (he preferred this term to 'sci-fi') may have prefigured the outlaw cyberculture of the late eighties and early nineties, based on the Internet before it became regulated and commercialised.

Delany did not have to wait long before his talent was recognised. *Babel-17* (1966) won a Nebula Award, as did *The Einstein Intersection* (1967), and the short story 'Aye, and Gomorrah' (1967). Reviewing *Nova* (1968), the critic Algis Budrys declared: 'Samuel R Delany, as of this book, is the best science fiction writer in the world.' Those who dislike sci-fi might take note of Delany's rhetorical style and his propensity for social comment dressed up as fiction, and interpret Budrys's announcement as an indictment of the whole genre.

< 76 >

In 1988 Delany accepted an academic appointment at the University of Massachusetts at Amherst. In 1994 he published *The Mad Man*, a novel about a graduate student who has unprotected, casual sex with scores of other men, even though he is living in the age of Aids.

MUST READ *Babel-17, The Motion of Light in Water, Nova, Triton*
READ ON **Philip K Dick**, Thomas M Disch, **Kurt Vonnegut**, Bernard Wolfe

Marquis de Sade

1740–1814
The pain of freedom

Donatien Alphonse François de Sade (known as Louis) was born in Paris. His family had been ennobled in the 12th century and remained a major power-broker in the southern region of Provence. Aged four, de Sade was sent to Avignon into the care of his uncle, whose sexual life was notoriously irregular. Back in Paris, de Sade attended the Jesuit college of Louis Le Grand, before being sent to his regiment (aged 14) to fight against Germany in the Seven Years War. In 1763 de Sade made a bad marriage and for the following five years he lived a life of scandalous debauchery, which often involved beating prostitutes with whips in *petites maisons* hired for this purpose. He was first arrested in 1763. On this occasion he was merely excluded from Paris and sent to his wife's family home in Normandy, but when de Sade continued to commit sex crimes the authorities became less lenient. From 1777 until the decree of the revolutionary Constituent Assembly of March 1790, de Sade was held in various prisons and asylums (Vincennes, Charenton, the Bastille), often in solitary confinement. At Vincennes he was sometimes fed through the bars of his cage, like an animal in a zoo. After his release from the Bastille, he took part in public affairs as part of the citizenry of the new France, but during the post-revolutionary Terror he was imprisoned for being too moderate. Later he was imprisoned again for intending to publish *Juliette* (1798), which was politically as well as sexually explosive. De Sade spent his last days under the merciful eye of the ex-abbé in charge of Charenton asylum. Although as a committed atheist he wished to be buried in unconsecrated ground, these wishes were ignored. However, his grave was later desecrated when phrenologists (a 19th-century pseudo-science which claimed to be able to analyse criminal behaviour in accordance with the size and shape of the perpetrator's skull) broke into it and carried off his head.

Some of de Sade's literary works were composed in prison, including a number of early plays which have never been performed. De Sade's published works include *One Hundred and Twenty Days of Sodom* (1784), *Justine or the*

Misfortunes of Virtue (1791), *The Philosophers of the Bedroom* (1793), *Juliette, and The Crimes of Love* (1800). All of these might be described as chronicles of 'sexual perversion', particularly the attainment of sexual pleasure in the infliction of pain upon others – the practice to which de Sade's name has been applied ever since. Those critics who believe that there is a continuum between pornographic words and images and real acts of sexual violence towards women have indicted de Sade as a multiple rapist, torturer and proto-murderer. Other critics point out that in his writing de Sade was exploring the extent and the limits of sexual and political freedom during the period of revolutionary upheaval which ushered in the modern world; they maintain that in its openness his work is progressive rather than degrading.

MUST READ *Juliette*
READ ON **Kathy Acker, Denis Cooper**

Philip K Dick

1928–1982
Saint Simulacra

Philip Kindred Dick was a twin, born six weeks premature. His twin sister Jane died and doctors gave Philip only a day to live. He survived, but may have been traumatised by Jane's death: he had asthma attacks, was riddled with phobias

< 78 >

(he couldn't eat in front of people), and went into therapy. Dick's insecurities may have arisen, though, from the fact that his father left the family home when he was six.

The young Dick wrote stories and poems for a local paper (by this time he and his mother had moved from Chicago to California, where Dick remained all his life). At 14 he wrote a novel, *Return to Lilliput*, which remains unpublished. This was the first of over 40 sci-fi novels and 200 stories. Fuelled by amphetamines, Dick could type 120 words per minute. Between 1963 and 1964, he wrote (or typed) 11 novels, 11 stories, 2 essays and scores of notes and letters. Amphetamine abuse led to rampant paranoia (he was convinced he was being followed/spied on/bugged by the CIA/FBI), but Dick thought he needed the pep pills to write. In a 1977 interview he recalled: 'I just had to write and that is the only way I could do it…I'm not sure I could have done it without the amphetamines.'

Time Out of Joint (1959) is the story of a man who gradually realises he is being kept in an illusory virtual reality by the military –industrial complex. *The Man in the High Castle* (1962) describes an alternative world where Germany and Japan were the victors in the First World War; at its centre is a man writing a novel in which Germany and Japan are imagined to have lost the war. In *The Three Stigmata of Palmer Eldritch* (1964) a powerful new social drug, Chew-z, is capable of plunging the user into a permanent world of carefree illusion, but only at a price – this world is controlled by Palmer the pusher. *Do Androids Dream of Electric Sheep?* (1968) is the story of Rick Deckard, a bounty hunter commissioned to track down and kill a group of androids that are virtually indistinguishable from humans. To compound this existential conundrum there is some suggestion in the book that Deckard himself may be an android.

Feted in France where he was awarded the Légion d'Honneur, Dick received less recognition in his native USA. His writing style has been found wanting, but for his supporters the carelessness of his high-speed prose is redeemed by the monumental scope of his prophetic ideas about human identity and social reality. Hollywood eventually caught up with Dick's advanced line in existential questioning, and *Do Androids Dream of Electric Sheep?* was filmed as *Blade Runner* (1982) by Ridley Scott. But Dick was not allowed to enjoy his new-found fame: he died in the year of the film's release after suffering a series of strokes.

'What is reality?' asked Dick in his essay 'How to Build a Universe that Doesn't Fall Apart Two Days Later?'. Posed in one form or another, this question occurs in everything he wrote. The dream states, other dimensions, parallel universes, drug-induced visions, virtual realities and identities, are all as 'real' as our phenomenal world. Or, if they're not real, then how 'real' are we? But, then again, was Dick

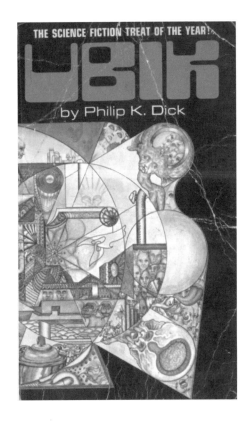

really interested in this question or did he just think it was a good way to spin a yarn? He once said: 'A successful writer can adopt any viewpoint which his characters must needs possess in order to function; this is the measure of his craft, the ability to free from his work his own prejudices.' On the other hand, he also declared that: 'People have told me that everything about me, every facet of my life, psyche, experiences,

< 79 >

dreams and fears are laid out so explicitly in my writing, that from the corpus of my work I can be absolutely and precisely inferred. This is true.' Really?

MUST READ *Divine Invasions: a biography of Philip K Dick* by Lawrence Sutin, *Do Androids Dream of Electric Sheep?*, *The Man in the High Castle, Time Out of Joint*
READ ON **William Burroughs**, Thomas M Disch, Luigi Pirandello

Joan Didion

1934–
California girl
(but not like the Beach Boys)

Born in Sacramento, Joan Didion was a student at the University of California in the mid-fifties, a decade before the Berkeley campus came to be associated with student protests. Moving to New York, she worked as associate features editor at *Vogue* magazine for seven years, during which time she also contributed to the *Saturday Evening Post, Esquire*, and the *National Review*.

Nineteen sixty-three was an eventful year for Didion: she left *Vogue*, suffered a kind of breakdown ('I had never understood what "despair" meant, and I am not sure that I understand now, but I understood that year'), and published her first novel, *Run River*. In 1964 she

married writer John Gregory Dunne, and together they left New York for California. Didion worked as a freelance journalist writing articles on Hollywood and the Haight–Ashbury hippies. Of California she wrote: 'The future always looks good in the golden land, because no one remembers the past.'

Combining personal reminiscences with cultural analysis and social commentary, Didion's non-fiction is a continuation of the New Journalism developed by Tom Wolfe, Truman Capote and Hunter S Thompson. But where they are energetic and excited like over-active children, she is calm and lucid. Three anthologies of her journalism were published in the sixties, seventies and eighties respectively: *Slouching Towards Bethlehem* (1968), *The White Album* (1979) and *Sentimental Journeys* (1983). *The White Album* is the stand-out of the three. With meditations on The Doors and the Manson Murders, California at the fag end of the sixties is depicted as a Babylon on the edge of cultural disintegration.

In addition, she has written two journalistic accounts of the complex, often-fraught relationship between the USA and the Hispanic culture of Latin America: *Salvador* (1982), and *Miami*. Along with Robert Stone, whose novel *A Flag for Sunrise* (1982) is set in a Spanish-speaking country in the throes of revolution, Didion was one of the first US writers to look closely at Uncle Sam's involvement in the region.

The combination of personal experience

< 80 >

Joan Didion

True Confessions (1972) which is based on the notorious Black Dahlia case (the same unsolved rape and murder case that has loomed large in the work of James Ellroy). The film version (1981) starred Robert De Niro and Robert Duvall.

Her individuality, subtlety and success as a novelist and journalist, are probably best described by Didion herself:

'My only advantage as a reporter is that I am so physically small, so temperamentally unobtrusive, and so neurotically inarticulate that people tend to forget that my presence runs counter to their best interests. And it always does. That is one last thing to remember: writers are always selling somebody out.'

MUST READ *Democracy, Salvador, The White Album*
READ ON John Gregory Dunne, **Robert Stone**, Anne Tyler, **Tom Wolfe**

and social insight is also characteristic of Didion's novels. *A Book of Common Prayer* (1977) is set in a post-colonial republic in search of its own history. *Democracy* (1984) is 'the story of a family, an affair, a murder – and a country that has lost its soul'. Its protagonist, Inez, is the wife of a man who wants to be US president and the lover of a behind-the-scenes political fixer.

Didion and Dunne collaborated on several screenplays, including one taken from his novel

D

D IS FOR DRUNK AS HELL
10 books about life with the bottle

A GOAT'S SONG
Dermot Healy
drinking through love and loss in the
west of Ireland

THE LOST WEEKEND
Charles Jackson
an alcoholic's descent into hell,
DTs and all

UNDER THE VOLCANO
Malcolm Lowry
one man's drunken crawl on Mexico's Day
of the Dead

JOHN BARLEYCORN
Jack London
an autobiographical account of the
alcoholic's life

IRONWEED
William Kennedy
drinking to forget with the bums on skid
row

TALES OF ORDINARY MADNESS
Charles Bukowski
fictional ditties from the
bar-room poet

HANGOVER SQUARE
Patrick Hamilton
set amid the hard-drinking
low life in the pubs of Earls Court

JERNIGAN
David Gates
fear and self-loathing with a New
Jersey drunk

A FAN'S NOTES
Frederick Exley
fear and self-loathing for a sports fan
and his bottle

THE DISENCHANTED
Budd Schulberg
fictionalised account of Fitzgerald's
last desperate days in Hollywood

< 82 >

Adam Diment

1944–
The Dolly Dolly Spy author

In 1967, the *Sunday Times* columnist known as Atticus described Adam Diment, author of the year's hit novel *The Dolly Dolly Spy*, as '23…tall, good-looking, with a taste for fast cars, planes, girls and pot'. In other words, just like the protagonist of *The Dolly Dolly Spy*, Philip McAlpine, who was in turn described by the *Daily Mirror* as 'the most modern hero in years…He's hip, he's hard, he likes birds, and, sometimes, marijuana.'

McAlpine had more style than a Len Deighton anti-hero and much less patriotism than Ian Fleming's James Bond: he was cynical about moral values but still romantically good-looking. The *Irish Times* noted that 'he has girls the way other people have cups of coffee'. The *Daily Express* had him down as 'the first Mod spy…a real Chelsea swinger'. Likewise, contemporary photos of Diment show a toothy young man with a mop of blond hair, Brian Jones-style, wearing a Swinging London jacket cut rather like a frock coat. The overall effect is somewhat reminiscent of a Regency fop.

The Dolly Dolly Spy sold well and was featured extensively in trendy magazines such as the large format *Intro*. But Diment's two Philip McAlpine follow-ups did not make the grade and Diment's outro from the glamour pages was as swift as his entry into the in-crowd.

MUST READ *The Dolly Dolly Spy*
READ ON Ian Fleming, John Le Carré, **Colin MacInnes**

E L Doctorow

1931–
Fictional mining at the truth of America's past

Born in New York and educated at the Bronx High School of Science, Kenyon College, and Columbia University, Doctorow worked as a script reader for Columbia Pictures, and from 1960 to 1964, was the editor of the New American Library.

His first novel, *Welcome to Hard Times* (1960), set the pattern for virtually all his subsequent work, in that it demythologised America's past (in this case, the West) and blended fact and fiction, a technique borrowed from the New Journalism school. It was filmed in 1967 starring Henry Fonda. Doctorow's second novel, *Big as Life* (1966), was a sci-fi satire set in New York which, contrary to its title, disappeared without trace.

Ragtime (1975), was a huge success, and his most effective fusion of reality and invention. Doctorow believed it was the writer's job to close the gap between history and fiction, because 'there is no fiction or non-fiction, as we commonly understand the distinction, there is

< 83 >

only narrative'. Through the novel's pages strolled J P Morgan, Freud, Henry Ford and Harry Houdini, mixing it up with the fictional characters as well as one another. When asked if Ford and Morgan had actually really met, Doctorow replied: 'They have now.' It was filmed in 1981, starring James Cagney in his final screen performance, and author Norman Mailer in, sadly, not his final performance.

Doctorow used this trick in other novels, including *The Book of Daniel* (1971; a brilliant oblique fictional account of the Rosenberg's trial and execution, filmed in 1983, with Doctorow co-scripting); *Loon Lake* (1980), a scathing diatribe against a Depression-wracked America; *Waterworks* (1994), and *Billy Bathgate* (1988), which chronicled the last days of gangster Dutch Schultz and was filmed in 1991, starring Dustin Hoffman. Explaining his fondness for this device, Doctorow asserted: 'The presumption of the interpenetration of fact and fiction is that it is what everybody does – lawyers, social scientists, policemen. So why should it be denied to novelists?'

MUST READ *The Book of Daniel, Ragtime*
READ ON **Thomas Berger, Robert Coover, Thomas Pynchon, Norman Mailer**, Simon Schama

J P Donleavy

1926–
Living in the shadow of the Ginger Man

Born to Irish parents in Brooklyn Heights, James Patrick Donleavy joined the navy after being expelled from school. His early literary efforts consisted of writing love letters for his young shipmates. A well-read naval instructor once likened the style of these letters to that of James Joyce. After the Second World War, Donleavy took advantage of the GI Bill to go to college. Mindful of his instructor's words, he chose to go to Joyce's alma mater, the University of Dublin.

In Dublin, Donleavy soon met Brendan Behan, another important influence, and Gainor Stephen Crist, a fellow American and the model for Sebastian Dangerfield, picaresque protagonist of Donleavy's first novel, *The Ginger Man* (1955). The history of this comic masterpiece is almost more fascinating than the novel itself. It took years to write, was rejected by 35 publishers, and was finally published (as erotica, not literature) by the notorious Olympia Press owned by pornographer Maurice Girodias, who was also the first to publish Nabokov's *Lolita*, Genet's *A Thief's Journal* and Beckett's *Molloy*. Donleavy and Girodias fell out, though. Having mouthed the words: 'I will see you in court,' Donleavy did just that and, after endless legal battles, won his novel

< 84 >

back, eventually wreaking his revenge on Girodias by outbidding him for the ownership of Olympia Press. Published legitimately, the book has sold over 5,000,000 copies worldwide and has never been out of print since 1955.

Donleavy wrote 11 more novels, some set in Ireland, others in New York and London. Some were successful, but none achieved the comic brilliance of his first book; and in this respect the figure of the Ginger Man has dominated his life and career. Although Donleavy was clearly influenced by Joyce and other Irish writers like Flann O'Brien and Brendan Behan (who suggested editorial changes in *The Ginger Man*), there is a lot of humour in his books that is unmistakably American, together with a potent mixture of barely supressed violence and aristocratic charm. 'I'll thank you not to fuck about with me you low cur' is a typical phrase and an indication of this engaging combination.

MUST READ *The Beastly Beatitudes of Balthazaar B, The Ginger Man, The History of the Ginger Man: an autobiography*
READ ON **James Joyce, Flann O'Brien**, Philip Roth

Fyodor Dostoevsky

1821–1881
Miserabilism writ large

Fyodor Dostoevsky was born in Moscow, where his father was a physician in the Tsarist army. The young Dostoevsky graduated from the military academy at St Petersburg in 1843 and received a commission in the Engineers' Regiment. He resigned from the army only three years later, and in 1849 was arrested and sentenced to death for being a member of the Petrashevsky circle of anti-Tsarist radicals. At the last moment his sentence was commuted to hard labour in Siberia, where he was imprisoned until 1854. After his release Dostoevsky was involved in the publication of various literary and topical journals, which tended to be short-lived. He was frequently in debt, not least because of his passion for gambling. Dostoevsky lived outside Russia for a number of years, but this only made him anti-European. After decades of poverty and difficulties with government officials, Dostoevsky returned to Russia in 1873; from that time until his death in 1881 he was widely revered as an editor, essayist and novelist.

Dostoevsky's masterpiece is *Crime and Punishment* (1865–1866), which he began in circumstances of extreme penury. It tells the story of an impoverished student, Raskolnikov, who is appalled by the the brutality of city life and by his own sordid existence. His problems

< 85 >

would be solved, he thinks, if he murdered the greedy, mean-spirited old woman who is his downstairs neighbour, and stole her money. He also thinks of the murder as a kind of test of character, as if by committing it he will prove his mettle. But as soon as Raskolnikov commits the crime he is wracked by the sense of having separated himself from the rest of humanity by the enormity of his own actions. This sense of separation prompts him to confess, even though he was not under suspicion. When the case comes to trial, the court is lenient to the gentleman murderer, and by the end of Dostoyevksy's mammoth tale (spinning out stories was a way of getting more money from magazine publishers who serialised them), Raskolnikov has found God, fallen in love, and feels reunited with the human race.

D IS FOR DRUGS
10 authors who just said yes

WILLIAM S BURROUGHS
act your Yage not your shoe size

ALDOUS HUXLEY
one should go mad on mescalin

HUNTER S THOMPSON
you name it, I'll take it; but look out for
the bats

ALEXANDER TROCCHI
pimping the wife for a hit of H

ALEISTER CROWLEY
two parts black magic to one part
opium

IRVINE WELSH
luv'd up – the Edinburgh Ecky advocate

PHILIP K DICK
speeding through those paranoid pulp
deadlines

DONALD GOINES
heroin junkie and king of ghetto pulpz

JIM CARROLL
young, free and on the nod in NYC

PAUL BOWLES
down and out–of–it in Tangiers

< 86 >

choose between Dostoevsky and Tolstoy: if you are a fan of one, you will dislike the other. Dostoevsky's critics complain that his characters' unremitting angst is over the top – like listening to too much Portishead. True, Raskolnikov is not the sort of character to 'lighten up'; nevertheless, his dark stuff provides some of the most rewarding and enlightening moments in modern literature.

Dostoevsky's other works of note include *Notes from the Underground* (1864), *The Idiot* (1869) (the story of an innocent prince which was particularly fashionable during the hippie, happy days of the late sixties and early seventies), *The Devils* (1871) and *The Brothers Karamazov* (1880).

MUST READ *Crime and Punishment, The Idiot, Notes from the Underground*
READ ON **Albert Camus, David Goodis, Jim Thompson**

Fyodor Dostoevsky

As an icon of young manhood, Raskolnikov is as important as Shakespeare's Hamlet. In his exhaustive treatment of the question of whether to kill or not to kill, Dostoevsky has spoken to successive generations of young people who share both Raskolnikov's feelings of alienation from society and his burning desire to reconnect with other people.

It has often been said that the reader must

Bret Easton Ellis

1964–
Affluent ennui and excess

Bret Easton Ellis was raised in Los Angeles. He graduated from Bennington College and lives in New York, but much of his fiction is set on the West Coast of America.

Less than Zero (1985), hailed by the New Yorker as 'an extraordinarily accomplished first novel', follows a group of affluent young Los Angeleños in their disaffection from society and their use of sex and drugs. In 1987 it was filmed by Twentieth Century Fox with Robert Downey Jr in a starring role. Picador, who published the book in Britain, described it as 'the shocking coming-of-age novel about the casual nihilism that comes with youth and money' – except that none of the characters is capable of coming of age: they are trapped in permanent adolescence and the novel is partly about how shock turns to schlock in the age of excess.

This last is the territory that Ellis developed more fully in his infamous third novel, *American Psycho* (1991) (his second effort, *Rules of Attraction*, 1987, was largely a recapitulation of his debut), which chronicles the sex crimes of a drug-fuelled serial rapist, torturer and murderer. Written in the yuppified eighties and set among the rich kids of New York, *American Psycho* is a brilliant satire on the moral collapse of the American Way of Life. Its protagonist is an ironic grotesque worthy of Jonathan Swift or Juvenal, but Ellis's deliberately excessive violence prompted an outraged response from those who could not tell the difference between realism and pantomime. In 1997 there were plans to make a toned-down film of the book; an over-the-top cartoon version would seem to be more appropriate.

The Informers (1994) returned to Los Angeles, and again described the slow death of the young, urban soul. This time Ellis approached his theme with greater maturity and more finesse. Critics finally recognised that in describing the collapse of old morality, Ellis is searching – if not finding – new values: the *Modern Review* dubbed him 'a profoundly moral writer' and compared him to F Scott Fitzgerald.

MUST READ *American Psycho, The Informers, Less than Zero*
READ ON **Michael Bracewell, Jay McInerney, Tom Wolfe, Dennis Cooper**

Harlan Ellison

1934–
Inventor of 'terror fiction'

At 15, Harlan Jay Ellison published his first short story in the *Cleveland News*. In 1953, he was writing regularly for, and occasionally co-editing, the Ohio State University magazine,

< 88 >

Sundial. The following year he was told by his English professor 'to forget ever trying to make a living from the craft of writing…I would never write anything of consequence.'

Expelled from college the following year, Ellison moved to New York and sold a story, 'Glowworm', to *Infinity* magazine. In 1956, he wrote and sold 100 stories. Since then he has produced a huge body of work: 69 books, including 26 volumes of short stories. Among these are the classics *I Have No Mouth and I Must Scream* (1967), and *Deathbird Stories* (1975).

Ellison drifts from fantasy to horror and back again. His writing has virtually created a new genre: terror fiction. Many of his characters are redeemed by surviving (or attempting to survive) the punishments they encounter in the deeply disturbing alternative worlds that imprison them. He once said:

'I want people's hair to stand on end when they read my work, whether it's a love story, or a gentle childhood story, or a story of drama and violence…It is in moments of violence that we have confrontation, that we find out what we believe in, whether we have soul and spirit, they are the pivotal points in our lives.'

Ellison clearly likes to play around with the idea of 'alternative reality'. In an autobiographical snippet in *The Essential Ellison* (1987), he claims he was born in India, 'spoke only Hindi and Urdu till the age of 13' and that his favourite foods 'are curried monkey brains scooped steaming from the trepanned skull, and french fries, very crisp'.

MUST READ *I Have No Mouth and I Must Scream, Deathbird Stories*
READ ON Ray Bradbury, Alfred Bester, Theodore Sturgeon

James Ellroy

1948–
Demon dog of crime fiction

Lee Earle Ellroy was born in Los Angeles to Armand Ellroy, a former manager of film star Rita Hayworth, and Geneva 'Jean' Ellroy, an attractive red-headed nurse, who drank and liked men. His parents divorced when he was eight and James/Lee Earle went to live with his mother in the seedy suburb of El Monte.

On 22 June 1958, Jean Ellroy was strangled and her body dumped in an ivy patch. Her killer was never found. Ellroy moved in with his father and started reading crime books and magazines. On his eleventh birthday he read about LA's most famous unsolved murder: the Black Dahlia case. The victim, Betty Short was attractive, red-headed, and liked men. She looked, as Ellroy said: 'like a 1940s shot of my mother…It sent me way off the deep end.'

Ellroy's father died when he was 17, and he bummed around, existing on a diet of booze, drugs and stolen steaks. He shoplifted, broke into houses, went homeless, was arrested, had a psychotic breakdown, was hospitalised, and,

James Ellroy

chronicle the underside of LA in the fifties and sixties, each one depicting the city of the angels as a town full of 'bad men doing bad things in the name of authority', each spurning Raymond Chandler's knight errant concept for 'shitbird cops out to fuck the disenfranchised'.

In 1987 he completed his masterpiece, *The Black Dahlia*, a brilliant work that finally fused the two murdered redheads who haunted him. Ellroy toured America, pushing the novel, and virtually reducing his mother's memory to a gimmick: 'I told the Jean Ellroy–Dahlia story ten dozen times. I reduced it to sound bites and vulgarized it in the name of accessibility.'

Hollywood bought options on Ellroy's novels and abandoned them as being too violent and crazy for mainstream audiences until, finally, his sprawling epic *LA Confidential* (1990) was made into an Oscar-nominated film.

In *My Dark Places* (1996) Ellroy retells the story of his mother's murder and of his recent attempts to solve it. He says of his efforts: 'It wasn't enough…I had to know more…I will not let this end. I will not betray her or abandon her again.' The book contains a picture of his mother's partially-clad body which is frankly erotic. Ellroy has confessed that 'when I was a kid, I wanted her and I wanted her bad…And I guess she still fascinates me in that way.' He has also admitted that 'her death made me a writer'. For all his research into the history of America, it is the ghosts of his own past that make Ellroy into the self-styled 'demon dog' of contemporary crime fiction.

once sober, got a job as a golf caddy. But he never forgot the Black Dahlia.

Ellroy later recalled that 'events changed after January 26 1979. That's the day I wrote the first page of my first novel. I knew right from the start that I had found what I was put on earth to do.'

His first novel was the semi-autobiographical *Brown's Requiem* (1981). After it was published he left the West Coast for New York (and subsequently the Kansas prairies) and wrote five more meticulously researched books which

< 90 >

E IS FOR EROTICA

5 places to find pleasure in the text

THE ROSY CRUCIFIXION
Henry Miller
sexistential search for life and its meaning

THE JOURNALS (SEVEN VOLS)
Anaïs Nin
women are sexistentialists too

OUR LADY OF THE FLOWERS
Jean Genet
the arousing beauty of degradation

FEAR OF FLYING
Erica Jong
in search of the zipless fuck

FANNY HILL
John Cleland
tales of a Victorian pleasure-giver

MUST READ *American Tabloid, The Black Dahlia, LA Confidential, My Dark Places*
READ ON Robert Campbell, **Raymond Chandler**, *City of Quartz* by Mike Davis, Ross Macdonald

Loren D Estleman

1952–
Motor City's Chandler

For someone who describes the Motor City as 'the place where the American Dream stalled and sat rusting in the rain', Estleman is a writer whose dyspeptic view of Detroit has stood him in very good stead. Only Raymond Chandler's love–hate relationship with Los Angeles has mined as rich a vein as Estleman's. The Chandler comparison extends beyond eloquently expressed urban disaffection, however, as Estleman has a worthy substitute for Philip Marlowe in Amos Walker. Walker is a private eye in the classic mould: touchy, stubborn, handy with a wise-crack and, when the pace hots up, armed with either a gun or (in dire emergencies) a slug or two from the office bottle. Cynical yet ruefully honest, Walker mercifully eschews Marlowe's tendency to feel sorry for himself.

Throughout the ten Walker novels and the many other noirish books Estleman has written, whether they are set in the Prohibition era (*Whiskey River*), the fifties boom years (*Edsel*), or the political unrest and violence of the sixties (*Downriver*), there is one constant: the Motor City itself, a Pandora's box whose flimsy lock has long since been sprung. Yet in Estleman's novels, Detroit, that ugly chunk of America, still has a little bit of hope remaining.

MUST READ *Edsel, Whiskey River*
READ ON **Raymond Chandler**

Frederick Exley

1930–1992
The fabulous failure

Born in small-town New York state, the son of a local football legend, Frederick Exley's own dreams of sporting success were ended by a car accident. He went to the University of Southern California to study dentistry yet graduated in English. On his return he began writing his masterwork in his mother's attic.

Finally published in 1968, and nominated for the National Book Award, *A Fan's Notes* received the William Faulkner Award and a whole slew of fellowships and grants

A Fan's Notes (subtitled a fictional memoir) and its two inferior follow-ups were a beguiling mixture of autobiography and fiction. In an introduction to the first, *A Fan's Notes* (1968), Exley wrote: 'Though the events in this book bear similarity to that long malaise, my life…I

Frederick Exley

ask to be judged as a writer of fantasy.' *A Fan's Notes* is largely concerned with Exley's desire for fame and the unfavourable comparison he draws between himself and his hero (and contemporary at USC) the football player Frank Gifford. Exley's fear was that it was his lot 'to sit in the stands with most men and acclaim others. It was my fate, my destiny, my end, to be a fan.' Some have claimed that the mixture of personal confession and sporting hero-worship made it the model for Nick Hornby's *Fever*

< 92 >

Pitch (Hornby is a keen student of recent American fiction).

Exley is similar to Henry Miller in his seamless fusion of fact and fiction, although less caustic than Miller. A key to his personality can be gained from a casual glance through the chapter headings of his final volume, *Last Notes from Home*: 'In the Days Before I Shot my Sister', 'Blowjob', 'Marriage and Resurrection' (although this last may sound tame, one should bare in mind, that the 'Resurrection' refers to Exley, on his Hawaiian honeymoon, with a grilling fork in his chest – stuck there by his new wife – drinking vodka, and watching the sunrise on Easter Sunday).

Throughout these volumes Exley life moves from bouts of troubled insanity and incarceration to drinking binges, through discussions of the writer's art and lyrical meditations on life, holding up his blemished life in a painfully raw and personal way. Exley died in 1990, leaving his brave account of a tragic life on the edge as his legacy. In a fine biography, *Misfit*, Jonathan Yardley describes Exley (who smoked three-packs-a-day and talked incessantly) as believing 'that hard drink, hard living and, if it be so ordained, early death were the appropriate ways of living the literary life.'

MUST READ *A Fan's Notes, Misfit* by Jonathan Yardley
READ ON **Charles Bukowski, Henry Miller, Nick Hornby**

E IS FOR EIGHTIES
5 novels about upwardly–mobile money monsters

MONEY
Martin Amis
grotesque excess and moral bankruptcy amid the film industry

THE CONCLAVE
Michael Bracewell
The English yuppie bildungsroman par excellence

BRIGHTNESS FALLS
Jay McInerney
Selling out amid take–over bids in the NY publishing set

BONFIRE OF THE VANITIES
Tom Wolfe
social panorama of the upwardly–mobile modelled on Vanity Fair

AMERICAN PSYCHO
Bret Easton Ellis
adding torture and dismemberment to the yuppie lifestyle

E
a reader's guide

< 93 >

F

CULT FICTION

John Fante

1909–1984
Down and out in LA

Born in Boulder, Colorado in 1909, Fante was educated at Regis High School, a Jesuit boarding school, and at the University of Colorado and Long Beach City College.

He began writing short stories in 1929, publishing the first in H L Mencken's magazine, *American Mercury*, in 1932, and continued a correspondence with the editor for over 20 years (Mencken and the *Mercury* were portrayed in Fante's fiction as Heinrich Muller and the *American Phoenix*).

He wrote a series of autobiographical novels featuring Arturo Bandini, a young writer eking out a living in Los Angeles, in poor, racially mixed areas, staying in cheap hotels. The first, *Wait until Spring, Bandini* (1938), was followed by *Ask the Dust* (1939), and two later volumes, including the posthumously published *The Road to Los Angeles* (1985), an early novel that had been lost.

For over ten years, Fante worked as a scriptwriter in Hollywood, churning out screenplays, of which the most memorable were the adaptations of his 1952 novel, *Full of Life*, and of Nelson Algren's classic, *Walk on the Wild Side* (1956), starring Laurence Harvey and Jane Fonda.

In 1955, Fante contracted diabetes and,

through complications, his eyesight failed, resulting in complete blindness by 1978. At this time, poet, novelist, and drinker Charles Bukowski championed Fante's work, and there was renewed interest in his writing. By dictating to his wife Joyce, Fante wrote one more book, a Bandini novel called *Dreams from Bunker Hill*, published in 1982.

After his death, several of his works were reprinted, and some unpublished novels, including *1933 Was a Bad Year* (1985) and two novellas, collected as *West of Rome* (1986), also appeared.

MUST READ *Ask the Dust, Wait until Spring, Bandini*
READ ON **Nelson Algren**, Edward Anderson, **Charles Bukowski**, Ethan Coen, **Knut Hamsun**, Sinclair Lewis

Richard Farina

1938–1966
Live fast, die young

With an Irish mother and a Cuban father, Farina was born a rebel. He grew up in Brooklyn, pre-revolutionary Cuba and Ireland. At 18 he was associated with members of the IRA, and was asked to leave Ireland. At Cornell University in the late fifties Farina was suspended for his part in a student protest, but was promptly rein-

< 94 >

stated when fellow students threatened to take further action to support him.

All these events are described in his only novel, *Been Down so Long It Looks Like Up to Me* (1966; so catchy was this title, that Doors singer Jim Morrison appropriated it for a song on the group's final album, *LA Woman*).

Leaving Cornell in 1959, Farina lived in Paris and London, surviving by 'music, street-singing, scriptwriting, acting, a little smuggling, anything to hang on'. In 1963 he returned to America and married Mimi Baez, sister of Joan, and they became a folk duo. Their debut album was recommended by the *New York Times* as one of the ten best releases of 1965, and their second record, *Reflections in a Crystal Wind*, was praised by the same newspaper as 'wild, imaginative, poetic, surprising'.

In an uncanny premonition of Seth Morgan's 1990 demise (fiancé of singer Janis Joplin, whose fatal drug overdose terminated their engagement; Morgan drove his bike off a New Orleans bridge shortly after the publication of his critically acclaimed first novel, *Homeboy*), Farina was killed in a motorbike accident, just two days after his book had been published. His Cornell contemporary and friend, reclusive author Thomas Pynchon (whose epic novel *Gravity's Rainbow*, 1973 was dedicated to Farina), heard the news on the radio: 'He'd been riding…where a prudent speed would have been 35. Police estimated that they must have been doing 90, and failed to make a curve. Farina was thrown off and killed.' Anxious for details, Pynchon phoned a mutual friend but she hadn't heard any more either. Finally, she had said: 'If that fucking Farina has only been seriously hurt – if he goes up to the edge of It, and then comes back, you realise we're never going to hear the end of it.' He hadn't and they had.

MUST READ *Been Down so Long It Looks Like Up to Me*
READ ON **Jack Kerouac, Ken Kesey, Seth Morgan, Thomas Pynchon**

William Faulkner

1897—1962
Cosmopolitan modernist or inbred Southerner?

Born in Oxford, Mississippi, William Faulkner left home to enjoy the bohemian fruits of New Orleans, where he wrote poetry under the influence of novelist Sherwood Anderson. During the First World War he trained with the Canadian Air Force, and afterwards encouraged the myth that he had seen action over France. But Faulkner never entered combat; nor did he escape to Paris at the end of the war, as so many other artists and writers did. Instead he returned home to Oxford, where for more than 40 years (except during his troubled sojourn in

< 95 >

Hollywood writing screenplays) he lived and wrote novels. There were times, however, when he lived at the bottom of his brandy glass; his drinking was legendary and he dedicated one of his books to a Mr Courvoisier.

The protagonist of *Soldier's Pay* (1927) is a blind veteran who fails to fit in with postwar society. *Mosquitoes* (1927) features a group of artists in New Orleans who are searching for an aesthetic that will transcend the mess that mankind has made of history without losing touch with real life. But the key to Faulkner's literary development is *Sartoris* (1929), in which he turns his gaze towards his Mississippi home and its history, and creates the people of Yoknapatawpha County – what novelist and critic Malcolm Bradbury has described as 'the Mississippi version of Hardy's Wessex'. Writing this novel, which again describes the uneasiness of a war veteran returning home, was something of a revelation to Faulkner himself: 'I discovered that writing was a mighty fine thing. You could make people stand on their hind legs and cast a shadow, and as soon as I discovered it I wanted to bring them all back.'

Accordingly, he set the bulk of his life's work in the fictional world of Yoknapatawpha County, including *The Sound and the Fury* (1929), *As I Lay Dying* (1930), *Light in August* (1932), and *Absalom, Absalom!* (1936) and *Go Down, Moses* (1942). These are experimental works which play games with the space–time continuum. In this respect they are characteris-

< 96 >

William Faulkner

tic of high modernism. On the other hand, they are rooted in the locality and history of the South, which seems to suggest a conservatism at odds with the accelerated pace of social change reflected in modernism. In fact, there is a common element underlying the two sides of Faulkner: alienation and the attempt to transcend it. In his alienation from the horrors of recent history and what has been done to the individual subject, Faulkner the conservative sought to escape the world of the modern city;

while Faulkner the modernist set about reconfiguring time, place and subjectivity in a manner that is both lyrical and avant-garde.

Faulkner veered away from the lean, mean prose of Ernest Hemingway et al. – a style which he described as 'scrupulous meanness'. His prose is lush – the density of the descriptive passages and the richness of the rhetoric are Faulkner's way of rising above solitude and re-establishing the world of our common humanity. Many critics believe that he succeeded; he was awarded the Nobel Prize for Literature in 1950. Others insist that some of his writing is unnecessarily difficult. Faulkner died in 1962, just before his paternalistic attitudes to black people might have got him into deep trouble with the burgeoning civil rights movement.

MUST READ *As I Lay Dying, Sanctuary, The Sound and the Fury*
READ ON **Harry Crews, James Joyce, Gertrude Stein**, Virginia Woolf

Ronald Firbank

1886—1926
Eccentric miniaturist

Ronald Arthur Annesley Firbank was the grandson of an illiterate miner from Durham who went on to make a fortune as a railway contractor, and the son of a Unionist MP (a supporter of the union of Britain and Ireland) who married into the aristocracy and was later made a baronet. At Cambridge University Firbank converted to Catholicism. Pathologically shy, he kept a palm tree in his flat and employed a gardener to water it twice a day. He wrote his sylph-like books on blue postcards in hotel rooms, sometimes abandoning his efforts when the comic scenes he had created became too absurd. In many ways, both his life and his writing career bear a marked similarity to Proust's: Firbank was homosexual, pampered by an over-indulgent mother whom he adored, obsessed with beauty and entranced by exotic pleasures. But there is an even more marked contrast between Firbank's slender output and Proust's magnum opus.

Championed by the Sitwells and W H Auden (the latter remarked: 'A person who dislikes Ronald Firbank, may, for all I know, possess some admirable quality, but I do not wish ever to see him again'), Firbank had to pay for the publication of his books himself until *Prancing Nigger* (1924) (UK title: *Sorrow in Sunlight*) established him in the USA. The American critic Edmund Wilson dubbed him 'one of the finest writers of his period.' Firbank was a frail man who drank heavily and was too nervous to eat properly (at a sumptuous dinner held in his honour, he refused to eat anything except just one pea). He died in Rome, leaving behind fragments of a New York novel, *The New Rhythm*.

Firbank's themes are derived from his privileged background: aristocratic aesthetes flit to and fro to different corners of the world, each a victim of what the French have described as a particularly English affliction: ennui. In his introduction to the American edition of *Three Novels*, critic Ernest Jones claimed that Firbank was 'afraid of feeling, a fear which seriously limited the range of his fiction, but which is directly responsible for his delightful ironies and flippancies'. Although some critics and fellow authors regarded his work with bemusement and even contempt, others adored him and his hilarious, somewhat surreal books. Anthony Powell, Ivy Compton-Burnett and Evelyn Waugh have all cited him as an influence. In *Vainglory* (1998), his second book, Firbank's description of a novelist (who can only be himself), coolly pinpoints his opinion of his novels: 'His work calls to mind a frieze with figures of varying height trotting all the same way. If one should turn about it's usually merely to sneer or to make a grimace. Only occasionally his figures care to beckon. And they seldom really touch.'

MUST READ *Prancing Niggers/Sorrow in Sunlight, Vainglory*
READ ON Anthony Powell, Marcel Proust, Edith Sitwell, **Oscar Wilde**

John Fowles

1926–
The Magus

Born in Leigh-on-Sea, in the south-east of England, John Fowles's childhood was typical of the suburban middle classes in Britain between the wars, but he also lived a strong imaginative life under the influence of books such as *Bevis* by Richard Jefferies. After attending the universities of Edinburgh and Oxford (New College), and military service in the Marines, Fowles did a prolonged stint of schoolmastering in France, Greece and back in England.

The first of Fowles's novels to be published was *The Collector* (1963), the story of a psychopathic lepidopterist who kidnaps an art student and treats her like one of his specimens: he loves her and cuts her up at the same time. Grotesque yet carefully controlled, this scenario allows Fowles to comment on all kinds of issues from class to the sense of stagnation in British society before the sixties started swinging. The novel was faithfully filmed by William Wyler (1965), with Terence Stamp and Samantha Eggar in the leading roles.

If *The Collector* brought Fowles a modicum of success, it was *The Magus* (1965, revised 1977) that put him fully on the literary map. Set on the fictional Greek island of Phraxos (based on Fowles's experience of the island of Spetsai, but not directly so; he once said that if he had fictionalised his spell as an English teacher at a boarding school there, the result would have been a comic novel), *The Magus* centres on a schoolmaster (Nicholas) who becomes a pawn in the 'Godgame' of the master-magician and manipulator, Maurice Conchis. In his introduction to the revised edition, Fowles explained that working on the original draft of *The Magus* was how he learnt to become a writer in the early fifties. He acknowledged the influence of psychologist Carl Jung, and divulged that his literary models were Alain-Fournier's *Le Grand Meaulnes*, Henry James's *The Turn of the Screw*, and Charles Dickens's *Great Expectations*. He also revealed that embarking on the novel was partly prompted by the renunciation of literary ambitions on the part of a fellow schoolmaster who had recently given up writing poetry. As to what *The Magus* means, Fowles kept his cards to his chest: 'If The Magus has any "real significance", it is no more than that of the Rorschach test in psychology. Its meaning is whatever reaction it provokes in the reader, and so far as I am concerned there is no given "right" reaction.' But he admitted that, despite his recent revisions, *The Magus* 'must always substantially remain a novel of adolescence written by a retarded adolescent'.

The French Lieutenant's Woman (1969) combines an apparently straightforward 19th-century romance with footnotes and documentary-style elements which remind the reader that the text is itself a 20th-century reading of an antique story and an equally anachronistic genre of writing. Many of its fans have praised Fowles for inventing such an imaginative hybrid. Critics complain that Fowles has only found a way of rendering the repressed sexuality of the Victorian era in a manner that our age can find titillating. The novel became especially popular in the eighties after it was filmed by veteran director Karel Reisz from a screenplay by Harold Pinter, with Meryl Streep and the young Jeremy Irons in the starring roles.

Fowles's subsequent novels are *Daniel Martin* (1977), *Mantissa* (1982), *A Maggot* (1985) and *Tessera* (1993). None of these received as much critical acclaim as his earlier work. A collection of his short stories, *The Ebony Tower*, was published in 1974. Fowles has written little of late, but long ago intimated that writing novels is not necessarily a lifelong occupation:

'It is a constant complaint in that most revealing of all modern novels about novelists, Thomas Hardy's agonized last fiction, *The Well-Beloved*, how much the younger self still rules the supposedly "mature" and middle-aged artist. One may reject the tyranny, as Hardy himself did; but the cost is the end of one's ability to write novels.'

MUST READ *The Collector, The French Lieutenant's Woman, The Magus*
READ ON **Jorge Luis Borges**, Alain-Fournier, Thomas Hardy, Dennis Wheatley

< 99 >

Kinky Friedman

1944–
The singing detective

Richard 'Kinky' or 'Big Dick' Friedman, alias 'The Kinkster' was born in El Paso, Texas to the Jewish faith. He attended the University of Texas and then joined the Peace Corps for two years in 1966. On returning he formed Kinky Friedman and The Texas Jewboys – 'a country band with a social message'. The songs tackled every subject from the Holocaust to abortion. Yet he has also had a lot of fun winding people up with song titles like 'They Ain't Making Jews Like Jesus Anymore' and 'Get Your Biscuits In The Oven And Your Buns In The Bed' for which he was voted male chauvinist pig of the year by the National Organisation of Women in 1974.

In the mid-seventies he moved to Greenwich Village, which inspired the settings and characters for most of his novels. He took up writing crime novels in the mid-eighties shortly after saving a woman from a New York mugger on his way home from a bar.

The hero of his novels is none other than Kinky Friedman, cigar-smoking, whiskey-drinking, Greenwich Village musician (rather like the real one) who aided and abetted by his Village Irregulars encounters among other things mysterious deaths, SS Troopers, pretty women and the FBI.

His has written 11 novels starting with *Greenwich Killing Time* in 1986 and stretching to *Blast From The Past* in 1998. Other titles include *Elvis, Jesus and Coca-Cola*, *God Bless John Wayne* and *The Love Song of J Edgar Hoover*. Though intricately plotted, the main attraction are Kinky's hilarious one-liners which are scattered throughout his books 'like crushed corn in a chicken pen'. Try: 'He looked like an accountant or serial killer-type. Definitely one of the service industries'. Or: 'That night it rained like a bitch with a charge account'.

The books have made him, in his own words, a 'cult fuck'. Among his fans number Nelson Mandela, Bill Clinton, Bob Dylan and Willie Nelson. Kinky now lives with his Smith-Corona typewriter, cats, dogs and armadillo on a ranch in Texas. He seldom performs except 'at bar mitzvahs, whorehouses and book signings'.

MUST READ *Greenwich Killing Time*
READ ON Joe R Lansdale, **Carl Hiaasen**, **James Crumley**

< 100 >

William Gaddis

1922–1998
The accountant of counterfeit culture

Born in New York, Gaddis was educated at Harvard but left without graduating. He lived and travelled abroad in Mexico and Central America until in 1945 he started his first, epic novel, *The Recognitions*, which was eventually published in 1955. From that point on, rumour alway surrounded Gaddis (in many ways, even more of a recluse than J D Salinger). Critics have from time to time suggested he is the alter ego of fellow recluse Thomas Pynchon. But then, they also thought he was a floorwalker at Macy's department store, or possibly a mercenary in a war in Costa Rica, or maybe a labourer on the Panama Canal. He has in fact supported himself through his lengthy literary silences by, among other things, writing public relations material for corporate clients. Gaddis has also worked as a fact finder for the *New Yorker*.

When his second novel *JR* (1975) won the National Book Award in 1976 (following its 20-year gestation period), Gaddis was confused at the awards ceremony with his friend, the critic and author William Gass, to the extent that, on the publication of *Carpenters Gothic*, a mere ten years later, the *New York Times* even attributed the book to Gass, not Gaddis. In 1984 acolytes John Kuehl and Steven Moore edited *In Recognition of William Gaddis* and, according to Gass: 'The honoured author turned artist and for the title page, self-drew himself suitably suited and bearing a highball glass. The figure has no head.'

Each of Gaddis's novels consisted almost entirely of dialogue, and each brilliantly lambasted different aspects of contemporary America: from the self-centred and superficial New York intellectuals in *The Recognitions*, through the corrupt business world of *JR*, and *Carpenters Gothic*'s fundamentalist hysteria and all-consuming greed (1985), to *A Frolic of his Own* (1994), with its masterly indictment of America's legal system and the country's mania for litigation. As Mary McCarthy said of Gaddis's work: 'His novels are massive in construction and dazzling in execution.' Experimental and difficult to categorise, they are encyclopedic works with meticulous, labyrinthine plotting and endless roll calls of characters. The characters are always without agency, enmeshed in some great unquantifiable system. In Gaddis's paranoid and conspiratorial fictional worlds everything seems to be counterfeit, hiding some elusive, never-to-be-found truth.

MUST READ *Carpenters Gothic, The Recognitions*
READ ON **Robert Coover, Don Delillo,** William Gass, **Thomas Pynchon**

< 101 >

Mary Gaitskill

196?–
Love and violation

Expelled from boarding school for a drug-related offence at 15, and then committed to a psychiatric hospital by her parents, the young Mary Gaitskill sold flowers, jewelry and candles on the streets of Toronto before finding work as a stripper and go-go dancer. She spent a few months in a squat in New York's Lower East Side, then went to college in Michigan, and came back to NYC to work in a bookshop and as a legal proofreader. She recalls her stripping days as 'an interesting experience for me, and often a pleasurable one. I had been inordinately shy and it was a way to act out a lot of fantasies.'

In 1988 Gaitskill made her debut with *Bad Behaviour*, a collection of short stories peopled by prostitutes, addicts, hustlers, sado-masochists, artists and johns. Its voices stood out well against the eighties rich kids and their angst (McInerney, Ellis et al.) and in contrast to the male-dominated Dirty Realists. In 1991 she published *Two Girls, Fat and Thin*. Set in Manhattan, its protagonists are a nervous, good-looking secretary connected to the New York art scene, and a fat, lonely VDU operator. Their contrasting lives are connected by their common experience of child sexual abuse. The book ventures into details of rape, masochism and malignant sex but the two girls are also linked by a commom interest in a controversial philosopher, Anna Granite (a loosely veiled caricature of Ayn Rand) and her theory of Definitism (Rand's Objectivism). *Because They Wanted To* (1997) her second collection of stories is again a raw vertiginous series of psychosexual portraits of characters who seem oddly at home living in emotional extremities.

In all her books Gaitskill's main concern is to examine the yearning to connect with other people in a world of isolation, and the self-destructive 'cul de sacs of behaviour' which often result from this desire. She believes that love and violation are not mutually exclusive, because 'violation is a form of contact'. In 1991 Gaitskill told Jon Wilde of *Blitz* magazine that 'I think you could love somebody and want to piss in their mouth. I know people who love each other and do things like that.'

MUST READ *Two Girls, Fat and Thin, Because They Wanted To*
READ ON **Kathy Acker**, **Tama Janowitz**, **Ayn Rand**, Catherine Texier

< 102 >

Jean Genet

1910–1986
The thief who wrote himself out of jail

Six months after he was born, Genet's unmarried mother surrendered him to a state orphanage in Paris. Farmed out to a family of artisans, Genet committed his first theft while a choirboy at the village church of Alligny-en-Morvan. Apprenticed to a typographer in Paris, he ran

Jean Genet

away; then absconded repeatedly from various institutions until he was locked up for two and a half years in the 'children's prison' of Mettray. He only got out when he joined the army, in which he served from 1929 until he deserted in 1936; at which point Genet went on the run through Europe – a criminal and sexual odyssey that provided source material for much of his subsequent writing. On his return to France he was discharged from the army for 'mental imbalance', but was repeatedly arrested and jailed for petty theft.

In prison in 1942, Genet began *Our Lady of the Flowers* (1944). His first published work, the poem 'The Man Condemned To Death', was also written in jail and later printed at his own expense. When Genet next appeared before the courts, he might well have been sentenced to life imprisonment as a recidivist, but was saved by the support he received from famous writers, notably Jean Cocteau.

In March 1944, Genet was released from prison, never to return. In the following decade or so he was a prolific writer. His output included books such as *Funeral Rites* (1947), *Miracle of the Rose* (1946) and *A Thief's Journal* (1949); poems such as 'La Galère' ('The Galley-ship'); a radio play entitled *The Criminal Child*; essays such as 'Fragments', published in Jean-Paul Sartre's magazine *Les Temps Modernes; A Song of Love*, a film that Genet wrote and directed, and stage plays such as *The Maids* (1946), *The Balcony*) and *The Blacks* (1958). Some of these

< 103 >

works were first published either clandestinely or without the publisher's name because of the highly explicit homosexual material that they contained.

Genet's books were banned in the USA at this time. He was repeatedly refused a visa to enter the USA, and twice crossed the border illegally. On the first occasion he had been commissioned by *Esquire* magazine to cover the 1968 Democratic Convention in Chicago, which was accompanied by militant anti-Vietnam War demonstrations in which Genet took part, culminating in a police riot. The second illicit border crossing occurred in 1970, when Genet did a two-month speaking tour in support of the Black Panthers and their jailed leadership. Genet was also a stalwart supporter of the Palestinian cause.

From the sixties to his death in the mid-eighties, Genet put less effort into writing new material and spent more time supervising productions of his plays and new editions of his prose. He also travelled a great deal through the Far East, Middle East and in Europe. This time round he journeyed in much greater comfort than before.

In his successful plea to the judge not to send Genet to jail for life, Cocteau described him as 'the greatest writer of the modern era'. Allowing, given the circumstances, for some exaggeration on Cocteau's part, Genet's literary standing is nevertheless extremely high. In particular, his determination to find aesthetic pleasure in experiences which, according to tra-

ditional standards, contain only brutality and degradation, has been an inspiration for a host of artists, musicians and writers during the last half century. Furthermore, in *Subculture: the meaning of style* (1990), cultural critic Dick Hebdige defined the whole purpose of subcultures and youth style in terms of Genet's reverence for artefacts – such as a tube of Vaseline to be used for sexual lubrication – which those in authority consider both sordid and laughable. For Hebdige and others, therefore, Genet is something of a template for youth culture. By the same token, Genet's capacity for making high culture out of lowlife is frowned upon by those conservative critics who insist that art and literature should be morally uplifting and a buttress to family values.

MUST READ *Our Lady of the Flowers, A Thief's Journal*
READ ON **Georges Bataille**, **William Burroughs**, **Jean Cocteau**, **John Rechy**

Sylvie Germain

1954–
Dreamer of the sacred earth

Born in Chateauroux, Germain received a doctorate in philosophy from the Sorbonne, and taught it at the French School in Prague from 1987 to 1993.

< 104 >

She claimed that philosophy, 'a continuous wonder' to her, was also too 'analytical', and she switched from Descartes and Heidegger to Kafka and Dostoevsky.

She grew up in rural France, in an area steeped in mythology and folklore, and she admitted 'that the power of place had a huge effect on me but it was an unconscious one'. That her prose was 'related to the earth…the soil, the peasants, the trees', was revealed in her first novel, *The Book of Nights* (1985), which won six literary awards. It tells the tragic history of a family living in Flanders, and their suffering as the countryside is ravaged in the Franco-Prussian War of 1870 and the two world wars of 1914 and 1939.

The second novel, *Night of Amber* (1987) continued from the first, and was followed by *Days of Anger* (1989). Despite this three-part structure, Germain claimed that she was 'trying only to express an obsessive image and to explain it to myself. I have no pretensions to creating a mythos. Each book begins with an image or a dream and I try to express that and give it coherence.'

The impact of dreams on Germain's writing should not be underestimated. Her work came from 'a plethora of unconscious images and revelations…childhood memories, emotions, sensations, dreams…I feel that the dream life, the life of the imagination, is very structured.'

Along with this overriding air of hallucination, all the books have a sense of religion.

Raised a Catholic, Germain stated that 'Catholicism – the pictorial, the statuary – has been very decisive in forming my imagery. All these images are important. They can lead to faith but at the same time they can eclipse faith …All my books are about the problem of evil.'

MUST READ *The Medusa Child, Immensities*
READ ON **Angela Carter**, Marguerite Duras, Virginia Woolf

William Gibson
1948–
Hard-boiled cyberpunk

Born in South Carolina, William Gibson's early childhood involved travelling around a lot, following his father's job (something to do with plumbing and contracting), and moving from one suburban housing development to another. Gibson remembers moving into one before they laid the turf: little houses set in 'Martian orange clay', like something out of J G Ballard. But his father died when Gibson was eight, and his mother took him to her family home in Virginia. Later he attended a boarding school in Arizona.

Gibson has described himself as part of 'the classic baby boomer demographic'. Growing up in the late fifties and sixties, his reference points were science fiction ('my home town'), rock-'n'roll music, Beat writing and Dashiell

< 105 >

G

Hammett. Traumatised at 18 when his mother died, Gibson got on a bus to Toronto and sat out the Vietnam War there (not technically a draft-dodger, he told the board where he was but they never came looking for him). He defines his Canadian existence as not so much hippie, more 'proto-slacker', adding that 'going through that sixties counterculture thing was my formative experience'. He got into writing by accident: 'I didn't do anything career-oriented, ever. I sort of backed into being a writer by accident at the very last minute. If I hadn't done that I'd probably be working in a second-hand bookstore or a record shop.'

Gibson's first published story was *Fragments of a Hologram Rose* (1976), which contains the fictional antecedents for virtual reality. The following year he gave up writing and collected a lot of punk records, until he was persuaded to take writing seriously by punk musician and author John Shirley. Soon afterwards Gibson met Bruce Sterling at a sci-fi convention in Austin, Texas, and along with Sterling, Shirley, Rudy Rucker and Lewis Shiner, became part of The Movement, which was later dubbed 'cyberpunk'. His short story 'The Gernsback Continuum', about a fascist-tinged parallel universe in which yesterday's dreams of the future have been fully realised, was included in Sterling's seminal cyberpunk anthology, *Mirrorshades* (1986).

Neuromancer (1984), the first part of Gibson's Sprawl trilogy (*Count Zero* came out in

1986, and *Mona Lisa Overdrive* in 1988), won all three major sci-fi awards in 1984 (the Hugo, the Nebula and the Philip K Dick). Combining Dashiell Hammett-style detail with eighties-style branding, *Neuromancer* took computer nerds, dressed them in leather jackets and made them into creatures of rock'n'roll. It was written on an olive-green Hermes portable typewriter made in 1927 (the sort that Ernest Hemingway might have used in the field), but this antiquated piece of technology was the machine that introduced the world to the concepts of cyberspace and virtual reality, defined by Gibson as 'the place where the bank keeps your money' and 'consensual hallucination'.

After seeing Ridley Scott's *Blade Runner*, Gibson is reported to have 'staggered from the cinema in despair', thinking that someone else had already depicted the landscape he had in mind for *Neuromancer*. But it is Gibson's work that has been referred to by a whole generation of architects and technologists. While he has no time for the kind of people who read *Neuromancer* every year to check how many more of the gadgets envisaged in it have now gone into production, he says that the aspect of computer technology that he most enjoys is that 'this is the revenge of the hippies'.

Gibson has said that his novels depict end-stage capitalism, and that his heroes 'live between the cracks'. This is certainly true of *Virtual Light* (1993) which hinges on a techno-counterculture in post-earthquake California.

< 106 >

Idoru (1996) deals with the dominant role of the media in our lives, to the point where we can fall in love with personalities that only exist in the media landscape. Gibson has also published a collection of short stories (*Burning Chrome*, 1986).

Few complaints have been made against Gibson. He is taken seriously by literary critics, revered by sci-fi readers, and lionised by techno-philosophers. But it is surely interesting that the man who is perhaps the best-known futurist in contemporary literature admits to having had his formative experiences in the counterculture of the sixties. Seems like Britpop is not the only cultural location where the future is retro.

MUST READ *Neuromancer, Virtual Light*
READ ON **Dashiell Hammett, Jeff Noon, Bruce Sterling**, Neal Stephenson

André Gide

1869–1951
Sex, sin and pendulum swings

Born in Paris, André Gide was an only child in a Calvinist household. His father was professor of law at the Sorbonne and the strict moral tone of his upbringing (Protestant school and private tuition) was the formative experience of his life. As a teenager Gide rebelled against Calvinism and became an almost religious believer in 'art

for art's sake'. His first book, *Les Cahiers d'André Walter* (*The Note Books of André Walter*; 1891) is the work of a perfectionist in both aesthetic and moral terms. It is surely the product of sexual repression, for at 24 Gide came to terms with his homosexuality in a relationship with Oscar Wilde. He entered into a period of sexual paganism, during which time he composed a paean to the pleasures of the senses entitled *Fruits of the Earth* and denounced chastity as 'peculiar [to Christianity], odd, morbid and abnormal'. But

André Gide

soon afterwards he returned to Calvinism, burdened with a sense of his own sin. This was the atmosphere in which Gide wrote the key cult novel *The Immoralist* (1902), which follows a journey to North Africa and a feverish descent into a decadent state of mind in which sex and depravity are synonymous.

In 1895 Gide married his cousin Madeleine Roudoux; their marriage was childless but he fathered a daughter by another woman. Two years earlier he had bemoaned his lack of sexual experience: 'I lived until the age of 23 completely virgin and utterly depraved; crazed to such a point that eventually I came to seek everywhere some bit of flesh on which to press my lips.'

Gide's soul continued its pendulum swings. At the outbreak of the First World War he converted to Catholicism but then drew back. Afterwards he wrote a manifesto in support of homosexuality (*Corydon*, 1924; around this time Gide made it public knowledge that he had a lover called Marc and enjoyed sexual encounters with Arab youths), an indictment of blind faith (*Strait is the Gate*, 1924) and a philosophical satire on organised religion (*The Vatican Swindle*, 1925). In the thirties he became involved with Communism, but later contributed to *The God that Failed* (1950), R H Crossman's anthology of ex-communist intellectuals who now rejected Marx as bad faith.

Gide's most experimental novel is *The Counterfeiters* (1926), a literary exercise based on musical patterns. But some critics prefer his straightforward *Journals* 1889–1949. These include such gems as: 'To be right…Who still wants to be?…A few fools', and Gide's changeable opinion of Robert Louis Stevenson's *Dr Jekyll and Mr Hyde*. 'Finished the Stevenson. Jekyll's confession is wonderful and what I wrote yesterday is absurd. If I do not tear out this page, it is for the mortification of rereading it someday.'

After many years of pro- and anti-religious zeal, Gide settled down and acquired a reputation as a liberal humanist (E M Forster described him as 'the humanist of our age'). At the age of 78 he received the Nobel Prize and an honorary doctorate from Oxford University.

MUST READ *The Immoralist, Journals 1888–1949, Strait is the Gate*
READ ON **Albert Camus**, John Knox, Marcel Proust, Evelyn Waugh

< 108 >

Donald Goines

1937—1974
Daddy Cool

Donald Goines was shot dead by a gunman (something to do with a drugs deal that back-fired) as he neared completion of a crime story appropriately entitled *Kenyatta's Last Hit*. The manner of his death was as fast, furious and unromantic as his short life and the many books he pumped out during his brief spell as a writer.

Born in Detroit, which was just then becoming known as 'motor city', Donald Goines was expected to go into his family's laundry business. But he enlisted in the US Air Force, falsifying his age to get in. By the time he got back from his last tour of duty in Japan (then under US occupation), Goines was a qualified heroin addict. He spent the 15 years from 1955 either robbing, pimping, or doing time. While in jail he tried his hand at writing Westerns, but his attempts were largely unsuccessful. However, around this time Goines was introduced to the work of Iceberg Slim (Robert Beck), whose semi-autobiographical writing proved a much more appropriate model (minus the homosexual aspects).

Goines wrote his first two novels in prison (*Whoreson*, a semi-autobiographical piece about the son of a prostitute who becomes a pimp, and *Dopefiend*, 1971, which focuses on two middle-class black girls who become enmeshed in drugs and crime). Released in 1970, he worked to a strict timetable (writing in the morning, shooting up heroin in the afternoon) and turned out eight books a year, including *Daddy Cool* and the *Kenyatta* (named after the 'father of Kenya', Jomo Kenyatta) series, issued under the pseudonym Al C Clarke. The whole of Goines's output was published by Holloway House in Los Angeles, an entirely unpretentious operation whose main outlets are not upmarket or even high street bookshops, but general stores and mom-and-pop shops in black America.

When Goines's novels were first published, they sold well but received no literary acclaim. In the eighties and nineties, a new generation of black Americans adopted Goines as part of their cultural heritage. Since 1993, when Goines first became available in translation, French readers have become all but addicted to him, comparing him to Chester Himes and even Jean-Jacques Rousseau. It is rumoured that sales of Goines's novels have now reached 10 million.

MUST READ Donald Goines wrote fiction the way other people package meat. There is little point in picking any of his titles as outstanding, since they are all formulaic. Equally, however, they are all outstanding in that they are street-real and avoid the romanticism of many of the films and books about black life in America.
READ ON **Clarence Cooper, Chester Himes, Iceberg Slim**

< 109 >

William Golding

1911–1993
Chronicler of the beast within

Although William Gerald Golding's father was a master at a top English public (i.e. private) school (Marlborough), the whole family was inclined towards radicalism. The Goldings supported the suffragist and socialist causes, and during the 1930s William Golding joined the Communist Party (briefly). He read English at Oxford before taking a commission in the Royal Navy during the Second World War. On D-Day (the Allied invasion of France in 1944) he commanded a small warship. After the war Golding became a schoolmaster himself.

All this makes Golding sound like the quintessential Englishman, an impression confirmed by his traditional dress, polite manner and penchant for riding. But the themes of his novels are a million miles away from a vicarage tea party.

When it was published in 1954, *Lord of the Flies* came like a breath of fresh air into the stuffy parlour of the English novel. Its exotic location (a tropical island), and its commitment to great themes – human nature itself – set it apart from the turgid renditions of English middle-class life that characterised the literature of the early 1950s. But the paradox of Golding's most successful novel is that its treatment of corruption and barbarism was very much of and for its time.

The plot of *Lord of the Flies* – a group of English public schoolboys find themselves alone on a deserted island – is lifted from the 19th-century adventure story *Coral Island*. But whereas in the Victorian yarn the young chaps reproduce the customs of the mother country and help bring civilisation to a dark corner of the globe, shouldering what used to be described as 'the white man's burden', in Golding's version the boys themselves become savages, eventually killing their own. The beast, Golding was suggesting, is not out there waiting to be tamed by civilised man, but is here within all of us, waiting for the right time to take over. Other writers, such as Emile Zola in *La Bête Humaine*, had suggested that some human beings are animals underneath; Golding is saying that this is the condition of mankind as a whole. In his novel, the lord of the flies is a dead airman, hanging from the trees with flies buzzing in and out of his head – a symbol of rotten humanity.

Golding often said that the Second World War drove all the idealism and optimism out of him: he could no longer believe in human betterment and perfectibility, as the Victorians had done. In *Lord of the Flies*, as in all his work, there is what he describes as an abyss that is barely covered by the veneer of civilisation and order.

But Golding's own power of imagination contradicts his low opinion of humanity. Each of his stories is told with a fabulous ability to mentally construct a new and different world.

< 110 >

He was once asked whether he had done a great deal of research into the building of medieval cathedrals for his novel *The Spire* (1964), which describes in minute detail how a man's dream of building a cathedral eventually comes about in reality. 'No,' Golding replied. He had just gone to Salisbury Cathedral, looked up at the spire and imagined what it must have been like to build it.

Golding's work deserves to be described as 'mythic'. From the wonderfully imagined world of the Neanderthals in *The Inheritors* (1955) to the Promethean struggle of the nearly drowned sailor in *Pincher Martin* (1956), he is constantly reworking the big themes of human evil and the loss of innocence.

Golding won the Booker Prize in 1980 for *Rites of Passage* (1980); in 1983 he was awarded the Nobel Prize for Literature. But it is for *Lord of the Flies*, the book that he once said was about 'grief, sheer grief, grief, grief, grief', that he is best known. In 1964 the novel was filmed by the theatre director Peter Brook, in an X-rated version that the boys who acted in it were barred from seeing. By 1967, *Lord of the Flies* was on the school O-level syllabus for 16-year-olds, and it looks set to remain the authoritative account of what country singer Johnny Cash calls 'the beast in me'.

MUST READ *Lord of the Flies, Pincher Martin, The Spire*
READ ON Nicholas Montserrat, Emile Zola

G IS FOR GANGS
5 novels about brotherhood in blood

THE WANDERERS
Richard Price
teenage gang wars in 60s Bronx

AWAY DAYS
Kevin Sampson
Catcher in the Rye with Stanley knives set amid 80s scally casual culture

THE FOOTBALL FACTORY
John King
on tour with the Chelsea firm, first and finest of his football trilogy

A CLOCKWORK ORANGE
Anthony Burgess
inspired slang in this ultra-violent futureshocker

CARLITO'S WAY
Edwin Torres
trapped in a NY Puerto Rican gangland career

G

a reader's guide

< 111 >

David Goodis

1917– 1967
Poet of the losers

Born and bred in Philadelphia, David Goodis grew up in a liberal, Jewish household in which his early literary ambitions were encouraged. After a short and inconclusive spell at the University of Indiana, he returned to Philadelphia to take a degree in journalism, graduating in 1937. Throughout the following year he wrote copy for a local advertising agency and worked on a Hemingwayesque novel about two couples and their involvement in the civil wars in Spain and China: *Retreat from Oblivion* was published in 1939, the year that Goodis moved to New York to work as a pulp writer paid (one cent) by the word. At Popular Publications he employed various pseudonyms which allowed him to write horror stories, mysteries and Westerns simultaneously. During this period Goodis was writing up to 10,000 words (i.e. $100) a day. But the Second World War brought paper shortages, even in the USA, and many pulp magazines were forced to close. By the end of the war, Goodis was putting more effort into serious fiction.

First published as a serial in the *Saturday Evening Post*, *Dark Passage* (1946) was sold to Warners as a film scenario (made by Delmer Daves with Humphrey Bogart and Lauren Bacall starring), and only then brought out as a hardback book. In 1947 Goodis published two more hardbacks, *Nightfall* (subsequently brought to the screen by Jacques Tourneur, starring Aldo Ray and Anne Bancroft) and the masochistic *Behold This Woman*. Hollywood beckoned, and although he packed his bags to go West, Goodis signed a deal which meant he would spend only six months of each year working on scripts and the remaining six months on his own novels. By the early fifties, though, the market for books had changed and Goodis was one of the first writers to enjoy a huge readership for his paperback (softback) novels. The first of these, *Cassidy's Girl* (1951), sold a million copies in the year of its publication. In total, Goodis wrote nine paperback originals for Gold Medal Books and three more for Lion. It has been said that these are not so much 12 different novels as a dozen different versions of the same one. The most famous titles from this period in his career are *The Moon in the Gutter* (1953, filmed much later by Jean-Jacques Beineix (*Diva*) with Nastassja Kinski and Gerard Depardieu), and *Down There* (1956, filmed by François Truffaut as *Shoot the Piano Player*, with Charles Aznavour in the lead role of bar-room piano-player Edward Webster Lynn).

In the introduction to the *Black Box* compilation (1983) of four novels by Goodis, Mike Wallington suggested that his protagonists are like Bogart in Casablanca, but gone seriously to seed: 'Imagine this crazy desperate world of

< 112 >

Bogart's five years on, recast him down there as a [John] Garfield or [Robert] Mitchum, give him a run of bad luck and have him trapped, hidden or hunted, and he enters that licensed zone of American fiction that David Goodis has made his own.'

Goodis, then, inhabits the sort of literary territory in which lead characters have long since abandoned hope; in fact, a reminder that they once had hopes is often as unwelcome as a smack in the mouth. This is the world of the victim, where a man can be accused of doing something he never did, and lose his own identity in the process of trying to prove that he did not do it (in *Dark Passage*, Parry has his face altered by a surgeon). The locations in his novels changed but he essentially wrote the same story again and again, chronicling a man's fall from grace and his landing in skid row among the other trapped and desperate lives. Goodis's characters are not so much subjects who initiate activity, but objects to whom things happen – whether they like it or not.

According to Wallington, Goodis is the acknowledged master of 'thing language' in which inanimate objects ('the room looked back at him') do things to people who are powerless to withstand the pressures impinging upon them. Wallington concludes that Goodis described the price to be paid for America's sudden loss of faith in itself. It is a loss that is still being felt, which makes Goodis's fiction all the more prescient and relevant today.

MUST READ *Dark Passage, Down There, Nightfall*
READ ON Steve Fisher, **Fyodor Dostoevsky, Jim Thompson**

Alasdair Gray

1934–
Lunacy in Lanarkshire

Alasdair Gray was born in Glasgow where he trained as a painter at the local school of art. He was 47 when he published his first novel, *Lanark* (1981), which combines all sorts of genres, from sci-fi to autobiography and literary criticism, into a fantastic account of the city of Unthank – a thinly disguised Glasgow. *Lanark* is held by some to be *the* postwar Scottish novel, at last offering the country a book in the modern idiom with Joycean ambition. *Janine, 1982* (1984) is a transcript of the various voices echoing through the mind of a sales rep as he masturbates in front of a mirror during a long night in a Scottish hotel. Each voice speaks, as it were, in a different typeface: this is characteristic of Gray's creative use of typography. *Poor Things* (1992), which is a book within a book (Gray pretends that he has written only the introduction and commentary to a story by 'Archibald McCandless MD, Scottish public health officer'), also contains drawings and graphics, some of them by the author, others

< 113 >

lifted from various sources such as the medical reference-book *Gray's Anatomy* (no relation).

Gray shows an interest in sex which borders on the unhealthy, as indicated by the title of his 1990 novel *Something Leather*, a novel that he himself compared to Chaucer. His other abiding interest is Scottish identity. Along with Agnes Owens and James Kelman, Gray was the third contributor to *Lean Tales* (1985), a work that prompted a revival of interest in Scottish writing. Gray's work always contains a satirical element, especially in *The Fall of Kelvin Walker* (1985), about a media person on the make, and *McGrotty and Ludmilla* (1990), which transposes the story of Aladdin into today's corridors of power.

Gray's fans claim that he is sexy, witty and uniquely challenging – his novels are invariably playful mosaics of intertextual reference where names, themes and motifs duly doff their caps to classic literature from Chaucer to Vonnegut. His critics dismiss him as no more than a provincial eccentric polymath. The latter no doubt hope that he will keep the promise he once made and give up writing for good.

MUST READ *Janine 1982, Lanark, Poor Things*
READ ON **John Barth, Jorge Luis Borges, John Fowles, James Kelman,** Laurence Sterne

G IS FOR PLAYING GOD
5 novelists who've entered their own fictions

ALASDAIR GRAY
Lanark
caught scribbling in bed by his own creation

HARRY CREWS
Where Does One Go...?
kidnapped by his own characters

MARTIN AMIS
Money
old Martin drops in for a game of chess with the loathsome John Self

KURT VONNEGUT
Breakfast of Champions
decides to pay a visit on his fictional alter-ego Kilgore Trout

NORMAN MAILER
Armies of the Night
Mailer is his own protagonist in 'the novel as history'

< 114 >

Radclyffe Hall

1880–1943

A woman called John

Marguerite Radclyffe-Hall was born in Bournemouth on the south coast of England. Her mother may have battered her, while her father, a playboy known as 'Rat', ignored her. In the drawing rooms of Edwardian society, Marguerite made a small name for herself as a poet and librettist. In 1907 she met a middle-aged fashionable singer, Mrs Mabel Batten, known as 'Ladye', who introduced her to influential people. Batten and Radclyffe-Hall entered into a long-term relationship. But before Batten died in 1916, Radclyffe-Hall, known in private as 'John', had taken up with the second love of her life, Una, Lady Troubridge, who gave up her own creative aspirations (she was the first English translator of the French novelist Colette) to manage the household which she shared with 'John' for 28 years. With Batten, Radclyffe-Hall converted to Catholicism; in the company of Una, she pursued an interest in animals and spiritualism. In later life, Radclyffe-Hall chased after a younger woman named Evguenia Souline, a White Russian refugee. Radclyffe-Hall died from cancer of the colon in October 1943.

As Radclyffe Hall (no hyphen; prefixed neither by 'John' nor 'Marguerite'), she published a volume of stories, *Miss Ogilvy Finds Herself* (1934), which describes how British society utilised 'masculine' women during the First World War and then dropped them afterwards, and a total of seven novels, including *The Forge and the Unlit Lamp* (1924), *A Saturday Life* (1925), *Adam's Breed* (1926), *The Master of the House* (1932) and *The Sixth Beatitude* (1936). However, the novel on which Radclyffe Hall's reputation rests primarily is *The Well of Loneliness* (1928).

The Well of Loneliness follows the trials and tribulations of Stephen Gordon (a woman so-named by a father desperate for a son) who is described as an 'invert' and as a member of 'the third sex', i.e. born with a male mind and a female body. Drawing on the work of sexologists Richard von Krafft-Ebbing, Edward Carpenter and Havelock Ellis, Radclyffe Hall describes her heroine as 'grotesque and splendid, like some primitive thing conceived in a turbulent period of transition' – a transitional period without happy resolution, however, since Radclyffe Hall depicts Stephen as destined to travel endlessly through 'the loneliest place in the world…the non-man's land of sex'.

The novel was successfully prosecuted for obscenity when it first came out, and remained banned in Britain until 1948. Vilified as 'the bible of lesbianism' by fire-and-brimstone reactionaries, *The Well of Loneliness* has been used by generations of lesbians as a coded message – from a daughter to a mother, in an attempt to tell her something that could not be spoken of;

< 115 >

from one friend to another in the hope that something more than friendship might be forthcoming. In the seventies, the halcyon days of radical feminism, it was hailed as the first portrayal of a 'butch' woman. But the seventies radicals who chose lesbianism as a challenge to 'patriarchy', were none too pleased by Radclyffe Hall's insistence that sexual orientation is pre-determined, and that homosexuality is something you are born with. More recently, Radclyffe Hall has been lambasted by Andrea Dworkin and others for anti-Semitism and harbouring fascist sympathies. But such criticisms could be levelled at many from the early 20th-century bourgeois class to which Radclyffe Hall belonged, and they have little or no bearing on her important contribution as a writer. Julie Burchill seemed to get the balance about right when she described *The Well of Loneliness* as 'quite beautiful – in a "wussy" kind of way'.

MUST READ *The Well of Loneliness*
READ ON D H Lawrence, **Jeanette Winterson**

Patrick Hamilton

1904–1962
Despair amid the drinking classes

Born in Sussex, Patrick Hamilton was the youngest of three children born to parents who were both divorced when they met and married in 1895. Bernard Hamilton, a wealthy barrister who preferred squandering his inheritance on drink and women to practising law, had married a prostitute who subsquently threw herself under a train. Ellen Hamilton had briefly married an incorrigible womaniser but the union was swiftly annulled. Although a rich vein for Patrick to mine in his fiction, it was clear to him that, as a human relationship, marriage was a failure.

A failed repertory actor, Hamilton published his first novel, *Monday Morning*, in 1925. Its success introduced him to London's literary life and allowed him to echo his father by drinking excessively and using prostitutes (at least one of whom he became hopelessly attached to). The book was followed by two others; in 1929, his play *Rope* was a smash hit, bringing him fame and fortune. A Nietzschean tale of two students who murder a third because they consider themselves superior beings, it was later made into a film by Alfred Hitchcock – although Hamilton hated it. The fictional world Hamilton made his own was that place which J B Priestley called 'a kind of No-Man's-

< 116 >

Land of shabby hotels, dingy boarding-houses and those saloon bars where the homeless can meet'. Hamilton had socialist leanings, which he expressed in compassion for the lives of his destitute characters. A trilogy of novels written between 1929 and 1934 featuring the inter-twining lives of a waiter, a prostitute and a bar-maid was published in 1935 under the title *Twenty Thousand Streets Under the Sky*. His 1947 novel *Slaves of Solitude* is a masterly study of the wretched lives of the inhabitants of a wartime boarding-house.

At the peak of his career Hamilton was accidentally run over by a car, sustaining multiple fractures and requiring plastic surgery. His already burgeoning affair with the bottle grew increasingly hard to control. While his love of drinking, pubs, and all things seedy provided unique inspiration for his fiction, it also impaired his health and ultimately, his ability to write. Even his constant champion, J B Priestley claimed that Hamilton 'spent too many of his later years in an alcoholic haze, no longer a social drinker but an unhappy man who needed whiskey as a car needs petrol'.

The interwar years of the thirties were Hamilton's bread and butter and his master-piece, *Hangover Square* (1941), and his 1950s Mr Gorse trilogy were all set in that time. *Hangover Square*, a destructive tale of fatal sex-ual obsession set amid the drinking classes of Earls Court in London is, along with Malcolm Lowry's *Under the Volcano* (1947), probably the finest account of drinking and its contradictory effects. The Gorse trilogy featured probably his most famous creation, the conman Ernest Ralph Gorse. Doris Lessing believed that Hamilton 'wrote more sense about England in the 1930s than anybody else I can think of, and his novels are true now. You can go into any pub and see it going on.' Hamilton finally suc-cumbed to his fatal passion for the bottle, dying of cirrhosis of the liver and kidney failure in 1962.

MUST READ *Hangover Square, Slaves of Solitude*
READ ON Charles Dickens, Graham Greene, Henry Green

Dashiell Hammett
1894—1961
Pioneer of the hard—boiled novel

Samuel Dashiell Hammett was born in St Mary's County, Maryland, and was brought up there and in Philadelphia. He left school aged 13. At 20, Hammett had held and lost a number of jobs, had started drinking, had contracted gonorrhea, and was directionless. The following year he joined the Pinkerton Detective Agency and changed his life forever.

Hammett left Pinkerton's to enlist during the First World War, in which he served as an ambulance driver and was invalided out with

< 117 >

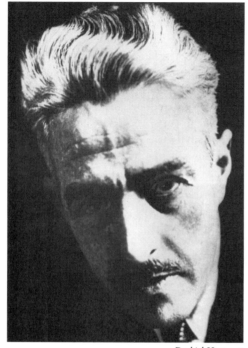

Dashiel Hammett

Dain Curse (1929), *The Maltese Falcon* (1930) and *The Glass Key* (1931), all in an intensely productive period between 1929 and 1932. With these novels and his wisecracking honest joe detective Sam Spade, Hammett virtually singlehandedly created the hard-boiled detective genre. They were bestsellers and snapped up by Hollywood. Moving to California, he wrote screenplays and befriended other writers, notably the playwright Lillian Hellman, with whom he had an intense love affair.

His final novel, *The Thin Man* (1934), was made into a series of films and a radio show. Between 1933 and 1950, as the hard-boiled paperback took off, launching a thousand would-be Sam Spades, Hammett's earnings from his books and their spin-offs approached one million dollars, allowing him to keep drinking, keep catching gonorrhea, and to remain directionless.

He fell foul of the McCarthy anti-communist witch-hunts in the fifties and was blacklisted for his communist beliefs, his royalties frozen. He died, penniless, of lung cancer in 1961.

'Hammett took murder out of the Venetian vase and dropped it into the alley', wrote Raymond Chandler of his *Black Mask* colleague. He added that Hammett's characters 'were not afraid of the seamy side of things; they lived there. Violence did not dismay them; it was right down their street…Hammett gave murder back to the kind of people who commit it for reasons, not just to provide a corpse.'

pneumonia, which led to tuberculosis. He rejoined the agency and worked for them intermittently, when his damaged lungs permitted. Sometimes, he was employed as a reluctant strikebreaker, which made his later espousal of Communism all the more apposite.

Married with a child, he started writing advertising copy and short stories which he sold to *Black Mask* magazine. Drawing on his Pinkerton experiences, he produced the brilliant detective novels *Red Harvest* (1929), *The*

< 118 >

Hammett's novels painted a realistic picture of America's social underbelly, while his vernacular prose style took on the staccato rhythm of the street, stripped down and ready for action: 'Another car came round the limousine and charged us. Out of it, gunfire.' No one else wrote like him; no one ever would.

MUST READ *The Glass Key*, *Red Harvest*
READ ON **Paul Cain**, **Raymond Chandler**, Joe Gores

Knut Hamsun

1859–1952
As miserable as Morrissey

Born in Norway, Knut Hamsun left school early and was apprenticed to a shoemaker. During the 1880s he visited the USA twice before settling in Europe permanently. His early fiction, written before his travels, is poor. *Hunger* (1890) is the first example of Hamsun's mature and meticulous prose style. Apart from Hunger, Hamsun published three more novels during the 1890s (*Mysteries*, 1892; *Pan*, 1894; *Victoria*, 1898): all deal with isolated individuals who feel threatened by their environment. *Hunger* focuses on a starving, homeless writer who shakes his fist at God while trying to scribble down his thoughts in a series of unfinished articles. The narrative shifts between first- and third-person accounts, combining immediate experiences with general observations. Some of Hamsun's later novels are satirical (*Children of the Age*, 1913; *Segelfoss Town*, 1915). Others (*Under the Autumn Star*, 1906; *Growth of the Soil*, 1917; *Vagabonds*, 1927) demonstrate what has been described as a 'strangely tangential and ambivalent relationship with the Norwegian pastoral tradition'. Though a modernist in style, in politics Hamsun leant towards a countrified conservatism and has been accused of harbouring fascist sympathies.

A poet and dramatist as well as a novelist, in all his work Hamsun strove to capture the 'fractional feelings' that are indicative of 'the unconscious and even today almost wholly uninterpreted life of the soul'. As far back as 1890, he demonstrated his concern for the fleeting moments in the workings of the mind:

'They last a second, a minute, they come and go like a moving winking light; but they have impressed their mark, deposited some kind of sensation before they vanished…Secret stirrings that go unnoticed in the remote parts of the mind, the incalculable chaos of impressions, the delicate life of the imagination seen under the magnifying glass; the random progress of these thoughts and feelings; untrodden, trackless journeyings by brain and heart, strange workings of the nerves, the whisper of the blood, the entreaty of the bone, all the unconscious life of the mind.'

He was greatly revered by Henry Miller and won the Nobel prize for Literature in 1920.

< 119 >

MUST READ *Hunger*
READ ON Arthur Koestler, Thomas Hardy,
Colin Wilson, Henry Miller

Jim Harrison

1937–
Eat, drink, hunt and be merry

A native of northern Michigan, where he lived until he was 12, Harrison suffered an injury to his left eye at the age of seven when, while playing 'doctor' with a young girl, she poked a broken bottle into the eye, which was subsequently blinded. 'For several painful months, the blind eye shone like a red sun in my head', wrote Harrison in his brilliant prose collection *Just Before Dark* (1991). In his 1976 novel *Farmer*, Joseph the narrator has a twisted left leg, an injury sustained when he was seven, and his nephew, one of the few relatives he likes, 'had lost an eye in an accident and Joseph supposed that gave them some sort of kinship'. Personal tragedy seems to have illuminated much of Harrison's work. The title poem of *The Theory and Practice of Rivers and Other Poems* (1989; the best received of his seven volumes of verse) was dedicated to the memory of his 14-year-old niece Gloria and again mentions the eye injury. Although his early novels are centred on the sixties and Vietnam, he hit his stride with *Farmer*, *Warlock* (1981), and *Sundog* (1985), all

more personal books, each one featuring a protagonist drawn from Harrison himself, complete with his usual obsessions: food, sex, and alcohol.

Harrison has often been compared to Hemingway and he shares many of the big man's passions. Indeed, Harrison himself says of those pursuits: 'If I had not learned to find solace in the most ordinary preoccupations – cooking, the forest and desert – my perceptions and vices by now would have driven me to madness and death. In fact, they very nearly did.' For a Hemingwayesque author however, Harrison has mined a rich vein of female characters. *Dalva* (1989), *The Woman Lit by Fireflies* (1991), and *Julip* (1994) all feature strong women. Ironically, Harrison used manly pursuits such as hunting, fishing and hiking as forms of therapy and combined them with 'enormous, complicated dinners' so that his writing 'began to revolve around more "feminine" subjects, the acquiring of new voices, and away from the "men at loose ends" that tend to characterize the fiction of most male writers'. Two of his novellas featuring revenge as their theme have been filmed (*Revenge*, starring Kevin Costner and *Legends of the Fall*, with Brad Pitt). Harrison co-wrote the screenplay for *Wolf*, starring his old drinking buddy Jack Nicholson, taken from a dream the author had had of a dying wolf passing her being into his mouth ('I remember idly thinking in the dream that I tried so hard to lose weight and now I was pregnant with a female wolf.'). Harrison's preoccupation with food is amply detailed in all his books. The opening section of pieces in *Just Before Dark* is titled simply 'Food'. At Jack Nicholson's house, Harrison succeeds in stuffing all the guests, only to have the host sagely proclaim: 'Only in the Midwest is overeating still considered an act of heroism.' Harrison counters with a maxim from Lermontov: 'Eat or die.'

MUST READ *Farmer, Sundog, Warlock*
READ ON **James Crumley**, Ernest Hemingway, **Thomas McGuane**, Rabelais, Walt Whitman

John Hawkes

1925–
'The whole panorama of dislocation and desolation'

An asthmatic only child, Hawkes was raised in New England, New York and Alaska. He spent six intermittent years at Harvard, interrupted when, in 1944, he volunteered as an ambulance driver and served in Italy and Germany. These war-torn areas surface in his novellas *The Goose on Grave* and *The Owl* (both 1954). His first book, *Charivari*, a novella, was published in 1949, swiftly followed by the novel, *The Cannibal* (1949). The latter, set in Germany between 1914 and 1945, was a bleak, unsettling account of the rise of Fascism.

Several of Hawkes's books featured violent sexual encounters, notably his psychotic parody of an English thriller, *The Lime Twig*. Published in 1961, it portrayed a sordid and decaying England, shrouded in fog, drenched by perpetual rain, where corruption and deformity seem the norm; a Graham Greene 'entertainment' via the Marquis de Sade, all the more astonishing since Hawkes had never visited England. As author Patrick McGrath noted: 'In *The Lime Twig* the sex is excessive, perfunctory, illicit, and quick, and marks the penultimate stage in a process of corruption that can end only in death.'

Similarly, his next novel *Second Skin* (1964), praised by Robert Coover for its 'inventiveness, awesome intensity, savage comedy, and verbal brilliance', was a harrowing tale, replete with images of, as Hawkes claimed: 'nightmare, violence, meaningful distortion...the whole panorama of dislocation and desolation in human relationships'.

Influenced by writers ranging from Europeans like Lautréamont and Céline to the American Gothic school of Flannery O'Connor and William Faulkner, he remained primarily a surrealist, attracted to 'a quality of coldness, detachment, ruthless determination to face up to the enormities of ugliness and potential failure within ourselves'. Paramount in his writing was the desire to experiment, to do away with the ordinary and the normal: 'I began to write fiction on the assumption that the true enemies of the novel were plot, character, setting and theme, and having once abandoned these familiar ways…totality of vision or structure were all that remained.'

MUST READ *The Cannibal, The Lime Twig*
READ ON **Robert Coover**, William Gass, **Céline**

Nathan Heard

1946–
Hatred on the street

Nathan Heard grew up in New Jersey. As a young man he was convicted of armed robbery and sent to Trenton State Penitentiary, where he wrote his first and most famous novel, *Howard Street* (1968). Based on the author's experience of life on the street, *Howard Street* intertwines the stories of various street people (from winos to bent cops, whores and junkies) and sets them against a background of menace, exclusion and smouldering resentment. Henry Miller commented: '[Heard] is a writer, no question about that. An almost frightening one – his hatred and violence are so intense.' Reviewing *Howard Street*, *Publishers' Weekly* wrote: 'Mr Heard tells it like it is. With no trace of condescension, without irony or sentimentality, with honesty and objectivity, he spins a raw and powerful story of ghetto life. Everybody in this story is a

loser, but each of Heard's fully realised characters is individual and distinct.'

After coming out of prison, Heard became a teacher. He has taught creative writing at Fresno State College and black literature at Rutgers University. He still lives in Newark and continues to write fiction, but the intensity of his debut remains unmatched.

MUST READ *Howard Street*
READ ON **Henry Miller, Seth Morgan, John A Williams**

Richard Hell

1949–
The voidoid

Born in Lexington, Kentucky, Richard Meyers was shipped off to a private school for troublesome kids in Delaware, which is where he met Tom (Verlaine) Miller. Together they ran away, trying to hitchhike to Florida, but only made it as far as Alabama before being picked up by the authorities. Meyers persuaded his mother to allow him to go to New York, where he worked in a secondhand bookshop (the Strand; later he was employed at Cinemabilia along with Patti Smith) and tried to become a writer.

Meyers arrived in the Big Apple at the tail end of the hippie scene. He took acid (and later heroin), but sought to develop a different sensibility in the manner of what he later referred to as 'twisted French aestheticism', i.e. more Arthur Rimbaud than Rolling Stones. Meyers printed a poetry magazine (*Genesis: Grasp*) and when Miller dropped out of college and joined him in New York, they developed a joint alter ego whom they named Theresa Stern. Under this name they published a book of poems entitled *Wanna Go Out?* (Dot Books, Hell's own imprint, 1971). This slim volume went almost unnoticed. It was at this point that Meyers and Miller decided to form a band, under the influence of the New York Dolls, The Stooges, sixties garagebands such as those featured on the Nuggets compilation, British Beat groups and, in Miller's case, free jazz. They changed their names to Hell and Verlaine, and called the band The Neon Boys. Meyers/Hell learnt to play bass, but they failed to find a suitable second guitarist (Chris Stein turned them down, the future Dee Dee Ramone could not play well enough).

During this hiatus, Hell wrote *The Voidoid* (1973), a rambling confessional which he says was inspired by French writers such as the dandy Gérard de Nerval and the first symbolist, the Comte de Lautréamont. *The Voidoid* might be said to represent the dandification of degradation. Hell wrote it in a 16 dollar-a-week room, fuelled by cheap wine and cough syrup that contained codeine. He reused the title in the name of the band (Richard Hell and The Voidoids) that he fronted after leaving

Television, which was the band he formed with Verlaine after the Neon Boys failed to light up. Hell is best known for having coined the term 'blank generation'. He intended 'blank' to mean fill-in-your-own-meaning, but the phrase was widely interpreted as the verbal embodiment of punk-style nihilism.

Hell recently returned to fiction with his 1996 novel *Go Now*. The story of a punk rock musician and heroin addict, Billy, on the road to escape his life in New York, it steadily creeps

Richard Hell

< 123 >

down the road to excess and oblivion. It gained a mixed critical reception. The *Times Literary Supplement* called it 'a splenetic journey that delights in changing lanes from one genre to the next without indicating', while the *Kirkus Review* called it 'a plotless and pointless fiction that lacks either the drug authenticity of a Burroughs or the transgressive aesthetic of an Acker'. Other reviewers compared it to everything from Jim Carroll and Irvine Welsh to *Huckleberry Finn* and Hunter Thompson.

MUST READ *From the Velvets to the Voidoids* by Clinton Heylin, *Go Now, The Voidoid*
READ ON Charles Baudelaire, **Jim Carroll**, Arthur Rimbaud, Paul Verlaine

Joseph Heller

1923–
Caught in his own Catch

As a flyer in the US air force, Jewish-born Joseph Heller went on 60 missions over Europe during the Second World War. The book that made him famous is set among a group of airmen stationed in Italy who are sent on an unending but apparently pointless series of missions. *Catch 22* (1961) introduced a new absurdist mode into American fiction: the title is taken from USAF regulations which suggest that to avoid combat duty an airman must be

< 124 >

certified insane; but the attempt to avoid combat duty is necessarily the act of a sane person: therefore no one is ever released from combat duty. Heller provides a cast of absurd characters, including conman Milo Minderbinder; Major Major, who is promoted to Major Major Major; Lieutenant Scheisskopf, who wants to turn his men into perfect parade ground robots; and mail clerk Wintergreen, who is really running the war. In the middle of this lunatic world, Captain John Yossarian struggles to retain his sanity and evade death. In fact, evasion is the only purpose left in his life: war is senseless ('There are now 50 or 60 countries fighting in this war. Surely so many countries can't *all* be worth dying for') and, burdened with death-dealing technology, humanity is going nowhere ('the spirit gone, man is garbage'). In the end, Yossarian deserts, but even then the Catch 22 of the human condition in an inhumane century will not desert him.

The anti-hero of Heller's *Something Happened* (1974) is Bob Slocum, a corporation man who lives in a world where everyone is permanently afraid of someone else (except a brain-damaged boy who knows no fear). Slocum yearns for a return to innocence ('when I grow up, I want to be a little boy'), but, like Yossarian, cannot extricate himself from the crazy, corrupt world. *Good As Gold* (1979) is both a continuation and a parody of the tradition of the Jewish novel in America. Bruce Gold, its protagonist, is an academic who tries to regain the Jewishness he has lost. But ethnicity offers no escape for Heller or his characters; rather it is further cause for self-doubt.

Published at the beginning of the sixties, *Catch 22* was adopted by a decade that often saw society in absurdist terms. With increasing American involvement in Vietnam, Heller's novel seemed even more relevant. The absurdist ethos of *Catch 22* was an influence on Richard Hooker's novel *M*A*S*H* (subsequently a Robert Altman film and a TV series), set in the Korean War; and on various radicals such as the Yippies, who came to believe that exposing the absurdity of a bureaucratic society was itself a revolutionary act.

Nothing Heller has written since has caught the public imagination in anything like the same way. When a journalist reminded Heller that he had not written anything else as good as *Catch 22*, he replied that no one else had either. He has a point: the fact that the title of his novel is now one of the most overused phrases in the English language indicates the accuracy with which it describes the absurdity of war, society and humanity itself. In the history of fiction, there are very few authors whose lives are large enough to accommodate more than one such masterpiece. That is Heller's own Catch 22.

But then again, is *Catch 22* really his own? In 1998 a fierce debate started on the Internet, as to whether some aspects of Heller's novel might have been borrowed from Louis Falstein's 1951 novel *The Sky is a Lonely Place*, which is also set on the Mediterranean base of a USAF bomber squadron.

MUST READ *Catch 22*
READ ON **Albert Camus, Norman Mailer, Kurt Vonnegut**

Gil Scott Heron

1949–
Musician turned soundreelist

Gilbert Scott Heron was born in Chicago in 1949. His mother was a librarian and his father a soccer player from Jamaica (Gilbert St Elmo Heron was nicknamed 'the Black Arrow' during his days with Glasgow Celtic Football Club). In his youth Heron displayed both sporting prowess and academic ability (he won a place at Pennsylvania Lincoln University, like his role model Langston Hughes, the Harlem Renaissance man). But he quit college after the first year to write his first novel, *The Vulture* (1970), which centres on a teenage gang-member (Eddie 'Spade' Shannon) who lives in a street world where a young man's reputation for toughness is almost his only asset. While Heron was writing *The Vulture* (welcomed by *Essence* magazine as 'a strong start for a writer with important things to say'), the ferment of black politics and student radicalism (Malcolm X, the Black Panthers, sit-ins at Berkeley, riots in Chicago) was coming to a head, and his second novel reflects these developments. *The Nigger Factory* (1972) is the story of a revolutionary uprising on the campus of Sutton University, Virginia.

Both novels are vehement and lucid, but stylistically unremarkable. Heron has been more adventurous in his work as a musician and rapper (his debut album was *Small Talk at 125th and Lennox*, 1970), which has been described as a 'soundreel' (an aural version of a newsreel) of the black experience in America. Together with The Last Poets (who appear on the soundtrack to *Performance*, starring Mick Jagger), Heron's mix of poetry with funk, Coltrane-style jazz, and sweet soul music in the manner of Curtis Mayfield provided the basis for the subsequent development of rap and hiphop. If only his successors had been as subtle and inventive as he is.

MUST READ *The Nigger Factory*
READ ON **Donald Goines, Chester Himes, Richard Wright**

Hermann Hesse

1877–1962
Prophet of free thought rediscovered by the sixties generation

Son of a Protestant pastor and missionary, Hesse intended to follow his father's calling, but rebelled and abandoned formal education to work as a bookseller, antiques dealer, and in a machine shop, the latter portrayed in his Nobel Prizewinning utopian masterpiece, *The Glass Bead Game* (1943).

Hesse published his first novel, *Peter Camenzind*, about a failed writer, in 1904, and its success prompted him to become a professional writer. His 1915 novel *Knulp*, a paean to being a vagabond, anticipated both the sixties hippie wanderer and the nineties New Age traveller.

Similar to Aldous Huxley in his espousal of Eastern philosophy and his belief in the need for spiritual self-realisation, Hesse, like the English writer, was condemned for his persistent pacifism. He was spurned by friends and readers alike, who were swept along with the patriotic fervour of the First World War. He spent the war in Switzerland, attacking the prevailing moods of militarism and nationalism.

When his publisher asked him in 1921 to choose a selection of his stories for publication, he replied that 'there was nothing there to select'. He claimed that he was 'by no stretch of the imagination a storyteller', realising that his work dealt not with the world, but only with his 'secret dreams and wishes', his 'bitter anguish'. A sense of personal crisis led Hesse to flirt with Jungian ideas and his 1919 novel *Demian* is a psychoanalytic study of incest. A journey to India after the war resulted in *Siddhartha* (1922), based on the early life of Buddha.

Although praised in Europe by writers such as Thomas Mann, André Gide, and T S Eliot, he was neglected in the USA; in 1949 *Time* magazine noted that, only three years after winning the Nobel Prize he was virtually ignored there. After his death, the *New York Times* obituary tactfully claimed he was 'largely unapproachable' for American readers.

Within a few years however, a new generation, tired of conforming, was reaching out for *Journey to the East*, *Siddhartha*, and *Demian*, looking to understand their own 'bitter anguish'. In 1969 the Californian rock group Sparrow changed their name to *Steppenwolf*, after Hesse's classic, and released 'Born to be Wild'. *Steppenwolf* (1927), a tale of the struggle between bourgeois society's demands and self-realisation, is Hesse's most personal masterpiece. In it, middle-aged Harry Haller, a reclusive intellectual, is angst-ridden and isolated in spiritual wastes of middle-class life and approaching crisis. His life then changes dramatically when he meets his opposite, Hermine, who introduces Harry to drinking, dancing, music, sex and drugs, teaching him to find his

true self. It is a sensuous and deeply poetic psychological exploration of Man's soul – a cult book at its time of publication and once again with the burgeoning sixties counterculture.

MUST READ *Knulp, Steppenwolf*
READ ON Heinrich Böll, **Aldous Huxley**, Thomas Mann

Carl Hiaasen

194?–
Hilarious chronicler of Florida's criminal underbelly

Carl Hiaasen was born and raised in the West Bromard County area of Florida. All of his adult life he has been a newspaperman, working as an investigative journalist. He wrote a series of award-winning reports on local corruption and crime for the *Miami Herald* before co-authoring, with colleague William Montalbano, three thrillers: *Powder Burn* (1981), *Trap Line* (1982), and *Death in China* (1984). It is a mark of his authenticity that when fellow novelist Elmore Leonard needed research for his Florida novels *Gold Coast* (1980), *Stick* (1983) and *La Brava* (1983), he used Hiaasen's journalism as his source.

Since 1986, he has written six novels, all bestsellers. *Striptease* (1993), was made into an atrocious film starring Demi Moore. All the novels have an equal measure of humour and a kind of surreal violence: a Mafia hitman is knocked out by a stuffed marlin's head; a villain, unable to prise a pit bull terrier from his arm, wears its decomposing head for the rest of the book. Virtually all have solid subplots concerning the systematic destruction of the environment, and the incessant corruption that is behind this devastation. The novels' dominant tension lies in Hiaasen's love for Florida and his hatred of the people (drug barons, unscrupulous politicians, and so on) who are ruining it.

As a columnist, all he could do was to report the gruesome facts and try to elicit support, but as a novelist he can play God. 'The best part is I can get to write a happy ending. I don't get to do that much as a journalist. When I write a novel the bad guys get what they deserve.' The writer P J O'Rourke summed up Hiaasen's books as being 'better than literature', and then claimed: 'Reading Hiaasen will do more to damage the Florida tourist trade than anything except an actual visit to Florida.' He should know. Hiaasen lives with his pet snakes and fishing boats on the Florida coast.

MUST READ *Double Whammy, Striptease, Tourist Season*
READ ON **Elmore Leonard**, James W Hall, Lawrence Shames, **Charles Willeford**

< 128 >

Chester Himes
1909–1984
Black American crime pioneer

Chester Himes was born in Jefferson City, Missouri, to a light-skinned, ambitious mother and a dark-skinned father. They had little in common and Chester grew up among their irreconcilable differences. On graduating from Cleveland East High School, he was admitted to Ohio State University, but was expelled for taking fellow students to one of the gambling houses he frequented. He went from studying to being an errand boy for pimps and hustlers. After numerous encounters with the law, Himes was arrested for armed robbery and sentenced to 25 years. He was just 19.

Learning the art of writing in prison, Himes wrote stories for black newspapers; in 1934 *Esquire* magazine published one of his stories, using his prison number as a byline. Paroled in 1936, Himes joined the Ohio Writers' Project and in 1945 published his first novel, *If He Hollers Let Him Go*, to critical acclaim. Subsequent works were deemed as being too bleak by the (white) critics, and in 1953 he moved to Europe where he remained until his death.

Gallimard, his French publishers, urged him to write a detective novel and Himes produced *A Rage in Harlem*, which won the prestigious Grand Prix de Litérature Policière in 1958 and was the first of nine crime novels dubbed by Himes 'domestic thrillers'. *A Rage in Harlem* was filmed in 1991, starring Gregory Hines and Danny Glover.

Through the black humour of the novel's protagonists, Coffin Ed Johnson and Gravedigger Jones, Himes captured both the garishness and ghoulishness of the black experience in America. At a lecture in Chicago in 1966 Himes claimed that the 'homicidal mania, lust for white women, a pathetic sense of inferiority…arrogance, hate and fear and self-hate' that could be revealed in an analysis of the black psyche were 'the effects of oppression on the human personality'. Later though, he countered: 'There is an indomitable quality within the human spirit that cannot be destroyed…we would be drooling idiots, dangerous maniacs, raving beasts – if it were not for that quality and force within all humans that cries "I will live".'

MUST READ *If He Hollers Let Him Go, A Rage in Harlem*

READ ON **Walter Mosley**, James Sallis, **Richard Wright**

H IS FOR HEROES

5 fictions in which famous authors have a walk–on part

The Lost Weekend
by Charles Jackson
– F SCOTT FITZGERALD

Shoeless Joe
by W Kinsella
– J D SALINGER

U and I
by Nicholson Baker
– JOHN UPDIKE

Inside Norman Mailer
by Max Apple
– NORMAN MAILER

Biography of a Buick
by Bill Morris
– VLADIMIR NABOKOV

H IS FOR HEROIN
it's their life and it's their wife – 10 novels about junk

JUNKIE
William S Burroughs
Bill's realist pulp account of his
addiction

TRAINSPOTTING
Irvine Welsh
picaresque antics of Leith's needling
schemie underclass

CAIN'S BOOK
Alexander Trocchi
autobiographical tale of life on a barge
in NYC with a habit

THE BASKETBALL DIARIES
Jim Carroll
Salingeresque innocence in the diaries
of a high-school junkie

THE MAN WITH THE GOLDEN ARM
Nelson Algren
Skid Row ex-soldier and card dealer with
a morphine problem

THE SCENE
Clarence Cooper Jr
cops, pimps, whores and plenty of junk
in the black ghetto

HOMEBOY
Seth Morgan
addict wrongly convicted of murder –
from Janis Joplin's ex.

DOPEFIEND
Donald Goines
need we say more – from legendary black
pulpfiend

GO NOW
Richard Hell
punk rocker with a habit hits the road
out of NY to oblivion

GUILTY OF EVERYTHING
Herbert Huncke
writings from the guy who turned Bill
Burroughs on to junk

< 130 >

S E Hinton

1950–
Camus for kids

Essentially a writer of fiction for 'young adults', S.E. Hinton was only 17 herself when she wrote *The Outsiders* (1967), a story of Middle American gang war between the 'socs' (rich kids) and the greasers from the wrong side of the tracks. The hero is Ponyboy, a 14-year-old greaser whose world crumbles when a soc is killed by his friend Johnny in a gang fight. In a similar vein Hinton also wrote *That Was Then, This Is Now* and *Rumble Fish*, the latter hinging on the relationship between a teenager (Rusty-James) and his existentialist elder brother (Motorcycle Boy) in an urban ghetto damaged by pointless gang wars. When Francis Ford Coppola directed the film version (starring Micky Rourke and Matt Dillon and with cameos from Dennis Hopper, Tom Waits and Susie Hinton herself – it was shot back to back with his film of *The Outsiders*) he dubbed it 'Camus for kids'. In the early nineties Hinton wrote the script for a prestigious advertising campaign for Pepe jeans. Shot in black and white by Bruce Weber, and incorporating archive footage and voiceovers from the original Beats, the campaign demonstrated the increasingly close convergence of would-be counter and corporate cultures. Despite this minor commercial compromise S E Hinton is still a big hit with rebels in short pants the world over.

MUST READ *The Outsiders, Rumble Fish, That Was Then, This Is Now*
READ ON **Albert Camus, Jim Carroll, Richard Price**

John Clellon Holmes

1926–1988
The first Beat generation novelist

Born in Holyhoke, Massachusetts, John Clellon Holmes studied at Columbia University and was a contemporary of Jack Kerouac and Allen Ginsberg in the New York bohemia of the late forties. As a teacher and a writer, he kept on the move throughout the fifties, sixties and early seventies, until 1977 when finally he found a long-term berth at the University of Arkansas.

Clellon Holmes was the first Beat to get into print. His earliest novel, *Go*, an attempt to encapsulate the restless energy of the emerging Beat scene, came out in 1952 – a full five years before Kerouac's *On the Road* arrived in bookstores. But as anthologists Gene Feldman and Max Gartenberg noted in their introduction to the seminal collection *Protest* (1958), Clellon Holmes was 'sober, dedicated, not quite given to the extravagances of mood and gesture of the others', and his measured prose is sometimes at odds with the spontaneity that he tried to express. Clellon Holmes's most adventurous work was *The Horn* (1958), a novel written in

< 131 >

homage to bebop saxophone player Charlie Parker and laid out like a jazz record (chorus, riff, chorus, riff…coda). Listening to his own authorial voice 20 years later, Clellon Holmes confessed to being 'embarrassed by its flat-out earnestness, its overflow of language, its obvious musical flaws'. But he also recalled 'the thrill of writing it' and 'the stubborn hope for our future that sometimes made the afternoons of writing pulse'. That pulse is still discernible in this remarkable piece of experimental writing.

Clellon Holmes's other works include *Get Home Free* (1964) and *Nothing More to Declare* (1967). His collected poetry appeared as *Death Drag* (1979), and he also published a series of essays. He received a Playboy Award for non-fiction, but his most historic piece of journalism is the article for the *New York Times* (1952) in which the term 'Beat Generation' first appeared.

MUST READ *Go, The Horn*
READ ON Geoff Dyer, **Jack Kerouac**, Art Pepper

Stewart Home

1962–
Porn + Hegel = ?

London-born Stewart Home worked in a warehouse for a few months when he was 16 – an experience that persuaded him never to hold down a day job again. He gained notoriety as the man behind the 'art strike' of 1990–92: a call for artists to join Home in taking three years off in which to reassess their work, aka a publicity stunt that got Home's name in the papers. More recently, he has been in close contact with Bill Drummond, half of the duo of pranksters known as the K Foundation, aka KLF, best known for 'burning' a million pounds (or did they?).

Likewise, Home's fiction is a joke – but a serious one. It employs every cliché in the book of pulp fiction and soft porn, and combines them into a high-speed trajectory through high art and lowlife. *Red London* (1994) features the Skinhead Squad led by one Fellatio Jones, a 'new breed of malcontents' who 'shoot, shag, stab, bludgeon and plunder their way from the mean streets of Mile End to aristocratic Belgravia'. *Slow Death* (1996), subtitled 'sexual violence and violent sex!', again features 'a gang of socially ambitious skinheads' running 'riot through the London art world, plotting the rebirth and violent demise of an elusive avant-garde art movement'. The blurb on the inside

< 132 >

cover of the Serpent's Tail edition claims that 'all traditional notions of literary taste and depth are ditched in favour of a transgressive aesthetic inspired by writers as diverse as Homer, de Sade, Klaus Theweleit, and 70s cult writer Richard Allen'. In the *London Review of Books*, Iain Sinclair commented:

'It's an exercise in futility to complain that Home's novels lack depth, characterisation or complex plots: that is the whole point. The project operates within its contradictions, subverting the spirit of redundant industrial fiction, while honouring the form…Home's language feeds on metropolitan restlessness, movement, lists of trains and buses, gigs in pubs, rucks outside phone kiosks, the epiphany of the grease caff.'

Reviews of Home's novels seem to suggest that they are the ultimate cult fiction. *The Face* described *Defiant Pose* as 'a future underground classic', and the *New Musical Express* labelled it 'the definitive cult novel'. Reviewing *Pure Mania* (1989), *Time Out* declared this 'is the stuff of which cults are made'. The *NME*'s assessment of Home's *Slow Death* insisted that he was the real thing, whereas some of his peers were only pretending: 'the skinhead author whose sperm'n'blood-sodden scribblings about the insaner fringes of pop culture make Will Self's writings read like the self-indulgent dribblings of a sad middle-class Oxbridge junkie trying to sound hard'. But this is to miss Home's point that in today's culture the real and the artificial are indistinguishable. He himself

Stewart Home

lives in the area of East London that was the breeding ground of the original skinheads, his hair is cropped and he often wears a Harrington jacket. But only the handful of anarchists who tried to disrupt his live gigs in 1996 are too stupid to realise that Home is a pretend-skinhead, playing with the image and its connotations (in any case his Neoist political views are a million miles away from the right-wing ideologies with which skins are traditionally – and sometimes erroneously – associated).

Stewart Home is also a scholarly essayist (one of the few people in Britain who even claims to have read the whole of Hegel's *Aesthetics*) and the editor of *Suspect Device: a reader in hard-edged fiction* (1998). In the publicity for the book Home declared: 'The literary establishment is now in retreat.' This may be the case; but now that everyone from gameshow hosts and television news producers to established novelists are busily 'subverting' and 'transgressing' genres, it does mean that Home's double take on trash is no longer as avant-garde as it used to be.

MUST READ *Red London, Slow Death*
READ ON **Richard Allen, William Burroughs**, G W F Hegel, Mickey Spillane

Nick Hornby

1957–
Reluctant voice of the 90s Lad

Born in prosperous Maidenhead in southern England (his father is the successful businessman Sir Derek Hornby), Nick Hornby read English at Cambridge but 'drifted' and ended up teaching English, first in a comprehensive and then to executives of the Korean company Samsung until the success (600,000 copies sold by the beginning of 1998) of his 1992 memoir *Fever Pitch* allowed him to concentrate solely on writing.

Fever Pitch is the record of Hornby's life through the prism of being an Arsenal Football Club supporter. In an amusing and imaginative way, it chronicles the most intense form of working-class consumer loyalty – being a football fan – but it was written by a middle-class man. As Hornby admits, in his younger days the class divide was wide enough to prevent him becoming truly part of what was then a semi-secret fraternity of football supporters. So he played the part of a modern-day George Orwell, reporting on a world that attracted him but which did not fully accept him. Hornby was not alone, however. If he was seeking a truly authentic experience in football and its fans, so were thousands more twenty- and thirtysomething middle-class males – the very people who went out in droves and bought his book along with their season tickets. Ironically, the success of *Fever Pitch* allowed them to come out as middle-class football fans. Taken together with other developments in the game, like the fallout from the Hillsborough disaster, fanzines, supporters' associations, academic institutions devoted to football, and even England's respectable performance in Italia '90, *Fever Pitch* was the cue for football to acquire a new literary respectability. Not only a personal memoir, *Fever Pitch* was also part of a social phenomenon.

With his first novel, *High Fidelity* (1995), Hornby applied the same technique to pop music instead of football: the life of a 35-year-old, and his relationships with women in par-

< 134 >

ticular, are chronicled in relation to his taste in music, and his obsessive categorisation of records. He again seemed to catch the zeitgeist perfectly, giving a voice to the denizens of dysfunctional males who communicate through lists and facts and find an alphabeticised record collection easier to deal with than a member of the opposite sex. Tony Parsons praised Hornby for writing 'like Martin Amis with a heart or Roddy Doyle with an unfeasibly large record collection'. *High Fidelity* has sold roughly as many copies as *Fever Pitch*, but since the middle classes have always owned pop culture anyway it does not represent a cultural shift in the same way that *Fever Pitch* summed up the 'Hornbyisation' of football.

In 1998 Hornby published *About a Boy*, centering on a selfish, immature, thirtysomething male (36 this time), who goes out cruising for single mothers because he enjoys the combination of sex and surrogate parenthood (no strings attached), until he learns the merit of responsibility and commitment when a 12-year-old boy turns to him for support. He does not feel able to be a father to the boy, however, but opts for the lesser role of elder brother instead. This is a Hornby hero actually growing up – but then again, not quite. The film rights went to Robert De Niro's Tribeca for £2 million.

Before he became successful Hornby wrote about soul music and films for *Time Out* and published a cultish work of criticism entitled *Contemporary American Fiction*. He still lives within the sound of the roar from Highbury.

MUST READ *About a Boy, Fever Pitch, High Fidelity*
READ ON **Michael Bracewell, Frederick Exley, Hanif Kureishi**, Giles Smith

Robert E Howard

1906—1936
Weird Tales pulp pioneer

Robert Ervin Howard, an only child, moved with his parents to the town of Cross Plains, Texas when he was nine. He was a voracious reader of history books, Western lore, and *Adventure* magazine. One of the earliest pulp authors, his first story, 'Spear and Fang', was published in 1925 in *Weird Tales*, and by 1928 he was submitting an average of eight stories yearly (in 1928 *Weird Tales* also published 'The Vengeance of Nitocris', an Egyptian story by 14-year-old Tennessee Williams).

Although Howard wrote detective, adventure, Western, and even romance stories, primarily he produced sword-and-sorcery epics. These featured a range of characters, including Solomon Kane, an Elizabethan Puritan (what else?) who fought savage natives and the supernatural in Africa; Kull, a king of lost Atlantis; and, most famous of all, Conan the Barbarian.

H

CULT FICTION

Apparently based on a mixture of several Texan roughnecks whom he knew and his own lurid fantasies, Conan was a huge success, and was adapted by the Marvel Comics Group in the seventies, who sold thousands of comics based on Howard's stories. In 1982 Arnold Schwarzenegger starred in the eponymous film (co-scripted by Oliver Stone), and the dreadful sequel, *Conan the Destroyer*, which co-starred singer Grace Jones.

Howard, who was subject to depression and had contemplated suicide, knew he was considered strange by his rather drab peers (one even calling him a 'weirdie'). He had written: 'It is no light thing to enter into a profession absolutely foreign to the people among which one's lot is cast.' Furthermore, his excessive devotion to his domineering mother and his lack of a wife or girlfriend encouraged speculation and increased his despair. Finally, his mother became seriously ill, and went into a coma. Howard, after an all-night vigil by her bedside, shot himself, and his mother died that evening. They were buried in a double funeral. His last written words were:

All fled, all done, so lift me on the pyre;
The feast is over, and the lamps expire.

The local justice of the peace, after being told the meaning of the word 'pyre', pronounced a verdict of suicide.

MUST READ *Conan the Barbarian*
READ ON Edgar Rice Burroughs, Fritz Leiber,
H P Lovecraft

❮ 136 ❯

Dorothy B Hughes

1904–
First Lady of hard–boiled crime

Born in Kansas City, Dorothy B Hughes graduated from the school of journalism at the University of Missouri and went on to postgraduate studies at Columbia and in Mexico. While working as a journalist and teacher, she wrote poems. Her first publication was *Dark Certainty* (1931), which was included in the series of slim volumes from younger poets put out by the Yale University Press.

Hughes's first crime story, *So Blue Marble* was not published until 1940, but in the following 12 years she produced another ten mysteries, including three which were made into major films (*The Fallen Sparrow*, 1942; *Ride the Pink Horse*, 1946; *In a Lonely Place*, 1947), and another which became a TV film (*The Davidian Report*, 1952). But at this point Hughes stopped writing novels (although she continued to review films and fiction for the *Los Angeles Times* and subsequently wrote a critical study of Erle Stanley Gardner entitled *The Case of the Real Perry Mason*, 1979). Later she explained that her domestic responsibilities made writing difficult at that time:

'My mother was very ill and lived with me. The children were in that state of getting started in marriage, with grandchildren for me to help care for. And I simply hadn't the tranquility required to write. I wasn't frustrated because I was reviewing mysteries, and reviewing has always been very important to me.'

Hughes's masterpiece is *In a Lonely Place*, the tale of psychopathic serial killer Dix Steele who is listlessly living in postwar Los Angeles, having been recently demobbed and simultaneously robbed of his identity. It is told in a spare, almost laconic fashion – in complete contrast to the hyperbole of *American Psycho* by Bret Easton Ellis. Perhaps what is most remarkable about *In a Lonely Place* is that, besides being a novel of relentlessly rising suspense, it is one of the quintessential stories of a peculiarly masculine form of rootlessness and alienation – and yet it was written by a middle-aged woman.

In a Lonely Place was filmed by Nicholas Ray in 1950, with Humphrey Bogart as Dix. Ray softened the story (the film insinuates that Dix isn't the killer), and relocated it in contemporary Tinseltown rather than in the aftermath of the Second World War. One critic said of the film 'never were despair and solitude so romantically alluring' – except, that is, in the original book, which surpasses even this remarkable film.

Dorothy B Hughes received a Grand Master Award from the Mystery Writers of America and a similar award from the Swedish Academy of Writers.

MUST READ *In a Lonely Place, Ride the Pink Horse*
READ ON **Leigh Brackett, David Goodis**

Herbert Huncke

1915–1996
Junkie, hustler and the real Beat

Born in Massachusetts, Herbert Edwin Huncke was raised first in Detroit and then in Chicago. When he was 12, his parents divorced. Huncke ran away from home and made for New York. He reached Geneva, a small town in New York State, when a policeman picked him up and returned him to Chicago. The lure of the road had snared him, however, and when he was 14 or 15 he left for California, following the Depression-struck Okies whom John Steinbeck later depicted in *The Grapes of Wrath* (1939). He rode the freight trains back to Chicago, but soon left again, this time going to Idaho, and then south to Nashville, Memphis and New Orleans. He hitched to Detroit to see a particular jazz singer, but was told to leave, as he was white. 'Just let me stay for one song,' he asked of the bouncer, who agreed.

Aged 24, Huncke finally arrived in New York and headed for 42nd Street, where he stayed for several years, hustling to support his heroin habit, but always finding time to scribble in his notebooks. He befriended jazz musicians, including Charlie Parker and Billie Holiday, and for a while partnered tenor-sax giant (and star of the 1986 film *Round Midnight*) Dexter Gordon, while they stole fur coats from cars and sold them to Harlem prostitutes.

During the war, Huncke joined the Merchant Marines (and was apparently scoring morphine on Normandy beach three days after the invasion). Afterwards, he returned to New York and was enlisted by Alfred Kinsey to help him in his research into America's sexual behaviour. Soon Huncke was recruiting hustlers for Kinsey and earning two dollars per recruit.

Around that time, he met William Burroughs (whom he introduced to morphine), Jack Kerouac and Allen Ginsberg. Kerouac was impressed by Huncke's street slang, in particular his use of the word 'beat' to mean tired and done in. Kerouac added another meaning: 'beat' as in 'beatific', and the Beat Generation was born. In a 1947 letter to Neal Cassady, Kerouac declared that 'He [Huncke] is the greatest storyteller I know, an actual genius at it in my mind.' Huncke is the basis for Elmo Hassel in Kerouac's *On the Road* (1957); he also appeared in Burroughs's *Junkie* (1953), Ginsberg's poem 'Howl' (1956), and John Clellon Holmes's novel *Go* (1952).

Although he stressed that he was more of a talker than a writer ('Talk is my stock in trade', he would often say), Huncke scribbled down notes constantly, except when he was in prison, where, although he would kick his habit, he couldn't write (throughout the fifties, Huncke was often incarcerated, either in Sing Sing, Dannemora, or Rikers Island). His first book, *Huncke's Journal*, was published in 1960; his second, *The Evening Sun Turned Crimson*, a story collection, appeared in 1980, and his autobiography, the aptly titled *Guilty of Everything*, in 1990.

In his later years, with his monkey-like face lined as deeply as W H Auden's, Huncke stayed in the notorious Chelsea Hotel, his bills paid for by the Grateful Dead. Shortly before his death he moved into a nursing home: 'I do very well in institutions,' he reasoned. Looking back at his life, Huncke said 'I wish I could say I'd hit upon the answers to the great mysteries of life…But it doesn't make any more sense than it did to me on day one.' As his friend Burroughs observed, 'Huncke had extraordinary experiences that were quite genuine. He isn't a type you find anymore.'

MUST READ *Guilty of Everything*
READ ON **William Burroughs**, Allen Ginsberg, **Jack Kerouac**

Aldous Huxley
1894–1963
Cynic, satirist and seer of our time

Aldous Huxley was born in Godalming, Surrey, into a family of famous intellectuals: his grandfather Thomas Huxley, known as 'Darwin's Bulldog', assembled the scientific evidence underlying the theory of evolution, his mother was the niece of poet and critic Matthew

< 138 >

Arnold, and his father, Leonard Huxley, was a biographer and editor of the prestigious *Cornhill* magazine.

But his early life was plagued by three tragedies which reverberate through his fiction. His mother died of cancer when he was 14, his elder brother Trevenen hanged himself at 24 and, at 16, Huxley developed an eye infection which blinded him for two years and from which he never fully recovered. A friend remarked: 'It was to Aldous the irreparable loss, a betrayal of his faith in life. He never got over it.' The pain of this period was reflected in *Eyeless in Gaza* (1936), his most autobiographical novel.

In the aftermath of the First World War, Huxley penned a series of acclaimed novels, as well as verse, short stories and essays. At 21, he was praised by Proust as one of England's most promising writers. Early novels such as *Crome Yellow* (1921) and *Antic Hay* (1923) are noted for their cynicism: they are satirical chronicles of literary and bohemian London which jibe at the pointless and superficiality of the modern world. *Brave New World* (1932), Huxley's most famous book, is partly a continuation of his satirical writing, and partly a serious investigation of what makes us human. It is also a prophetic vision of the social impact of genetics and drug-use.

During the thirties Huxley toyed with various ideologies including socialism and pacifism. On the eve of the Second World War he toured America, lecturing on the need for peace,

Aldous Huxley

prompting Evelyn Waugh and J B Priestley to brand him a coward. By 1936 he was writing in praise of 'the unattached man', a stance which prefigures the existentialism of postwar Paris. In 1937 Huxley moved to California, where he remained until his death. It was in California that he turned away from secularism towards a kind of do-it-yourself mysticism involving a sacramental use of hallucinogenic drugs. (In his odyssey from ironism to po-mo spirituality, the Canadian author Douglas Coupland seems to

< 139 >

be following in Huxley's footsteps.)

Huxley advocated his own brand of drug-aided mysticism in lectures and in essays such as *Heaven and Hell* (1956) and *The Doors of Perception* (1954), from which Jim Morrison took the name of his band. In his final novel, *Island* (1962), Huxley envisioned a society based around hallucinogens, communal living and sexual freedom. It was derided by most critics. This was five years before the summer of love, when Huxley's face appeared on the sleeve of the Beatles's Sergeant Pepper album.

On his deathbed Huxley was given mescaline by his wife. He died of cancer on 22 November 1963 but his demise went largely unnoticed at the time because it occurred a few hours after the assassination of John F Kennedy.

MUST READ *Antic Hay, Brave New World, Eyeless in Gaza, Island*
READ ON Edward Bellamy, Robert Heinlein, Timothy Leary, **George Orwell**, Evelyn Waugh

Joris Karl Huysmans

1848–1907
Decadent and unnatural acts

Born of mixed parentage (a French mother, a Dutch father) in Paris in 1848, the young Huysmans was traumatised by the death of his father. As a young man he became a clerk at the Ministry of the Interior; there he remained for 32 years. Huysmans's inner life and work, however, were as exotic and, some would say, decadent, as his outer life was boring and banal.

Huysmans's first book (*Le Drageoir à Epices*, Sugar and Spice, 1874) was a collection of prose-poems in the manner of Charles Baudelaire. His early prose reflected the influence of contemporary French novelists Gustave Flaubert and Emile Zola; for a time, Huysmans was a member of the circle of Zola's disciples known as the Medan group. But with *A Rebours* (1884; translated into English as *Against Nature*), he broke new ground, stylistically and thematically.

Whereas Zola and the literary school of Naturalism encouraged writers to engage with modern society, Huysmans – in the form of the protagonist of *A Rebours*, the wealthy aesthete Duc Jean Floressas des Esseintes – recommended shutting oneself away and giving oneself over to exotic pleasures. Likewise, where the Naturalists' language was direct and dynamic, Huysmans' use of words became mellifluous and intoxicating. Of *A Rebours*, Oscar Wilde

< 140 >

wrote: 'The heavy odour of incense seemed to cling about its pages and to trouble the brain.'

Before his death from cancer in 1907, Huysmans wrote five more novels, *En Rade* (1887), *Là-Bas* (Down There; 1891), *En Route* (1895), *La Cathédrale* (1898) and *L'Oblat* (1903). Their subject matter includes sex, satanism and monastic life. In the introduction to the Penguin edition of *A Rebours*, translator Robert Baldick notes that they all 'tell the story of the efforts made by one character, under different names, to achieve happiness in various forms of spiritual and physical escapism'. Whether Huysmans is describing fasting or feasting, his concern is to find spiritual meaning beyond the day-to-day world. In this respect, his work marks the onset of disillusion with the man-made world. Huysmans found God and was readmitted into the Catholic church in 1892.

In the late 19th century, *A Rebours* was 'the Bible and bedside book' (Paul Valéry) of the Decadence, the movement of French and English aesthetes who craved seclusion, artificiality and emotion rather than society, nature, and rationality. It receives a highly favourable mention in Oscar Wilde's *The Picture of Dorian Gray* (1890). The antisocial ethos expressed in A Rebours still exerts a powerful influence. In the dandyism of his protagonists and their self-consciously neurotic lifestyles, Huysmans might be regarded as the precursor of modern icons like Johnny Rotten and Morrissey.

His fans champion Huysmans as one of the

Joris Karl Huysmans

first writers to combine exoticism, eroticism and spirituality. His detractors claim that Huysmans lived in fear and loathing of the modern world, and is therefore partly responsible for inaugurating the victim mentality that is so widespread today.

MUST READ *A Rebours, Là-Bas*
READ ON Charles Baudelaire, **Oscar Wilde**, Paul Verlaine, Emile Zola

John Irving

1942–
The world according to John

Irving was a faculty child who lived at and attended Exeter Academy, New Hampshire, where his stepfather taught history. A poor student because of his dyslexia, and despite hating most sports, he nevertheless discovered his abiding passion for wrestling there. He studied for a year in Vienna (scene of his first novel, *Setting Free the Bears*, 1969, and parts of his second big success, *The Hotel New Hampshire*, 1981) and returned to America in 1964, where he enrolled at the Iowa University Writers' Workshop.

Here he befriended fellow hopefuls André Dubus and James Crumley, studied briefly under Nelson Algren (who considered his writing 'too fancy'), and then with Kurt Vonnegut, who asked him if he 'thought there was something intrinsically funny about the verbs peek and peer'. (Later, in a moment of typical prescience, Vonnegut told Irving: 'I think capitalism is going to treat you okay.') Irving went on to teach at Iowa, along with author John Cheever, numbering among his students such future luminaries as T C Boyle, Ron Hansen and Stephen Wright.

It wasn't until his fourth novel, *The World According to Garp* (1978) – a surreal serio-comic tale of an illegitimate boy conceived during sex between a nurse and a fatally-injured pilot who can only utter the word 'Garp' – that Irving

became a critical and commercial success. The book sold in excess of 3 million copies. Among its pages lurked his obsessions: wrestling, psychoanalysis, strange relationships; only Vienna was absent. It was filmed in 1982, starring Robin Williams and Glenn Close, with Irving in a cameo role as, naturally, a wrestling match referee.

The Cider House Rules (1985) adopted a more humane approach, and both this and *A Prayer for Owen Meany* (1989) possessed notes of profundity absent from his earlier work. Yet both preserved Irving's terrain, particularly the sense of tragedy and horror that invades people's lives. Irving is an acknowledged admirer of Dickens and his books have much in common with those of the eminent Victorian novelist: exaggerated yet well-rounded characters, a broad, sweeping canvas and an overriding social conscience.

Although lauded by some critics as a star of the postmodern idiom, Irving's success and 'blockbuster' approach have left him in a curious position among American writers. His paean to Graham Greene in *The Imaginary Girlfriend* (1996), might easily have been written about himself: 'Greene's manipulation of popular forms …obviously cost him the critical appreciation that is withdrawn from writers with too many readers.' His most recent novels are *Son of the Circus* (1994) and *A Widow for One Year* (1998).

MUST READ *The World According to Garp*
READ ON Robertson Davies, Charles Dickens, Günter Grass

< 142 >

I IS FOR INBRED
10 American Gothic greats

Flannery O'Connor
A GOOD MAN IS HARD TO FIND
twisted tales of original sin in southern
backwaters

Cormac McCarthy
BLOOD MERIDIAN
hell—fire reading of the American West

William Faulkner
AS I LAY DYING
tragi—comic capers around the burying
of a body

Davis Grubb
NIGHT OF THE HUNTER
a preacher with the Bible on his lips and
a knife in his hand

Harry Crews
FEAST OF SNAKES
deadend white trash gather for an
annual rattlesnake hunt

James Dickey
DELIVERANCE
city—slickers get a taste of hillbilly law

Carson McCullers
THE HEART IS A LONELY HUNTER
smalltown lives seen through the prism
of a deaf mute

Herman Melville
MOBY DICK
mad captain Ahab and his crew chase
damnation

Edgar Allen Poe
THE FALL OF THE HOUSE OF USHER
insanity, incest and death come to
haunt Frederick and co.

Nick Cave
AND THE ASS SAW THE ANGEL
superior Southern pastiche from the
gallows balladeer

Tama Janowitz

1957–
The Downtown doyenne

Born in San Francisco, Janowitz moved from the West Coast to the East and was educated at Columbia University. Her first novel, *American Dad*, was published in 1981 and was immediately acclaimed. A hilarious account of young Earl Przepasniak ('a name as unwieldy as a tumour') who, at 5 foot 6, is dismayed and stunned by his 6-foot-tall father's physical excellence, especially his sexual capabilities, it was a streetwise and sassy debut which set Janowitz apart from her nearest rivals.

Her next book, *Slaves of New York* (1986), was a linked group of stories set on the seedier fringes of the artistic/bohemian world of the East Village, where grotesque gallery rats, lowlife writers and unfunded film-makers all lurk, hoping for the big one. Rather like Robert Altman's treatment of Raymond Carver's stories in the film *Short Cut*s, the book was filmed (with nothing like as much success) by the director James Ivory in 1989. Janowitz herself wrote the screenplay and had a small role (presumably replacing the absent Helena Bonham Carter).

Her third book, *A Cannibal in Manhattan* (1987) was a blackly comic parable involving a native of the South Seas who is dragged to New York by an eccentric and beautiful heiress.

Her other books are *The Male Cross-Dresser Support Group* (1992) and *By the Shores of Gitchee Gumee* (1996), in which Janowitz for once leaves the ultra-hip downtown demimonde for, of all things, a modern-day parody of Longfellow's *Song of Hiawatha* in which the 'forest primeval' has been replaced by a town with a pizza joint called Minnie-Wawa's.

In contrast to her 'brat pack' colleagues Jay McInerney and Brett Easton Ellis, Janowitz writes entirely from her imagination and very little of her work seems autobiographical. As the *Kirkus Review* stated, Janowitz sports 'an ironic intelligence and new-wave sensibility unparalleled among contemporary chroniclers of postmodern life'.

MUST READ *American Dad, Slaves of New York*
READ ON **Mary Gaitskill**, Lorrie Moore, Dawn Powell, Catherine Texier

Sebastien Japrisot

1931–
Simenon proof-read by Robbe-Grillet

Educated in Marseilles and then at the Sorbonne, Jean-Baptiste Rossi changed his name for the anagrammatic pseudonym Sebastien Japrisot. By the time he was 17 he was a published author; in his early twenties he translated J D Salinger's *Catcher in the Rye* into French.

He worked in advertising for several years and during that time wrote his first two crime novels, *10.30 from Marseilles* (1962; filmed in 1965 starring Simone Signoret and Yves Montand as *The Sleeping Car Murder*) and *Trap for Cinderella* (1962), which won the Grand Prix for Detective Fiction. Japrisot's customary mathematical plot led to it being described as 'Simenon proof-read by Robbe-Grillet'.

His third novel, the succinctly titled *Lady in the Car with Glasses and a Gun* (1966) won the Prix d'Honneur and was filmed in 1970 starring Samantha Eggar and Oliver Reed, the Gerard Depardieu of his day. Seduced by the film industry, Japrisot spent most of the next ten years scriptwriting (eventually, all of his books were filmed); he also directed.

In 1978 he returned with his steamy thriller *One Deadly Summer*, featuring a sultry girl obsessively (and elaborately) seeking revenge, using sex to get it. In the 1983 film Isabelle Adjani played the girl. As in the novel, the script, by Japrisot, featured several of the characters sharing the narration.

This trademark device of viewing the scene from different characters' perspectives (possibly influenced by the American poet and crime writer Kenneth Fearing's *The Big Clock*), was displayed perfectly in his 1989 novel *Women in Evidence*, which starts at 8.15 pm and ends at 9.10 pm, featuring stories in between from eight different women: Emma the bride, Belinda the whore, Frou-Frou the manicurist turned porn star, etc.

His last novel, *A Very Long Engagement* (1993), was set during the First World War and concerned a crippled woman trying to discover the reason behind her fiancé's mysterious death.

MUST READ *Lady in the Car with Glasses and a Gun, One Deadly Summer, Trap for Cinderella*
READ ON Friedrich Dürrenmatt, Kenneth Fearing, Georges Simenon

Alfred Jarry

1873—1907
Pistol-toting père of pataphysics

Born in Laval, Meyenne, and educated at Rennes, Alfred Jarry – an unparalleled eccentric – wrote from his early teens and had completed the first draft of his most famous dramatic work, *Ubu Roi*, by the time he was 15.

Though a midget, his presence was huge – a walking, talking work of art, part madman, part genius. A notorious drinker with a taste for absinthe, he was famous for the cyclist's garb he would wear around Paris complete with his two pistols. He would fish daily in the Seine, making catches at will by all accounts. He lived in a bizarre apartment where each storey had been cut horizontally in half to make double the original number of floors. This was fine for the diminutive Jarry who would write on the floor stretched out on his stomach, but not for some of his taller guests like Apollinaire, who also describes a stone phallus Jarry kept on his mantelpiece which he always covered with a velvet purple sheath after once frightening a literary lady.

Ubu Roi, which premièred in 1896, was an attack on bourgeois conventions and their greed for power. It is the story of Père Ubu, who slaughters the royal family of Poland in order to ascend to the throne. Ubu was a malicious parody of Jarry's former mathematics teacher who subsequently entered politics. Jarry's behaviour and views made him the scourge of respectable Parisian society and *Ubu Roi* became a focus for this disgust after a riot broke out during its opening performance. Thirty years later it was being championed by the Dadaists and Surrealists as the first work of absurdist drama.

Through Père Ubu and his later character Dr Faustroll, Jarry developed a science of 'pataphysics' – an almost-impossible-to-define logic of the absurd, which for Jarry stretched beyond literature to life itself (pataphysics has been formally defined as 'the science of imaginary solutions, which symbolically attributes the properties of objects, described by their virtuality to their lineaments'). The 'science' was later taken up and developed by other French novelists such as Boris Vian, George Perec and Raymond Queneau.

Although remembered primarily as a playwright (in particular for his Ubu plays – there were several sequels) Jarry of course crossed every literary boundary, writing in many forms: poems, essays and novels – all of which blurred into something new, hallucinatory and very much his own. His fictions, which include *Days and Nights: a Novel of a Deserter, Supermale* and *Exploits and Opinions of Dr Faustroll, Pataphysician*, if anything, resemble a cross between Lewis Carroll and Flann O'Brien at his most surreal.

Always one to blur art and everyday life, Jarry steadily began to emulate his absurd creations in life: drinking, hallucinating, swearing, talking about himself in the third person and threatening bystanders with his pistols. He finally died from the drink on All Saint's Day in 1907.

MUST READ *Exploits and Opinions of Dr Faustroll, Pataphysician, The Ubu Plays*
READ ON **Antonin Artaud, Flann O'Brien, George Perec, Raymond Queneau, Boris Vian**

< 146 >

J IS FOR JAZZ
5 novels that can really blow

THE HORN
John Clellon Holmes
written in the form of a jazz
improvisation

YOUNG MAN WITH A HORN
Dorothy Baker
loosely based on the career of Bix
Beiderbecke's life

COMING THROUGH SLAUGHTER
Michael Ondaatje
reconstructing the violent life of
Buddy Bolden

WORLD IN A JUG
Roland Grant
the restless life of a peripatetic
piano-player

PARIS BLUES
Harold Plender
Yankees in Paris who just don't want
to go home

Jerome K Jerome

1859—1927
The original slacker

Jerome K(lapka) Jerome was born in the Black Country (Walsall, Staffordshire) in 1859. His father was an ironmonger, but his business was not profitable and Jerome was brought up in north London where he attended Marylebone Grammar School. Leaving at 14, as was customary in those days, he worked first as a railway clerk and subsequently as a schoolmaster, journalist and actor. Jerome married in 1888. During the First World War he served as an ambulance driver on the Western Front. He died in 1927.

In the 1880s Jerome K Jerome published two volumes of humorous essays, which sold respectably but unexceptionally. In 1889, however, he produced the comic novel that made his name and his fortune. 'There were four of us – George, and William Samuel Harris, and myself, and Montmorency' is the first sentence of the multi-million-selling *Three Men in a Boat (to say nothing of the dog!)* chronicling the minor misfortunes of three middle-class Victorian chaps holidaying in a boat on the Thames. The tone of the novel is remarkable: no writer before or since has bettered Jerome's lampooning of the Victorians' high opinion of themselves. Moreover, the games Jerome plays with his own narrative – hardly a paragraph goes by without the introduction of some diversion or other – are so inventive and so self-conscious that if *Three Men in a Boat* had been written a century later it would almost certainly have been dubbed the ultimate 'postmodern' text.

Jerome had fond recollections of writing *Three Men in a Boat*. Years later, he wrote:

'I remember only feeling very young and absurdly pleased with myself for reasons that concern only myself. It was summer time, and London is so beautiful in summer. It lay beneath my window a fairy city veiled in golden mist, for I worked in a room high above the chimney-pots; and at night the lights shone far beneath me, so that I looked down as into an Aladdin's cave of jewels.'

The author's pleasure in being a young man-about-town is still discernible in the book today.

With the money he made from *Three Men in a Boat* Jerome co-founded the *Idler*, a magazine that published articles by, among others, the American humourist and author of *Huckleberry Finn,* Mark Twain. In its celebration of laziness, Jerome's *Idler* was the forerunner of the eponymous publication established in London in the 1990s by Tom Hodgkinson. Furthermore, in their sheer determination to do nothing in particular, Jerome's protagonists bear a certain resemblance to the characters in Richard Linklater's film *Slackers* – except that Jerome's characters must have seemed much more mischievious to the Victorians, given the

< 148 >

overwhelming influence of the Protestant work ethic at the time.

In 1900 Jerome published a sequel to *Three Men in a Boat*. Entitled *Three Men on the Bummel,* it is the story of three chaps on a walking tour through Germany. But it was not an instant hit and its chances of becoming a gradual success were subsequently wrecked by the rise in Britain of anti-German chauvinism. Jerome went on to write plays in a similar style to that of his friend J M Barrie, the creator of *Peter Pan*; in 1926 he published an autobiography, *My Life and Times*. Critics might complain that Jerome K Jerome was never more than light and fluffy, but that's like complaining because the Wombles are not Wagner.

MUST READ *Three Men in a Boat*
READ ON **Richard Brautigan, Jack Kerouac,** J B Priestley

B S Johnson

1933–1973
'Fuck all this lying'

Novelist, poet, playwright, film-maker and all-round Renaissance man, Bryan Stanley William Johnson was born in Hammersmith, London and, except for a period during the war when he was evacuated, spent all his life in the city. He read English at King's College and, after writing short fictional pieces (later collected in the posthumous *Aren't you Rather Young to be Writing your Memoirs?*, 1974) published his first novel, *Travelling People*, in 1963. Recalling the styles of several of the more exploratory Irish writers, Flann O'Brien, James Joyce, and Samuel Beckett (who considered Johnson to be a most gifted writer), the book also featured typographical devices to break up the narrative.

His second novel, *Albert Angelo* (1964) seemed relatively conventional, until the midway appearance of Johnson himself and his notorious interjection: 'Fuck all this lying.' This was followed by *Trawl* (1966), winner of the Somerset Maugham Award, which Johnson described as 'all interior monologue, a representation of the inside of my mind but at one remove', a state he effected by cutting holes in the pages.

Such playfulness reached its apogee with his infamous 'novel in a box' *The Unfortunates* (1969), in which the 27 loose-leaf sections (except the first and last) could be arranged and read in any order.

As well as being poetry editor at the prestigious *Transatlantic Review* and publishing two volumes of verse, Johnson also wrote several plays including *Entry* (1965), a BBC radio play; *One Sodding Thing after Another* (1967), and the modestly titled *B S Johnson v. God* (1971). His films, which he occasionally directed as well as scripted, were, like everything he undertook, experimental, but still found audiences, with both the BBC and the British Film Institute commissioning work, notably the award-winning short *You're Human Like the Rest of Them* (1967), and the charming *Up Yours Too, Guillaume Apollinaire!* (1968).

Johnson's last two novels, *House Mother Normal* (1971), and *Christie Malry's Own Double-Entry* (1973) were both critically acclaimed, with the normally middlebrow Auberon Waugh praising the latter for being undoubtedly a masterpiece.

A victim of recurring depression, Johnson killed himself in 1973.

MUST READ *Christie Malry's Own Double-Entry, Trawl*
READ ON **William Burroughs, Donald Barthelme, Iain Sinclair**

Erica Jong

1942–
In search of the zipless fuck

A native New Yorker, Erica Jong's earliest writing was confessional poetry with a strong emphasis on her Jewish identity (*Fruits and Vegetables*, 1971). But the sexual revolution of the late sixties and early seventies had an impact on Jong, and she, in turn, wrote a book which contributed to the further development of the sexual revolution. *Fear of Flying* (1973) focuses

< 149 >

on Isadora Wing, a woman who, while riddled with self-doubt, nevertheless goes in search of the 'zipless fuck'. Wing wants to be able to enjoy sex in the same carefree and unattached manner as her male counterparts. In other words, she is out to control her sex life and thereby gain control over her own personality.

Jong wrote three further instalments in the life of Isadora Wing: *How to Save your own Life* (1977), *Parachutes and Kisses* (1984), and *Any Woman's Blues* (1990). The latter, as its title suggests, is more downbeat in tone. Jong also wrote *Fanny, Being the True History and Adventures of Fanny Hackabout-Jones* (1980), a pastiche of classic porn novels such as *Fanny Hill*, with the emphasis on female rather than male enjoyment of sexual intercourse.

More recently, Jong produced *Fear of Fifty* (1994), a book about middle age in which she describes the sexual impotence of her fourth (and current) husband. In 1998 she published another non-fiction book, *What do Women Want?*

When *Fear of Flying* was published, sexual pleasure for women was a right-on slogan. Feminists, generally speaking, wanted to be more like men, and their idea of liberation included the right to be sexually irresponsible. Nowadays, feminists are more keen on nurturing; anything that smacks of irresponsibility is frowned upon, and Erica Jong is persona non grata with the political-correctness police.

< 150 > MUST READ *Fear of Flying*

READ ON **Simone de Beauvoir**, Marilyn French, Harold Robbins, Henry Miller

James Joyce

1882–1941
The greatest modernist of them all

Born in Dublin into a background of genteel poverty, from the age of six James Augustine Aloysius Joyce was educated by Jesuits, whom he thanked for teaching him to think straight, although straight thinking later required him to reject all their religious instructions. As a student at University College, Dublin, Joyce became interested in the plays of Henrik Ibsen; the latter's determination to question social conventions was his most attractive feature. Joyce also came under the literary influence of W B Yeats.

Joyce set most of his subsequent fiction in Dublin, but as a young man he was frustrated by the parochialism of the city and by the difficulties he experienced in earning a living there. He spent a year in Paris on next to no money, returning when a telegram arrived saying his mother was dying. Not long after her death, Joyce was travelling again – this time to the Italian city of Trieste on the Adriatic coast. He gave English lessons and talked about setting up an agency to sell Irish tweed. Refused a post teaching Italian literature in Dublin, he continued to live abroad.

At the outset of the First World War, Joyce and Nora Barnacle, his lifelong and long-suffering companion (Joyce drank too much and was sometimes obsessive about other women), moved to Zurich in the neutral country of Switzerland, where they sat out the war alongside Lenin and the Dadaist Tristan Tzara (a coincidence that provides the basis for Tom Stoppard's 1974 play *Travesties*). After the war the Joyces moved on to Paris, where they resided until the Nazi occupation of France prompted them to cross over into Switzerland once more. There James Joyce died of a duodenal ulcer in 1941. Joyce had been plagued by failing eyesight for many years, and it has been suggested that this was the legacy of a syphilitic father; in which case hereditary syphilis may also have been a factor in his death.

Except for the slim volume entitled *Pomes Penyeach* (1927), and *Finnegans Wake*, which some people maintain is incomprehensible, the publication of all Joyce's work was delayed because of what at the time was considered to be its controversial nature. The short stories grouped under the title *Dubliners* (1914) were eventually published in the USA after British publishers had turned them down and an Irish printer destroyed the 1,000 copies which Joyce, out of desperation, had intended to publish himself. *A Portrait of the Artist as a Young Man*, the history of the soul of Joyce's alter ego Stephen Dedalus (originally named Stephen Hero, latterly – but only briefly, Stephen Daly)

James Joyce

appeared as a serial in the avant-garde literary magazine the *Egoist* (1914–1915). The first copy of *Ulysses* (1922), the monumental life-in-the-day of Leopold Bloom, a Jewish shopkeeper in Dublin, was delivered into Joyce's hands on his fortieth birthday. When a second copy was displayed in the window of the Paris bookshop Shakespeare & Co, there was so much clamour and excitement that it had to be removed. *Ulysses* was not published in Britain for another 14 years.

Opinion is divided over *Finnegans Wake,* published in Paris four months before the outbreak of the the Second World War in 1939. Some claim that it amounts to 628 pages of mumbo jumbo. Others regard it as the masterpiece of the century. There is not much plot to speak of. A publican serves his customers, gets drunk, tries to make love to his wife but falls asleep – that's all there is, and even this does not get going until Chapter 9. There are no characters as such. The publican turns up in hundreds of different forms – animal, vegetable and mineral. So does just about every figure from history, real and mythological. The book is set in Dublin, but Dublin is an analogue for everywhere else; in this respect *Finnegans Wake* does not even have a setting.

Joyce's disciple and onetime secretary Samuel Beckett said of *Finnegans Wake* that it 'is not about something, it is that something itself'. There is no straightforward description here, as in an ordinary novel. Form and content dissolve into one another. Or, to put it another way, Joyce was trying to write a book that approximated to music. Music does not have to be about anything, it just is – and it therefore allows greater scope for the exploration of form. This is what Joyce was trying to achieve with words.

Although in one sense *Finnegans Wake* is an ultra-modern experiment, in another respect it is quite traditional. The structure of the book follows the three stages of history as laid out by the 18th-century Italian philosopher Giambattista Vico: the Divine, the Heroic and the Human, followed by a period of flux, after which the cycle begins all over again. Joyce imitated this cyclical notion, to the point where the last sentence of the book runs into the first.

Born in Dublin into a background of…

MUST READ *Dubliners, Finnegans Wake, The Portrait of the Artist as a Young Man, Ulysses*
READ ON **Samuel Beckett**, Ezra Pound, **Thomas Pynchon**, Virginia Woolf

< 152 >

Franz Kafka

1883–1924
Alienation and absurdity

The Austrian novelist Franz Kafka thought of himself as 'a wandering Jew' in exile from the modern world. He was brought up in the Czech city of Prague, which was part of the decaying Austro-Hungarian empire until the Treaty of Versailles (1918–1921) redivided Europe after the First World War. Kafka, therefore, spent most of his life in the part of the modern world which was least comfortable with modernism, where professional men and senior government employees could lose their positions for being 'modernists'. It was the divide between the new and the old generations which prompted Kafka's father to refer to his son as an 'insect', which in turn inspired the famous story 'Metamorphosis' (1916) in which the clerk Gregor Samsa wakes to find that he has turned into a beetle.

The stories published during Kafka's lifetime were poorly received and he died in obscurity. Had his deathbed wishes been respected, his executors would have destroyed the manuscripts of what subsequently came to be recognised as the classic documents of 'the modern individual's endeavours to penetrate life's purposes, to elucidate the mysteries of existence, in a world in which indefinable but implacable forces confront the aspirations of the self'

Franz Kafka

(Malcolm Bradury and James McFarlane, *Pelican Guide to Modernism*). For these are the tasks which Kafka set himself in *The Trial* (1925), *The Castle* (1926) and *Amerika* (1927), all published posthumously.

Kafka recognised that not only the world but also writing about the world is problematic. In a letter written in 1914, he seemed to suggest that authentic communication is as elusive as the Holy Grail: 'What I write is different from what I say, what I say is different from what I

< 153 >

think, what I think is different from what I ought to think and so it goes further into the deepest darkness.' But even if life and art both mock our intentions, Kafka is determined to pursue them to the last.

After the Second World War Kafka was adopted by a new generation looking for a literature that would mirror its own disdain for society. If their lionisation of Kafka rescued him from obscurity, their reinterpretation has robbed him of his original subtlety. Kafka's intention was not simply to provide a post-morality play depicting the individual's struggle (good) to survive against the pressures of a bureaucratic existence (bad). He once declared that 'in the struggle between yourself and the world you must take the side of the world', and in stories like 'Metamorphosis' and 'The Hunger Artist' he is careful to balance the vitality of the world against the desire of the alienated individual to transcend it. Likewise, in *The Trial* the painter Titorelli is not ignorant of the values held by Josef K; in some respects he is K's spiritual guide. Thus Kafka suggests a more subtle relationship between the individual and society than some of his latterday champions would allow.

To the modern reader Kafka's style of writing may seem dry, even mechanical. But it is this same precision and accuracy that prevent Kafka's themes from becoming unwieldy and unworkable.

< 154 >

MUST READ *The Castle*, 'Metamorphosis', *The Trial*
READ ON Saul Bellow, Alfred Doblin, John Dos Passos

Anna Kavan
1901–1968
The enigma of violence

Anna Kavan's real name was Helen Wood, and although her parents were British, she spent much of her childhood on the Continent and in California. Her early novels were written under her married name, Helen Ferguson, but *Let Me Alone* (1930) and *A Stranger Still* (1935), both featured a character called Anna Kavan – the name she used as the byline for her later novels.

Her 1940 collection *Asylum Piece* includes stories detailing her experiences of drug addiction and insanity. *Change the Name* (1941) was a transitional work that led (following her discovery of Kafka's writings) to much more experimental fiction.

Kavan lived with her first husband in Burma, and this experience is featured in her 1963 novel *Who Are You?*, in which a typical female character is victimised by a sexually aggressive male while trapped in a strange land. Author Jean Rhys may have borrowed this theme for her 1966 novel *Wide Sargasso Sea*: in a letter dated 1964 to her champion, the writer Francis Wyndham, she said: 'Anna Kavan's stories I like, and I have her novel *Who Are You?*. Very short but what a splendid title. If only I'd thought of it.'

Kavan's most famous novel, *Ice* (1967), was deemed by author Brian Aldiss to be a sci-fi book, as it detailed a bleak landscape in which nuclear tests had frozen the world. It also featured another victimised female protagonist, this time fleeing across icy wastes attempting to elude two sadistic lovers, with the glacial imagery symbolising the numbness and pain of the author's heroin addiction. The novel formed part of a posthumous collection called *My Madness* (1990), a selection of stories and autobiographical writings.

MUST READ *Ice, Who Are You?*
READ ON **Kay Boyle, William Burroughs, Jean Rhys**

James Kelman

1946–
The lyricist of Scotland's excluded

Born in Glasgow, James Kelman was apprenticed to a typesetter at 15, left Scotland at 17 when his family emigrated to the USA, returned shortly afterwards, odd-jobbed around Scotland and London, spent time on the dole reading books, enrolled as a philosophy student but dropped out during his final year.

In the 15 years between the short story collection *Not Not While the Giro* (1983) and his 1998 collection *The Good Times,* Kelman has focused on the durability and dry humour of the west of Scotland's disaffected. His style has been described as 'Beckett with a west coast accent'. His first novel, *The Busconductor Hines* (1984), exhibited his trademark technique: blurring the distinction between the authorial voice and the voices of his characters. Moving fluidly from the thoughts to the spoken words of his characters, without regard to traditional punctuation, Kelman has tried to find a new way of representing ordinary thought processes and speech. 'Working in that way,' he explains, 'from within the perceptions of the people within the world…it won't be like an observation…I don't want to tell stories about this community, rather the stories are created within the community. Therefore, those divisions between dialogue and narrator all have to go.'

Kelman believes that this makes for a non-judgemental, non-hierarchichal form of writing:

'There's not a judgement from within the narrative form itself, whereas in most English literature there's a judgement from within the narrative, in terms of language, for instance – that this person's language isn't as good as this person's and therefore that person's culture is inferior to this culture, which is the culture of the authorial God-voice, "standard English", which is usually the counterpoint for everything to be evaluated from.'

A Chancer (1985) is the story of a 20-year-old loner and compulsive gambler, Tammas, who lives for betting because the rest of the world seems closed off to him. The sense of closure is also a strong element in *The Burn* (1991), a collection of stories including 'The Streetsweeper' and 'The Ins and Outs'. The novel that brought Kelman to the attention of a wider public was *A Disaffection* (1989, shortlisted for the Booker Prize), the tale of a schoolmaster who cannot bring himself to believe in what he is meant to be teaching. The character of Patrick Doyle prompted comparisons with John Osborne's Jimmy Porter, the original Angry Young Man in the play *Look Back in Anger* (1956). Kelman himself has written three plays (*Hardie and Baird and Other Plays,* 1991).

In the novel *How Late it Was, How Late* (1994), Kelman's sense of Scottish identity has become even stronger. He insists that 'Affirming your culture is a terribly important and subversive thing to do.' His critics are concerned that an author of universal significance might have succumbed to the current fashion for parochial particularism.

MUST READ *A Chancer, A Disaffection, How Late it Was, How Late*
READ ON Agnes Owens, **Samuel Selvon**, Jeff Torrington, **Irvine Welsh**

< 156 >

K IS FOR KITCHEN SINK
5 of the best from 60s Britain's dirty realism

SATURDAY NIGHT AND SUNDAY MORNING
Alan Sillitoe
factory workers have fun (and all the rest is propaganda)

ALFIE
Bill Naughton
the life and loves of a cockney rogue

THE L—SHAPED ROOM
Lynne Reid Banks
bringing up baby in bedsit land

THIS SPORTING LIFE
David Storey
playing dirty up North, rugby's finest literary moment

BILLY LIAR
Keith Waterhouse
dreaming up escapes from a dull Northern life

William Kennedy

1928–

The fighting Irish

The focus of all William Kennedy's books is Albany, the Irish-American town in New York State where he was born and raised, and where he has lived all his life except for the two years he spent in the army. The core of his output is the Albany cycle of novels, which intimately trace immigrant experience written through an expansive Irish-American family history

Kennedy's non-fiction work *O Albany* (1983), a beguiling tribute to his home town, is dedicated 'to people who used to think they hated the place they grew up, and then took a second look'. His first novel, *The Ink Truck* (1969), is a witty, sometimes surreal, tale of a newspaper strike (the author was for many years a reporter on the local paper) and civic corruption, complete with tabloid headlines and 'Extra!' notices. Like his subsequent work, it exudes an earthy aroma of life and death, sex and redemption.

Kennedy's reputation was cemented by his next three novels, collectively known as *The Albany Cycle*, and praised by Saul Bellow as 'a memorable series'. *Legs* (1975) is a fictionalised account of dashing bootlegger Jack 'Legs' Diamond (who was the role model, apparently, for Scott Fitzgerald's Gatsby) and his supposed slaying by Albany's police chief. *Billy Phelan's Greatest Game* (1978) introduced pool hustler Billy and his family, including father Francis, a baseball player and bum, and hero of *Ironweed* (1983). This last book won Kennedy the Pulitzer Prize and was filmed (with a Kennedy screenplay), starring Jack Nicholson and Meryl Streep. *Very Old Bones* (1992) *The Flaming Corsage* (1998) continue the complex archaeology of the legendary Phelan family.

Kennedy's other cinematic contribution was as screenwriter on Francis Coppola's Harlem epic *The Cotton Club*; his account of the production is hilarious. Appalled as the film's budget zoomed from 25 to 43 million dollars, Kennedy slaved away on 30 to 40 versions of the script. Coppola, apparently, reckoned Kennedy would soon be making his own films, but the writer felt differently: 'He [Coppola] is suited to the ringmaster role, but I believe I would gnash my teeth to cinders in a matter of weeks.'

Instead, Kennedy continued writing about Albany, constructing the Phelan family tree, every novel a new branch.

MUST READ *The Albany Cycle, Quinn's Book*
READ ON Saul Bellow, **William Faulkner**, F Scott Fitzgerald, John O'Hara

Jack Kerouac

1922–1969
King of the road

Jack Kerouac was born in the New England mill-town of Lowell, Massachusetts. His parents were from French-Canadian families who had emigrated from Quebec, and Jack did not learn English until he attended a primary school run by Catholic nuns.

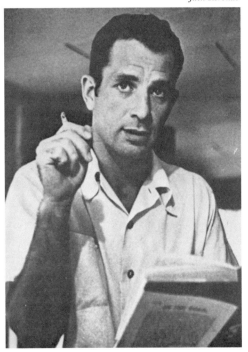

Jack Kerouac

In his late teens Kerouac spent a year at Horace Mann School in New York, then took up an athletics scholarship at Columbia College near by. But Kerouac's hopes of becoming an American football hero were dashed when he suffered a split leg-bone in his second game. Invalided out of the team, Kerouac also exited from the commonly accepted view of the American Way Of Life.

First he enlisted in the navy, from which he received a none-too-honourable discharge. But Kerouac's most important journeys were to be of a different kind. He had kept up his connections with the Columbia campus, and soon hooked up with a coterie of spiritual adventurers led by Allen Ginsberg, who was still a student there. Together with other embryonic luminaries of the Beat Generation such as William Burroughs and Herbert Huncke, and inspired by the hi-energy of the young delinquent from Denver, Neal Cassady, they set out on a series of quests – coast to coast across the United States, to Europe, to Mexico and beyond – in search of something with which to replace the lost horizons of the American Dream and its now-tarnished images of material wealth and technological progress.

Documented most famously in *On the Road* (published 1957, written and rewritten between 1948 and 1956), these journeys also provided the backdrop for Kerouac's *The Dharma Bums* (1958), *Visions of Cody* (1959), *Mexico City Blues* (1959), *Lonesome Traveller* (1960) and

< 158 >

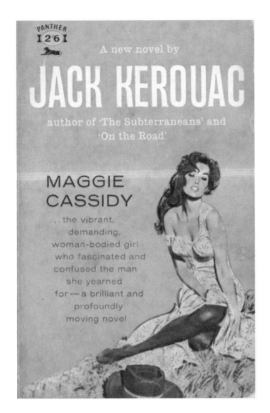

self-seekers touched upon many of the values and notions that have since become embedded in contemporary culture. Drawing from the lowlife experiences of hustler Huncke and the spiritual visions of Ginsberg, Kerouac hit upon the notion that being 'beat' (defeated by the world and its machinations) also meant being 'beatific'. Initiated by Kerouac, the deification of defeat and victimhood is now commonplace.

The Beats were also rejuvenating founding American values of the past, as set out by transcendentalists like Emerson and Thoreau who believed in self-reliance, spontaneity and spiritual freedom.

Kerouac's critics claim that his writing is childish (Truman Capote declared: 'this is typing, not writing'); they reject his celebration of madness ('the only ones for me are the mad ones') as a kind of voyeuristic dilettantism (also noting that the author of *On the Road* never did the driving); and they recognise that his restlessness never really challenged the American Way Of Life, which is perhaps why towards the end he sometimes sounded like a raving redneck. But there is no denying that the icon of Kerouac, typing furiously in an attempt to document the undirected dynamism of his generation, has loomed large ever since he set out on the non-linear road to nowhere in particular.

Satori in Paris (1966), among others. But by the sixties Kerouac the lonesome traveller was in fact spending most of his time back home with his beloved Mémère (mother). He died an alcoholic in 1969, disconnected from mainstream America but equally disaffected from the hippies who succeeded the Beats.

In their quest for a different kind of enlightenment, Kerouac and his company of

MUST READ *The Dharma Bums, On the Road, Memory Babe: a critical biography of Jack Kerouac* by Gerald Nicosia, *Visions of Cody*

Gerald Kersh

1911–1968
British noir

Gerald Kersh was born of Jewish stock in Teddington, Middlesex, southern England, and died in New York State a naturalised American citizen. His occupations were as varied as his places of residence: nightclub bouncer, cook, wrestler, soldier, scriptwriter and journalist. In Fleet Street he was known as a feature writer who could turn his hand to almost anything.

As a writer of fiction, Kersh was equally adaptable. Short stories such as 'Men without Bones' and 'The Extraordinarily Horrible Dummy' (possibly the best mad-ventriloquist tale ever written) continue to appear in horror anthologies. Of the 23 full-length novels written by Kersh, probably the most famous is *Night and the City* (1938), a story of London's underworld which was made into a film (a rare example of film noir set in Britain) starring Richard Widmark, Gene Tierney and Herbert Lom; it was filmed again in the 1990s by Irwin Winkler, with Robert De Niro and Jessica Lange in the lead roles. With its unravelling morality and shadowy streets, *Night and the City* reads like a cross betwen Graham Greene and the American hard-boiled school.

But Kersh's literary range was even broader. His 'straight' novel, *Fowler's End* (1957), has been assessed as 'one of the outstanding novels of this century'. His fictionalised account of the Lidice massacre was described as 'a great book; a formidable and irresistible book'; and his warts-and-all account of soldiery in the Second World War was judged by the left-wing weekly the *New Statesman* to be 'the most original and distinguished contribution to the literature of [the] war'.

Of all the half-forgotten writers of the mid-

Gerald Kersh

< 160 >

century, Kersh is the most ripe for rediscovery. In the early nineties a tiny imprint by the name of Brainiac Books had the bright idea of republishing *Night and the City* to coincide with the release of Winkler's remake of the film. But the movie was not a great success, and Brainiac Books lacked the marketing muscle to bring Kersh to a wider readership. The job remains to be done...but probably not for long.

MUST READ *Fowler's End, Night and the City*
READ ON **Norman Mailer, Horace McCoy**

Ken Kesey

1935–
The Merry Prankster

Ken Kesey was born in Colorado and educated at the University of Oregon and at Stanford, where one of his tutors was Malcolm Cowley, editor of the *New Republic* and champion of Faulkner, Fitzgerald, Cheever, and Kerouac. In the fifties and early sixties he was a paid volunteer at a veterans' hospital, where he took LSD, mescaline, and other drugs under clinical supervision. He also worked as a night ward attendant in the psychiatric ward of the same hospital.

All this went into Kesey's first novel, *One Flew Over the Cuckoo's Nest*, published in 1962 to immediate critical success (the film version made in 1975 won five Oscars, including best film for director Milos Forman and best actor for Jack Nicholson). Narrated by an American Indian chief who lets people think he is a deaf mute, *One Flew Over the Cuckoo's Nest* follows petty criminal and prankster McMurphy in his efforts to subvert the bureaucratic nightmare of a mental hospital. Kesey is suggesting that society is a madhouse, and that the really dangerous lunatics are those in positions of authority. Our only defence against them is the anarchic energies of the McMurphys, who dare to stand up for free expression in a world of repression and mind control. Kesey's second novel, *Sometimes a Great Notion* (1966), confused critics and fans alike, with Orville Prescott of the *New York Times* declaring that: 'His monstrous book is the most insufferably pretentious and the most totally tiresome novel I have had to read in many years.' Kesey's next move was to abandon literature. He set up a commune in La Honda, California and appointed himself the spearhead of the nascent hippie/protest/drugs movement – a move which had much more impact than his literary career. King Kesey's psychedelic reign was described in Tom Wolfe's factional classic, *The Electric Kool-Aid Acid Test* (1968). His band of Merry Pranksters included Kerouac's buddy and muse, Neal Cassady, as well as several malcontents who became irritated with Kesey's autocratic style: 'We used to be equals. Now it's Kesey's trip. We go to his place. We take his acid. We do what he wants.' Arrested on a drugs charge, Kesey fled to Mexico where he faked an unconvincing suicide. Captured eventually, he received a relatively light sentence and retired to Oregon to farm. Two more books, *Demon Box* (1987) and *Sailor Song* (1990), have appeared, but failed to attract much attention.

MUST READ *One Flew Over the Cuckoo's Nest,* *Sometimes a Great Notion*
READ ON **Robert Stone,** **Hunter S Thompson, Tom Wolfe**

Stephen King

1947–
Horror bestseller and a serious writer

Stephen Edwin King was born in Maine. His first stories combined horror and science fiction. He was suspended from high school for publishing a spoof newspaper, the *Village Vomit*. He also printed stories on an small offset printing press that belonged to his brother.

King was encouraged to write by faculty members at the University of Maine (during his student days he was active in the anti-Vietnam War movement), who showed him that it was possible to be popular and literary at the same time. In the wake of *Soul on Ice* by the influential black power leader Eldridge Cleaver, one staff member asked King's class whether there was such a thing as the 'suburban soul'. In a sense, King has spent his whole literary career

answering this question in the affirmative. He subsequently described his own writing style as 'the literary equivalent of a Big Mac and a large fries'.

Having graduated in English, King failed to find a teaching job immediately. Married with two children, he began to think that he had lost the chance to be a writer, but when Doubleday published *Carrie* (1974, filmed by Brian de Palma in 1976), an 'updating of High School Confidential' in which the female protagonist is estranged from her peers, Stephen King's reign of terror had begun. The paperback rights were bought by the New American Library, enabling King to give up high school teaching (he later taught creative writing at university) to concentrate on writing full time.

Whether in *The Shining* (1977, filmed by Stanley Kubrick in 1980 with Jack Nicholson in the lead role) or in *Misery* (1984), King laces his horror with love. He insists that the reader must come to love characters in order to share fully in their horror: in the case of *The Shining's* Jack Torrance (who is partly based on King's own situation before he became a publishing sensation) he further complicates matters by inviting the reader to love a man who 'is being driven to destroy all he loves'.

King has also said that if he feels unable to frighten the reader, he is not too proud to go for the 'gross out'. At times he is unashamedly vulgar, but the key to King's success is his subtle ability to imbue the banality of mainstream surburban

< 162 >

life with the magical intensity of infinite horror.

King is so prolific that in 1977 he adopted the pseudonym Richard Bachman (taken from the group Bachman–Turner Overdrive) in order to get more books on the market than would have been possible in just his own name. But in 1985 he abandoned 'Bachman', saying that he had died of 'cancer of the pseudonym'.

King's critics complain that his first published book, *Carrie*, which was written largely in the form of letters, commentary and spoof documentation of the imaginary events in the narrative, was his last experimental work. His straightforward storytelling is too, er, straightforward, they say. Others claim that this master of the macabre is also the poet of suburbia, whose literary depth depends on the combination of the ordinary and extraordinary that is his hallmark.

MUST READ *Bare Bones: conversations on terror with Stephen King* edited by Tim Underwood and Chuck Miller, *Carrie, Gerald's Game, It, Salem's Lot*
READ ON Clive Barker, Ramsay Campbell

Jerzy Kosinski

1933–1991
The painted bird

Born in Lodz, Poland, Kosinski was separated from his parents during the war at the age of six. Wandering through Russia and Poland, living on his wits, he was only reunited with his family in 1945. Such a traumatic experience caused him to lose the power of speech for several years; he only recovered it in 1947, as the result of a skiing accident.

Kosinski was utterly opposed to the totalitarian regime in postwar Poland and, as a student at Lodz University, managed, by an elaborate hoax, to receive an 'invitation' to study in America. In 1958 he became a graduate student at Columbia University and in 1962 joined the New School for Social Research. During this time, he published two non-fiction works, both sociological studies of the individual snared in totalitarian societies, and both written under the Americanised name of Joseph Novak.

His first novel, *The Painted Bird* (1965; the first time he published under his own name), was a fictional account of his bizarre wartime childhood during the Nazi occupation of Poland and Russia. The title of the novel derives from the act of capturing and painting a bird: when the bird is set free to join its flock it is ripped apart because of its differences. The book received widespread critical acclaim and some notoriety for its sadistic and violent vision of humanity. During the story the boy is captured, several times brutalised and narrowly avoids being murdered on two occasions.

It was the start of a five-part cycle of books: *Steps* (1968), *Being There* (1971), *The Devil Tree* (1973), and *Cockpit* (1975), with the common theme of an individual totally isolated, in an alien environment, marooned from his past. *Steps*, an erotically charged novel, won the National Book Award and was unanimously praised, with author Geoffrey Wolff (brother of Tobias) calling it 'a beautifully written book …precise, scrupulous and poetic', while *Time* magazine acknowledged 'the savage purity of Kosinski's vision'.

Being There was filmed in 1979, starring Peter Sellers, and with Kosinski's script. In many ways his key book, the childlike silences and Zen-style mutterings of the protagonist Chance, misconstrued by his superiors (including the president) to be signs of wisdom, had obvious links with Kosinski's harrowing past. Kosinski was found dead in his bath in New York in 1991.

MUST READ   *Being There, The Painted Bird, Steps*
READ ON   **J G Ballard**, Saul Bellow, Stan Elkin

Milan Kundera
1939—
The Czech who bounced back from censorship

Milan Kundera was born in Czechoslovakia (a single entity while the Communist Party ruled it, the country has since split into two parts). He worked as a labourer, a jazz musician and a lecturer in literature. For several years he worked as a professor at the Prague Institute for Advanced Cinematographic Studies. Some of his students went on to become the prime movers behind the New Wave in Czech cinema.

Kundera was one of the metropolitan intellectuals associated with the liberalisation of Czecholsovakia during the premiership of Alexander Dubcek. In the summer of 1968, the Soviet bureaucracy clamped down on the Czech 'experiment', Warsaw Pact tanks rolled into Prague – and occupying Russian soldiers stole pears from the garden of the American embassy. Along with thousands of others, Kundera lost his job, and his books were removed from public libraries. In 1975 he settled in France. Four years later the Czech government revoked his citizenship, and Kundera applied (successfully) to become a French citizen. In 1980 he was appointed professor at the Ecole des Hautes Etudes en Sciences Sociales in Paris. He writes in Czech and French. His books were reinstated in his home country after the 'velvet revolution' of 1989.

< 164 >

Along with a collection of short stories, *Laughable Loves*, Kundera's first novel, *The Joke* (1967), was published in Prague before the Russian invasion, although he later said that he was surprised it ever got past the censor. In the author's preface to the 1984 Penguin edition, Kundera explained that *The Joke* is 'a melancholy duet about the schism between body and soul'. He began writing it in 1962, at the age of 33, prompted by the arrest of a girl for stealing flowers from a cemetery and giving them to her lover. Kundera's Lucie is a character for whom 'sexuality and love are two completely different, irreconcilable things'. His male protagonist, Ludvik, 'concentrates all the hatred he has accumulated during his life in a single act of love'. The joke is on man (a single character and also representative of mankind) who, 'caught in the trap of a joke, suffers a personal tragedy which, seen from without, is ludicrous. His tragedy lies in the fact that the joke has deprived him of the right to tragedy. He is condemned to triviality.'

In the West, reviewers sought to endow *The Joke* with a political message. During a television panel discussion in 1980 someone described it as 'a major indictment of Stalinism', to which Kundera replied: 'Spare me your Stalinism, please. *The Joke* is a love story!' In the first version to be published in Britain and America, crucial passages were omitted and Kundera later commented: 'The ideologues in Prague took *The Joke* for a pamphlet against

socialism and banned it; the foreign publisher took it for a political fantasy that became reality for a few weeks and rewrote it accordingly.' They all missed the point that *The Joke* 'was always meant to be…merely a novel'.

Kundera's subsequent novels were not published in his homeland until recently. They include *Life is Elsewhere* (1973, winner of the Prix Medicis for the best foreign novel published in France in that year) and *The Farewell Party* (1976, winner of the Premio Mondello Award for the best foreign novel published in Italy in 1978). In 1981 he received the American Commonwealth Award in recognition of all his work up to that time.

In 1984 Kundera published *The Unbearable Lightness of Being*, which was filmed in 1987 by Philip Kaufman, with Daniel Day Lewis and Juliette Binoche in the starring roles. The plot focuses on a womanising doctor who is in the process of rethinking his lifestyle at the very moment when the Russian tanks arrive in Prague. The film has been described as a 'faithful' telling of Kundera's story, although the narrative of the film is linear (i.e. traditional) whereas the form of the novel is more experimental.

Malcolm Bradbury dubbed Kundera 'a writer who really matters'. Ian McEwan described *The Unbearable Lightness of Being* as 'a dark and brilliant achievement', and David Lodge heralded *The Joke* as 'a funny, sad, gripping, wise, marvellous book'. The main complaint against Kundera seems to be that his

< 165 >

philosophical interpolations can be woolly and sometimes get in the way of his storytelling.

Kundera has published three more novels: *Immortality* (1991), *Slowness* (1995) and *Identity* (1998). This last features two lovers at a loose end in an out-of-season seaside resort, and a former revolutionary who recycles slogans from the sixties in order to sell nappies. In some of his recent work Kundera seems to be retreading ground that he has broken before.

MUST READ *The Joke, The Unbearable Lightness of Being*
READ ON **Mikhail Bulgakov**, Vaclav Havel, Bohumil Hrabal, Ivan Klíma, François Sagan, Josef Skvorecky

Hanif Kureishi

1954–
The buddha of multiculture

Born in Bromley, Kent, of Pakistani parentage, Hanif Kureishi went to university in London and afterwards wrote plays for fringe theatres (notably *Outskirts*, 1981, about two violent racists from South London), financing himself by writing pornography. His screenplay for Stephen Frears' film *My Beautiful Laundrette* (1985) featured a gay relationship between two men of different races, and was hailed in the London listings magazine *City Limits* under the headline 'Victim Victorious'. It has subsequently been interpreted both as a description of the near-impossibility of cross-cultural relationships, and as a literary map for new 'hybrid' cultural mixes. Kureishi said he was aiming for an effect that was partly Godfather-style gangster epic and partly like the slushy romances shown on TV on Sunday afternoons. His second screenplay for Frears, *Sammy and Rosie Get Laid* (1987), covered some of the same territory but to less effect.

Kurieshi's film *London Kills Me* (1991) is a fitting tribute to the capital city of a country that he once described as 'an intolerant, racist, homophobic, narrow-minded, authoritarian rat-hole'. In the same year, Kureishi published his first novel (later televised by the BBC), *The Buddha of Suburbia*, a satirical piece focusing on the cultural confusions of a successful Asian businessman and his son. The story, featuring a pop star character based on Kureishi's Bromley schoolmate Billy Idol of Generation X (Banshee Siouxsie Sioux went to the girls' school down the road), reflected Kureishi's abiding interest in pop music: he went on to co-edit the mammoth *Faber Book of Pop* with Jon Savage, premier chronicler of punk. *The Black Album* (1995) is a more ambitious novel – and a more problematic one – examining aspects of cultural disintegration among Muslims in Britain as they are more or less integrated into British society. In 1997 Kureishi issued a collection of short stories (*Love in a Blue Time*). *Intimacy* (1998), a novel about desertion (man leaves woman and children) and moving away from one's youth, is narrated by a character who sounds a lot like Kureishi himself and who confesses, 'I think I have become the adults in *The Catcher in the Rye*.' It prompted some critics to suggest that Kureishi is maturing nicely; others suggested that Kureishi is a multicultural version of Nick Hornby, destined never to grow up. But critical analysis was overtaken by complaints from Kureishi's ex-partner to the effect that *Intimacy* is not a novel at all, but a fictionalised rendition of the breakup of their relationship. 'Hanif says it's a novel,' Tracy Scoffield observed, 'but nobody believes it's just pure fiction. You might as well call it a fish.' Most recently he wrote the film script for *My Son the Fanatic* (1998).

MUST READ *The Buddha of Suburbia, Love in a Blue Time*
READ ON **Michael Bracewell**, E M Forster, **Nick Hornby**, V S Naipaul, Meera Syal

K IS FOR 'KILL YER IDOLS'
10 bands who are named after books

THE GO-BETWEENS
(L P Hartley)

THE SOFT MACHINE
(William Burroughs)

THE DOORS
(Aldous Huxley/William Blake)

STEPPENWOLF
(Herman Hesse)

BOO RADLEYS
(Harper Lee)

SWANN'S WAY
(Marcel Proust)

THE DIVINE COMEDY
(Dante Alighieri)

THE TRIFFIDS
(John Wyndham)

THE VELVET UNDERGROUND
(Michael Leigh)

PERE UBU
(Alfred Jarry)

K

a reader's guide

Gavin Lambert

1923–
Hollywood on the slide

London-born Gavin Lambert went to St George's prep school (a private junior school), Windsor, and from there to Cheltenham College, where he befriended the future film director Lindsay Anderson. Together they produced a musical which was denounced by the headmaster as 'disgusting'. The admissions tutors at Oxford were not put off by it, however, and Lambert went to Magdalen College to read English, leaving after one year because 'The prospect of learning medieval English was no more appealing than the personality of my extraordinarily self-satisfied tutor, C S Lewis.' Before leaving, Lambert met the future theatre director Peter Brook and appeared as a 'drunken slut' in Brook's 16 mm film of Laurence Sterne's *Sentimental Journey*.

In 1947 Lindsay Anderson founded a film magazine, *Sequence*, and invited Lambert to be co-editor. The magazine was a success, and Lambert was subsequently asked to become director of publications at the British Film Institute. He also wrote and directed *Another Sky*, a low-budget feature shot in Morocco and funded by the eccentric Sir Aymer Maxwell (brother of Gavin, who wrote *Tarka the Otter*).

Introduced to Nicholas Ray, who was in London for the opening of his film *Rebel*

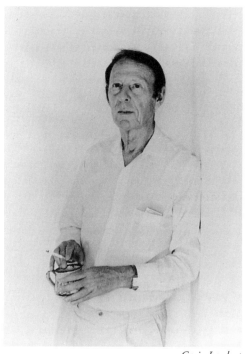

Gavin Lambert

Without a Cause, Lambert was invited to go to Hollywood as Ray's personal assistant. There he worked on *Bigger Than Life*, starring James Mason; back in Europe, Lambert and Ray co-scripted *Bitter Victory* with Richard Burton in the lead role.

On the recommendation of the novelist Paul Bowles, Lambert moved to Tangiers to escape the years of 'creeping [president] Nixonism' in the USA. But after 14 years in North Africa, the lure of Tinseltown proved too much and he moved back to Hollywood, where he confirmed his reputation as an important scriptwriter.

Lambert was Oscar-nominated for his screenplay of D H Lawrence's *Sons and Lovers*. He worked with the playwright Tennessee Williams on *The Roman Spring of Mrs Stone* and wrote the script for the film of his own novel, *Inside Daisy Clover* (1963). Natalie Wood took the title role and Robert Redford was introduced to the big screen as her gay husband – a risqué part back in 1965.

Lambert's best work deals with the underbelly of the film industry. *The Slide Area* (1954), reissued in 1998 by Serpent's Tail, is set in Hollywood's Pacific Palisades, where the land could slide into the ocean at any time – hence the signs by the roadside which read 'slide area'. But what's really on the slide in Lambert's 1959 classic are the souls of his protagonists. Christopher Isherwood, another British expat in Hollywood, described *The Slide Area* as 'the most truthful stories about the film world and its suburbia I have ever read. How I wish I had written this book.' The eminent film critic Dilys Powell designated it 'the best book about Hollywood'. Summarising Lambert's output (his other novels are *Running Time* and *The Goodbye People*), Armistead Maupin wrote that 'decades before it was fashionable, Gavin Lambert expertly wove characters of every sexual stripe into his lustrous tapestries of Southern California life...His elegant, stripped-down prose caught the last gasp of Old Hollywood in

a way that has yet to be rivalled.' This is a fitting tribute from another author who has clearly been influenced by Lambert's elegantly cool yet also coyly camp writing style.

Lambert's non-fiction includes *On Cukor* and *The Dangerous Edge*, biographies of Norma Shearer and Alla Nazimova, and a memoir of the late Lindsay Anderson.

MUST READ *The Goodbye People, Inside Daisy Clover, The Slide Area*
READ ON Armistead Maupin, **Vladimir Nabokov, Budd Schulberg**

Ring Lardner

1885–1933
The sad sportsdesk cynic

Born in Niles, Michigan, Ringgold Wilmer Lardner studied engineering briefly in Chicago and worked as a book-keeper and clerk before joining the *South Bend Times* in 1905. In 1910 he was editing the *Sporting News* in St Louis, and from 1913 to 1916 became a popular columnist on the *Chicago Tribune*. Celebrated as a sportswriter, especially for his baseball writing, he started writing cynically humorous and misanthropic stories, which were published in the *Saturday Evening Post* in 1914 and collected in *You Know Me Al* (1916), *Own Your Own Home* (1919) and *How to Write Short Stories* (1924).

< 169 >

His disillusionment with baseball began with the infamous Black Sox scandal in 1919, when the Chicago White Sox were bribed by gamblers to throw the World Series – an incident immortalised in F Scott Fitzgerald's *The Great Gatsby*. Lardner himself was depicted in print in Fitzgerald's *Tender is the Night*, and eventually on screen in John Sayles's 1988 film *Eight Men Out*, featuring Sayles himself as Lardner, and 'guerrilla journalist' Studs Terkel.

By the twenties Lardner was writing stories for *Cosmopolitan* magazine; by 1927 his popularity was so high they were paying him $4,500 a story, making him the most highly paid short-story writer in America. In spite of his success, Lardner was frequently despondent and already drinking self-destructively. A fellow author and friend, Elizabeth Hardwick, put her finger on this strange disparity when she said, 'He came from a charming, talented family and married a woman he loved. He was kind, reserved, hard-working; his fictional world is loud, cruel, filled with desperate marriages, hideous old age, suburban wretchedness, fraud, drunkenness.' When asked once to name the ten loveliest words in the English language he included wretch, mange, scram and gangrene in his choice. Despite adding a successful Broadway play to his achievements (*June Moon*, 1929) Lardner was still depressed and asked his collaborator George Kaufman if his intended suicide would hurt the play's box office sales. In 1933, tuberculosis and alcoholism finally com-

bined to rule out the need for suicide.

MUST READ *Own Your Own Home, You Know Me Al*
READ ON F Scott Fitzgerald, **Dorothy Parker, Nathanael West**

Sheridan Le Fanu
1814–1873
Victorian Gothic master

Related by marriage to the dramatist Richard Sheridan, Le Fanu was educated at Trinity College, Dublin, where he read law. Although called to the Irish Bar in 1839, he abandoned the legal profession for journalism, publishing poems and stories in the *Dublin University Magazine*, an important periodical that later printed early verse by Oscar Wilde. In 1858 Le Fanu's wife died, having suffered for seven years from nervous depression, and he was devastated. His habitual shyness hardened into reclusiveness, and, coupled with his now nocturnal lifestyle, earned him the nickname 'the Invisible Prince', a title that might have come from one of his stories. Henceforth, madness featured in most of his work, notably the connection between the supernatural and the ghosts and demons that inhabit people's minds. His celebrated collection *In a Glass Darkly* (1872), featured not only the classic vampire story

< 170 >

'Carmilla' (a huge influence on Bram Stoker's *Dracula*, 1897, replete with lesbianism, an aberration so inconceivable, Queen Victoria refused to believe it existed) but also 'Green Tea', in which the victim, a Reverend Jennings, is pursued by an evil spirit until he kills himself. Le Fanu refused to reveal whether it came from some arcane world or the priest's deluded brain. M R James, a distinguished ghost story writer, and one influenced by Le Fanu, wrote of the supernatural tale: 'It is not amiss sometimes to leave a loophole for a natural explanation, but…let the loophole be so narrow as not to be quite practicable.' Many of the tales from *In a Glass Darkly* featured this loophole, in order to (as academic and editor Robert Tracy has stated) 'tease us with its failure to reassure. There are demons in Le Fanu's world. We cannot always see them, but when we do, they take shape from our guilt, or from our obsessive fears.'

MUST READ *In a Glass Darkly*.
READ ON M R James, John Polidori, **Anne Rice, Bram Stoker**

L IS FOR LONDON
5 alternative tours of the capital's byways

ABSOLUTE BEGINNERS
Colin MacInnes
in at the start of Swinging London

DOWNRIVER
Iain Sinclair
frenetic experimental tour of London past and present

ADRIFT IN SOHO
Colin Wilson
50s literary life in bohemian London

IN SEARCH OF THE CRACK
Robert Elms
looking for the spice of life in 80s–style W1

RED LONDON
Stewart Home
post–pulp speed, sex and violence in the metropolis

L
a reader's guide

Elmore Leonard

1925–
Short titles, great dialogue

Elmore John Leonard, born in New Orleans, lived in Dallas, Oklahoma City and Memphis before settling in Detroit in 1935. After serving in the navy, he studied English literature at the University of Detroit where he entered a short-story competition. From 1949, he worked as an advertising copywriter and also wrote stories and novels, mainly Westerns, for the pulp and pocketbook market.

Having sold a novel, *Hombre*, to Hollywood in 1966, he began to write full-time, producing Westerns and thrillers. None performed spectacularly, although some were filmed (notably *Valdez is Coming*, 1968, starring Burt Lancaster). Churning out unsuccessful bread-line novels to support his family, Leonard soon took the customary American writer's route to alcoholism. In the book *The Courage to Change*, a collection of essays by reformed drunks, he wrote: 'Not until the very end did I drink before noon. Noon was always that magic time when it became all right…Hangovers never bothered me because all I had to do was drink a few ice-cold beers or a real hot, spicy bloody mary and I was back.'

Leonard finally eschewed horses and hooch to produce a series of crime novels set in Detroit and Florida, all with snappy one-word titles, in which dialogue and pace took precedence over plot. *Swag* (1975), *Stick* (1983), *Glitz* (1985), and *Bandits* (1982) were all bestsellers and most were filmed. His novel *Get Shorty* (1990) was screened with much critical and commercial success. Leonard spurned the conventional 'good guy/bad guy' theme for confrontations between flawed, well-meaning men and violent, if amusing, opportunists. His Westerns had a similar, though less popular approach. *Forty Lashes Less One* even had an Indian and a black as protagonists. This was too radical for most John Wayne fans, as Leonard discovered: 'People said my Westerns were too grim, didn't have enough blue sky in them, no romance.'

The best aspect of Leonard's work, however, is the dialogue, which reflects the years he spent hanging around the bars and streets of Detroit. He has a perfect ear for the (mainly black) rhythms of Motor City speech. Long-term fan Quentin Tarantino admitted to copying the style of *Pulp Fiction*'s dialogue from Leonard's work and his film, *Jackie Brown*, was the best-received adaptation of a Leonard novel (*Rum Punch*, 1992) yet. His recent novel *Cuba Libre* (1998) is to be filmed by the Coen Brothers. After 40 years, Leonard has finally arrived.

MUST READ *Get Shorty, Rum Punch*
READ ON Charles Williams, **Charles Willeford**, Laurence Shames, **Carl Hiaasen**

< 172 >

Doris Lessing

1919–
The Angry Young Woman

Doris Tayler Lessing is the daughter of a British army officer who was serving in Persia (Iran) when she was born. In 1924 the family moved to the British colony of Rhodesia (Zimbabwe) in southern Africa, and Doris was brought up in Salisbury (Harare) and on the family farm, where she read voraciously and started to write her own fiction. After two failed marriages, Doris Lessing (she abandoned the children from her first 'uncooked' marriage and kept the surname of her second husband) left Rhodesia to come to London in 1949, carrying with her an insomniac small son and the manuscript of *The Grass is Singing*.

While in Salisbury, Lessing had helped to found a non-racial party of the left, and her writing has always contained strong elements of socialism and feminism. *The Grass is Singing* (1950) is a fictional study of white colonialists and their doomed domination over Africa – a theme which also figures in the short-story collection *This Was the Old Chief's Country* (1951). In the following year Lessing published the first in a quintet of novels with the collective title *The Children of Violence* (*Martha Quest*, 1952; *A Proper Marriage*, 1954; *A Ripple From the Storm*, 1958; *Landlocked*, 1965; and *The Four-Gated City*, 1969), exploring social issues and the

problems of contemporary consciousness. In 1957 Lessing was the only woman in a prestigious anthology of essays, *Declaration*, written by Angry Young Men such as John Osborne and Colin Wilson. In her contribution she attacked the existentialism of Wilson and others. Together with film-maker Lindsay Anderson she posited political engagement rather than the celebration of alienation, although by this time, following the invasion of Hungary in 1956, she had ended her brief dalliance with the Communist Party. Lessing's continued interest in politics is evident in her most recent work, such as the prizewinning novel *The Good Terrorist* (1985) and *The Fifth Child* (1987).

During the sixties and early seventies Lessing was best known for two fictional accounts of mental collapse (*The Golden Notebook*, 1962; *Briefing for a Descent Into Hell*, 1971), which challenged the traditional distinction between sanity and insanity (a similar line of questioning was being pursued at the time by the charismatic 'anti-psychiatrist' R D Laing). *The Golden Notebook* was hailed as a landmark in the evolution of the feminist novel. Lessing has also used the science fiction genre as a platform from which to speculate on philosophical questions. Her sequence of sci-fi novels (she prefered the term 'space fiction'), *Canopus in Argos: Archives*, contains five titles: *Shikasta* (1979), *The Marriages between Zones Three, Four and Five* (1980), *The Sirian Experiments* (1981), *The Making of the Representative for Planet 8* (1982), and *The*

Sentimental Agents in the Volyen Empire (1983).

Her other work includes poetry; short stories; five novellas published under the title *Five* in 1954, the autobiographical account of her arrival in London, *In Pursuit of the English* (1960), and the plays *Each His Own Wilderness* and *Play with a Tiger*. During the fifties Lessing was championed by the *Sunday Times* reviewer C P Snow for eschewing stylistic experimentation and continuing to write in the traditional narrative form. Other commentators have cited this as grounds for criticism. But in her ideas, if not in the form in which she expresses them, Lessing has never stopped experimenting.

In 1997 Lessing published the second volume of her autobiography, *Walking in the Shade*, which ends in 1962. Volume one, *Under My Skin* (1994), was praised by Hilary Mantel as 'her greatest work of art'. She has said she will not write a third volume because she cannot name names.

MUST READ *The Golden Notebook, The Good Terrorist, Under My Skin*
READ ON Pat Cadigan, Emma Goldman, Germaine Greer, Katherine Mansfield

< 174 >

L IS FOR LOSING IT
5 novels about cracking up

THE BELL JAR
Sylvia Plath
a successful young woman's
breakdown in 1950s New York

ONE FLEW OVER THE CUCKOO'S NEST
Ken Kesey
lunatics take over the asylum in a
parable of modern America

CATCHER IN THE RYE
J D Salinger
classic adolescent angst over a
winter weekend in 1950s Manhattan

BRIEFING FOR A DESCENT INTO HELL
Doris Lessing
a personal account of a descent
into madness

THE TRICK IS TO KEEP BREATHING
Janice Galloway
claustrophobic tale of succumbing to
a dark depression

Ted Lewis

1940—1982
British and brutal

Born in the northern industrial city of Manchester, Ted Lewis spent four years at art college in Hull before going into advertising. He later worked on films (including the Beatles' *Yellow Submarine*) and television programmes as a specialist in animation. As a writer he specialised in gangster novels which were peculiarly British and brutal – an unusual combination in the days when British crime writers either set their stories in the USA or sounded like Agatha Christie.

Lewis made his debut with *All the Way Home and All the Night Through* (1965), followed by *Plender* (1971), *Billy Rags* (a gritty tale of lifelong criminal Billy Cracken, 1973), *Jack Carter's Law* (1974), *The Rabbit* (1975), *Boldt* (1976), *Jack Carter and the Mafia Pigeon* (1977) and *GBH* (1980). But he is remembered primarily for having written *Jack's Return Home* (1970). The story of a professional hardman returning to an unnamed town near Doncaster to find out who had killed his brother, it was filmed as *Get Carter* (1971) by Mike Hodges with Michael Caine in the sinister but still likeable leading role of Jack Carter. The plotline of *Get Carter* was reprised and reworked in *Radio On* (1979), a road movie directed by Chris Petit and starring Sting of the pretend-punk band The Police, which sought to excavate the dark side of Britain in the seventies just as Lewis's Carter dug into the provincial underbelly of the Sixties sex industry.

Opinion is divided over Lewis: was he a true originator, or did Mike Hodges make a masterful film out of what was only a middling novel? Cult fiction critic John Williams rates Lewis highly. He wrote a posthumous portrait of Lewis for *Arena* magazine, bemoaning his premature death at the age of 42 and identifying him as a forgotten genius.

MUST READ *Billy Rags, Jack's Return Home, Plender*
READ ON *Big Breadwinner Hog* by Robin Chapman, Christopher Petit, **Derek Raymond**

Mark Leyner

1956—
MTV for the printed page

As a child, Mark Leyner wintered in Jersey City and spent his summers in the coastal town of Deal, New Jersey. He decided he wanted to be an 'artist' after seeing the Beatles on television in 1963; at Columbia High School he wrote a column for the school paper and played in a rock'n'roll band. Leyner recalls wanting to sound like Bowie or the New York Dolls, but the other guitarist preferred the Allman

Brothers. In 1972 his poem about Tina Turner was published in *Rolling Stone* magazine; while at college (Brandeis) he began writing fiction. He then moved to Boulder, Colorado to take up a postgraduate writing fellowship (MA, 1979). Back on the East Coast, Leyner worked as an advertising copywriter while compiling what became an acclaimed collection of short stories, *I Smell Esther Williams* (1983). While working on his best-known book, *My Cousin, My Gastroenterologist* (1990), parts of which first appeared in magazines such as *Harper's* and *Esquire*, Leyner again supported himself by copywriting: his oeuvre includes adverts for biodegradable incontinence briefs and artifical saliva. Most of the girls he dated as a youth seem to have gone on to become successful lawyers. In 1984 Leyner married Arleen Portada, a psychotherapist.

Described as 'a cult novel that has been selling like Ray-Bans and reads like the MTV version of a David Lynch script', *My Cousin, My Gastroenterologist* is held together not so much by plot or character as by Leyner's wit and intelligence. Cross-cutting between genres (cyber-sci fi, hard-boiled detective), he mixes in cultural trivia and literary allusion – all at a fast and furious pace. *Rolling Stone* recommended it as 'weird, supercharged prose'. In *Fiction International*, Larry McCaffery concluded that *My Cousin, My Gastroenterologist* 'establishes Mark Leyner as the most intense, and, in a certain sense, the most significant young prose writer in America'. But if this is what constitutes 'significant', what must 'trivial' be like?

MUST READ *I Smell Esther Williams*, *My Cousin, My Gastroenterologist*
READ ON **Donald Barthelme**, Russell Bone, **Douglas Coupland**

Jack London
1876–1916
The great American adventurer

While Jack London was growing up in San Francisco, making a living on the poverty line by means both legal and illegal, the city was growing into the cultural centre of California. But London could not wait to move on. He signed up for the merchant navy (his maritime experiences were recalled in *The Sea Wolf*, 1904, and *The Mutiny of the Elsinore*, 1914) and then joined the gold rush to the Klondyke. His experience of panning for gold in Alaska was recycled in *The Call of the Wild* (1903) and *White Fang* (1906), two books ostensibly written from the point of view of a dog in a sled-team.

Opinion is divided as to whether London's identification with the wilderness makes him the antecedent of the Beats and the Green movement, or whether his writing should be relegated to the schoolroom along with Anna Sewell's *Black Beauty*. This view could perhaps

< 176 >

through the bottom of a bottle, puts him in the same sorry line-up as Jack Kerouac and Charles Bukowski. *Martin Eden* (1909), subtitled *Alcoholic Memoirs*, is an autobiographical novel which, as Malcolm Bradbury has pointed out, tells the story of his own confused idealism, which seems to have combined left-wing theories with Nietzscheanism. *The People of the Abyss* (1903) a documentary of the poverty in London's East End prefigures George Orwell's *Down and Out in Paris and London*.

MUST READ *The Call of the Wild, The Iron Heel, John Barleycorn, Martin Eden*
READ ON Bertolt Brecht, **Malcolm Lowry**, Upton Sinclair, Robert Tressell

Jack London

be confirmed by Jerry of the Islands (1917), a heart-warming (or stomach-churning) tale of an Irish Setter pup in the South Sea Islands. London's stripped-down prose style – in marked contrast to the Latin sentence constructions of his Victorian contemporaries – certainly helps to locate him in the modern world. And the left-wing philosophy underlying his novel of class struggle *The Iron Heel* (1908) has tended to confirm his street-cred; while *John Barleycorn* (1913), the story of his own tendency to see life

H P Lovecraft

1890—1937
A 20th-century Poe

Born in Providence, Rhode Island, Howard Phillips Lovecraft was an only child. When HP was three, his father went insane and was sent to an asylum, where he died five years later. Smothered by his neurotic mother, Lovecraft attended school intermittently. At 18 he was prevented from graduating by a 'nervous collapse'.

Influenced by Poe, Arthur Machen, and the aristocratic fantasy-writer Lord Dunsany, Lovecraft wrote hundreds of stories, many of which were published in *Weird Tales* magazine. In 1924 he married and moved to Brooklyn in New York, the first time he had left Providence. In a story called 'The Horror at Red Hook', he depicted Brooklyn as 'a maze of hybrid squalor…a babel of sound and filth'; in a later story, he described New York in similar terms: 'Garish daylight showed only squalor and alienage and the noxious elephantiasis of spreading stone where the moon had hinted of loveliness and elder magic…and the throngs of people… were squat, swarthy strangers.' Although his wife was of Russian-Jewish extraction, the xenophobic Lovecraft wrote vitriolic passages about 'twisted, ratlike vermin from the ghetto' and 'the organic things – Italo/Semitico/Mongoloid – inhabiting that awful cesspool'. No wonder he didn't like Brooklyn. After travelling to New Orleans and Quebec, though, he grudgingly admitted that 'the French are not bad'. He even became close friends with Jewish writer Robert Bloch, the author of *Psycho*.

After publishing 62 stories, Lovecraft died of intestinal cancer. After his death his work became better known than when he was alive. In the sixties his name was even adopted by a psychedelic guitar band.

Lovecraft's main achievement was the creation of the Cthulhu Mythos, a legend of prehistoric Earth that is featured in many of his stories. He also invented an epic tome called the *Necromicon*, from which he 'quoted' in many of his tales. Numerous fans thought that such a book existed, especially after pranksters smuggled an index card for it into the files of the Yale University Library.

MUST READ *At the Mountains of Madness, The Case of Charles Dexter Ward, Dagon and Other Macabre Tales*
READ ON August Derleth, **Robert E Howard, Edgar Allan Poe**

< 178 >

Malcolm Lowry

1909–1957
Ultra-drinker

Born in Cheshire, probably the richest county in north-west England, Malcolm Lowry (he hated the first name which his parents had given him: Clarence) ran away from school to enlist in the merchant navy and sail on a cargo ship to China. Despite his hasty exit from school, he was accepted by St Catherine's College, Cambridge University, where he completed his degree – and started drinking heavily. Before long Lowry was entirely dependent on alcohol. Twice-married, his personal affairs became increasingly chaotic and he died by choking in his sleep. The coroner recorded a verdict of 'death by misadventure'.

Lowry's better novels draw heavily on the events of his own life. *Ultramarine* is a fictionalised version of his voyage to China, and centres on the young protagonist's frustrated desire to prove his manhood and become accepted by his fellows. It was eventually published in 1933 after Lowry had rewritten it following the theft of the original manuscript. *Under the Volcano* (1947, filmed much later with Albert Finney in the starring role of Geoffrey Firmin) is a life-in-the-day story (appropriately, the day in question is the Day of The Dead) which follows the final hours of a British consul in Mexico, overdosing on a powerful cocktail of hallucinogenic mescal (the local brew) and corrosive self-doubt about his wife, his whole life, and the meaning – if any – of civilisation.

Lowry, who had lived in Central America with his first wife, wrote *Under the Volcano* while in British Columbia with his second spouse. After his death, three further novels were put together from the huge pile of papers that he left behind.

With the possible exception of Patrick Hamilton, there is no finer chronicler of the spiral of self-pity and self-criticism in which the alcoholic often finds himself enmeshed. While with most hard-drinking writers it is true to say that they would have written better without so much recourse to the bottle, in Lowry's case the insights of the former are inextricably linked to the debilitating, and ultimately fatal, effects of the latter: what made him a writer also destroyed him.

MUST READ *Under the Volcano*
READ ON **Brendan Behan**, F Scott Fitzgerald, **Patrick Hamilton**

< 179 >

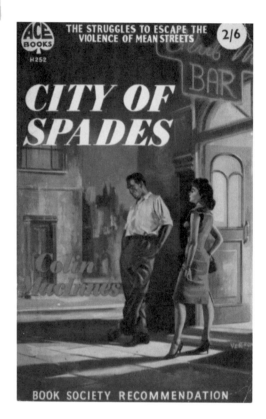

THE STRUGGLES TO ESCAPE THE VIOLENCE OF MEAN STREETS

ACE BOOKS

2/6

H252

CITY OF SPADES

Colin MacInnes

BOOK SOCIETY RECOMMENDATION

Colin MacInnes

1914–1976
The original Cool Britannia

Great-grandson of Sir Edward Burne-Jones (the pre-Raphaelite painter), cousin to Stanley Baldwin (the British PM) and Rudyard Kipling (the novelist of the British Empire), son of writer

Angela Thirkell, Colin MacInnes was born into the Australian branch of what his biographer Tony Gould refers to as a 'Victorian cultural dynasty'. But MacInnes would have none of it. When he moved to London as a young man he gravitated first to the bohemian territory of Soho and then to the new multicultural district of Notting Hill in west London – but this was before 'multiculturalism' had been invented.

In his own lifetime, MacInnes's reputation as a writer rested largely on his non-fiction. He documented the rise of 'the classless class' of youth ('the children's crusade') for the broadsheets and for influential magazines such as *Encounter*. He took up now-fashionable causes before they became so. As a homosexual, MacInnes was always sensitive to the censorship of sexually explicit material on grounds of 'obscenity'. He campaigned to end discrimination against black people; he defended the 'Mangrove Nine' against their police accusers; and he was one of the first intellectuals to put down 'the white man's burden' (of civilising the rest of the world) and declare that the West had a lot to learn from Africa. Such sentiments are commonplace today, and MacInnes must take some credit for their introduction into public debate. To his detractors, however, something of the missionary always remained in MacInnes, albeit in a perverse fashion: while foraging for sex among black men he seems to have behaved almost like a minister in search of converts to his own personal religion.

< 180 >

Nowadays, MacInnes is remembered mainly for his trilogy of London novels, written and published on the cusp of the sixties. *City of Spades* (1957) follows the fortunes of a Nigerian immigrant in London, and is somewhat derivative of Samuel Selvon's seminal novel of black life in the metropolis, *The Lonely Londoners* (1956). The final part MacInnes' trilogy is *Mr Love and Justice* (1960), a tale of policing and poncing; but his best-loved work is *Absolute Beginners* (1959) in which he captures the look, the sound and the overall feel of the first London teen scene as it emerged in Soho's jazz clubs and coffee bars and the decaying Victorian housing stock of Notting Hill. Based on Italian fashion, anti-racism and post-politics, this is 'pop culture' even before pop music became the central element in it.

What makes *Absolute Beginners* so attractive is that MacInnes portrays both the confidence and the nervousness of a generation that knows its time has come. Republished by Allison & Busby in the early eighties, *Absolute Beginners* became a revered part of a new scene revolving around clubs like the Beat Route, coffee bars such as the Bar Italia in Soho's Frith Street, and the *Face* magazine. Starring Patsy Kensit, director Julien Temple's disastrous film (1987) failed to kill it absolutely; MacInnes's novel is now an inspiration to the latest generation of 'cool Britons' who have made Soho their stamping ground.

MUST READ *Absolute Beginners, City of Spades, Inside Outsider* by Gould, *Mr Love and Justice*

READ ON **Richard Allen, Samuel Selvon**, Andrew Sinclair, **Colin Wilson**

Norman Mailer

1923–
A fighter and a writer

Born in New Jersey of Jewish stock and brought up in Brooklyn, Norman Mailer went to Harvard aged 16 and it was there, heavily influenced by the novels of John Dos Passos and Ernest Hemingway, that he decided to become a writer. On the night in 1941 when Japan attacked the American naval base at Pearl Harbor and the USA entered the Second World War, Mailer was wondering whether he would be up to the job of writing the definitive war novel. He was. Based on his own active service in the Pacific, *The Naked and the Dead* (1948) is a biting satire on the military establishment and a vivid rendition of the humanity of those who fought in what Mailer later described as 'a mirror to the human condition which blinded all those who looked into it'. The conventions of the period forced Mailer to hold back on some of the actuality of war, however. In the published version of *The Naked and the Dead*, the word 'fug' – a euphemism for 'fuck' – appears several hundred times.

Although *The Naked and the Dead* was well received, Mailer's second book, *Barbary Shore*

< 181 >

(1952) was derided as a 'socialist' novel (it came out during the Korean War when red-baiting was at its height) and dubbed 'paceless, tasteless and graceless' in its depiction of a sexually impotent orphan, symbolising the powerlessness of the individual against the state. Mailer himself described it as the first existentialist novel set in America. *The Deer Park*, published in 1955 after Mailer had fallen seriously ill and taken up smoking marijuana, is the story of a Hollywood movie director and his ill-fated affair with a younger woman, as told by a cool but confused young narrator named Sergius O'Shaughnessy. It picked up some abominable reviews: 'the year's worst snake pit in fiction', 'sordid and crummy' and 'moronic mindlessness'.

Mailer was a founder and columnist of the first magazine of the counterculture, the *Village Voice*. Around this time he experimented with drugs, group sex and occasional wife-beating. He also acquired a reputation for sorting things out with his fists. In 1957 he wrote *The White Negro*, an illuminating account of the fashion for black styles among whites. In the early sixties Mailer had high hopes of John F Kennedy's Camelot. In *The Presidential Papers* (1963) he tried to make connections between the ethos of the Kennedy administration and his own brand of individuated anarchism, and in *An American Dream* (1965) the hipsterish protagonist has personal connections with the Kennedy crew. After Kennedy's assassination Mailer saw him-

Norman Mailer

self as 'an American Jeremiah', and became something of a thorn in the side of the establishment and its war in Vietnam; although the New Left found him pretty prickly too – especially when he became pugilistic and self-consciously Hemingwayesque. He stood (unsuccessfully) for election to the office of mayor of New York. In 1970 he directed a film, *Maidstone*, in which he starred as himself in the role of an avant-garde film-maker and presidential candidate who has heated debates with all

< 182 >

and sundry. It was dismissed as '110 minutes of pure Megalomailer'.

In 1971 Mailer attracted the ire of the women's movement, and feminist author Kate Millett in particular, with an essay on sex and violence entitled 'The Prisoner of Sex' (on one occasion he is reported to have said that violence prevents cancer). In 1979 he won the Pulitzer Prize for the second time: he had already won it in 1968 with *Armies of the Night*, a factional account of the anti-war march on Washington in 1967, with the author as the main character in the story – indicative of Mailer's readiness to make himself the star of his own writing and also illustrative of his ambitions for 'the novel as history, history as novel'. Mailer's second prizewinner was *The Executioner's Song*, a gargantuan account of the life and crimes of the convicted murderer Gary Gilmore (whose execution was also described in a song by the punk band The Adverts). *Ancient Evenings* (1983) is another huge book, this time a novel. *Tough Guys don't Dance* (1984) is a thriller – filmed in 1987, it was described by one critic as 'a conservatoire of false notes'; *Harlot's Ghost* (1991) is a spy novel – if that is an adequate description of a mammoth, fictionalised description of life in the CIA from 1945 to the time of President John F Kennedy's assassination. Mailer's latest novel (1997) is an autobiography of Jesus.

The vigour and vivid character of Mailer's writing is undeniable, although sometimes he seems to be flailing around to no great purpose, and on other occasions he appears to be carried away with his own tough-guy image. But these are minor blemishes on the huge and colourful canvas of an immensely combative writer.

MUST READ *The Executioner's Song, Harlot's Ghost, The Naked and the Dead, The White Negro*
READ ON **Truman Capote, Hunter S Thompson, Gore Vidal**

Dan Mannix

1911–
The carny man

Dan Mannix was expected to follow his father's example (and his grandfather's, and his great-grandfather's) and become an officer in the US navy. However, even as a child he felt like a misfit, partly because of his great height, but also because of his eccentric interests such as witchcraft and folklore. When Mannix left school he told his parents that he was going to become a witchdoctor; they enlisted him in the US naval academy.

After a year Mannix could stick it no more. He walked out of the naval academy and registered as a student at the University of Pennsylvania, aiming to become a professional writer. When he sold an article to the *Saturday*

< 183 >

M IS FOR THE MUSIC BIZ

5 novels about the rock'n'roll life

EXPRESSO BONGO
Wolf Mankowitz
scuffling and skiffling in the
coffee-bar craze

THE JOHNNY ANGELO SERIES
Nik Cohn
the pills and thrills of pop stardom

PLATINUM LOGIC
Tony Parsons
a story of The Biz by the NME's young
gunslinger

ESPEDAIR STREET
Iain Banks
former songwriter's account of a
70s rock band

GREAT JONES STREET
Don DeLillo
fear and self-loathing in the record
industry

< 184 >

Evening Post he thought he was on his way, but this proved something of a false start, and when Mannix left college he still had no clear idea of what he was going to do with his life. Almost by accident he joined a 'carny' or travelling circus and spent the next three years crossing America and learning how to be a fire-eater and sword-swallower. The first time he tried fire-eating he blistered his mouth so badly he could not eat for days; he later learnt to ram lit-up neon tubes down his gullet so that he glowed in the dark.

Mannix began recording his 'carny' experiences in a series of articles for *Collier's* magazine. He then collected and adapted these into a book, a fictionalised autobiographical piece entitled *Memoirs of a Sword Swallower*. This was enough to launch him as a professional writer. As well as writing articles and making films about wildlife, he went on to produce a biography of Aleister Crowley, *The Beast*, a book about the 18th-century reprobates known as the Hellfire Club, and the bestselling novel *Those About to Die*. He lives on a farm in Pennsylvania, not that far away from the city of his birth (Philadelphia).

Mannix's best book is *Memoirs of a Sword Swallower*. From its opening line ('I probably never would have become America's leading fire-eater if Flamo the Great hadn't happened to explode that night in front of Krinko's Great Combined Carnival Side Shows'), it is a witty and compelling tale of carnival life. It is also redolent of a young man's search for a place where he can feel relaxed, away from his strait-laced family: Mannix's carnival is where would-be counterculturists could go before there was any such thing as a counterculture.

MUST READ *The Beast, Memoirs of a Sword Swallower*
READ ON Joseph Conrad, **Harlan Ellison**, John Masefield

William March

1893—1954
The writer who nearly went to seed

As a schoolboy in Mobile, Alabama, the young William March won prizes and was generally regarded as a talented young man in the making. Suddenly, his father moved the whole family to a small sawmill town out in the sticks; the son resented his forced removal from the prospective life of a Southern gentleman. His resentement was reinforced when his father reputedly burnt one of his early literary efforts and thrashed him for good measure.

March Jnr could not wait to get away from his family. He left home at 16 (later he said that he could never have fallen for the Southern penchant for incest because the members of his family were so ugly), fought and was decorated in the First World War (he subsequently felt the need to exaggerate his war record). He worked his way up through menial office jobs to various executive positions, which he held until the mid-1940s when he turned to writing full time, with financial backup from the stocks and shares he had accumulated previously. During the course of his life March suffered at least two mental breakdowns (one of these occurred while he was a company rep in Berlin). He was interested in the theories of Freud, was wont to talk about everyone else's personal and sexual relations, but never had a relationship with a woman himself (perhaps after being slighted as a boy by a girl named Bessie). All of this has prompted the social critic Elaine Showalter to suggest that March may have been a case of repressed homosexuality.

March's work as a writer is largely unremarkable. He drew on his war experiences in the writing of *Company K. The Little Wife* and the stories in the anthology *Some Like Them Short* have been described as 'Southern Gothic'. The journalist and broadcaster Alistair Cooke was a close friend, and even he admitted that March's literary standing was never very high. He was referred to as a 'third-rate Sherwood Anderson' and known as much for the parties he gave in New York as for his output as a writer. But everything changed in 1954 when March published *The Bad Seed*, the story of a child serial killer named Rhoda Penmark told through the eyes of her mother. The novel, which March seems to have regarded as something of a potboiler, was hailed as the book of

< 185 >

1954 and caused a publishing sensation. Staged on Broadway, the play ran for a year. Filmed by Mervyn Leroy (who gave it a happy ending), *The Bad Seed* terrified audiences across America, who had to be told that it was only fiction, not reality. Sadly, after a lifetime on the margins of the literary scene, March hardly had time to enjoy his long-awaited success. He died before the year of publication was out.

MUST READ *The Bad Seed*
READ ON Stanley Ellin, Henrik Ibsen, Gitta Sereny

Cormac McCarthy

1933–

A hell-fire Melville on horseback

Born in Rhode Island, Charles McCarthy (Cormac is a family nickname), moved with his family to Knoxville, Tennessee and enrolled at the University of Tennessee. He didn't complete his degree, leaving instead to join the US Air Force where he stayed for four years.

McCarthy's first novel *The Orchard Keeper*, started while he was at college, appeared in 1965 and set the pattern for his subsequent work in its Faulknerian tone and evocation of a receding rural America, with the ubiquitous threat of violence. It won the William Faulkner Foundation Award for first novel and an American Arts and Letters Grant which sent him to Europe for two years.

On his return to Knoxville, McCarthy published *Outer Dark*, a cheerful tale of incest, illegitimacy and infanticide that received no awards. Equally gloomy was his third book *Child of God*, about a backwoods serial killer and necrophiliac who hides his victims' corpses in a cave.

In 1976, McCarthy collaborated with director Richard Pearce on a TV movie called *The Gardener's Sow*, about a murder in South Carolina. He wrote another script, which Pearce described as 'very dark, and very difficult', and for which, unsurprisingly, there was no finance forthcoming. Apparently, McCarthy used it as the basis for *Cities of the Plain*, the final part in his acclaimed *Border Trilogy*.

McCarthy's fourth novel *Sutree* offered some clues to his early life in that the protagonist is a man who turns his back on his family and their middle-class world and spends his days in a rotting houseboat on a fetid river, hanging out with drunks, petty crooks and disenfranchised grotesques – 'a fellowship of the doomed, where life pulsed obscenely fecund'.

After *Sutree*, a book which he had been gestating and rewriting for over 20 years, McCarthy's bitterness over his lack of commercial success surfaced, and he moved West to El Paso to write what his ex-wife Annie DeLisle called 'the great Western novel'. In 1981, however, he was awarded the MacArthur Fellowship

< 186 >

(the panel of judges included Saul Bellow, who praised McCarthy for his 'absolutely overpowering use of language, his life-giving and death-dealing sentences'), freeing him from immediate financial constraints.

Blood Meridian was eventually published in 1985, the apocalyptic story of 'the kid', a nameless orphan who has 'a taste for mindless violence', and a work that totally strips the West of any notion of heroism, leaving behind the sense of the utter cheapness of life. Death and violence literally stalk the book, and one critic calculated that a murder is averaged every five pages.

McCarthy's breakthrough came with *All the Pretty Horses*, the first part of his *Border Trilogy*, the story of two young men who saddle up and ride into dark adventures in Mexico. It sold almost 200,000 copies and won among other prizes the National Book Award. It was the book in which McCarthy finally left the shadows of his mentors Faulkner and Melville (apparently McCarthy reads *Moby Dick* eight times a year, possibly one reason why he's a recluse). This reclusive nature has lately made him the subject of Salingeresque speculations and attentions. It was rumoured that he lived enigmatically for many years from day to day out of a suitcase. Journalists have crossed continents to search him out detective-like, yet he refuses all interviews.

Put simply, his masterpiece, *The Border Trilogy*, is little more than a rites of passage adventure underlined by a tragic sense of man as a fallen creature. What excites critics and readers alike to such a state of euphoria is McCarthy's epic use of language on the page. He is a master craftsman, a polisher of fine natural detail and a virtuoso of free-range lyrical description – writing at times with little or no punctuation – with a majesterial tone that lies, as one critic put it, 'somewhere between Melville and God'.

MUST READ *Blood Meridian, All the Pretty Horses*
READ ON **William Faulkner, Herman Melville, Davis Grubb**

Horace McCoy
1897–1955
Tinseltown's dark poet

Born in Nashville to parents whom he described as 'book-rich and money-poor', by 12 Horace McCoy was selling newspapers. At 16 he left school to become, variously, a mechanic, travelling salesman and cab driver. During the First World War he flew several missions behind enemy lines as a bombardier and reconnaissance photographer, was wounded and received the Croix de Guerre. In a letter to his parents he wrote: 'I love a battle, and am willing to go anywhere to get into one.' After the war he settled for dreaming up dogfights and selling them as

< 187 >

stories to pulp magazines such as *Battle Aces* and *Man Stories*. In 1927 *Black Mask* published the first of 17 McCoy stories, all featuring tough, Hemingwayesque prose.

As an out-of-work writer and actor in Hollywood during the Depression (in his own words: 'a road bum'), McCoy gathered the material for his first novel *They Shoot Horses, Don't They?* (1935), the story of a dance marathon and two of its participants. Gloria looks forward to death as a release from the hard labour of life, and her partner Robert finally grants her wish. McCoy's text is both nihilistic and socially aware. Sartre, de Beauvoir and others welcomed it as the first existential novel to come out of America (Albert Camus reserved this accolade for James M Cain's *The Postman Always Rings Twice*; but McCoy always disliked comparisons between his work and Cain's.) Sydney Pollack's film, made in 1969 with Jane Fonda starring (and the inspiration for a song of the same name by the seventies band Racing Cars), is slightly softened and has been described as the 'Hollywood chic view of the Depression'.

McCoy's second novel, *No Pockets in a Shroud* (1948), draws on his experience as a newspaperman to tell the story of a doomed attempt to launch a magazine that tells the stories other papers will not print. *I Should Have Stayed at Home* (1938) follows two Hollywood extras in their desperate efforts to climb the greasy pole to stardom. It also includes a por-

trait of McCoy as Johnny Hill, a studio publicist and budding writer. By this time (1938), McCoy was a successful scenarist and respected novelist, but his involvement in 'the whoring' and 'bottomless muck' of Hollywood ('a cheap town filled with cheap stories and cheap people') filled him with self-loathing and he considered himself a failure. His final novel, *Kiss Tomorrow Goodbye* (1948), is ostensibly about gangsters but is really an allegory for the criminal and morally degraded film industry.

For some, McCoy is just too twisted. The *Saturday Review* lambasted *I Should Have Stayed at Home* as a 'bitter, name-calling novel'. *Time* magazine described *Kiss Tomorrow Goodbye* as 'one of the nastiest novels ever published in this country' and dismissed its author as 'a literary caveman'. But McCoy's depiction of the human flotsam swept along by the tide of the Depression has probably never been bettered. He died of a heart attack, aged 58.

MUST READ *I Should Have Stayed at Home, They Shoot Horses, Don't They?*
READ ON **James M Cain, David Goodis,** John Steinbeck

Carson McCullers

1917–1967
Belle of the Southern Gothic ball

Carson McCullers was born in Georgia, also the birthplace of Harry Crews, although her social station was much more elevated than his. She left the South to attend classes at Columbia and New York University (she had intended to study music at the Juilliard school but managed to lose the money set aside for her tuition). After a brief stay in North Carolina, she moved back to New York to live in the bohemian district of Greenwich Village. Her relationship with lifelong partner Reeves McCullers was loving but fraught: they were twice married and twice divorced (he committed suicide after their second parting; she wrote the bitter-sweet comedy *The Square Root of Wonderful* (1958) in an attempt to expiate these experiences). McCullers's facial features were delicate, and so was her health. Throughout her life, she suffered from bouts of illness; after withstanding a number of strokes she finally succumbed to cancer and a brain haemorrhage.

McCullers's first novel, *The Heart is a Lonely Hunter* (1940), is about a deaf mute who becomes confidante to a number of disturbed individuals. The latter only realise his worth after he commits suicide. Well-received when it came out, it was widely interpreted as an anti-fascist book. In 1968 it was filmed with Alan Arkin in the lead role.

Throughout her literary career, McCullers continued to combine 'anguish and farce'. These elements are discernible in *Reflections in a Golden Eye* (1941, filmed with a twinkling sense of humour by John Huston in 1967 with Marlon Brando and Elizabeth Taylor in the starring roles), which describes various illicit sexual activities on an army base in the South. They are also evident in *The Member of the Wedding* (1946), which describes in detail the loneliness of a young girl at her brother's wedding; *The Ballad of the Sad Cafe* (1951); and *Clock without Hands* (1961), which depicts the race question in the South.

All McCullers's novels are elegantly written, with a well-trained eye for evocative detail. Her oeuvre is often described as 'Southern Gothic', but it is surely significant that her novels about the South were written after she herself had left it behind. It is as if the South was more distinctive as a virtual presence in McCullers's mind's eye than it was in reality. In this respect, her work is not unlike Evelyn Waugh's *Brideshead Revisited* (1945, written around the same time as McCullers's prolix period): an ambiguous elegy to a world that was fast disappearing, if indeeed it ever existed at all.

MUST READ *Reflections in a Golden Eye, The Heart is a Lonely Hunter*
READ ON **Harry Crews, William Faulkner,** Mark Twain, Evelyn Waugh, Eudora Welty

M

Ian McEwan

1948–
Poet of the perverse

Born in the southern English garrison town of Aldershot, Ian McEwan went to Sussex University during the days of student radicalism, and afterwards to the University of East Anglia, where he attended the postgraduate course in creative writing soon after it was established by Malcolm Bradbury. His first collection of short stories, *First Love, Last Rites*, won the Somerset Maugham Award in 1976, only six years after McEwan started writing. It also attracted controversy for its cool study of obsession and sexual perversion, as did McEwan's second book of short stories, *In Between the Sheets* (1978) and his first novel, *The Cement Garden* (1979).

The Comfort of Strangers (1981) is another elegant but chilling story, this time of a young English couple (Colin and Mary) who are at a loose end in Venice until they come under the psychological influence of a mysterious but menacing ex-pat called Robert. The novel was nominated for the Booker Prize and subsequently filmed by Paul Schrader, with a masterful rendition of Robert by a mask-faced Christopher Walken. McEwan also wrote the screenplay for *The Ploughman's Lunch* (1983), a topical but ultimately unsatisfying film about life in Thatcher's Britain.

In more recent work such as *The Child in Time* (1987; about coping with loss after the kidnapping of a child), *The Innocent* (1990; a story of the Cold War published a year after it had ended with the fall of the Berlin Wall in 1989) and *Black Dogs* (1992), McEwan seems to be striving for greater emotional depth. But some readers seem to prefer the perversity of his earlier work, even if at times it borders on gimmickry.

In 1997, after a five-year lay-off, McEwan published *Enduring Love* – a novel of erotomania in which a 28-year-old drifter forms a morbidly intense attachment to the book's narrator, a science journalist, after they both witness a terrible accident. Compared by some critics to the work of film director Alfred Hitchcock, McEwan's writing aims for what he himself once described as 'an exceptional visual clarity, like a super-realist painting'. In *Enduring Love* he also experimented with comic writing.

McEwan is a voracious reader of science books: he believes that the best writer who is also a practising scientist is the Harvard biologist E O Wilson. McEwan's 1998 novel *Amsterdam*, an ingeniously-plotted but slight tale of a death-pact gone wrong, won him the Booker Prize.

MUST READ *Black Dogs, The Cement Garden, The Comfort of Strangers*
READ ON Malcolm Bradbury, **Paul Bowles**

< 190 >

Patrick McGrath

1950–
Knowing Gothic pastiche

McGrath's background reads like one of his stories. He was born in London, and his father was medical superintendent at Broadmoor (mental) Hospital. Asylums and sanatoria have become the main stages on which his evocative tales of sexual obsession, madness and evil are played out. McGrath has lived in various parts of the USA and, for many years, on a remote island in the North Pacific. In 1981 he moved to New York, the setting for some of the stories featured in his first book, *Blood and Water* (1989).

The Grotesque, his next novel, was a brilliant parody of an English country house horror story. The character of Fledge, the butler, was so impressively malignant that Sting promptly snapped up the film rights just so he could play him. Despite McGrath's screenplay, the film, which also starred Trudie Styler, aka Mrs Sting, was swiftly consigned to straight-to-video limbo. Jeanette Winterson declared of this novel: 'McGrath's roots are in Poe but his imagination inhabits some bestial Hell where Swift and Baudelaire run the butcher's shop.'

In addition to his own upbringing lending itself to a Gothic sensibility, McGrath seems to have immersed himself in every primary Gothic source available, not to mention the wealth of modern literary and psychological commentary, to construct his neo-Gothic world. To call it pastiche is not to debase it: his books are intelligent and knowing, but never smothered by their knowledge. They are invariably immaculately pitched – sensual yet psychologically harrowing – and as rich as any original of the genre.

Alongside all the blood and lunacy that usually dwell in his books, there is often the theme of obsessive love. Add to this a liking for unreliable narrators, as well as a pulsing vein of mordant black humour, all set against an evocative backdrop of an austere England in either the Victorian era, the thirties or the fifties, and you have the classic McGrath recipe. The recipe is followed to good effect in his two latest novels, *Dr Haggard's Disease* (1992) and *Asylum* (1995).

MUST READ *Dr Haggard's Disease, The Grotesque*
READ ON **Sheridan Le Fanu**, Bradford Morrow, **Edgar Allan Poe**

< 191 >

Thomas McGuane

1941–
Satirist of the New West

McGuane was educated at Michigan State University, Yale School of Drama and Stanford University. His first novel, *The Sporting Club* (1969), set a pattern for the next two books, with its Hemingwayesque hero and use of Western ingredients: disaffected loners, who can be provocatively antisocial and often violent, struggling to make some sense of their lives.

McGuane wrote a screenplay for his next book, *The Bushwacked Piano* (1971), but it was never filmed. The 1973 novel *92 in the Shade* was filmed, however, and McGuane also directed. The *Time Out Film Guide* described it as 'one of the most enjoyable messes ever to be suppressed as unsaleable…McGuane here exhibits a totally appealing incompetence as director.' The film featured *Easy Rider* star Peter Fonda (presumably fairly comfortable with chaotic working methods) and actress Margot Kidder, whom McGuane both married and divorced in 1976.

Although he never strayed behind a camera again, he also wrote the screenplays for *Rancho Deluxe* (1975), *The Missouri Breaks* (1976; starring Marlon Brando and Jack Nicholson, and brilliantly scripted) and *Tom Horn*. Initially to be directed by whizz kid record producer James William Guercio, this was completed by one William Wiard. McGuane's script was endlessly rewritten, and the star, Steve McQueen, was dying of cancer. Other than that, it was a fine Western. *Cold Feet* was co-scripted with his friend, author Jim Harrison, and starred Keith Carradine, Tom Waits and Rip Torn.

Once McGuane's film career was on hold, he produced several more novels, including *Something to be Desired* (1984), *Keep the Change* (1989) and *Nothing But Blue Skies* (1993), his most comic work even though it was about loss and madness. His writing has been consistently acclaimed, with the critic L E Sissman claiming that he 'shares with Céline a genius for seeing the profuse, disparate materials of everyday life as an organised nightmare'.

MUST READ *The Bushwacked Piano, Nothing But Blue Skies*
READ ON **James Crumley, Jim Harrison,** Ernest Hemingway, Larry McMurtry

Jay McInerney

1955–
Salinger of the eighties bratpack

Before becoming a New York celeb (McInerney's early career was a classically staged piece of eighties hype – the novelist as a star), McInerney worked as a reader at Random House, as well as a fact-finder on the *New Yorker* – an occupation shared by the narrator of

< 192 >

his first novel, *Bright Lights, Big City* (1984). The book, written notably in the second person, launched the young, hip McInerney as a perfect mixture of F Scott Fitzgerald's doomed romanticism, (replace the decadent twenties with the meretricious eighties and the cocktail with coke) and Hunter Thompson-style drug-fuelled high jinks. In his wake came a wave of young disaffected urban writers: Bret Easton Ellis, Tama Janowitz, Lorrie Moore.

Fuelled by endless supplies of 'Bolivian Marching Powder', the nameless narrator of *Bright Lights, Big City* has everything: a good job, marriage to a gorgeous model ('the face that launched a thousand trips to Bloomingdales'), and a life in the fast lane, but eventually he discovers he has nothing. The book was filmed in 1988, with McInerney's screenplay, and starred the hopelessly miscast Michael J Fox.

With one exception (his second novel, *Ransom*, 1985, set in Japan), all McInerney's books have featured (at least in part) New York, drugs, and modern cynics. *Story of My Life* (1988) is a first-person, female version of *Bright Lights*, chronicling the directionless, coke-fuelled social life of leisured rich-kid Alison Poole. *Brightness Falls* (1992) has moved on from twentynothings to thirtysomethings and centres on a New York publishing house during the hostile takeover bids of the moneyed eighties. *The Last of the Savages* (1996) broke the mould somewhat, in that as well as drugs, cynicism, etc. it featured politics and music

(McInerney is a fan of old rhythm and blues; *Bright Lights* is the title of a Jimmy Reed song), whereas his latest novel, *Model Behavior* (1998), is about a NYC model and her long-suffering boyfriend.

The best of McInerney is enlivened by a keen irony, a sense of humour and a generous quota of one-liners: 'Her voice…is like the New Jersey State Anthem played through an electric shaver.'

MUST READ *Bright Lights, Big City, Brightness Falls, Story of My Life*
READ ON **Brett Easton Ellis**, F Scott Fitzgerald, David Handler

Gustav Meyrink

1868–?
Occult expressionist

Born Gustav Meyer (later Meyrink) in Vienna, the illegitimate son of Baron Karl Varnbuler von und zu Hemmingen, minister of state for Wurttemburg, and Maria Meyer, a Bavarian actress, Gustav Meyer was educated in Munich, Hamburg and Prague. He joined the Meyer and Morgenstern bank in Prague, and became a director. He attempted suicide in 1891, and immersed himself in occultism, joining the Theosophical Lodge of the Blue Star. Over the next few years, Meyrink studied the cabala (ancient Jewish Mysticism), and investigated freemasonry, yoga, alchemy and hashish.

Following a vision in Moldau (apparently, all his writing was the result of visionary experiences), he wrote his first story, 'The Burning Soldier' while recovering from an illness in a Dresden tuberculosis sanatorium, and later published the collection of that name in 1903.

As a result of his flirtation with Philomena Bernt, a banker's daughter, Meyrink (a married man), fought a series of duels with several officers of a Prague regiment; at the same time he was thought to be directing his bank's affairs using financial advice from the spirit world. Money was missing and he was imprisoned, his incarceration leading to temporary paralysis. Eventually he was released but ruined.

He published his masterpiece, *The Golem*, in 1915, basing it on an ancient Yiddish legend. The fantasy writer Jorge Luis Borges revered the book, praising it accordingly: 'Gustav Meyrink uses this legend…in a dreamlike setting on the Other Side of the Mirror and he has invested it with a horror so palpable that it has remained in my memory all these years.' It was filmed four times, twice by Paul Wegener, the only surviving print being Wegener's second version – the 1920s classic of German expressionist cinema.

While working on the novel, Meyrink translated the complete works of Charles Dickens into German, a colossal labour which must have influenced his own work, as novelist Robert Irwin noted: 'Dickens' taste for city life, for grotesque characters, and heightened sentiment

< 194 >

was Meyrink's too and is patent in *The Golem*.'

MUST READ   *The Golem*
READ ON   **Franz Kafka, Edgar Allan Poe, Mary Shelley**

Martin Millar

1959—
The P G Wodehouse of the Brixton squat

Tattooed (discreetly), and bedecked with earrings, Martin Millar is the godfather of grunge literature. His characters are creative, idiosyncratic individuals who were simply not built for a lifetime of mind-numbing work. Instead, they get by as best they can, scamming this and making the occasional bundle out of that, in the manner of what has been dubbed 'the giro generation' (from the practice of living off the welfare). Set in riot torn Brixton, the eponymous protagonist of *Lux the Poet* (1988) tries to do all right by his girlfriend Pearl but gets caught up in a right-wing genetic conspiracy. The main character in *Milk, Sulphate and Alby Starvation* (1987) is a sympathetic dealer. *Dreams of Sex and Stage Diving* (1994) focuses on a tomboyish female called Elfish. All five of Millar's novels are populated by the kind of people who moved to Brixton because it was relatively cheap to live there, and then discovered they could not afford to move out. Millar has been compared to Tom Sharpe and Geoffrey Chaucer. The most frustrating aspect of his characters is that they seem to think they are experimental and way-out, when in fact their chosen lifestyle is extremely mannered and self-limiting. In this respect, Millar might accurately be described as the P G Wodehouse of the squat-punk scene in Brixton.

MUST READ *Lux the Poet, Milk, Sulphate and Alby Starvation*
READ ON Nicholas Blincoe, **Damon Runyan**, Tom Sharpe, P G Wodehouse

Henry Miller

1891–1980
Celebrant of sex and sensuality

Born of American-German parents, Henry Valentine Miller grew up in Brooklyn and later recalled: 'From five to ten were the most important years of my life; I lived in the street and acquired the typical American gangster spirit.' After two months at New York City College, he left and worked for a cement company, before travelling around Alaska and the south-west, financing himself with the money intended for his university career. Working briefly in his father's tailoring workshop, he left after trying to unionise the workforce. He also worked as a ranch-hand, a bellhop and a garbage collector.

Henry Miller

Eventually he became employment manager at the Western Union Telegraph Company, a position that provided him with a rich vein of anecdotes which he used to good effect in *Tropic of Capricorn* (1939), and *Sexus* (1949), *Plexus* (1953), and *Nexus* (1960), which jointly comprise his trilogy *The Rosy Crucifixion*.

Miller's writing is always about himself; moreover, it is nearly always about his struggle to free himself from the world of bourgeois respectability and enter a new kind of existence in which a man can feel truly alive. Ironically, it was a woman who prompted him to make this attempt.

Of his five marriages, the most significant was his second, to June Mansfield Smith (portrayed, along with Miller, in the 1990 film *Henry and June*). She convinced him to become a writer and to move to Europe. Stepping off the career-ladder for good and embarking on a lifetime of self-discovery, Miller extricated himself from moneygrubbing America, went to Paris and entered into a well-documented affair with Anaïs Nin. This was the beginning of a life of material poverty and sexual abundance, as described in *Tropic of Cancer* (1934; an erotic tour-de-force that was lauded by the likes of Beckett, Eliot and Pound), published in Paris and banned everywhere else.

In 1940, Miller moved back across the Atlantic to California, but continued to write about Paris (*Quiet Days in Clichy*, 1956) and New York (*Black Spring*, 1936; *The Rosy Crucifixion*). His time came in the sixties: his books finally became available and he was feted as a pioneer of the counterculture. In the seventies Kate Millett and other members of the women's movement accused him of misogyny.

Miller always thought of himself as an outsider. He once remarked: 'All my life I have felt a great kinship with the madman and the criminal.' Self-obsessed but always honest, Miller's ecstatic appetite for the joys of life is usually infectious and only occasionally irritating.

< 196 >

Author and critic Robert Nye said of him: 'Miller is one of the few modern writers who can move a reader to tears, quite simply, by the pressure of his own feeling. He can also communicate and induce in the reader a delicious delight in being alive.' Miller's own personal hero was Walt Whitman, the transcendental poet, celebrant of sensuality and critic of mainstream America.

MUST READ *The Rosy Crucifixion*
READ ON **Charles Bukowski**, Lawrence Durrell, **Jack Kerouac, Anaïs Nin, Fred Exley**

Yukio Mishima

1925—1970
Masochistic militarist

Yukio Mishima was born in the 1920s at a time when Japan was industrialising and militarising simultaneously. But his first book, the autobiographical *Confessions of a Mask* (1949), was published post-Second World War, during the occupation of Japan by the US army. Apart from the peculiarities in his own psychological makeup, this was the historical twist in the tortured life of Mishima, which culminated in 1970 when he had himself ritually beheaded after he and a handful of followers overran a military base and vainly attempted to rouse the troops with nationalist ideology.

Confesssions of a Mask made Mishima a literary luminary at the age of 24. It is a largely autobiographical account of a young man trying to cope with his own homosexual and masochistic fantasies. In its aestheticism and preoccupation with the body (Mishima wished to create for himself a beautiful body that age could not make ugly: he began body-building in 1955, took up kendo in 1959, and in 1966 started to learn karate), it set the tone for Mishima's later novels. In all his work, Mishima couched his obsessions in terms of traditional Samurai (warrior) codes and Confucian philosophy (knowledge through activity rather than contemplation). Ironically, given Mishima's burning desire to re-establish the East in contradistinction to the West and what he saw as its oppressive influence, all over Europe and America at that time young people were picking up on similar themes (in terms of lifestyle and of the body as a medium of expression) but articulating them through very different idioms such as rock'n'roll, Beat literature and fashion. In this respect, the career of Mishima shows that youth culture is truly global, but with local variations that can be highly distinctive. The common ground betwen Mishima's life and the concerns of Western youth is further demonstrated by the movie about him, simply entitled *Mishima* (1986) directed by *Taxi Driver* screenwriter Paul Schrader.

Grafton Books, who published *Confessions of a Mask* in Britain in the seventies, felt it necessary to 'warn the reader that…its final effect is bleak beyond words'. The *Times Literary Supplement* praised it as 'a haunting, hopeless tale, told without self-pity but with true art and with a desperate humour'. Critics might say that if only Mishima had learnt to lighten up and laugh a little more he might even have kept his head.

On the day of his death by seppuku (ritual suicide), Mishima delivered to his publishers the final pages of a four-volume sequence of novels, *The Sea of Fertility*, which encapsulates his vision of the Japanese experience in the 20th century. 'I have put into it', he wrote, 'everything I have felt and thought about life and this world.' Mishima chose the title of his tetralogy because 'it superimposes the image of cosmic nihilism on that of the fertile sea'.

Spring Snow (1968), the first book in the series, is set in the closed circles of Tokyo's Imperial Court in 1912. Its protagonist is caught in the tensions between the old and the new. The following three novels (*Runaway Horses*, 1969; *The Temple of Dawn*, 1970; *Five Signs of a God's Decay*, 1971) continue Mishima's examination of social, aesthetic and moral life in Japan through to the sixties. His other novels are *Thirst for Love* (1950), *Forbidden Colours*, *The Sailor who Fell from Grace with the Sea* (1963), *After the Banquet* (1960), *The Temple of the Golden Pavilion* (1956), *The Sound of Waves* (1954) and *Madame de Sade* (1965). He also wrote five modern No plays.

MUST READ *Confessions of a Mask, The Sailor who Fell from Grace with the Sea, The Sea of Fertility*
READ ON **Kathy Acker, Jean Genet**, Friedrich Nietszche

Michael Moorcock

1939–
Fantasy writer for the Hawkwind generation

Some of Michael Moorcock's earliest memories are of the bombing of London during the Second World War; these memories feature prominently in a long and distinguished literary career. Besides the Blitz, Moorcock is also associated with London in the Swinging Sixties: he did a stint as a blues singer, and later, as Swinging London evolved into psychedelia and hippiedom, Moorcock was involved with the band Hawkwind which included the infamous Lemmy (Motorhead) on bass. He subsequently (1975) made an album entitled *The New Worlds Fair*. Moreover, the protagonist of Moorcock's best-known novels, the Jerry Cornelius series, is a stereotypical sixties swinger, and Moorcock's work as the editor (1964–1971) of 'New Wave' sci-fi magazine *New Worlds* is also regarded as an integral part of the London scene and the flowering of English pop culture.

At school Moorcock hand-produced his own magazines, and wrote his first published story for *Tarzan Adventures* (1955). Under the pseudonym of Desmond Reid, he wrote a thriller for the Sexton Blake Library of crime stories. Moorcock's first sci-fi/fantasy was *The Sundered Worlds*, published in serial form in *SF Adventures and Science Fantasy* in 1962–1963, republished as a book in 1965. He continued to use the format of the heroic fantasy series for many years, during which he produced the Sojan stories, the Erekose sequence, the Elric stories, the Hawkmoon series and the Corum books. Indeed, the 1979 *Encyclopaedia of Science Fiction* suggests that all Moorcock's stories are part of a single meta-series which explores different facets of the 'multiverse' – a term probably borrowed from fellow novelist John Cowper Powys and loosely defined as 'a universe in which multiple alternate realities co-exist, sometimes destroying one another, though never permanently, and in which some of the same cosmic dramas are played and replayed by various characters in various worlds'.

The notion of alternate realities is not so far from another idea that was fashionable in the sixties: 'instantaneity', meaning that reality is not a chronological progression, as (mis)interpreted by the fiction known as rationality, but should be experienced and understood as a rainbow of simultaneously occurring impulses and sensations. Another sixties-style feature of Moorcock's writing is the setting up of a stock character like Jerry Cornelius, just to knock

< 198 >

him down – and set him up again. In other words, Moorcock distances himself ironically from his own characters, but this does not preclude identification with those same characters on the part of the author and his putative audience. In this respect, Moorcock is 'camp', like pop art and many of the pop singers of the sixties.

His appreciation of wider cultural trends has taken Moorcock beyond the substantial but narrow readership of genre sci-fi, and in 1977 his *Condition of Muzak* won the fiction prize awarded by the *Guardian* newspaper. Moorcock's critics would say that it is just as well there is an element of playful self-mockery in his writing, otherwise all that 'sword and sorcery' stuff would be totally unreadable.

MUST READ The Jerry Cornelius series
READ ON **J G Ballard, Iain Banks, Jeff Noon**, Terry Pratchett, J R R Tolkien

Seth Morgan

1949–1990
Over the edge

Having grown up in a large family with five brothers and sisters, Seth Morgan enrolled at the Berkeley campus in California, but dropped out at around the time that student radicalism reached its peak, i.e. when quitting college seemed like a radical thing to do. Morgan became involved with the rock scene on the West Coast, and was the singer Janis Joplin's boyfriend when she died of a heroin overdose in 1970 at the age of 27.

Soon afterwards Morgan quit California and moved to New York, where he became a strip joint barker on Broadway. He was convicted of armed robbery and sent back to California to serve time in the state penitentiary. While in the pen, Morgan was awarded a prize by PEN, the international authors' organisation, for an essay he had written. He then embarked on his first novel, *Homeboy* (1990), a semi-autobiographical tale of a strip joint barker and dope addict who finds a missing diamond and is falsely convicted of murder. *Homeboy* was widely praised. *Washington Post Book World* reported: 'Seth Morgan makes the ugly streets of San Francisco's Tenderloin…into mythical characters and places, much larger than life and highly colored.' *Vanity Fair* described *Homeboy* as 'Armistead Maupin meets Mickey Spillane and Fritz the Cat'. Citing William Burroughs and Henry Miller as Morgan's antecedents, the *New York Times Book Review* welcomed him as 'an important new novelist…[who] writes with the picaresque authority of a Joycean Hell's Angel', while the *Los Angeles Times Book Review* simply hailed him as 'the conquering literary hero'. But Morgan may have been conquered by success itself. Although he had already started work on a second novel, not long after the publication of *Homeboy* he rode his new motorcycle off the

Golden Gate bridge and plunged to an untimely death in the waters of the San Francisco Bay.

MUST READ *Homeboy*
READ ON **Jim Carroll**, Joe Gores

Walter Mosley

1952–
Chandler's LA painted black

After studying writing at the City College of New York, Mosley returned to his home town, Los Angeles, and in 1990 published *Devil in a Blue Dress*, the first of his crime series featuring Ezekiel 'Easy' Rawlins. Set in post-Second World War Los Angeles, the novel is a retelling of Raymond Chandler's *Farewell My Lovely* from a black perspective, with Easy searching for a missing white woman and stumbling into organised crime. Others in the highly successful series are *A Red Death* (1991), *White Butterfly* (1992), *Black Betty* (1994), and *A Little Yellow Dog* (1996).

In 1995 *Devil in a Blue Dress* was filmed, with Mosley writing the screenplay. *Gone Fishin'*, his first novel, written in 1988 and a kind of prequel to the Easy Rawlins series, was published in 1997. *RL's Dream* (1995), a novel telling the story of an old blues guitarist living in contemporary New York, borrows heavily from the short life of Robert Johnson, legendary King of the Delta Blues singers.

< 200 >

Although similarities certainly exist between the Easy Rawlins books and the novels of Raymond Chandler (notably the beginning of *Devil in a Blue Dress*), where Chandler wrote of the white world of Sunset Boulevard and off-shore gambling boats in the Pacific, Mosley's LA is in the ghettos of Watts, with its street smarts, casual violence and police brutality. The latter having an added political, i.e. racial, edge entirely absent from Chandler's writing. Each novel in the series sees Easy growing older, more successful and increasingly reluctant to go rummaging in the hotbed of the LA netherworld, although this is the only place where he can shake off his hard-earned complacency and feel alive again. Perhaps he needs to feel the tension and violence he experienced as a young man, in order to retain some glimmer of his youth.

In many ways the real star of the novels is Mouse, Easy's friend from their childhood in Houston. Mouse is a brilliant creation, elevating the series above its status of slick crime thriller. Pint-sized and murderous, he represents Easy's dark side and the excitement that lures Easy away from his comfortable life.

With *Blue Light* (1999) Mosley switched to sci-fi with mixed results. His stories *Always Outnumbered, Always Outgunned*, though set in Watts, are another foray beyond the crime genre.

MUST READ All the Easy Rawlins novels
READ ON **Raymond Chandler, Chester Himes**, Joe R Lansdale

Ryu Murakami

1952–
Alienated offspring of postwar Japan

Born in 1952, Ryu Murakami was raised in Sasebo, a port in Western Japan. While a student at Musashino College of Art in Tokyo, Murakami wrote *Almost Transparent Blue*, a story of sex, drugs and self-destructive alienation, and entered it in a competition for new authors organised by the influential literary monthly *Gunzo*. Subsequently published as a novella, *Almost Transparent Blue* won the Akutagawa Literary Prize for 1976.

Murakami went on to present a radio programme and a TV show. He continues to write and publish fiction, but with sales of over a million copies, *Almost Transparent Blue* is still his best-known work. Japanese youth welcomed it as a homegrown version of the alienated sensibility that they had previously imported from Western pop music and cult novelists such as Albert Camus. For Western readers, it served to dispel the clichéd image of Japan as a country of conformist salary-men and their submissive females. Instead of bespectacled men in suits and kimono-clad women, Murakami's Japan is populated by characters who might just as easily have come from Andy Warhol's Factory or from the New York punk scene of the mid- to late seventies.

Newsweek described *Almost Transparent Blue* as 'a Japanese mix of [Anthony Burgess's] *A Clockwork Orange* and [Albert Camus's] *L'Etranger* [The Outsider]'. The *Washington Post* noted Murakami's 'combination of exotica, erotica and indigenous literary technique'. But *Almost Transparent Blue* seems about as indigenous to Japan as Hubert Selby's *Last Exit to Brooklyn* (1964): both writers use the same vocabulary of sex, violence and degradation.

MUST READ *Almost Transparent Blue*
READ ON Russell Bone, **Albert Camus, Seth Morgan, Hubert Selby**

Robert Musil

1880–1942
A man with many qualities

Born in Vienna, Robert Musil's family expected him to follow a career in the army of the Austro-Hungarian Empire, but instead he studied engineering at the Technical University of Brno, then read philosophy at the University of Berlin, from where he graduated in 1908. He wrote a novel (*Young Torless*, 1906) about the brutality of life in a military academy. But when war broke out in 1914, while Musil was working in Berlin as a freelance editor, he volunteered immediately and served on the Italian front as an officer in the Austrian army.

After the war Musil embarked on his great

M

work, *The Man Without Qualities*. He completed the first part while living in Berlin. In order to escape the Nazis and the economic inflation which had ruined him financially, he returned, temporarily, to his native city, Vienna, before going into exile in neutral Switzerland. He died before editing the numerous drafts of his masterpiece.

The Man Without Qualities is a huge novel without a plot. Its protagonist is Ulrich, who is the same age and of the same background as the author. Ulrich is talented but, as one critic put it, he 'cannot summon up a sense of reality'. To Ulrich, 'truth is not a crystal one can put in one's pocket, but an infinite fluid into which one falls headlong'. Ulrich has no wish to fall headlong into the real world; indeed it seems to him that to do so would be to lose sight of his own personality. Accordingly, Ulrich decides to put his qualities on hold and to stand outside of life for a year – this is the year that begins in August 1913, the last year in the life of the Austro-Hungarian Empire, which was broken up under the terms of the Treaty of Versailles at the end of the First World War.

Ulrich is in suspension. He exists only in the realm of possibilities, hence for all his culture and learning he is the man without qualities. Likewise, the second strand of the novel deals with a campaign by leading Viennese figures who seek to celebrate the Austrian soul. But they can never quite decide what this is, nor can they get anything done. They too cannot connect with reality. The third major element in Musil's great work is the character of Moosbrugger, a murderer awaiting trial who represents the beast in us all and the slaughter that, in the form of the First World War, was just around the corner. This is reality all right, but is it of a kind that we can live with?

Part 3 of *The Man Without Qualities*, with which Musil had originally intended to begin the novel, demonstrates his complexity and ambiguity: sides are constantly switched and his prose fuses such opposites as male and female, intellect and imagination, science and art. Duality is a constant theme; it was the focus of two early stories entitled *Unions* (1891), and it is indicated by Musil's early working title (*The Twin Sister*) for his masterpiece.

If for no other reason than the great length of their novels, Musil is often compared to Marcel Proust. But they have more in contrast than in common, as noted by novelist and essayist V S Pritchett: 'Where Proust seeks to crystallise a past, Musil is always pushing through that strange undergrowth to find out, if possible, where he is, where life is tending, and what is the explanation.' Elias Canetti, author of *Auto-da-Fé*, once remarked that 'There are few writers I admire as much as Musil. For fifty years I have found myself reading and rereading him.'

MUST READ *The Man Without Qualities*
READ ON Elias Canetti, Marcel Proust

M IS FOR NO, BUT I SAW THE MOVIE
10 cult classics more famous as films

DARK PASSAGE
David Goodis
Bogart and Bacall play Goodis's
doomed lovers

NIGHT OF THE HUNTER
Davis Grubb
Robert Mitchum as the psycho
southern preacher

LITTLE BIG MAN
Thomas Berger
Dustin Hoffman in Berger's epic
post—Western

INVASION OF THE BODY SNATCHERS
Jack Finney
the sci—fi original made into
classic McCarthy era movie

THE HUSTLER
Walter Tevis
Tevis's pool shark hero brought
to life by Paul Newman

DELIVERANCE
James Dickey
dark adventure masterpiece filmed
by John Boorman

STRAW DOGS
Gordon M Williams
rape and violence at an
isolated country cottage

JULES AND JIM
Henri—Pierre Roche
two men who share everything,
especially women

THE GRADUATE
Charles Webb
Here's to you Mrs Robinson...

BELLE DE JOUR
Joseph Kessel
Catherine Deneuve as respectable
women turned prostitute

Vladimir Nabokov

1899–1977
Trilingual polymath and dirty old man

Born in St Petersburg to wealthy parents, Nabokov attended the progressive Tenishev School in St Petersburg, where he was accused of 'not conforming' to his environment.

His father was a liberal serving in Kerensky's provisional government. In 1919, after the Bolshevik Revolution, the family fled Russia and went into exile. Nabokov and his brother were awarded scholarships to Cambridge, where he studied Russian and French literature. In 1922 his father was murdered, and Vladimir rejoined his family in Berlin. There he remained for 15 years, publishing, under his real name of Vladimir Sirin, three novels: *Mary* (1926), *The Gift* (1937), and *Glory*. Although he translated them into English when they were published many years later in the West, he was scornful of them, particularly *Glory*, which he dismissed in a letter to critic Edmund Wilson, as 'blevotina' (vomit). On the rise of Nazism, he left Berlin for Paris, where he met James Joyce. Paris was his home until it too fell to the Nazis in 1940. Nabokov sailed to the USA on one of the last boats out of France that year. He received his citizenship papers in 1945, and claimed to be 'as American as April in Arizona'.

In 1955 the Olympia Press in Paris published his masterpiece, *Lolita*, the tale of a middle-aged

teacher's insatiable lust for a 12-year-old girl. The relationship between Humbert and Lolita is a metaphor for the writer and his art, and for the old world encountering the new in all its vivacious vulgarity. But it was the literal meaning of the story that attracted the attention of moralists and censors. The book was branded as immoral and banned in a number of countries, while at the same time hailed by some commentators as a major aesthetic achievement. It has been filmed twice: first by Stanley Kubrick (1962; Nabokov wrote a film script for Kubrick but his published text bears little resemblance to the dialogue onscreen) and second by Adrian Lyne (1998). Both versions made Lolita appear older than in the novel but still ran into serious trouble.

Lolita's notoriety allowed Nabokov to leave teaching and abandon the USA for a solitary life in a Swiss hotel. He has been referred to as a parodic explorer of the storehouse of literature. If his books are short on moral humanism, this is because they are primarily a playful exploration of the literary art. He is famously on record as saying: '"Reality" is a word that means nothing except in quotes.' But on another occasion he wrote: 'Men have learned to live with a black burden, a huge aching hump: the supposition that "reality" may only be a dream. How much more dreadful it would be if the very awareness of your being aware of reality's dream-like nature were also a dream, a built-in hallucination.' Nabokov wrote in three languages (Russian, French, English) and for him the textual world reigns supreme.

A number of authors have put the figure of Nabokov into their work. In Bill Morris's debut novel, *Biography of a Buick* (1992), Nabokov is inspired to write *Lolita* after seducing a young student. In *The Emigrants* by W G Sebald (1996) he appears or is mentioned in each segment. Nabokov even has a cameo role in 'Don't Stand

N IS FOR NEW YORK, NEW YORK
5 different bites at the
Big Apple

BONFIRE OF THE VANITIES
Tom Wolfe
yuppie gets come-uppance in ethnic America

LADIES' MAN
Richard Price
down and out of love on the streets of NYC

A SINGULAR MAN
J P Donleavy
paddywhackery on the other side of the water

BRIGHT LIGHTS, BIG CITY
Jay McInerney
fact-checking in a city without truth

BUTTERFIELD 8
John O'Hara
raw tales of the damned during the speakeasy era

So Close To Me', a song by The Police, in which the words 'shake and cough' are forced, kicking and screaming, to rhyme with his name.

MUST READ *Lolita*
READ ON William Gerhardie, **Jerzy Kosinski**, Philip Roth

Anaïs Nin

1907–1977
Passionate eroticist and diarist

Born in Paris, Anaïs Nin was the eldest child of a Spanish–Cuban father and a Danish–French mother. She lived in Paris until she was 11, when her father, a composer, abandoned his wife and children, and the family moved to New York.

After ten years, she married banker Hugh Guiler and moved back to Paris. There she studied psychoanalysis under Otto Rank, later becoming his lover. She also met other writers and artists, including Lawrence Durrell, William Carlos Williams, and Henry Miller, who became her lover for many years. This fiery relationship, along with their mutual artistic influence, formed the basis of much of Nin's work and is best viewed through their correspondence, published in 1987 as *A Literary Passion*. Nin returned to New York in 1934, and resumed her affair with Rank (who had relocated there), playing him and Miller off against

each other, while still married to Guiler, possibly the world's most understanding man. Instinctively, she was searching for 'the man who would deliver me from all of them'. Here, she wrote novels, including *House of Incest* (1936), *Winter of Artifice* (1939) and *Spy in the House of Love* (1954), and a collection of stories, *Under a Glass Bell* (1948), all of them drawing heavily on her relationships (intellectual and physical) with both Rank and Miller. She also wrote (surprise, surprise), several volumes of erotica, which were published in the late sixties as *Delta of Venus* (1969) and *Little Birds*.

There lies in her prose an obsession with female identity, with a woman's sense of self, that the feminists of the seventies took wholeheartedly to their bra-less bosoms. Coupled with her analyst's fascination with dreams and unconscious desires, she can be seen as a surprisingly cerebral writer, notwithstanding the earthy eroticism of her work.

Her diaries and journals, ranging from the twenties to the seventies, are a seminal portrait of a unique era as well as being a riveting account of her self-discovery. 'It is true that because of my doubts and anxieties I only believe in fire…That this is the story of my incendiary neurosis! I only believe in fire. Life. Fire. Being myself on fire I set others on fire. Never death. Fire and life. Les Jeux.'

MUST READ *The Journals, Spy in the House of Love*
READ ON Lawrence Durrell, **Erica Jong**

< 206 >

N IS FOR NOIR

10 original pulp classics from the hard—boiled school

THE GRIFTERS
Jim Thompson
the life of smalltime cons from the
dimestore Dostoyevsky

SHOOT THE PIANO PLAYER
David Goodis
honour among thieves from the
poet of the losers

THEY SHOOT HORSES DON'T THEY?
Horace McCoy
nihilistic Depression era view of the
Hollywood circus

SOLOMON'S VINEYARD
Jonathan Latimer
kinky sex and California cults get
the noir treatment

THE POSTMAN ALWAYS RINGS TWICE
James M Cain
the classic of fatal sexual compulsion

THE LONG GOODBYE
Raymond Chandler
a masterpiece from LA's white knight
of noir

I WAKE UP SCREAMING
Steve Fisher
Hollywood writer framed for murder by
a dying cop

RED HARVEST
Dashiell Hammett
the first full—length outing from the
man who invented noir

IN A LONELY PLACE
Dorothy B Hughes
a psychopath on the loose in LA

NIGHT AND THE CITY
Gerald Kersh
noir comes to the shadowy streets
of London

Jeff Noon

196?–
'Kids' stories but with weird sex and drugs thrown in'

Jeff Noon studied fine art and drama at Manchester University and was subsequently appointed writer in residence at the city's Royal Exchange theatre. But Noon did not stay too long in the theatrical world, possibly because the realism associated with the theatre was not conducive to the fantastical worlds he was itching to invent. While doing an upmarket McJob behind the counter at the local Waterstone's bookshop, a colleague suggested he write a novel. The result of that suggestion, *Vurt* (1993), was a sci-fi story which reflected the concerns of crusties and cyberculturists, who reciprocated by making it the hippest sci-fi novel to be published in Britain since the headiest days of Michael Moorcock in the late sixties. Noon's reputation was confirmed with the publication of *Pollen* (1995) and *Nymphomation* (1997), set in a near-future Manchester which is enthralled by a Lottery-based game called Domino Bones.

Like Moorcock, Noon is not preoccupied with technology per se, but incorporates technological developments into a world of magic and fantasy. He owes a great deal to Lewis Carroll (Noon cites his rereading of the Alice books at the age of 16 as the defining moment of his artistic career), and in *Automated Alice*

(1996) he updated Carroll's young heroine and made her into a gun-toting robot. As a teenager, Noon was addicted to American comic heroes, and still turns to them for inspiration. He has said that music is more of an influence on his writing than novelists: he 'usually writes to music', and his record collection ranges from classical to drum 'n' bass.

Noon does not like being bracketed with the middle-class Martin Amis school of soul searching; nor does he fit in with the 'E-scene' writers, although he did contribute a story to *Disco Biscuits* (1997), an anthology for the 'chemical generation'. Noon would like to offer a less cynical view of the world: he describes his output as 'like kids' stories…but with weird sex and drugs thrown in', and says he wants to be thought of as the man who reintroduced 'whimsy' into English fiction. Critics might say that Noon's predilection for the childlike and naive is itself a somewhat cynical escape route from the task of developing an adult worldview capable of assimilating the end of the 20th century. His politics can be equally trite: the subtext of *Nymphomation* seems to be that the soul of the nation is being destroyed by the Lottery and the greed it represents. As if we have not heard that killjoy argument enough times already, without having a whole novel dedicated to it.

MUST READ *Automated Alice, Vurt*
READ ON **Lewis Carroll, Michael Moorcock, Mervyn Peake**

< 208 >

Flann O'Brien

1911–1966
The laughing civil servant

Born in Strabane, Co Tyrone, Northern Ireland, as Brian O'Nolan, the third of 12 children, O'Brien attended University College, Dublin, to study German, Irish and English, but, reputedly, spent most of his time drinking the black stuff (stout) and playing billiards. He joined the Irish civil service in 1935, staying until his retirement from ill health in 1953.

His first novel, *At Swim-Two-Birds*, was published under the name Flann O'Brien in 1939, at the behest of Graham Greene. Samuel Beckett loved it, as did the nearly blind James Joyce (by whom O'Brien was heavily influenced), who read it using a magnifying glass, noting: 'That's a real writer, with the true comic spirit.' A dextrous and utterly surreal novel, it is among other things both a multilayered examination of Irish culture and a commentary on the art of fiction itself.

His next novel, *The Third Policeman*, was rejected by his publisher, and his disappointment was such that he claimed he had lost the manuscript. It was only published posthumously, in 1967.

In 1941, his novel *An Béal Bocht* was published in Gaelic and wasn't translated (as *The Poor Mouth*) until 1967. As civil servants were

Flann O'Brien

forbidden to publish under their own names, for over 25 years from 1940 he wrote a daily column in the *Irish Times* called the 'Cruiskeen Lawn' ('Little Brimming Jug'), as Myles na Gopaleen. After a reader once requested 'something that may interest and help us in our daily lives', O'Brien, or rather Myles, replied with the following advice on how to help an inebriated 'friend': 'Your 'friend' has consumed 48 pints and has now fallen down on the broad of his back. Today's Hint is this: DON'T lift his head

< 209 >

CULT FICTION

…Keep his body completely horizontal. If you lift his head and shoulders, you'll probably spill some.' Extracts from these hilarious pieces were printed in various collections, notably *The Best of Myles* (1968) and *The Hair of the Dogma* (1977). The novelist Nicholson Baker praised them as being: 'intoxicatingly funny…A priceless estate-sale of alien and gorgeous vocabuary.'

Following the reissue of *At Swim-Two-Birds* in 1960, O'Brien wrote *Hard Times* in 1962, and *The Dalkey Archive* in 1964. Sadly, it is only posthumously that he has been regarded as a great Irish writer; privately he regarded himself as something of a failure. He died rather fittingly on April Fool's Day, and many people at first thought it was just another of his pranks.

MUST READ *At Swim-Two-Birds, The Poor Mouth, The Third Policeman*
READ ON **Samuel Beckett, James Joyce**, Patrick McGinley, S J Perelman

Flannery O'Connor

1925–1964
Grotesques of the Deep South

Born in Savannah, Georgia, O'Connor was raised a Catholic in a fanatically Protestant 'Christ-haunted' area of Georgia. As described in her essay 'The Catholic Novelist in the Protestant South' (1969), this anomaly fundamentally shaped her writing, which often concerns tortured figures racked by issues of faith. When she was 12, her family moved to Milledgeville, her mother's birthplace, because of the ill health of her father, who died when she was 15.

Educated at Georgia State College for Women, and the State College of Iowa, she published her first story, 'The Geranium', in 1946, while still at college. The following year, she won the Rinehart–Iowa Fiction Award for a first novel. The novel was actually just a part of what would become *Wise Blood*, which was not published until 1952. The tragi-comic story of a young religious fanatic, it was later filmed by John Huston in 1979, starring Brad Dourif and Harry Dean Stanton.

In 1950, O'Connor contracted lupus, the disease that had killed her father, but was not told of it until 1952. According to Sally Fitzgerald, her friend and the editor of her posthumously published letters and essays (*Habit of Being*, 1979; *Mystery and Manners*, 1969), 'She took stock characteristically, and began to plan her life in the light of reality.'

O'Connor's second novel, *The Violent Bear It Away*, which again has a tortured religious fanatic at its heart, appeared in 1960; her story collection, *A Good Man is Hard to Find*, which she called 'nine stories of original sin', came out in 1955. Her second collection, *Everything That Rises Must Converge* appeared posthumously in

< 210 >

1965, its tone blackened further by the pain she was by then suffering.

Particularly acclaimed for her stories, O'Connor, along with writers like Carson McCullers and Eudora Welty, belonged to a Southern Gothic tradition that focused on the decaying South and the 'tragic sense of life' that lurked there, probing the overriding sense of loneliness and the constant taint of evil. The view of the human situation that she presents is nothing short of grotesque. Some claim her freakish portraits are cruel, but in truth she manages to maintains a stance that is simultaneously detached yet sympathetic.

MUST READ *A Good Man is Hard to Find*, *Wise Blood*
READ ON **Nick Cave, Harry Crews, William Faulkner, Carson McCullers**, Katherine Anne Porter, Eudora Welty

Joyce Carol Oates

1938–
Commentator at the ringside of life

Joyce Carol Oates grew up in the country around Lockport, New York. She received degrees from Syracuse University and the University of Wisconsin, where she taught English until moving first to the University of Detroit, then across the Canadian border to the University of Ontario, and finally south again to Princeton University, New Jersey – not that far from where she grew up. Oates has been a prolific writer. Since the early sixties she has published 15 novels among a total of 50 books. *With Shuddering Fall* (1964) was her first novel; *Them* (1969) won the 1970 National Book Award. Other titles include *Unholy Loves* (1979), *Marya: A Life* (1986), *Angel of Light*, *Bellefleur* (1980), *A Bloodsmoor Romance* (1982), *You Must Remember This* (1987), and a dozen volumes of short stories, as well as plays, critical essays and poetry. Oates has a longstanding interest in boxing, and her essay 'On Boxing' (1987), first published in the *Ontario Review*, ranks with anything written on the subject by the pugilistic Norman Mailer. Oates seems to regard boxing as an appropriate metaphor for modern life; from the moment she made her debut with the publication of *With Shuddering Fall*, her fiction has often contained elements of intense physicality and fierce contestation. If life is like a boxing match, Oates is one of the foremost ringside commentators. Along with social observation, her work is noted for its American Gothic sensibility. Whatever the geographical setting (the slums of Detroit, the groves of academe), her fiction is placed in the psychic landscape of the Gothic. For Oates, this is a mode of expression that allows her to connect the violence of the past with the antagonisms of present-day America. She puts particular emphasis on the representation of women,

< 211 >

and draws on a wide range of literary and cultural artefacts in the construction of her own, richly distinctive authorial voice.

MUST READ *A Bloodsmoor Romance, American Appetites, On Boxing, With Shuddering Fall, Them*
READ ON **Richard Brautigan, Truman Capote, Anne Rice**

George Orwell

1903—1950
Ambivalent about Englishness

Born in Motihari, India (then part of the British Empire), Eric Arthur Blair was the second son of a middle-ranking British official in the Indian civil service. When he was four, Blair's family returned to England, to a house near Henley on Thames. At 8 he was sent to a private school in Sussex where he remained until the age of 13. He won a scholarship to Wellington School (he only stayed for one term), and then to Eton. Afterwards, he said that coming from a family of modest means, he felt most uncomfortable being surrounded by the sons of the wealthiest families in Britain. His schooling completed, Blair joined the Indian Imperial Police and served in Burma for five years. While home on leave in 1927, he decided to resign. During the first six months of

< 212 >

1928 he went on what he thought of as an expedition to discover the life of the poor in the East End of London. Then he went to Paris, where he worked as a dishwasher and wrote two novels, which have been lost. Towards the end of 1929 he fell ill with pneumonia and returned to England. When he recovered, he continued to go 'tramping' – working and travelling with hop-pickers and hobos. He used his parents' home in Suffolk as a base until 1936, when he moved to Wallington, Hertfordshire, where he ran the village store. A few months later he married Eileen O'Shaughnessy, an Oxford graduate in English.

By this time Eric Blair had established the identity of George Orwell, author. In Suffolk, he earned money by writing articles and teaching; he also wrote up his experiences of the lower depths of Paris and the East End, which were published in 1933 as *Down and Out in Paris and London* (the author was not too happy with the title: he said he would rather own up to being a dishwasher than 'down and out'). Blair did not wish the book to be published under his own name; partly because it might have made it more difficult for him to earn a living as a teacher, but also to symbolise his rejection of the life of a middle-ranking officer in the colonial service, for which he had been trained and educated. Blair may have been rejecting Englishness, with all its imperial connotations, but he chose for himself the most English of names – the country had just been ruled by one George (the fifth) and was about to be ruled by another; Orwell is the name of a river in rural Suffolk. Herein lies the contradiction at the heart of Orwell/Blair: a deep dislike of his class and country, offset by an equally profound affection for both.

Burmese Days (1934), based on Orwell's experiences in Burma, was first issued in the US because the publisher feared it would give offence to ex-colonials. The novels *A Clergyman's Daughter* (1935) and *Keep the Aspidistra Flying* (1936) both demonstrate a love–hate relationship with Englishness and the class system. But at this stage Orwell's reputation was primarily that of a chronicler of social conditions; and it was on this basis that the Left Book Club commissioned him to go on an expedition to northern England and write *The Road to Wigan Pier* (1936). Its publication marked Orwell's embrace of the socialist cause – though he was already strongly critical of most forms of the organised socialist movement, particularly those dominated by the middle classes.

While Orwell was finishing work on *The Road to Wigan Pier*, he was making plans to go to Spain; primarily to report on the Spanish Civil War, but possibly to fight against General Franco's fascists. In the event, Orwell did join the militia of the Partido Obrero de Unificación Marxista, later transferring to the British Independent Labour Party contingent. He was wounded, but only left Spain after the Republican authorities outlawed the POUM.

George Orwell

Orwell's socialist commitment was confirmed, but his experience of the rivalry between Stalinist-type communists and the POUM made him fiercely critical of orthodox leftists, as shown in his account of the war, *Homage to Catalonia* (1938).

Orwell planned to go to India to write a new book, but he had contracted tuberculosis and, with a loan from another author, he spent the winter of 1938–1939 recuperating in Morocco. There he wrote *Coming up for Air*, a bitter tale of an England swamped by mass production and the waste and destruction it apparently entails. During the Second World War Orwell worked as a talks producer for BBC radio and served in the Home Guard as a firewatcher. In 1943 he left the BBC to become literary editor of *Tribune*, a left-wing paper which at that time exercised considerable influence. Between 1943 and 1944 Orwell wrote his best-known story – *Animal Farm* (1945), the fable of revolution among the animals which suggests that power corrupts absolutely, no matter who wields it. But in 1944 British policy was pro-Soviet, and no one would publish *Animal Farm* until the Second World War had ended and the signs of the coming Cold War were already evident. In March 1945 Orwell's first wife died during an operation. He took their adopted son to the island of Jura, off the Scottish coast, where he lived until 1948. During that time he drafted and redrafted *Nineteen Eighty-Four* (1949), while suffering from increasingly virulent attacks of tuberculosis. In September 1949 he went into a TB hospital in London, and the following month married Sonia Brownell. In January 1950 Orwell died.

Orwell is revered as the exemplar of a great writer who could also be political and, furthermore, as an example of political commitment without orthodoxy and narrow ideology. His critics, on the other hand, complain that he never went the whole way: he hated the British Empire but never broke from Britishness.

< 214 >

Sometimes his attitude to common people and their tastes seems pompous and patronising, as when, in an essay on the fashion for violent crime novels in the forties, he suggested that snobbery is perhaps an 'underrated virtue'. So don't expect to see the ghost of Orwell queueing up to see the latest Tarantino movie.

MUST READ *Animal Farm, Keep the Aspidistra Flying, Nineteen Eighty-Four*
READ ON **Nelson Algren**, J B Priestley, **Franz Kafka**, Rudyard Kipling, Henry Green

---

O IS FOR ORACLE
5 novelists whose predictions have come true

WILLIAM GIBSON invented cyberspace on a manual typewriter (Neuromancer)

ISAAC ASIMOV announced the age of robotics (I, Robot)

ARTHUR C CLARKE'S Hal heralded artificial intelligence (2001)

J G BALLARD saw the collapse of the fashion for high-rise living (High Rise)

GEORGE ORWELL envisaged CCTV and called it the 'telescreen' (1984)

Dorothy Parker

1893—1967
The Algonquin queen of the one-liner

Born Dorothy Rothschild to prosperous Jewish parents in New Jersey, the last of three children, her sister being nine years older, Dorothy Parker was an infant when her mother died and her father remarried an extremely religious woman, whom Dorothy resented bitterly and referred to as 'the housekeeper'. Much of her verse and fiction would deal with her inability to find love, and her harsh upbringing undoubtedly inspired that.

In 1916, she started writing verse and reviews for *Vogue* magazine. The following year she wrote for *Vanity Fair*, and married Edwin Parker, a Wall Street broker. Shortly after the wedding, Parker went to serve in France (following all-night drinking binges, he was so pale at parade, his fellow soldiers named him 'Spook').

Mrs Parker, or Dottie, as she was known, swiftly became known as the wittiest woman in America. At the famous Round Table in Manhattan's Algonquin Hotel she would preside over the wits and raconteurs (Robert Benchley and Robert Sherwood among them) and mutter dazzling puns and put-downs ('a girl's best friend is her mutter,' she remarked later).

Underneath the wisecracks lay an insecure woman, whose alcoholic husband, ruined by the war, loved the bottle more than her. A woman, furthermore, who stumbled through unhappy love affairs, had abortions, attempted suicide, drank excessively and was escorted by gigolos (many of whom were homosexual), whose celebrity status was used openly by men to further their own careers. Critic and author Gilbert Seldes considered her to be 'a sad person, unable to take real pleasure – as if being enormously satisfied with anything would not be in her character, or would have diminished her'.

She moved to Hollywood, wrote film scripts (including *A Star is Born*), espoused socialism, married writer Alan Campbell (twice!), and made money, but never enough – she complained that the studios' payments were 'like so much compressed snow. It goes so fast it melts in your hand.'

She died of a heart attack in 1973, a lonely old woman, befuddled by alcohol and senility. Her stories and poems are still available in *The Collected Dorothy Parker* (1977). In 1994 Jennifer Jason Leigh played her in the film *Mrs Parker and the Vicious Circle*.

MUST READ *The Collected Dorothy Parker*
READ ON Robert Benchley, **Ring Lardner**, Edna St Vincent Millay

< 215 >

P IS FOR PSYCHOPATH

killing with confidence — 13 of literature's Most Wanted

WILLIAM WHARTON
MY IDEA OF FUN by Will Self
killing for the reality distorting Fat
Controller

NORMAN BATES
PSYCHO by Robert Bloch
more from Norman's perspective than in
the Hitchcock film

LOU FORD
THE KILLER INSIDE ME by Jim Thompson
a small town sheriff is harbouring a
sadistic psychopath

FRANK CAULDHAME
THE WASP FACTORY by Iain M Banks
roaming his Scottish island home killing
animals and islanders

FRANCIE BRADY
THE BUTCHER BOY by Patrick McCabe
an Irish psycho's coming of age, Huck
Finn meets Hannibal Lecter

GRENOUILLE
PERFUME by Patrick Suskind
a twisted Gothic murderer with a
discerning nose

LESTER BALLARD
CHILD OF GOD by Cormac McCarthy
a backwater serial killer roams the
Tennessee hills

PATRICK BATEMAN
AMERICAN PSYCHO by Bret Easton Ellis
yuppie killer extraordinaire

DR HANNIBAL LECTER
RED DRAGON by Thomas Harris
the first fictional encounter with the
star of Silence of the Lambs

CHAPPY
THE END OF ALICE by A M Homes
inside the mind of a pederast child killer

THE COMPTONS
EXQUISITE CORPSE by Poppy Z Brite
blood—soaked cannibalistic serial killer
gay romance

RHODA PENMARK
THE BAD SEED by William March
serial killing at the age of eight in small
town Alabama

< 216 >

Pier Paolo Pasolini

1922–75
The Catholic Marxist

Born in Bologna, traditionally the most left-wing of Italian cities, Pier Paolo Pasolini saw poetry in the peasantry and spirituality in the urban proletariat. In the fifties, his two novels (*The Ragazzi*, 1955 and *A Violent Life*, 1959) brought him notoriety. Although Pasolini continued to write fiction and poetry, he became primarily interested in film-making, and his first feature, *Accattone*, centred on the life of a pimp in Rome. Using non-professional actors, Pasolini's films are an attempt to combine the reverent and the revolutionary in an aesthetic that finds beauty in the unexpected and the everyday – no wonder he referred to himself as a 'Catholic Marxist'. Pasolini was a homosexual, and he was murdered one night after cruising for rough trade.

MUST READ *A Violent Life*
READ ON **Céline**, Graham Greene, **Iceberg Slim**

Mervyn Peake

1911–1968
Francis Bacon for kids

Mervyn Peake, like J G Ballard, spent his childhood in China, which may explain why in his life and work he never quite fitted into the pattern set by his English contemporaries. His Outsider orientation was exacerbated by a particularly traumatic experience which occurred at the close of the Second World War: Peake was one of the first British soldiers to enter the concentration camps and, as a war artist, it was his job to draw the horrors that he saw there. Memories of the camps haunted him for the rest of his life, casting a shadow over his subsequent work. While Peake's peers were dabbling in socialist realism or inventing the Angry Young Man, Peake created *Gormenghast*, a huge gothic fantasy of fear, innocence and youthful determination. The *Gormenghast* trilogy has been described as Dickensian but is probably just as close to the magic realism associated with the Latin American writers of the late sixties and seventies. Futhermore, in its emphasis on the grotesque, Peake's prose is not altogether dissimilar to the work of another outsider from the same period, the painter Francis Bacon. Peake's nightmares, however, were intended for a younger readership. The protagonist of *Titus Groan* (1946), *Gormenghast* (1950) and *Titus Alone* (1959, unfinished) is Titus, the son and

P

CULT FICTION

heir to the great but decaying house of Gormenghast. The trilogy follows his progress from birth to young manhood, spotlighting his battles with a dynamic but demonic social climber, Steerpike, who started out as a kitchen boy and rose to become the unofficial ruler of the household.

The atmosphere of dust and decay in the Gormenghast trilogy has something in common with the grim routine of George Orwell's *Nineteen Eighty-Four* (1949), but Gormenghast is more in tune with what later became the rock'n'roll sensibility. It was adopted by a new generation of avid readers in the early seventies. In their mind's eye, Titus appeared as a kind of Marc-Bolan-in-the-making, embodying the latter's combination of delicacy and drive. A few years later, the pop critic Jon Savage, who wrote the definitive history of punk, *England's Dreaming* (1992), averred that there was more than something of Steerpike in the stage act of Johnny Rotten. Hence the two sides of the rock'n'roll persona – the innocent and the demonic – may have been prefigured by Peake in the Gormenghast trilogy. Peake also worked as an illustrator of books (mainly children's). In this field too, he emphasised the Gothic and the grotesque

He died of Parkinson's disease.

MUST READ The Gormenghast trilogy
READ ON **J G Ballard, Lewis Carroll, Jeff Noon**

<218>

Georges Perec
1936–1982
French lover of puns and puzzles

Georges Perec was the only son of Isie and Cyrla Peretz, Polish immigrants who had moved with their families to Belleville, a working-class, largely Jewish area of Paris, in the twenties. As Perec grew up, all he heard was how terrible things were in Poland, in Germany, in Czechoslovakia, in Austria. In 1940, his father, who had enlisted in the army, was killed, and Perec was sent to Grenoble for the war's duration. His mother was taken to Drancy, where Jews were being rounded up before being sent to Auschwitz–Birkenau. When Red Army soldiers liberated the camp in 1945 (among the survivors was the novelist Primo Levi), Perec's mother was not there.

Perec wrote eloquently but fictitiously (as if to distance himself) about his childhood experiences in *W or the Memory of Childhood* (1975). He was raised by relatives, and after graduating from school announced to his friends that he wanted to be a writer ('Moi, je serais écrivain'). His first novel, *Things* (1965), won the Prix Renaudot in that year, yet lasting literary success eluded him until his epic *Life: a user's manual* was published in 1978 and won him the prestigious Prix Medicis. Perec was obsessed by language as a science; in 1967 he joined OuLiPo (Ouvroir de Littérature Potentialle, or

Workshop for Potential Literature), a group of writers and mathematicians that included Raymond Queneau, Italo Calvino and Perec's friend the American author Harry Mathews.

Under their influence, in 1969 Perec produced the bizarre novel *La Disparition* (*A Void*), a book that doesn't include a single letter 'e'. Redressing the balance, he later wrote *Les Revenentes* (1972), which means 'The return of the "e"', containing no vowels other than 'e'. It was his only work to deal directly with sex, possibly because of the 'e' words in French that have sexual connotations: lèvre, membre, pénétrer etc. Perec's fondness for lexicographic intricacies may explain his poorly paid job as an archivist at a scientific research funding council, a position he kept for 17 years. Perec also earned money by writing a radio serial sponsored by Eveready, the battery company. Perec's *The Extraordinary Adventures of Mr Eveready*, a mixture of Tintin, Jules Verne, The Goons and his own work, was broadcast on the Ivory Coast (presumably a fertile area for battery sales).

Changing tack somewhat, he also wrote the dialogue for *Serie Noire*, the French adaptation of Jim Thompson's novel *A Hell of a Woman*. All his life, Perec was a huge fan of American culture, lowbrow or otherwise, and his work was a fascinating mix of this, European intellectualism and his intensely personal feelings. Referring to his kaleidoscopic mix of styles Perec remarked: 'This systematic versatility has baffled more than one critic seeking to put his finger on the "characteristics" of my writing…It has earned me the reputation of being some sort of computer…for producing texts…I should rather compare myself to a farmer with many fields.'

MUST READ *Life: a user's manual, A Void*
READ ON Harry Mathews, **Raymond Queneau**

Robert M Pirsig

1928–
A mechanic for the soul

Robert M Pirsig was born in Minnesota, where his father was dean of the university law school. Pirsig Jnr became a teacher of philosophy and rhetoric, but his mind would not accept the mechanistic character of academic learning or the dualism (the split between mind and body) of Western self-consciousness. He suffered from mental breakdowns and was hospitalised on a number of occasions. He later said that being in hospital taught him to get along with people and make compromises. Meanwhile, the uncompromising side of his personality came to be represented in the character of Phaedrus (the name is taken from the Socratic dialogue written by the Ancient Greek philosopher Plato), the intellectual and spiritual voyager in Pirsig's highly successful first book, *Zen and the Art of*

Motorcyle Maintenance: an inquiry into values (1974). Conceived as a short essay in 1968, *Zen* took four and a half years to complete, with support from James Landis, who edited it for publishers William Morrow. Ostensibly an account of a motorcyle journey involving Pirsig and his son Chris, it is really an account of the Eastward-looking search for mental and spiritual fulfilment in an exhausted Western culture. The hardback copies sold as fast as Morrow could print them; when it was published in Britain *Zen and the Art of Motorcyle Maintenance* became the first book ever to be featured on the front cover of the *New Musical Express* (then at the height of its influence). Meanwhile Pirsig, who had experienced 20 years of rejection before leaving the academic world and becoming a technical writer, was learning to live with success and thinking about how to guard his privacy. Nearly 20 years later Pirsig produced *Lila: an inquiry into morals* (1991), primarily an investigation into the nature and inevitability of conflict. It was warmly received in some circles but never acquired the same kudos as his earlier work.

MUST READ *Zen and the Art of Motorcycle Maintenance: an inquiry into values*
READ ON **Aldous Huxley, Ken Kesey**, Alan Watts

P IS FOR PEN—ITENTIARY
5 tales of life behind bars

FALCONER
John Cheever
flying in search of freedom

THE FIXER
Bernard Malamud
life in a Tsarist jail

ONE DAY IN THE LIFE OF IVAN DENISOVICH
Alexander Solzhenitsyn
life in a Stalinist jail

BILLY RAGS
Ted Lewis
clever crim leads jailbreak

GREEN RIVER RISING
Tim Willocks
psycho leads prison riot

Sylvia Plath

1932–1963
Patron saint of suicidal angst

Sylvia Plath was born in New England. Her early years were partly blighted by an authoritarian father who died when she was eight. As she grew up she appeared to be a model student: she won prizes and scholarships, and her writing (both fiction and non-fiction) was published. But at 20 she underwent a nervous breakdown which culminated in a suicide attempt. These events were fictionalised in *The Bell Jar* (1963, initially published under the pseudonym 'Victoria Lucas'), the semi-autobiographical novel which takes place in New York at the height of the Cold War during the hot summer in which the Rosenbergs were sent to the electric chair, convicted of spying for the Soviets. Written in a lucid manner which belies the underlying psychological confusion of the female protagonist, *The Bell Jar* is widely regarded as a powerful indictment of the American Way Of Life – the restricted role of women, the Cold War, mechanised men in suits – which provides the emotional backdrop to the breakdown and near-death of its heroine. Alongside J D Salinger's *Catcher in the Rye* (1951), it is recognised as a classic of adolescent angst and anxiety.

The Bell Jar was Plath's only novel, but the suicide attempt described in it was not her last.

In 1956, she came to Cambridge, England, as a Fulbright scholar. At Cambridge University she met the young poet Ted Hughes, married him, then lived with him in London and subsequently in Devon. In 1962 they separated. Plath committed suicide in 1963, soon after the publication of *The Bell Jar*.

Plath's literary reputation rests mainly on her poetry, particularly the verse that she composed in the months leading up to her death (these poems were published in three posthumous collections: *Ariel*, 1965; *Crossing the Water*, 1971; and *Winter Trees*, 1972). But in her prose as well as her poetry, Plath speaks in a mode both confessional and fatalistic.

MUST READ *Ariel, The Bell Jar*
READ ON Ted Hughes, **Joyce Carol Oates**, **J D Salinger**, Elizabeth Smart

Edgar Allan Poe

1809–1849
Poet of the damned, master of the macabre

Born in Boston, the son of travelling actors, Poe was orphaned at the age of three and adopted by John Allan, a wealthy merchant from Richmond, Virginia who moved his family to England between 1815 and 1820.

When he was 17, Poe enrolled at the

University of Virginia, but because of his gambling debts and alleged drunkenness, his foster father removed him. Poe fled to Boston, where, within a year, he published a collection of verse, *Tamerlane* (1827), at his own expense. He then spent two periods in the army between 1827 and 1831, finally being dismissed for wilful neglect of duty.

In 1831 Poe moved to Baltimore and lived with his aunt, whose daughter, Virginia (his cousin), he would marry in 1836, three months before her fourteenth birthday. Escaping the cholera epidemic that raged in Baltimore in 1831, he employed his experience of it to good use in such tales as 'King Pest' (1835) and 'The Masque of the Red Death' (1842). This last, along with several Poe stories, was filmed by maverick film-maker Roger Corman in the 1960s.

Concentrating on stories and newspaper work, Poe became editor of the *Southern Literary Messenger* in 1836, but soon left, stating that 'the drudgery was excessive, the salary was contemptible'. Another reason might be that he yielded 'to the temptation held out on all sides by the spirit of Southern hospitality', for, as he later admitted: 'it sometimes happened that I was completely intoxicated'.

Poe moved to New York, then Philadelphia, wrote his famous novel, *The Narrative of Arthur Gordon Pym* (1838), published a story collection, *Tales of the Grotesque and Arabesque* (1840), and became editor of *Graham's Magazine*.

When he left the magazine (its circulation having risen from 5,500 to 40,000) his salary was $800 a year, while George Graham, the owner, was making a fortune. Poe's poem, 'The Raven', was published in 1845, winning him fame, if not riches, and he moved to New York with his ailing wife, who died of tuberculosis two years later. Poe attempted suicide the following year, and though he recovered, he suffered from the DTs as a result of his excessive drinking. In 1849, engaged to a wealthy woman, he returned to Baltimore to settle his affairs. Found semi-conscious from alcohol and in some kind of seizure, he died days later in a hospital, and in his words, 'the fever called "Living" was conquered at last'.

Poe is most famous for his short stories, which have seen him heralded as a pioneer of the detective, horror and sci-fi genres. He was admired by Baudelaire in France and by Oscar Wilde. The stories are in the macabre Gothic tradition and feature minds in mental collapse, families in decay, incest, necrophilia and sadistic torture, with Death getting at least a walk-on part in most tales. He is also seen by some as an existential forerunner with parables like 'The Pit and the Pendulum' (1843), 'The Masque of the Red Death' and 'The Cask of Amontillado' (1846) laying bare the bleak truth of the human condition.

MUST READ *The Narrative of Arthur Gordon Pym, Tales of the Grotesque and Arabesque*
READ ON Algernon Blackwood, Nathaniel Hawthorne, **H P Lovecraft**, Herman Melville

Richard Price

1950–
The law of the streets

The young Richard Price made a sensational debut with *The Wanderers* (1974), a story of gang war and racism in the Bronx with Vietnam looming on the horizon. He explored similar themes in *Bloodbrothers*, followed by *Ladies' Man* (1978), which depicts the painful self-realisation of an unemployed salesman whose girlfriend has just walked out on him. His largest and most expansive novel to date is *Clockers*, a story of drug-dealing, murder and the quest for morality in the ethnic landscape of New York. Comparing 'majestic' *Clockers* to Tom Wolfe's *Bonfire of the Vanities*, London's *Time Out* observed that 'while Wolfe's high-rollers only dipped a toe into the dark side, Price gives us all the raw detail of the street'. The *Washington Post* praised Price for 'that combination of muscularity, insight and compassion we might call heart.' Price's later energies have been directed toward Hollywood. His screenplays have been lauded: his script for *The Colour of Money* was Oscar-nominated, and the screenplay of *Sea of Love* is also highly regarded. But the film versions of Price's own novels have received mixed reviews. Philip Kaufman's *The Wanderers* (1979) is viewed with respect, not least for its intelligent soundtrack, but Spike Lee's *Clockers* (1994; Lee took the director's

chair after Martin Scorsese pulled out) was not so successful with the critics. Forget the films and check out the far superior originals.

MUST READ *The Wanderers, Ladies' Man, Clockers*
READ ON **Jim Carroll**, S E Hinton, **Charles Bukowski**

Thomas Pynchon

1937–
Polyphonic paranoia

Born in Glen Cove, New York, in 1937, little is known of the notoriously reclusive Pynchon. There is only one known picture of him. In the mid-fifties, he spent two years in the navy, then went to Greenwich Village where he 'enjoyed only a glancing acquaintance with the Beat movement...I spent a lot of time in jazz clubs...I put on hornrimmed sunglasses at night. I went to parties in lofts where girls wore strange attire. I was hugely tickled by marijuana humour.' He then studied at Cornell University, where he befriended Richard Farina, folk singer and author of *Been Down So Long It Looks Like Up To Me*.

In 1958 he began writing stories, which were published in magazines and appeared eventually in the collection *Slow Learner* (1984), graced with Pynchon's humorous introduction: 'My first reaction, rereading these stories, was oh my God, accompanied by physical symptoms we shouldn't dwell upon.' After Cornell, Pynchon spent two years in Seattle as a technical writer for the Boeing Aircraft Corporation, later recycling this experience in the technological, quasi-scientific content of his more epic work.

Lying at the core of much of Pynchon's vast polyphonic work (he can shift voice and style with ease) are labyrinthine systems of plotting, conspiracy and paranoia by the bucketload, and the constant, shifting sands of undermined meaning and signification. His first novel, *V* (1963), featured his trademark, two opposed, and absurdly named protagonists (Benny Profane and Herbert Stencil) in a double narrative, each wandering respectively through the distorted present and the mysterious past in search of *V*. But *V* is an enigma that keeps shifting – a woman, a place, a theory – and is constantly out of comprehensive reach. Pynchon's next book, *The Crying of Lot 49* (1966), was a fable satirising, as did the later *Vineland* (1990), the excesses of the Californian lifestyle (continuing in the tradition of Nathanael West, Terry Southern, Joan Didion and many others). In Oedipa Maas's search for the mysterious (and again constantly shifting) Trystero, *The Crying of Lot 49* shares many themes with *V*. This was a mere scrap, however, compared to the sprawling *Gravity's Rainbow* (1973). Described by some critics as a post-modern *Ulysses*, this huge novel, whose plot and structure are almost impossible to describe, fuses history, paranoia and technology into one vast glorious whole. The critic Richard Poirier called Pynchon a novelist who 'has caught the inward movements of our time in outward manifestations of art and technology'.

His latest mammoth offering *Mason and Dixon* (1997) – a parodic historical reconstruction of the lives of the two English surveyors who mapped out the Mason-Dixon line – shows that he has lost none of his now legendary versatility and creative genius.

MUST READ *Gravity's Rainbow, V*
READ ON **Don DeLillo, William Gaddis, Kurt Vonnegut, Nathanael West**

< 224 >

Raymond Queneau

1903–1976
Poet of the pataphysique

Born in Le Havre in 1903 and educated at the Sorbonne in Paris, Queneau worked on the famous *Encyclopédie de la Pléiade* and for 20 years was its director. He was secretary of the reading panel at the famous French publishers Gallimard, and helped writers, including Georges Perec, to publish their work there.

Queneau was largely inspired by Alfred Jarry, author of the classic anti-bourgeois play *Ubu Roi* (1896), who coined the term *pataphysique*, a logic of the absurd that Jarry referred to as a 'science of imaginary solutions'. Queneau and other French writers (including Boris Vian), formed the College of Pataphysics and from this grew OuLiPo (Ouvroir de Littérature Potentialle, or Workshop of Potential Literature), paradoxically, a sort of freedom through restriction and self-imposed limitations.

Always experimental, during the fifties Queneau was at the cutting edge of French culture (singer and actress Juliette Greco used to sing his poems in bohemian cellars, clad in a black plastic raincoat, performing a kind of existential cabaret), and his 1959 novel *Zazie in the Metro* was filmed successfully by Louis Malle.

Among his works were the novels *The Bark Tree*, an amusing pastiche of Descartes; the verse-novel *Oak and Dog*; *The Blue Flowers* (1965); and the quaintly titled *We Always Treat Woman Too Well*. His most famous book was probably *Exercises in Style* (1947), which gave 99 variations on a simple scene: a man getting on a bus, who accuses another man of treading on his toes, then leaves the bus to meet a friend who advises him to put an extra button on his coat! It was the book he most wanted to see translated; when it was, he wrote congratulating the translator: 'I have always thought that nothing is untranslatable. Here is new proof.' Along with Perec's *A Void* (a novel written without using a single letter 'e'), it was the finest example of the OuLiPo ethos.

MUST READ *Exercises in Style, Zazie in the Metro*
READ ON **Georges Perec**, Harry Mathews, **Boris Vian**

Thomas De Quincey

1785—1859
Drug—taking in pursuit of a higher
morality

Born in the burgeoning northern industrial city of Manchester, Thomas De Quincey met the poet Samuel Taylor Coleridge on a visit to the fashionable town of Bath. Coleridge introduced De Quincey to Robert Southey and William Wordsworth, and in 1809 he went to live with them in the Lake District village of Grasmere. But it was in London that De Quincey first took opium, after suffering a series of debilitating illnesses between 1812 and 1813. Seven years later (1821) the *London Magazine* serialised *Confessions of an English Opium Eater*, De Quincey's account of both the ecstasies and the torments he experienced as a result of taking opium and subsequently becoming an addict. His chronicle was an instant success, and has been widely revered ever since. In recent years, it has been suggested that De Quincey prefigured modern Outsider-writers such as Alexander Trocchi (who was fond of quoting him) for whom drugs served as confirmation of their alienation from mainstream society. But what De Quincey wanted from opium was quite different from the more recent expectations invested in it. Instead of using opium as part of a deliberately amoral, alienated lifestyle, De Quincey praised the drug for the sense of

harmony and high moral tone that it seemed to engender in him. A serious-minded man of the Enlightenment, whose account of the effects of opium includes quotes in Greek, Latin and Italian, he took the drug in the hope of increasing his rationality rather than obliterating it, as his modern counterparts are wont to do. It would seem, therefore, that De Quincey's current reputation as a 'cult' writer rests more on what some people are reading into him than on what he really wrote in *Confessions of an English Opium Eater*.

MUST READ *Confessions of an English Opium Eater*
READ ON Charles Baudelaire, **Jean Cocteau**, Samuel Taylor Coleridge

< 226 >

Raymond Radiguet

1903—1923
The Rimbaud of the novel

Radiguet's short life was very similar to that of the narrator's in his first book, *Devil in the Flesh* (1923). He had already composed verse when he wrote the novel between the age of 16 and 18. It told of an affair beween a schoolboy and a young married woman whose husband is fighting at the Front (based on Radiguet's own adolescent liaison with an older woman).

The novel received unanimous praise, with the *Times Literary Supplement* calling it 'one of the most outstanding twentieth century novels'. It was filmed in 1946 (starring, among others, the French comedian Jacques Tati). A huge hit, the film won the Grand Prix and the International Critics Prize. According to the critic Pauline Kael, the film had 'the beauty and despair of lovers attempting to save something for themselves in a period of hopeless confusion'.

His next book, *The Count of Orgel's Ball* (1924), was published posthumously, and was similarly received. The novelist F Scott Fitzgerald tried in vain to persuade his editor to publish it ('Raymond Radiguet's last book…is a great hit here'), although he was unaware that Radiguet had already died. A year later he was still singing its praises: 'I still think that *Count Orget's Ball* would sell like wildfire. If I had the time I'd translate it myself.' (He never found the time.)

Radiguet too ran out of time, dying of typhoid fever at the age of 20. He was buried in the famous Père-Lachaise cemetery alongside Oscar Wilde and Proust. (Doors singer Jim Morrison arrived later.) He left behind two literary gems, and as Jean Cocteau (who wrote the preface to *Devil in the Flesh*) attested: 'He belonged to the solemn race of men whose lives unfold too quickly to their close.'

MUST READ *Devil in the Flesh*
READ ON Harry Crosby, **Jean Cocteau**, F Scott Fitzgerald

Ayn Rand

1905—1982
A radical for Capitaliism

Alisa Rosenbaum was born in pre-revolutionary St Petersburg to a prosperous Jewish family. When the Bolsheviks requisitioned the pharmacy owned by her father, Fronz, the Rosenbaums fled to the Crimea. Alisa returned to the city (renamed Leningrad) to attend the university, but in 1926 relatives who had already settled in America offered her the chance of joining them there. With money from the sale of her mother's jewellery, Alisa bought a ticket to New York. On arrival at Ellis Island, she changed into Ayn

R IS FOR ON THE ROAD
10 novels to fill up your backpack

ON THE ROAD
Jack Kerouac
from East to West Coast and back again,
the original blacktop poem

BEATNIKS
Toby Litt
the Beat life sort of relived in
90s Britain

THE GRAPES OF WRATH
John Steinbeck
Okies go West in search of the
promised land

HUNGRY MEN
Edward Anderson
riding the roads and rails in search of
work in Depression America

FACTOTUM
Charles Bukowski
home is where the next drink is

NEARLY ROADKILL
Caitlin Sullivan & Kate Bornstein
crunches and prangs on the
information highway

THE ODYSSEY
Homer
everything that can happen to a man
on his way home

SOMEBODY IN BOOTS
Nelson Algren
tramping through Depression America

ZEN AND THE ART OF MOTORCYCLE
MAINTENANCE
Robert M Pirsig
a roadmap for the soul on two wheels

EVEN COWGIRLS GET THE BLUES
Tom Robbins
big thumbs keeps on hitchin'

< 228 >

(the name of a Finnish writer) Rand (taken from the brand name of her Remington-Rand typewriter). She moved swiftly to Hollywood, where she learnt English, worked in the RKO wardrobe department and as an extra (Cecil B De Mille called her his 'little caviar'), and – fuelled with Dexamyl – wrote screenplays and novels through the night. She also married a bit-part actor called Frank O'Connor because he was 'beautiful' – and because her original visitor's visa had run out.

Rand sold her first screenplay in 1932, but nobody would buy her first novel. Set in Russia, *We the Living* (1936) is a melodrama that prefigures the anti-communism of all Rand's work. Her first real success was *The Fountainhead* (rejected by more than ten publishers before publication in 1943), which follows the fortunes of Howard Roark, an architect who demolishes his own public housing scheme rather than allow its design to be compromised by the authorities. Rand was a libertarian, opposed to state interference of all kinds, and her follow-up novel *Atlas Shrugged* (1957) describes a group of entrepreneurs, artists and scientists who set up a community in Colorado in an attempt to escape American bureaucracy and its 'conspiracy of mediocrity'.

Rand's fiction is not art for art's sake but a novelisation of a philosophy that she labelled 'Objectivism' and defined as 'the concept of man as a heroic being, with his own happiness as the moral purpose of his life, and reason as

his only absolute'. Her novels elevate an idea of the rational individual struggling against collectivism and the pressure to act according to the 'good of society'. For Rand, there was no such thing as society. Although virulently anti-communist herself, Rand always regretted agreeing to appear before the red-baiting House Commission on Un-American Activities on the grounds that it too was a tool of the state. Ignored or despised by literary critics, Rand's fiction attracted a dedicated following among the American public (her keenest disciples called themselves 'the Collective' – an eerie echo of the personality cults associated with Communism). *The Fountainhead* made her a millionaire. The proceeds from *Atlas Shrugged* allowed her to set up an institute for Objectivism, headed up by her lover Nathaniel Branden (who was to become an unperson when he ended the affair and went off with a younger woman). At the peak of its influence in the mid-sixties, the institute was running courses in 80 American cities from a base in the Empire State Building.

Photographs of Rand wearing a dress covered in dollar signs suggest an eccentric, isolated figure. She may have lacked empathy with others (to the point where critics have suggested she did not even understand authors like Nietzsche, whose ideas were closest to her own), and she could be remarkably arrogant: asked to cut *Atlas Shrugged* she quipped: 'Would you cut the Bible?' But when Rand appeared on the *Johnny Carson Show* she made such an impression that

Carson cancelled his other guests and let her have the whole of the programme. By the mid-eighties, 5 million copies of *Atlas Shrugged* had been sold. A survey undertaken by the Library of Congress in 1991 concluded that, after the Bible, it has been the most influential book in the USA. Worldwide, total sales of all Rand's books have reached 30 million.

Critics complain that her work has no literary merit. Of *The Fountainhead*, which came out during wartime, the New York critic Diana Trilling wrote: 'Anyone who is taken in by it deserves a stern lecture on paper rationing'. *Time* magazine dismissed *Atlas Shrugged* with the rhetorical question, 'Is it a novel, is it a nightmare?' Feminists take issue with Rand's submissive women; but Rand described herself as a 'male chauvinist' and encouraged other women to play the heroic role previously associated with men only. Today's Greens are as alienated by her enthusiasm for technology as the New Left was in the sixties (Rand wrote a polemic against the New Left, entitled *The Anti-Industrial Revolution*). But her admirers are legion: Barbara Stanwyck and Clark Gable, who competed for the film rights to *The Fountainhead*; Michael Caine, whose daughter Dominique is named after the heroine of *The Fountainhead* (not a lot of people know that); Billie-Jean King; Federal Reserve bank chief Alan Greenspan; shockjock Rush Limbaugh; Mussolini's brother and the heavy metal band Rush.

In the seventies and eighties prominent free-marketeers contributed to the objectivist journal and some critics tried to associate Rand with the fascist far-right. But Rand herself criticised right-wing Ronald Reagan for his paternalistic anti-abortion stance, and even the left-leaning Gore Vidal conceded that her heroic characters are 'almost perfect in their immorality'. It remains to be seen how Rand, whose cigarette holder was her trademark, will fare in the anti-smoking atmosphere of contemporary America; maybe it will only reinforce her standing as one of the most influential (if cranky) libertarians of the 20th century

MUST READ *Atlas Shrugged*
READ ON Friedrich Nietzsche

Simon Raven

1927–
A black sheep among the British establishment

At Charterhouse, one of England's most prestigious public (i.e. private) schools, Simon Raven was a notable scholar in Latin and Greek and was tipped to become head of school until his pleasurable activities with persons of both sexes (intercourse with ladies of the night, mutual masturbation and oral sex with boys) were brought to the attention of the headmaster.

< 230 >

Sacked from school (a contemporary said that Raven went 'trailing an odour of brimstone' behind him; in later years the novelist and critic Angela Carter put it about that Raven had tasted human flesh), he nevertheless went up to King's College, Cambridge (noted for its sexual tolerance), where he was compared to the legendary Greek beauty (and interlocutor with Socrates) Alcibiades. He left Cambridge under something of a cloud and afterwards tried the army, but after running up a series of debts he was lucky not to be court-martialled. Back in civvies, he applied to be a spy but was turned down. Raven only turned to writing when there was nothing else left.

With publisher Anthony Blond as his patron, Raven retired to Deal in Kent, where he lived in lodgings (Raven has never owned a house or a flat or even a television set), wrote religiously for four hours a day, and spent the rest of his time reading and drinking, with only an occasional trip to London or some other fleshpot (after the age of 30, Raven began to 'prefer a good dinner to a good fuck'). Blond gave him an allowance of £15 a week, which was later cut to £12 10s in order to pay off a gambling debt. In exchange, Raven sent Blond the typescripts of a ten-volume series of novels, *Alms for Oblivion*. (Raven recalls that the aim of a ten-book deal was to get Blond to provide for him for at least ten years.) *Alms for Oblivion* follows the unravelling of the British establishment during the 30 years after the Second World War and, according to Raven, is concerned with 'time and chance and the malice of most of the human race, and occasional goodness mixed up with malice, lust and sloth'.

Much has been made of the real-life precursors of some of the fictional characters in *Alms for Oblivion*: William Rees-Mogg/Somerset Lloyd James; the Tory minister James, now Lord, Prior/Peter Morrison MP; Anthony Blond/Gregory Stern, the Jewish publisher who is crucified by the PLO; Simon Raven himself/the disfigured ex-army officer turned writer Henry Fielding. Raven does not deny that these characters are based on real individuals, many of whom he went to school with, but maintains that they contain fictional elements as well.

Raven is an optimist in style and a pessimist about human history. Steeped in the classics, he says that aesthetic excellence is the reward of talent and effort. His sentences appear effortless, but only because they are crafted in the classical manner (his publisher reports never having to change a comma of Raven's work). Although Raven believes that beauty can be achieved, he is by no means so sure about progress. He avers that there has been 'technical progress, but no one seems to a jot happier'. He thinks that 'we keep ending up in the same place' – like one of the heroic figures of Greek mythology who is condemned to repeat his fate over and over again. In short, he is a self-confessed snob (the way to mantain high-quality institutions, he says, is to keep people out) who hates 'growth, development and democracy'. The last novel in the *Alms for Oblivion* series, *The Survivors*, was published in 1975. Nine years later, in 1984, Raven published the first (*Morning Star*) in another, shorter sequence (*The First-Born of Egypt*). He wrote the screenplay for the James Bond film *On Her Majesty's Secret Service*, and he has adapted the work of other novelists (Aldous Huxley, for example) for television. He now lodges in a home for impoverished Old Carthusians (old boys of Charterhouse – so he has been accepted into the fold which rejected him in the late forties), where, sexually impotent and unable to drink with anything like his former gusto, he takes pleasure in reading the classics which he says he skimped in his 'spunky youth'.

MUST READ *Alms for Oblivion* – all ten volumes
READ ON **Anthony Burgess**, Ian Fleming, Anthony Powell, Edward Upward

Derek Raymond

1931–1994
He lived with his eyes open

Robert Cook failed to follow the career path that his prosperous southern English family had laid out for him. Turning his back on public

(private) school and a life of privilege he changed his name to Robin Cook and went looking for bad company. He used his experiences as the basis for *The Crust on its Uppers* (1962), chronicling the connections between the Chelsea Set and the underworld on the cusp of the Swinging Sixties. By the time the sixties were in full flow, however, Cook had already made another escape.

In *A State of Denmark* (1970), his protagonist is on the lam from a near-fascist Britain. Cook himself also went into exile. He lived in Morocco, Italy, Turkey and the USA before settling in France, where he remained for 18 years during the seventies and eighties. During this period he did casual work in the vineyards, and also produced four 'Factory' novels featuring an unnamed policeman who uses his own alienation from society and the police force in order to get into the minds of psychopaths. By this time, the name Robin Cook was associated with the bestselling American author of *Coma*, and Cook was forced to choose another new name for publication purposes. He opted for 'Derek Raymond', partly in homage to the crime writer Raymond Chandler. For many years the Factory novels of Derek Raymond were well received in France (Claude Chabrol made a film based on one of them) but almost unknown in Britain. In the late eighties a number of British critics picked up on Cook/Raymond, and this encouraged him to return to London. He took a modest flat in West Hampstead (which is closer in spirit to the tough district of nearby Kilburn than to the literary life of Hampstead proper), where he bashed out his autobiography (*The Hidden Files*, 1992) and another Factory novel (*Dead Man Upright*, 1993) on an ancient Amstrad wordprocessor. Cook/Raymond enjoyed a drink (he was often to be seen, wearing his trademark beret, in the French House in Dean Street and afterwards in various Soho drinking clubs), and took great pleasure in making a record (his speaking voice was both delicate and raspish) with a group of musicians and admirers known as Gallon Drunk. Cook's body came in for plenty of punishment over the years and he died prematurely in 1994.

The Factory novels contain incredibly detailed descriptions of gruesome killings. One publisher is said to have been physically sick after reading the manuscript of *I Was Dora Suarez* (1991), and Cook/Raymond said that he too felt queasy after entering into the personality of his psychopathic killers. Some critics maintain that the violence in his novels is never gratuitous, and that his descriptions of human degradation contribute to an uplifting investigation of what makes us human in the first place. This seems especially true of *He Died With His Eyes Open* (1984) which combines the sensitivity of Samuel Beckett's *Krapp's Last Tape* with the brutality of Mickey Spillane's *I, The Jury*. The *Sunday Times* summation – 'a gripping study in obsession and absolute, awful evil' – does not tell the half of it. Others insist that

Cook/Raymond was simply a sensationalist; and at least one senior London-based critic thought that he was 'a complete fraud'.

MUST READ *The Crust on its Uppers, He Died With His Eyes Open, The Hidden Files, I Was Dora Suarez, A State of Denmark*
READ ON **Samuel Beckett, David Goodis, Patrick Hamilton, Malcolm Lowry**

John Rechy

1934–
Strangers in the night

Texas-born John Rechy leapt to prominence in 1963 with his unflinching account of life in the homosexual underbelly of America, *City of Night*. This was a fictional narrative. In 1978 Rechy published *The Sexual Outlaw*, an equally influential documentary journey through roughly the same terrain. In most of his work Rechy projects an image of gay life as a self-enclosed world that reverses the taboos of straight society. *Bodies and Souls* (1983) was something of a departure, in that its main character is the city of Los Angeles: 'the most spiritual and physical of cities, a profound city which drew to it the various bright and dark energies of the country'. Rechy's Los Angeles is populated by porn superstar Amber; punk-rocker Manny Gomez; Dave Clinton, a male

City of Night by John Rechy

The Vampires); a one-act play *Momma as She Became – But Not as She Was*; and *Rushes*, a novel that was subsequently turned into a play.

MUST READ *City of Night, Bodies and Souls*
READ ON **Donald Barthelme, Jean Genet**

Ishmael Reed

1938–
Postmodern hoodoo guru

Born in the South (Tennessee), Ishmael Scott Reed was raised in Buffalo in New York State. In the mid-sixties he founded his own magazine as a vehicle for avant-garde writing, the *East Village Other*.

The central themes of Reed's fiction are paranoia and the absurd, as located in the black experience. His plots are filled with intelligently playful comicbook mischief. *The Freelance Pallbearers* (1967) is a free-form satire on radical black politics. In *Yellow Back Radio Broke Down* (1969), Reed used the term 'Hoodoo' to describe absurd combinations of racial and cultural mythologies. *Mumbo Jumbo* (1972) is an allegorical account of the effects of jazz on the West. *The Last Day of Louisiana Red* (1974) and *Flight To Canada* (1976) are more straightforward and less experimental in their protest against the position of blacks in the USA. But with *Reckless Eyeballing* (1986) – the

stripper who is past his prime; Mandy Lang-Jones, a tough TV personality; street-hustlers Billy and Stud; and televangelist Sister Woman. They inhabit paradise lost, yet they are still in search of redemption. The suggestion of the redemptive potential of personal and sexual relationships is a hallmark of Rechy's work, which also includes novels such as *Numbers*

< 234 > (1967), *This Day's Death, The Fourth Angel* and

title is taken from an infamous charge against a black man who was later lynched – Reed is back at his satirical best. The novel tells the tale of a black playwright who has been 'sex-listed' by a feminist mafia, and who is trying to get back into the sisters' good books. Reed was satirising political correctness before most people knew it existed.

Reed is an academic (as well as respected poet) and his 1992 novel, *Japanese by Spring*, is set on a campus that is taken over by the Japanese. (With typical boundary-dissolving playfulness, Reed himself appears in the book as a champion of multiculturalism.) His critics complain that he is a professional maverick who has to be outside current trends, regardless of whether or not they are valid.

MUST READ *The Freelance Pallbearers, Mumbo Jumbo, Reckless Eyeballing*
READ ON **Chester Himes**, LeRoi Jones, P J O'Rourke, **Thomas Pynchon**

Luke Rhinehart

d.o.b. not known
The Dice Man

George Cockcroft (aka Luke Rhinehart) is something of a mystery man.

He was educated at Cornell and Columbia Universities, gaining a Ph.D in American literature from Columbia. He then taught creative writing for 12 years at a number of colleges, resigning after the success of his first novel.

The Dice Man (1971), called 'the most fashionable novel of the early 1970s' by *Time Out* magazine, is narrated by its eponymous protagonist, aka Dr Luke Rhinehart, a bored psychiatrist who decides to dispense with his own free will and 'let the dice decide' what he will do next: he throws the die and starts a new life by going downstairs to rape his colleague's wife. The rest of the book is a picaresque account of Dr Rhinehart's eventful career according to Chance. The book was perfect for the children of the 70s – the Me generation, jaded by the failure of the 60s counter culture, yet still heading further into lifestyle experiments and hedonistic excess. The idea of stepping outside both morality and purposive activity was attractive and simple to follow, although next to no one pursued it for real – despite what that old hippie in the pub tells you. Rhinehart/Cockroft continued to play with this idea in subsequent books (*The Search for the Dice Man, Adventures of Wim, Matari, Long Voyage Back*) but none of these received as much attention as the original. Film rights were sold to Paramount in 1971, but it is yet to be filmed although there have been more than a dozen screenplays generated including one from Rhinehart himself in 1995. But it looks as if the book, very much a product of its time, has had its role of the dice.

MUST READ *The Dice Man*
READ ON Graham Greene, **Albert Camus**, Henry Fielding

Anne Rice

1939—
Queen of the Damned

Anne Rice is known primarily as the author of *The Vampire Chronicles*, a series of five books in which the vampires are both heroes and villians, beginning with the publication of *Interview with the Vampire* in 1976 (subsequently filmed by Francis Ford Coppola with Tom Cruise and Keanu Reeves in the starring roles) and followed by *The Vampire Lestat* (1985) and *Queen of the Damned* (1988). In an interview broadcast in an edition of BBC television's *Bookmark*, Rice explained that 'I write to fight' the sense in which 'life is almost unbearable – pain, loss, destruction and chaos'. Her own life story gives some indication of why she feels compelled to

Anne Rice

write and fight against the 'almost unbearable' nature of existence.

Rice was born in a house on St Charles Avenue on the edge of the garden district of New Orleans. The elegance and mystery of the surrounding houses made a profound impression on her, as did going to church, which she recalls as a 'sensuous drench' involving the heavy perfume of flowers, incense and graphic images of Christ's suffering. During her earliest years Rice's father was away fighting in the

< 236 >

Second World War, and she became particularly close to her mother, who was both a fine story-teller who wanted her daughters to become geniuses, and a chronic alcoholic who drank herself into long stupors and ultimately, via severe liver-damage, to death. At 16, Rice left the 'Gothic atmosphere' of her New Orleans childhood and went to high school in Texas, where she met her husband-to-be, Stan. After she went to work in San Francisco Stan tracked her down and they embarked upon a 'hot correspondence' that culminated in marriage.

The newly weds lived in the Haight –Ashbury district of San Francisco, and witnessed the hippie scene magically mushrooming around them. Stan Rice soon became a prominent poet on the local literary scene, while Anne stayed in the background. When Stan got a job teaching at university, they decided to have kids. Their daughter Michelle was conceived almost immediately and their life seemed idyllic, until Michelle died of leukaemia. Stan and Anne entered their 'Scott and Zelda' period, drinking all the time because they no longer cared what happened. Then, three years after their daughter's death, Anne began to stay up all night, typing her first vampire story. Her writing made them wealthy, but as Anne Rice, dressed in black, sits writing among her vast collection of dolls (substitutes, perhaps, for the daughter she no longer has), it seems as if money and fame are a poor recompense for the carefree contentment that her own life has denied her.

If writing is a way of keeping her demons at bay, it is also a form of cathartic release in which Anne Rice's experiences are recapitulated and expressed in an imaginative form. Rice has been compared to Bram Stoker (author of the original Dracula story), but her ability to find beauty in the macabre, and her evocation of being damned like a vampire, are probably unsurpassed in their intensity.

Another take on Rice is that she puts an existential slant on the vampire myths. Through her reinterpretation of the vampire, we encounter various existential truths: the absence of God and the existence of flesh, blood and soil; the boredom of our lives; the need to find a moral universe, even if we must fabricate it for ourselves. We are also invited to confront their/our helplessly destructive tendencies, as expressed in the thirst for blood.

Rice has also written a trilogy, *The Mayfair Witches*; *Witching Hour* (1990), *Lasher* (1993), *Talos* (1994), and three other novels, including *The Violin*. She has published under two pseudonyms: as Anne Rampling she wrote the erotic novels *Exit to Eden* (1985) and *Belinda* (1986), and as A N Roquelaure she wrote another trilogy, *Beauty* (1983–5).

MUST READ *The Vampire Chronicles*
READ ON **Poppy Z Brite, Albert Camus, Edgar Allan Poe, Bram Stoker**

R

Rainer Maria Rilke
1875–1926
The Santa Claus of loneliness

Rainer Maria Rilke was born in Prague, lived mainly in Vienna, and wrote in German. In life he was as fastidious – obsessive, even – as he was meticulous in art. Rilke's critics have suggested that being forced to wear girls' clothes as a child might have had an adverse effect on him.

In his poetry and prose, Rilke's main subject is the distance between himself and the rest of the world. W H Auden dubbed him 'the Santa Claus of loneliness'. His sense of alienation is summed up in the declaration that it is our 'fate to be opposite and nothing else, and always opposite'. Although Rilke was acutely conscious of his own separation from everything else, he strove to find a way of looking and describing that was holistic rather than fragmented. There are mystical elements in his early lyric poetry, but his later work is more concerned with material things and their meaning. Rilke's prose, notably *Das Buch vom lieben Gott und Anderes* (*Tales of God and Other Things*; 1900); *Die Weise vom Leben und Tod des Cornets Christoph Rilke* (*The Lay of the Life and Death of Cornet Christoph Rilke*; 1906); and *Die Aufzeichnungen des Malte Laurids Brigge* (*The Notebooks of Malte Laurids Brigge*; 1910) tend towards the quality and density of poetry. His last poems, *Die Sonette an Orpheus* (*Sonnets to Orpheus*) and

Duineser Elegien (*Duino Elegies*; 1923) are concerned with 'the identity of terror and bliss' and 'the oneness of life and death'.

There are one or two sunny passages in Rilke, but he is not designed for holiday reading. He died in an appropriately intense but absurd fashion: of blood poisoning after being cut by the thorn of a rose that he had picked for a young woman.

MUST READ *Duino Elegies*
READ ON John Keats, Thomas Mann, Vladimir Mayakovsky

Tom Robbins

1936–
Cosmic counterculture ideals, outrageous comic plots, outlandish characters

Born in Blowing Rock, North Carolina, the son of two Baptist preachers, Robbins was writing stories at the age of five. Educated at Lee University (journalism) and the University of Washington (Far Eastern studies), he then worked as a meteorologist, journalist and broadcaster until the publication of his first novel, *Another Roadside Attraction* (1971), which gradually became a cult success. After that, he produced a novel every four or five years, writing them from his home in Seattle.

The second novel, *Even Cowgirls Get the Blues* (1976) received effusive praise. Thomas Pynchon deemed it as 'one of those special novels…that you just want to ride off into the sunset with'. Surrounding the hitchhiking adventures of big-thumbed Sissy Hankshaw, the book also features one Dr Robbins: 'preventative psychiatrist and reality instructor'. The novel was filmed in 1993 by director Gus Van Sant. The film expert Leonard Maltin described the film as 'a candidate for the decade's worst movie: there is not enough peyote in the entire American Southwest to render scenes set in the feminist-collective ranch comprehensible or possible to endure'. Ever charitable, he also described the novel as 'hopelessly outdated'.

Summaries just don't do the surreal rollercoaster rides of Robbins's novels any justice: *Still Life with Woodpecker* (1980) takes place in the confines of a packet of Camel cigarettes; *Jitterbug Perfume* (1984) is the story of two people who discover the secret of immortality through sex and perfume; while *Another Roadside Attraction* features circus hippies who send Jesus's corpse into space. Robbins is one of those writers you either love or loathe; you rarely find readers sitting on the fence. His fans see his books as more than just a good read: they're life-affirming, even life-changing. Ancient culture and myths, and how they relate to our modern entrenched cynicism are a frequent theme for Robbins. In amongst all the wacky play he tries to re-enliven our tired hearts

R

with timeless philosophical truths and the latent wonder of the world. And importantly for many of his readers, most of the heroic leading roles are played by complex women characters. Those who don't like Robbins find his prose unbearably cutesy and naïve.

Summing up his own intentions, Robbins said 'Too many people mistake misery for art. You don't have to be somber to be serious about a subject. My characters show that. One of my main themes is joy in spite of everything.'

MUST READ *Even Cowgirls Get the Blues, Jitterbug Perfume*
READ ON **Richard Brautigan, Ken Kesey, Thomas Pynchon**

Henry Rollins
1961—
Total commitment, but to what?

Raised in Arlington, Virginia (near Washington DC and home to the largest military cemetery in the world), Henry Garfield was beaten by his father. He left home as soon as he could and took a series of dead-end jobs, including working in a Häagen Daz ice-cream shop, in order to avoid having to go back to his parents. He also left his name behind and became Henry Rollins.

Pumping iron, punk music and performance poetry were the three main interests in the life of the young Henry Rollins. He built up his own physical bulk, formed the archetypal American punk band Black Flag, renowned for its total commitment in attitude and performance, and started to publish prose poems. Black Flag broke up in 1986, and Rollins went on to front his own outfit. Just before Christmas 1991, Rollins's best friend and former Black Flag roadie Joe Cole was shot dead; Rollins himself was lucky to be left alive. The following year he declared 'I'm not an ordinary guy, I'm not. I'm damaged.'

Rollins's early writing was published by the Illiterati Press; later he formed his own publishing company, named after his date of birth: 2 13 61 (13 February 1961). He is a prolific writer (*Bang!*, *Eye Scream*, and *Pissing in the Gene Pool*, are just some of the many volumes

< 240 >

he has produced), who has done thousands of spoken-word performances all over the world. Nearly all Rollins's writing and performances take the form of a stream-of-consciousness confessional. He once said that 'writing is the stitching that stops me from exploding'. Writing may well be therapeutic for Rollins, but this does not necessarily translate into literary merit.

Rollins appeared in a cameo role as the bodyguard in the film *Heat*. He also performed a notoriously sexy scene on video with the post-punk performance artist Lydia Lunch.

MUST READ *Eye Scream*
READ ON **Norman Mailer**, Friedrich Nietzsche

Damon Runyon

1884–1946
The verbal cartoonist of life on Broadway

Demobbed from the American army at the end of the war with Spain (1898), Damon Runyon became a sports journalist with the *New York American* (1911), and subsequently a feature writer of syndicated columns such as 'The Brighter Side' and 'Both Barrels', which combined social comment with satirical humour. But his reputation rests on his short stories depicting life among the colourful criminal classes of New York's Broadway. Runyon took the argot of petty criminals and the idiomatic use of the historic present tense, and combined them into a highly stylised form of writing which is very much a literary creation, while also containing an authentic-sounding tone. One of Runyon's anthologies (*Guys and Dolls*, 1932) was used as the basis for a musical, which was then made into a film starring Frank Sinatra and Marlon Brando. In the last years of his life Runyon himself became a film producer.

Many of Runyon's stories were collected into two anthologies and republished by Picador in the seventies. At around the same time, a music writer by the name of Penny Reel started writing articles in the *New Musical Express* in the characteristic Runyon style (historic present, plenty of street-slang). Most *NME* readers remained ignorant of its origins, however, and assumed that this style of writing was a creation of the post-punk era.

MUST READ *On Broadway*
READ ON **Dashiell Hammett**, James Thurber

R IS FOR LITERARY RECLUSES
10 writers who want to be alone

CORMAC MCCARTHY
if you're passing through El Paso, just ride right on stranger

J D SALINGER
the original pace-setter – even publishing is too high profile

THOMAS PYNCHON
master of paranoia of whom there's only one known photograph

DON DELILLO
even wrote a novel about a literary recluse, but he's getting better

GOD
the original 'don't ask, its all in the book' merchant

EMILY DICKINSON
published under a pseudonym, didn't leave the house for 20 years

RALPH ELLISON
wrote the Invisible Man and then disappeared

WILLIAM GADDIS
a self-perpetuating literary Zelig, his self-portraits are headless

B TRAVEN
mysterious pseudonym of the Mexican desert chronicler

SALMAN RUSHDIE
would dearly love to get out more, but...

Leopold von Sacher-Masoch

1836–1895 (1905?)
Whip crack away

In January 1836 Leopold von Sacher-Masoch was born into a family of high-ranking officials in the Austro-Hungarian Empire. He grew up in the Galician town of Lemberg in Eastern Europe. One day, during a game of hide and seek, the young Leopold was hiding in a cupboard in the bedroom of a relative of his father, Countess Xenobia, who customarily wore a house jacket trimmed with fur. She entered the room with her lover and Leopold watched as the couple made love – until the Countess's husband charged into the room. The Countess hit him in the face and then beat him on the back with a whip, prompting him to retreat; when Leopold stirred noisily and was discovered, he received much the same treatment. From then on Leopold von Sacher-Masoch seemed to have associated arousal and sexual pleasure with infidelity and pain – preferably inflicted by a woman dressed in fur. This association became the centrepiece of both his life and his work.

When Anna de Kottowitz left her husband for Sacher-Masoch, he pushed her into the arms of yet another man – a con artist who was pretending to be a Polish count. This episode subsequently provided the basis for Sacher-Masoch's story 'The Separated Wife'. During his relationship with Fanny Pistor, Sacher-Masoch volunteered to obey her unconditionally for six months, and even dressed as her servant. Meanwhile, she promised to treat him cruelly and to wear fur while abusing him. This relationship later served as the basis for Sacher-Masoch's most famous story, 'Venus in Furs'. Some years afterwards, he came to an arrangement with his first wife Aurora – who appears in her own memoirs as 'Wanda', the dominatrix of 'Venus In Furs' – whereby he would stop writing about women with furs and whips if she would agree to dress in fur and whip him herself. Sacher-Masoch's voyeuristic tendencies were not satisfied, however, until he persuaded Aurora/Wanda to take a young Hungarian named Sandor as her lover.

After this marriage was dissolved, Sacher-Masoch married Hulda Meister, who bore him three children in what seems to have been a relatively orthodox relationship. The official version of Sacher-Masoch's demise is that he died peacefully in the German town of Hessen in March 1895; some reports suggest that he was committed to an asylum where he lived in complete obscurity for another ten years.

During his lifetime, Sacher-Masoch was a widely respected writer. His volume of stories *The Heritage of Cain*, comprising 'The Wanderer', 'Platonic Love', 'Venus in Furs' and others, was published in 1870 by the reputable

Stuttgart firm of J A Cotta. As well as erotic elements, these stories contain Sacher-Masoch's observations on marriage, the state and society. When Leopold and Aurora/Wanda were resident in Leipzig, he edited a journal of international affairs, *Auf der Hohe* (*On the Summit*), and was regarded as second only to Heine as a writer of German prose. After 25 years as a man of letters, Sacher-Masoch was awarded the Légion d'Honneur by the French government. It was his strong reputation as a writer that prompted Krafft-Ebbing and then Freud to adopt his name as the label for the age-old syndrome whereby sexual pleasure is derived from the experience of pain and suffering.

Sacher-Masoch's writing is less stilted and verbose than most Victorian prose. It is crisp and matter of fact, and in this respect not totally dissimilar to that of early William Burroughs (*Junky, Queer*). But Sacher-Masoch's reputation far exceeds his actual readership and, rather than the story itself, it was surely the idea of a Venus in Furs that in recent years has excited pop musicians such as the Psychedelic Furs and the Velvet Underground, who lifted the title of Sacher-Masoch's story and used it as the basis for one of their best-known songs.

MUST READ *Venus in Furs*
READ ON Georges Bataille, **Marquis de Sade**, John Cleland, D H Lawrence, **Alexander Trocchi**

< 244 >

J D Salinger
1919–
Reclusive guru of disaffected youth

Salinger was born in New York to a Scottish mother and a Jewish father who was an importer of Kosher cheese. He was largely educated at Valley Forge Military Academy (the 'Pencey Prep' of *The Catcher in the Rye*) where he was literary editor of the class yearbook, 'Crossed Sabres', in which he was nicknamed 'Salinger the Sublime'. Leaving school at 17, Salinger worked on a cruise liner as a dancing partner for wealthy spinsters along with a friend called Holden, whose name Salinger appropriated for his immortal creation Holden Caulfield. He dabbled as a student at various universities, and travelled to Europe around 1937, writing stories en route, sending them to magazines and beginning to learn 'how not to mind when the manuscripts came back'. His first story, 'The Young Folks', was published in 1940. In 1948 he published 'A Perfect Day for Bananafish', the earliest reference to the Glass family, whose stories would go on to form the main corpus of his writing. The family, who appear in the collections *Franny and Zooey* (1961), *Raise High the Roof Beam, Carpenters* (1963) and *Seymour: An Introduction* (1963) are the intellectual kids of two vaudeville veterans; their stories are narrated by Buddy Glass, Salinger's self-confessed alter ego. The books display, thinly veiled,

J D Salinger

would catapult him to an unlikely star status and upon which his reputation largely rests.

The Catcher in the Rye was finally published in 1951, becoming a bestseller, introducing to an unsuspecting world Holden Caulfield, the first hero of adolescent angst. It is the story of a depressed prep school kid who plays truant from school and heads off for a weekend in New York. After several depressing encounters he ends up at the end of the novel in a psychiatric clinic. Holden was the figure that launched a thousand literary caricatures. When described now, the character sounds hackneyed: he is cynical about everything and secretly frozen by the thought of impending adulthood. But before Holden the state of adolescence didn't really exist in print and it has still rarely been bettered. He describes everything as 'phoney' (his favourite word) and is constantly in search of sincerity and lost innocence. In retrospect, the book's greatest achievement is its mimicking of the teen vernacular, making Holden a kind of Cold War Huckleberry Finn. If a criticism had to be raised it would be of Salinger's tendency toward sentimentality. By 1970, the book had been translated into 30 languages; it still sells a quarter of a million copies in English each year.

When the stage and screen director Elia Kazan begged for permission to produce the novel on Broadway, Salinger replied: 'I cannot give my permission. I fear Holden wouldn't like it.' Similarly, when Hollywood wanted to buy the film rights and Salinger refused, movie

Salinger's reverence for Zen Buddhism (he was also an ardent devotee of *The Gospels of Sri Ramakrishna*, a huge study of Hindu mysticism). Franny herself proclaims: 'I'm just sick of ego, ego, ego. My own and everyone else's.'

In March, 1948 *Uncle Wiggily in Connecticut* appeared and was bought for the screen and filmed the following year as *My Foolish Heart*, the only Salinger piece to be screened. He then turned to the novel he'd been writing intermittently for years, the work that moguls sent him a grand piano to try to change his mind. He sent it back. Holden presumably wouldn't have liked that either.

Salinger grew so sick of media attention that he retreated to the wilds of New Hampshire and has virtually disappeared behind a 40-year wall of silence. His close friend the humorist S J Perelman visited him and noted that 'Jerry's in fine shape (though looking a little hunted because of those acolytes who steal up his mountain in their bare feet to get The Word).'

But that was it for Salinger. With the curious exception of one story recently published on the internet by a friend, he has stayed a recluse, seeking enlightenment, writing for himself and not for an audience (and definitely not for publishers). Or, as fellow New Yorker author John Cheever speculated, was it a case of 'hiding in the bathroom like Salinger who never seemed to find his way out'? Who knows? Salinger has been married and divorced twice and a book about their relationship by one of his wives is pending.

MUST READ *The Catcher in the Rye*
READ ON **Douglas Coupland**, Kaye Gibbons, *In Search of J D Salinger* by Ian Hamilton, *Shoeless Joe by* W Kinsella (in which Salinger appears as a character), **Jay McInerney**

< 246 >

James Salter

1925–
Unsung hero of American letters

Born in New Jersey, Salter was raised in New York City and educated at Georgetown University and West Point Military Academy. He served in the air force for 12 years, leaving in 1957, the year after his first novel, *The Hunters*, was published. Among Salter's squadron were Edward White, the first American to walk in space ('I watched as on screens everywhere he walked dreamily in space…I was sick with envy…Whatever I might do, it would not be as overwhelming as this'), and Buzz Aldrin, one of the first men on the moon.

Hunters, like his second book, *The Arm of Flesh* (1961), is set in the world of jet pilots during the Korean War. About boredom, uncertainty and the limits of personal ability as much as the traditional questions of battle, it is one of the finest novels to come out of the conflict. The book was filmed dreadfully in 1958, starring Robert Mitchum as the major who, because of his coolness in combat, is known as *The Iceman*. During a ten-year film career Salter wrote numerous screenplays (including one for Robert Redford's 1969 film *Downhill Racer*) and occasionally directed.

In 1961, Salter moved to France, where he lived for a year. His style, as he admitted, was influenced by French authors, including André Gide and Jean Genet. His 1967 erotic tour de force, *A Sport and a Pastime* (as he put it: 'licentious yet pure, an immaculate book filled with images of an unchaste world more desirable than our own') was loosely based on his experiences there. It is the story of a sexual relationship between a French waitress and an American graduate, as related by an American student staying at his house – one man's fantasies of another's adventures.

Despite being praised by other authors – Joseph Heller, Graham Greene, John Irving and Michael Ondaatje – Salter, unjustly, remains on the outskirts of literary fame.

MUST READ *A Sport and a Pastime, Hunters*
READ ON John Cheever, **Jean Genet**, Peter Matthiessen

Jean-Paul Sartre

1905–1980
In search of freedom

Born in Paris, Jean-Paul Sartre attended the Ecole Normale Supérieure where he read philosophy and psychology. In 1928 he failed his *agrégation* (the competitive examination for the state teaching qualification) but the following year came top, with the love of his life Simone de Beauvoir in second place. After military service he taught philosophy at the *lycée* (high school) in Le Havre, in 1933 succeeding Raymond Aron as fellow at the Institut Français in Berlin, where he studied phenomenology. Returning to Paris in 1937, he continued teaching (intermittently) until 1944. At the outbreak of the Second World War he was called up, but was taken prisoner in 1940 without seeing action. Released in 1941 he was loosely associated with the French Resistance until the end of the war.

In the immediate postwar period Sartre was hailed as the brains behind existentialism – the philosophy (and fashion statement) which maintains that the present moment is all that exists (everything else is 'bad faith'). Existentialism caught on among young people in Paris and swiftly became an international phenomenon. But from the early fifties Sartre began to move away from existentialism and its disconnectedness, and to integrate himself into the politics of the left. In May 1968 he identified himself with student radicalism, and subsequently became associated with the Maoist version of Marxism.

Sartre's fiction belongs to the earlier period of his philosophical journey. *Nausea* (1938, English translation 1949) describes a man (Roquentin) who suddenly finds normal life nauseating (his feelings of nausea are reduced when he hears a black woman singing the blues – surely one of the first literary references to

< 247 >

S

CULT FICTION

white boys searching for salvation in the black experience). The trilogy *Roads to Freedom* (*The Age of Reason*, 1945; *The Reprieve*, 1947; *Iron in the Soul*, 1949) follows the fortunes of teacher Mathieu Delarue from the prewar Parisian world of nightclubs and cafés, through the heatwave week of September 1939 when the world hovered on the brink of war, to his call-up into the French army, the fall of France and the moments before his death, in which Delarue felt more sure of himself than at any other time in his life. In the final part of the last book, attention shifts to the story of Bruno, a communist and prisoner of war – perhaps a presentiment of the shift in Sartre's own thinking, away from existentialism towards political commitment.

In the sixties and seventies Sartre the philosopher, essayist, novelist, dramatist and editor of the magazine *Les Temps Modernes*, was probably the most widely known French intellectual in the English-speaking world. *Roads to Freedom* was televised by the BBC in a series which was both controversial and groundbreaking. Sartre was also satirised as the epitome of needlessly obscure French intellectualism; in the comedy series *Monty Python's Flying Circus* his very name became a mantra of silliness. Some critics suggested that Sartre was making a fool of himself with his apparent embrace of extreme left politics. The image of him – a short, middle-aged man wearing spectacles, standing at factory gates trying to sell copies of a Maoist

workers' paper – prompted frequent criticism and much hilarity.

MUST READ *Nausea, Roads to Freedom*
READ ON **Simone de Beauvoir, Albert Camus,** Iris Murdoch

Budd Schulberg

1914–
A child of Hollywood

Budd Schulberg grew up in Hollywood, where his dad was one of the founding fathers of the American film industry. His first novel, *What Makes Sammy Run?* (1941), is a satirical account of the film world, in which a talentless but manipulative Jew makes it to the top while more creative men fail. *The Harder They Fall* (1947) focuses on racketeering in professional boxing, and has been compared to the muckraking protest novels of Upton Sinclair such as *The Jungle* (1906). Schulberg wrote *On the Waterfront* for the screen (1954), and subsequently produced a 'novelisation' (1955) of the tale of union corruption and gangsterism in the docklands of New York. He was to return to the same subject a quarter of a century later in *Everything that Moves* (1980).

Schulberg also published two collections of short stories, *Some Faces in the Crowd* (1950) and *Love, Action, Laughter and Other Sad Tales*

< 248 >

Budd Schulberg

Shep cannot help admiring Manley, even as he destroys himself.

Anthony Burgess proclaimed: 'Halliday is a three-dimensional creation who will haunt the imagination of all who have the good fortune to be coming, for the first time, to this remarkable novel.' Though by no means as attractive, the character of Shep is equally credible and, at times, poignant. Whereas Schulberg's other writing is 'not quite literature', Burgess noted that in *The Disenchanted*, 'by taking as his protagonist a master of language, Schulberg was forced into the development of a style which is sometimes distinguished and always assured'. This is the undisputed peak of his achievement.

MUST READ *The Disenchanted, On the Waterfront*
READ ON F Scott Fitzgerald, Elia Kazan, **Gavin Lambert**, Upton Sinclair

(1990). The autobiographical *Moving Pictures: memories of a Hollywood prince* came out in 1981. But Schulberg will be remembered most for *The Disenchanted* (1950), which follows the breakdown of a famous but failing author (Manley Halliday in the story, F Scott Fitzgerald in real life) as seen through the eyes of a younger man, Shep. The latter is politically active and morally upright, whereas the former represents the decadence of the roaring twenties and of living only for aesthetic pleasure; but

Bruno Schulz

1892–1942
The Polish Kafka

Schulz spent the whole of his short life in Drohobycz, a small and predominantly Jewish town in south-eastern Poland, where he taught art at the local secondary school. Aged 40, he sent some of his stories to Zofia Nalkowska, a leading novelist in Warsaw; they were published in 1934 as *Cinnamon Shops* (later known as *The Street of Crocodiles*), and his reputation grew. Awarded a prize from the Polish Academy of Letters, Schulz's school gave him a professorship, but no extra money!

Having translated Kafka's *The Trial* into Polish (Kafka was an important influence), in 1937 Schulz published another story collection, with his own illustrations, entitled *Sanatorium under the Sign of the Hourglass*. Like its predecessor, it was, in Schulz's words: 'An attempt at eliciting the history of a certain family…that aura that thickens around any family history, can occasionally disclose to a poet its second, mythical face…a depth in which the secret mystery of blood and race is hidden.'

Although his books were critically acclaimed in Poland, Schulz desired international renown, and was hopeful of 'breaking the borders of Polish language', but never lived long enough to see it. Only five years after his debut, war was declared and, as a Jew, Schulz was transferred to a ghetto in Drohobycz.

Always a shy, lonely man, Schulz craved solitude for his art, and his whole purpose in life was 'to use it creatively'. The war finished all that, and towards the end of his life he sent folders containing his work to friends. Manuscripts containing stories, a novel called *The Messiah*, and much of his voluminous correspondence, were lost, and never resurfaced after the war.

In September 1942 he was returning home

< 250 >

with a loaf of bread, when a Gestapo officer, as a grudge against another Nazi (an admirer of Schulz's drawings), shot and killed him.

MUST READ *The Street of Crocodiles*
READ ON **Franz Kafka, Robert Musil, Rainer Maria Rilke**

Delmore Schwartz

1913—1966
hard-drinking boho poet who died too young

Born to Jewish immigrant parents in Brooklyn, Schwartz was educated at Harvard and New York University, and later taught at various colleges around the country. One of his students and fans was Lou Reed, future songwriter and leader of the Velvet Underground.

His first collection of poems, *In Dreams Begin Responsibilities*, was published in 1938 and was instantly acclaimed, with poet and critic Allen Tate proclaiming it to be 'the first real innovation that we've had since Eliot and Pound'. The title-piece of the book was not a poem but a story, which Schwartz had written in 1935 and which had been published in the first issue of *Partisan Review*, in preference to work by such luminaries as Edmund Wilson and James Farrell. An autobiographical masterpiece, it was selected by Vladimir Nabokov as one of 'his half dozen favourites' in contemporary American fiction.

Following that, Schwartz translated Rimbaud's *Season in Hell*, and ensconced himself among the Greenwich Village bohemians, enjoying his literary fame and drinking excessively. Much of this was portrayed in his first story collection (which originally had been intended as a novel), *The World is a Wedding* (1948). Three of the stories, along with the 1941 poem, 'Shenandoah', featured the autobiographical character, Shenandoah Fish, a 'young writer of promise', somewhat alienated, who 'had for long cherished the belief that if he were an interesting and gifted author, everyone would like him and want to be with him and enjoy conversation with him'.

Schwartz's verse collection *Galahad I* (1943) was to have been his *Waste Land*, but the critics were unimpressed, and he was bitterly disappointed. Much of his work in the mid-forties consisted of unfinished stories about failed authors, and this (along with his drinking) signalled the beginning of his mental and physical decline.

He died alone in a Times Square hotel, but was resurrected on the Velvet Underground track 'European Son to Delmore Schwartz' and, more significantly, as Von Humboldt Fleisher, poet, intellectual, and drunk, in Saul Bellow's novel *Humboldt's Gift* (1975). Bellow sums up the Schwartz/Humboldt predicament as follows: 'It was, as he saw it, Humboldt versus madness.

Madness was a whole lot stronger…He was a great entertainer but going insane.'

MUST READ *Galahad I, In Dreams Begin Responsibilities, The World is a Wedding*
READ ON Isaac Babel, Saul Bellow

Hubert Selby, Jr

1928–
No exit urban life

Selby left school at 16 to join the Merchant Marines and serve in the war. He contracted tuberculosis and was hospitalised for almost five years, during which time he became addicted to morphine, a state he would later depict grimly, if effectively, in his fiction (interestingly, Frankie Machine, the narrator of Nelson Algren's 1949 novel *The Man with the Golden Arm*, is a sailor who develops a morphine habit while recovering from wounds).

He started writing stories and publishing them in magazines like *Black Mountain Review* and *Kulchur*. They would later appear in his 1986 collection *Song of the Silent Snow*.

Some of the pieces he wrote during this time were sections of his first novel, the notorious *Last Exit to Brooklyn*, which was published in the US in 1964 and the UK in 1966, where it was the subject of a controversial and protracted obscenity trial, eventually winning on

author and novel, saying: 'Mr Selby's stream of reality, an urgent ticker-tape from hell, works stunningly…The taste of this stew of callousness, savagery and hatred, and the pitiful, blind gropings towards substitute tenderness, is one of compassion for the subterraneans and rage at the averted eye.'

It was filmed in 1989, starring Jennifer Jason Leigh, and featured Selby in a cameo role as a cab driver.

Later novels *The Room* (1971) and *The Demon* (1976) dealt with imprisonment and sexual obsession respectively. As with most of his writing, they were concerned with the dark underside of the American Dream, as was his 1978 novel, *Requiem for a Dream*, a tale of two morphine addicts. Underneath the squalor, Selby argued that conventional palliatives like television, or consumerism in general, were crutches every bit as insidious as hard drugs. His first novel in 14 years, *The Willow Tree*, appeared in 1998, but it is almost certainly for *Last Exit to Brooklyn* that he will finally be remembered.

MUST READ *Last Exit to Brooklyn*
READ ON **Nelson Algren, William Burroughs, Alexander Trocchi**

appeal. Before the trial, author Anthony Burgess wrote in the novel's defence: '*Last Exit* presents social horrors out of reformist zeal, not out of a desire to titillate or corrupt.'

The charge of obscenity was deeply ironic, considering Selby's powerful moralistic tone, and his genuine concern (present in all of his work) for the impoverished victims of urban decay. Critic Kenneth Allsop praised both

Will Self

1962–

The sweet smell of satire

'Nouveau Jew' Will Self scraped a third-class degree in politics, philosophy and economics at Oxford before devoting himself to heroin. Novelist, satirist, short-story writer, columnist and journalist, he later described himself as 'a hack hired because I do drugs'.

Self's first collection of short stories, *The Quantity Theory of Insanity*, appeared in 1991. The following year he published *Cock and Bull*, two novellas of the grotesque in which a woman sprouts a prick and a man grows a cunt. *My Idea of Fun* (1993) is a satirical novel of money and psychosis which was described by a reviewer in the *London Evening Standard* as 'the most loathsome novel I have ever read'; but that did not stop the said reviewer from reading it repeatedly. Meanwhile, Salman Rushdie merely said: 'Will Self is already a cult figure.' Martin Amis described him as 'thrillingly heartless, terrifyingly brainy'.

In 1994 Self published another collection of nine short stories, *Grey Area*, and the following year issued a collection of essays and journalism, *Junk Mail*. In 1996 he produced *The Sweet Smell of Psychosis*, followed by *Great Apes* (1997), a novel in which a middle-aged London painter wakes up to find himself and his girlfriend transformed into chimps. *Great Apes* was written in response to those who have failed to understand Self's true calling as a satirist.

Self has nothing but admiration for Jonathan Swift, whom he regards as 'the satirist's Shakespeare'. He also acknowledges the influence of William Burroughs and J G Ballard; he recalls going to interview Ballard for a 1,000-word piece and staying to talk to him for more than four hours. As an enfant terrible of contemporary Eng Lit, Self has been described as a sort of younger brother to Martin Amis. Word by word, his prose certainly has the same fizz and sparkle that Amis achieves and he has a wonderful ability to concoct perfectly off-key descriptions to furnish his off-kilter paranoid worlds. As with Ballard and Burroughs, Self's characters are often the helpless inhabitants of warped realities where an explanation is perversely always one Kafkaesque step away.

The 1998 short-story collection *Tough, Tough Toys for Tough, Tough Boys* is set in a world of crack dealers, fast cars, quick sex and drinking binges. But in the *Evening Standard* Melanie McDonagh remarked that, for all that, 'Mr Self…strikes me as rather a moral writer.'

During the run-up to the British general election of 1997, Self was sent on the campaign trail by the *Observer* newspaper. The spin doctors of New Labour were wary of his 'reputation and possible behaviour', and refused to let him travel on Tony Blair's battlebus. Self was allowed on prime minister John Major's plane, but was kicked off (not while in flight, of course) for allegedly snorting heroin in the lavatory. The *Observer* sacked him from his £40,000 a year job, even though the contrast between outlaw-Self and stuffed-shirt Major had been the angle all along. Self said he 'abjured[d] the anti-libertarian tone' taken by the *Observer* and others. These others might seem to include the New Labour government, for he subsequently said: 'There are no words to describe my contempt for Tony Blair and what he represents.'

In spring 1998 Self was the victim of a spoof magazine, simply entitled Self, which seemed to have stemmed from his satirical pen, whereas in fact he had nothing whatsoever to do with it. In early April 1998 the publishers of his latest work pulped the entire first edition after the printers had produced the wrong version. For whatever reason, it seems that Will Self is never far from the headlines.

MUST READ *Great Apes, My Idea of Fun*
READ ON **Martin Amis, J G Ballard**, Jonathan Swift

Samuel Selvon

1923–1994
The cognoscenti's Colin MacInnes

Following the film of *Absolute Beginners*, a new generation of readers has been introduced to the two other books in Colin MacInnes's London trilogy (*City of Spades*, 1957; *Mr Love and Justice*, 1960), and has become accustomed to the idea that MacInnes was the first chronicler of the new wave of black immigrants who arrived in Britain in the mid-fifties. Not so. In 1956 Alan Wingate published *The Lonely Londoners* by Sam Selvon, which follows the fortunes of a group immigrants (with their 'cardboard grips and felt hats') headed by Moses Aloetta. Selvon served in the British navy before finding a berth in London in 1950. His protagonist Moses was already settled in London by the time the *Empire Windrush* sailed from the West Indies in 1948, and he finds himself acting as a guide and mentor to those who have just got off the boat train at Waterloo, including the naive but optimistic 'Sir' Galahad. The narrative compares the world-weariness of Moses with the high expectations of Galahad. At one point – the only point at which Moses feels truly positive about himself – the character of Moses and the persona of the author seem to merge, and they both dream about being an ordinary 'fellar' who writes a novel that 'everybody would buy'.

< 254 >

There is plenty of dialect in *The Lonely Londoners*. Moreover, the story is told in the historic present tense; in this respect the form of the narrative is redolent of speech patterns in the West Indies. But linguists from the Caribbean have pointed out that Selvon's writing is not 'authentic': it does not correspond with the use of language on the part of real people from the social groups depicted in the novel. These are mainly working-class characters. (The position of the intellectual who came from the West Indies to London is discussed in a series of essays by George Lamming, *The Pleasures of Exile*, 1960.) The language of *The Lonely Londoners* is therefore a fabrication on the part of the author, perhaps designed to symbolise the separation which all the new Londoners felt from their adopted environment.

A character named Moses also appears in two later books by Selvon: *Moses Ascending* (1975) and *Moses Migrating* (1983, by which time Selvon had moved to Canada). Some critics, though, dispute the existence of a 'Moses trilogy', claiming that the character in the later books bears only a superficial resemblance to the protagonist of *The Lonely Londoners*. What is indisputable, however, is that for all his world-weariness the Moses of the first book retains a readiness to question and to engage with the world as he finds it: a combination that makes him one of the most alluring – and one of the most neglected – characters in the literature of postwar London.

MUST READ   *The Lonely Londoners*
READ ON   E R Braithwaite, George Lamming, **Colin MacInnes**, Andrew Salkey

Mary Shelley
1797–1851
The woman who created a monster

Mary Shelley was born in London on 30 August 1797, daughter of the English radical William Godwin and the proto-feminist Mary Wollstonecraft, who died in childbirth. In 1814 she ran off to the Continent with the poet and essayist Percy Bysshe Shelley, whom she married two years later after his first wife committed suicide. In 1823 Mary Shelley returned to England after her husband drowned at sea off the coast of Italy. She lived on until 1 February 1851.

One night in 1816, the Shelleys were in the company of the Romantic poet Lord Byron, who suggested that as a form of amusement they should each write a ghost story. Byron's and Percy's efforts came to nothing, but Mary produced probably the most famous horror story in the English language: *Frankenstein, or the Modern Prometheus* (1818) – the tale of a Swiss scientist who gives life to an inert body and so discovers the secret of life itself.

Mary Shelley wrote *Frankenstein* in the manner of a Gothic story – the preferred form of light reading among the literati of the late

18th and early 19th centuries. In the light of Mary's own dramatic life and her connections with Byron, various critics have tried to classify *Frankenstein* as a work of the Romantic imagination. When Hollywood took over the story, notably with Boris Karloff in the role of the monster, it tended to dwell on the notion of the eccentric scientist and his uncontrolled experiments. More recently, a phalanx of feminists has descended on Mary Shelley in an attempt to make her one of their own. All these interpretations have sometimes obscured the most important theme of Frankenstein: alienation in the modern world.

The key is in the second half of the title, '*the Modern Prometheus*'. This is a reference to *Prometheus Bound*, the play by the ancient Greek tragedian Aeschylus which describes the plight of Prometheus, the mythical titan who gave fire to human beings and whose punishment was to be chained to a rock, with his liver pecked out by a bird of prey, for all eternity. This story is generally interpreted as a metaphor for human civilisation and its limitations. Writing at the height of the historical period known as the Enlightenment, Percy Shelley reinterpreted the myth in a dramatic poem entitled *Prometheus Unbound* (1819–1820), which depicts Prometheus – and by implication, humanity – overcoming the constraints imposed upon him by the gods and the natural world. Mary Shelley's further reinterpretation of the myth suggests that mankind's ability to impose his will on the world may have the effect of confusing him and alienating him, ie he will become a monster in his own eyes. The monstrous character of Frankenstein is not to be found in his physical appearance, but is rather derived from his terrible loneliness and separation from the pattern of relationships all around him. He is Man Alone, and also a man with no name. In this respect the monster in Mary Shelley's *Frankenstein* has more in common with *The Man With No Name* created by film director Sergio Leone and actor Clint Eastwood than he does with the ugly creature of the vintage Hollywood versions.

In *Billion Year Spree* (1973), Brian Aldiss cited *Frankenstein* as the first science fiction novel, in that it is the first modern representation of the relationship between humanity and science (incidentally, Mary Shelley's father William Godwin is often credited with having written the first-ever detective novel, *Caleb Williams*, 1794). Mary Shelley's *The Last Man* (1826), which tells of a future world wiped out by plague, is also proto-sci-fi.

MUST READ *Frankenstein*
READ ON Aeschylus, Lord Byron, Karl Marx, Percy Bysshe Shelley,

< 256 >

GREAT PAN

SATURDAY NIGHT AND SUNDAY MORNING
Alan Sillitoe

A novel of today with a freshness and raw fury that 'makes *ROOM AT THE TOP* look like a vicarage tea-party'
DAILY TELEGRAPH

Filmed by
WOODFALL PRODUCTIONS
starring
ALBERT FINNEY

2'6

Alan Sillitoe

1928–
The long-running lonely man

Alan Sillitoe was born in a working-class district of Nottingham in the Midlands. As a boy he endured real poverty: his father remained out of work for most of the thirties. Having failed the 11-plus exam for entrance to grammar school, Sillitoe left school at 14 and went to work in a factory as a capstan lathe operator. After three years' service in the RAF, X-rays showed that Sillitoe had contracted tuberculosis. Pensioned off at 21 on 45 shillings a week, he lived in France and Spain for seven years in an attempt to recover from this debilitating condition. It was during his sojourn on the Continent that Sillitoe started to write; and his first novel (*Saturday Night and Sunday Morning*) was published in 1958, soon after his return to England. His literary apprenticeship had lasted nine years; he celebrated the acceptance of his novel by the publishers W H Allen by treating himself to lunch at a Lyons corner house.

Arthur Seaton, the young protagonist of *Saturday Night and Sunday Morning* lives for the good times to be had at the weekend, and declares at the outset that 'all the rest is propaganda' – and that includes politics and traditional moral values. Sillitoe was articulating a new mood among the young, in which relative economic prosperity co-existed with the discrediting and impoverishment of the political and moral ideologies that had held sway until then. Seaton was a rock'n'roller even before rock'n'roll had had much of an impact in the English provinces. His motto could have been the message at the beginning of the seminal sixties pop programme *Ready Steady Go*: 'The weekend starts here.'

The protagonist of 'The Loneliness of the Long Distance Runner' (the title-story of

Sillitoe's 1959 collection) is equally alienated from society's expectations of him. An inmate of a borstal (junior prison), he finds solace and a kind of freedom in the isolated activity of running. Refusing to allow the world to make demands upon him, he stands by and lets another competitor win a race that he himself could have won, deliberately dashing the hopes that the institution's governor had pinned on him.

Sillitoe's career path is marked by the same kind of estrangement. In the early sixties he was feted as the golden boy of gritty realist writing – an Angry Young Man without the self-obsession of John Osborne (*Look Back in Anger*, 1956) or the slightly plummy vowels of Kingsley Amis (*Lucky Jim*, 1954). *Saturday Night and Sunday Morning* and 'The Loneliness of the Long Distance Runner' were filmed by Karel Reisz (1960) and Tony Richardson (1962) respectively, and heralded as triumphs of the new school of British realism (although *Time* magazine complained that Richardson's film was 'prolier-than-thou'). Sillitoe was tipped to be a central figure in British cultural life, but instead he has remained largely on the outside looking in. His later works include children's books, plays, and fiction such as *The Key to the Door* (1962, based on his experiences as a wireless operator in Malaysia) and *Lost Loves* (1991).

MUST READ 'The Loneliness of the Long Distance Runner', *Saturday Night and Sunday Morning*

< 258 >

READ ON John Braine, John Harvey, David Storey, Leslie Thomas

Herbert Simmons

1931–
The revolutionary on the corner

Born in St Louis on the banks of the Missouri, Herbert Simmons made his debut with *Corner Boy* (1957), the documentary-style story of a drug dealer trapped in a life of corruption and despair. *Corner Boy* won the Houghton Mifflin Literary Fellowship for Simmons (his victory in this competition was the source of some controversy at the time), which helped to finance the writing of his next novel. *Man Walking on Eggshells* (1962) follows the life-chart of trumpet player Raymond Douglas as he transforms himself from musician to revolutionary. Though it received critical acclaim, Simmons believes that his publisher did not wish to be too closely associated with the revolutionary message of the book, and so failed to promote it properly.

Three years later, the rioting in the Watts district of Los Angeles made Simmons's work seem all the more prophetic. After the riots, however, Simmons stopped thinking of himself as primarily a writer. Instead, he became more committed to the Watts 13 Foundation, which he had co-founded as a way of providing educational and creative opportunities to the girls and boys in the 'hood.

MUST READ *Corner Boy*
READ ON **Clarence Cooper, Gil Scott Heron,** Charles Mingus, **John A Williams**

Iain Sinclair

1943–
Archivist of omens and the occult past

Born in Cardiff, Sinclair moved to London in the early sixties and studied at the London School of Film Technique. He graduated from Trinity College, Dublin and returned to London, where he has lived ever since, absorbing all the myriad influences the city and its past have to offer.

Sinclair spent the next 15 years teaching, occasionally doing odd jobs but mainly trying to crash the London film world, as scenarist, cameraman, dogsbody. His account of this lengthy attempt in *Lights Out for the Territory* (1997) is superb. 'My brilliant career in cinema was over before it began, and there was nothing brilliant about it...Film is ninety-nine per cent hassle to one percent fruitful accident. It's Russian roulette with thousands of blanks and a single golden bullet.' Sinclair started writing and self-publishing several volumes of poetry,

mostly critically acclaimed. His 1975 collection *Lud Heat* contained the major prose piece 'Nicholas Hawksmoor, His Churches', which was to be a huge influence on Peter Ackroyd's 1985 novel *Hawksmoor*.

His first novel *White Chappell, Scarlet Tracings*, was published in 1987, an experimental, multilayered work disinterring the Jack the Ripper mystery while focusing on the desperate antics of four down-at-heel bookdealers (including Sinclair himself) and their futile search for a rare Conan Doyle volume.

Two more novels followed: *Downriver* (1991; praised by the late Angela Carter as 'a great, strange, possibly definitive piece of fiction about London...a work of conspicuous and glorious ill-humour'), and *Radon Daughters* (1994), each book stripping the flimsy layers of 'history' aside to reveal what *Watchmen* author Alan Moore describes as 'the concealed guts of our culture'.

Sinclair possesses a kind of alchemist's touch, using sleight of hand to convert arcane myths into semi-believable accounts, knowing all along that truth is where you find it.

MUST READ *Downriver*
READ ON Peter Ackroyd, William Hope Hodgson, Christopher Petit

Iceberg Slim

1918–1992
Pimping the word

Iceberg Slim was born Robert Beck, the son of a chef who cooked for a large hotel in Chicago, and who left his family not long after Beck was born.

His mother married again to a man named Henry Upshaw. The family was happy for several years, until she fell for a hustler named Steve; their marriage was over, with Upshaw dying the following year.

On Beck's fourteenth birthday, Steve beat his mother senseless, then disappeared. Her jaw wired, and in agony, his mother 'was desperate to save at least fragments of her image, to hold fast the love and respect I had for her in Rockford. I had seen too much, had suffered too much, The jungle had started to embalm me with bitterness and hardness…I was sopping up the poison of the street like a sponge.'

Beck graduated from school with a 98.4 average and won a scholarship to Tuskegee, a Southern Negro college, but already 'had started to rot inside from street poisoning'. In his second year he started selling bootleg liquor and pimping. He was caught and sent to prison, where he changed his name to Iceberg Slim; for 'The best pimps keep a steely lid on their emotions and I was one of the iciest.'

In the forties and fifties, Slim was the king

Iceberg Slim

of the pimps in Chicago, with 'stables' of girls bringing in money. He became addicted to heroin and cocaine, but after a third stretch in prison, he cleaned up his act, moved to Los Angeles, and became a writer. Iceberg Slim's seven books describe the condition of rage in which the black man has been said to live, with particular emphasis on the sex and violence that go with it. Slim described himself as 'insane', and as an 'inmate of the torture chamber behind America's fake facade of justice and

< 260 >

democracy', who, despite being 'mauled' by the system, had set about constructing a 'new life' by his own, literary efforts. *Pimp* (1967) is the story of his own criminal career. *Trick Baby* (1967) tells the tale of a black man who is so light-skinned he could pass for white, but refuses to do so on account of his black consciousness (the author was a vociferous supporter of the Black Panthers). *Mama Black Widow* focuses on 'comely' homosexual queen Otis Tilson and follows the fortunes of a Southern black family who migrate to the North. Published in the sixties and seventies by Holloway House, these books were an important influence on the black rappers of the eighties, especially Ice-T who admitted that 'I took my rap name in tribute to him and I've never regretted it. He was a true hustler.'

MUST READ *Mama Black Widow, Pimp, Trick Baby*
READ ON **Donald Goines, Chester Himes, Walter Mosley, Richard Wright**

Susan Sontag
1933–
The Marilyn Monroe of the intellectuals

Born in New York, Susan Sontag grew up in Arizona and California, where she attended North Hollywood High before going on to the University of Chicago and thence to Harvard. She first came to prominence as a journalist and critic. On the bohemian New York scene of the early sixties, she swiftly acquired a reputation as the American woman who had not only appropriated the best of ancient and modern European culture, but could also reinterpret it in the American idiom. The resulting combination was heralded as a 'new sensibility' in which the 'beauty of a machine or of the solution to a mathematical problem, of a painting by Jasper Johns, or a film by Jean-Luc Godard, and of the personalities and music of the Beatles is equally accessible'. The British satirist and director Jonathan Miller was prompted to describe the creator of this sophisticated, sexy and quintessentially sixties sensibility as 'probably the most intelligent woman in America'. During this period Sontag was also an enthusiastic radical-liberal.

Sontag's fiction reinvents the European tradition, and the European avant-garde, in an American context. *The Benefactor* (1963) is partly a pastiche of the 19th-century *Bildungsroman* (a novel about the formation of character, such as Stendhal's *The Red and the Black*). *Death Kit* (1967) is a nightmarish meditation on life, death and the relationship between the two. *The Volcano Lover* (1992) draws on the love triangle between Emma, Lady Hamilton, her husband, and her lover Admiral Lord Nelson. It is also a story of revolution and the position of women, written in a manner that approaches the formality of late 18th-century English.

Sontag's short stories, collected and published as *I, etcetera* (1977), tend towards the experimental: 'Debriefing' (1973), which follows a woman on the way to suicide, is written in the sort of truncated sentences and telegrammatic phrases which the epic American crime novelist James Ellroy learnt to use 20 years later. 'Unguided Tour' (1978) is about the restless longing to be somewhere else, and the sense that the world used to be more real than it is now. In some senses it is a fictional representation of the essay *On Photography* (1977) for which Sontag won the National Book Critics Circle Award. Her later essays include *Illness as Metaphor* (1978) and *Aids and its Metaphors* (1989).

The Times of London said of Sontag: 'she offers enough food for thought to satisfy the most intellectual appetites'. The *New York Times* claimed that 'Sontag makes thought grow'. But whether she always makes it 'grow' in any particular direction, or whether with Sontag eclec-

< 262 >

ticism sometimes becomes an end in itself, is an open question.

MUST READ *The Benefactor, The Volcano Lover*
READ ON **Simone de Beauvoir**, John Berger, **Joan Didion**

Terry Southern

1924—1995
Sixties king of black comedy

Terry Southern was educated at various universities including Dallas, Chicago, Evanston, and Paris (France, not Texas). In the early fifties he was living in Paris and contributing to the *Paris Review*, a new magazine edited by George Plimpton. Excerpts from Southern's novels *Flash and Filigree* (1958) and *The Magic Christian* (1960), as well as his short stories, appeared there. His novel *Candy* (1958) first published by the notorious Olympia Press, was banned in France and then republished word for word under the new title *Lollipop* (1958), after the obscenity laws had been relaxed. It remained banned in America until 1964.

One fan of *The Magic Christian* was film director Stanley Kubrick, who was trying to film a Cold War drama called *Red Alert* until Southern came on the scene. He helped to transform Kubrick's film into *Dr Strangelove, or:*

How I Learnt to Stop Worrying and Love the Bomb, a black comedy starring Peter Sellers which was made in the shadow of the Cuban Missile Crisis. Southern's contribution to Kubrick's film is typical of the black humour and pranksterish mentality that characterises the best of his fiction.

Following his involvement in *Dr Strangelove*, Southern abandoned what he termed the 'Quality Lit Game' and concentrated on screen work, writing or contributing to scripts for *Barbarella*, *The Loved Ones*, *The Collector*, *Casino Royale* and *Easy Rider*. He also co-wrote the script for the film of his own novel *The Magic Christian*, starring Peter Sellers (again) and Ringo Starr (it was the sixties!).

Although he wrote more short stories and journalism (including his hilarious coverage of the Rolling Stones' mid-seventies US tour), Southern never again reached the heights of his early days, when envious peers such as Gore Vidal had called him 'the most profoundly witty writer of our generation'. Even Norman Mailer had compared him, as had several others, with another blackly comic genius: 'Terry Southern writes a clean, mean, coolly deliberate, and murderous prose – and in it we may have at last found the rightful heir…of Nathanael West.' George Plimpton probably summed up Southern best by merely noting his position on the Beatles' Sergeant Pepper sleeve: 'Terry is tucked in behind Lenny Bruce and Edgar Allan Poe…next to the master of the macabre on one hand and the great practitioner of black humour on the other.'

MUST READ *Candy, The Magic Christian*
READ ON **Richard Brautigan, Robert Stone, Nathanael West, Tom Wolfe**

Gertrude Stein

1874–1946
The modernist's modernist

Born in the USA, Getrude Stein studied psychology and experimented with automatic writing under the direction of William James before relocating to Paris in 1903. She later said: 'America is my country and Paris is my home town.' On arrival in France she set about collecting paintings and arranging a circle of up and coming artists around her, including Matisse and Picasso (after differences emerged between the Cubists and the post-Impressionists, Gertrude Stein sided with the former while her brother Leo championed the latter). When a new generation of American expats settled in Paris during the twenties, Stein – with her salon at 27 rue de Fleurus – was the bohemian guru to whom they looked for advice and, sometimes, money.

But Stein was a writer of note as well as a high-class hostess. *Three Lives* (1909), her first prose work, is clearly influenced by the Jameses (novelist Henry and psychologist William) and the French novelist Gustave Flaubert. *Tender Buttons* (1911) is a collection of still lives in prose. For example:

'APPLE. Apple plum, carpet steak, seed clam, coloured wine, calm seen, cold cream, best shake, potato, potato and no gold work with pet, a green seen is called bake and change sweet is bready, a little piece a little piece please. A little piece please. Cane again to the presupposed and ready eucalyptus tree, count out sherry and ripe plates and little corners of a kind of ham. This is use.'

The Making of Americans was written before the First World War but not published until 1925. In it, Stein tries to translate Cubist painting into a prose form. Her aim was to produce 'a whole present of something that it had taken a great deal of time to find out'. In other words, like the Cubists, she wanted to present an object or an experience from every angle simultaneously; to this end her writing eschews linear narrative for simultaneity and alogicality. Moreover, the effect of her prose is dependent on repetition and verbal patterns which accumulate. The cumulative effect is reinforced by unconventionally minimal use of punctuation. Stein later recalled: 'When I first began writing, I felt that writing should go on, I still do feel that it should go on but when I first began writing I was completely possessed by the necessity that writing should go on and if writing should go on, what had colons and semi-colons to do with it.'

Stein's other works include *The Autobiography of Alice B Toklas* (1933), ostensibly the life-story of her sexual partner and companion, and *Paris France* (1940). Although her output is characteristic of high modernism (she once said that this was the only form of 'composition' that could encapsulate the composition of the modern world), she also had a strong influence on more popular, less difficult writers. Ernest Hemingway, onetime habitué of Stein's Paris circle, combined her use of repetitive patterns with vernacular speech to arrive at a style that is both modern and streetwise. On the other hand, it is wrong to claim that William Burroughs and other practitioners of the cut-up technique were her direct descendants. Although Stein played around with logic and rationality, her aim was to re-present rather than destroy them, as Burroughs sought to do.

Stein's champions claim she is 'dazzling'. The usual counter-claim is that her prose is 'impenetrable'. Stein is often referred to by historians of modernism, but apart from *The Autiobiography of Alice B Toklas* very little of what she wrote is actually read nowadays. She may well be remembered as the woman who coined a phrase which was originally applied to suburbanised American cities, but is increasingly used to describe the de-centred Internet: 'There's no there, there.'

MUST READ *The Autobiography of Alice B Toklas*

< 264 >

READ ON **Paul Bowles**, Gustave Flaubert, Henry James, **James Joyce**

Bruce Sterling

1954–

The man who invented cyberpunk

Texas-born Bruce Sterling made his literary debut at the age of 23 with *Involution Ocean* (1977), set on the inhospitable planet of Nullaqua (no water). In 1980 he published *The Artificial Kid*, about a video star who lives in a state-sponsored anarchy zone called Reverie. Sterling's reference points were as much derived from pop music as from sci-fi, and he began publishing a fanzine, *Cheap Truth*, in which under the pseudonym of Vincent Omniaveritas (AllTruth) he polemicised against old-fashioned s-f and called for a new, hard-hitting genre in touch with contemporary culture. His polemics eventually led to the publication of a short story collection, *Mirrorshades*, under Sterling's editorship. It featured two contributions by William Gibson and is generally regarded as the seminal document of first-wave cyberpunk.

Since the early eighties Sterling has been interested in the correlation and the contradictions between biology and technology, and his concern is demonstrated in the novel *Schismatrix* (1985). In 1988 he published a prescient novel about the effects of the information age, particularly on those countries that are left behind. Co-written with William Gibson, *The Difference Engine* (1990) was dubbed 'steampunk'. It is set in a parallel version of Victorian London, where the 19th-century mathematician Charles Babbage has succeeded in building the computer that in real life he was never able to perfect. Sterling has published two collections of short stories and many other novels, including *Heavy Weather* (1995, about an adrenaline-driven team who go looking for hurricanes) and *Holy Fire* (1996).

Sterling's factual account of law enforcement on the information superhighway, *The Hacker Crackdown* (1992), remains a model explanation of the vexed relationship between computer culture and those in authority. He writes regularly for *Science Fiction Eye* and produces a popular science column for the *Magazine of Fantasy and Science Fiction*. Sterling's first-person accounts of new media technologies are both witty and perceptive. Complaints have sometimes been made against his novels and stories, to the effect that they are really essays dressed up in fictional form.

MUST READ *The Difference Engine, Mirrorshades: a cyberpunk anthology, Schismatrix*
READ ON **William Gibson**, Neal Stephenson, Rudy Rucker

S IS FOR SCOTS
5 cult classics from the
new tartan army

TRAINSPOTTING
Irvine Welsh
picaresque tales of drugs and
degradation in Edinburgh's schemes

MORVEN CALLAR
Alan Warner
an opaque-souled modern heroine on
a trail of blank hedonism

HOW LATE IT WAS, HOW LATE
James Kelman
a dark tale of blinded rogue's
meanderings around Glasgow

BUNKER MAN
Duncan McLean
horror yarn of a man who stalks a
school

COMPLICITY
Iain Banks
a journo is implicated in the murder
he is covering. RLS for the 90s

Robert Louis Stevenson
1850—1894
Adventure stories and tales of evil

Born into a family of lighthouse engineers, Stevenson was a perpetual invalid as a child and never enjoyed good health as an adult, suffering from colds, bronchial complaints and, eventually, tuberculosis. He was educated at the Edinburgh Academy before the harsh winters drove him and his family to the south of England and prompted an extended trip to Germany and Italy in 1862/3. He was grimly aware that his poor health precluded any hopes of remaining in his beloved Scotland: 'I have been a Scotsman all my life, and denied my native land!' Stevenson studied law and became an advocate in 1875, but writing was his real passion. After trying his hand at travel writing, a series of adventure novels, *Kidnapped* (1883), *Treasure Island* (1886) and *The Master of Ballantrae* (1889), finally brought him fame. Yet the cult of Stevenson rests firmly on his most famous tale of evil.

Stevenson's tale of split personality, *The Strange Case of Dr Jekyll and Mr Hyde* (1886), was written in, of all places, Bournemouth, a seaside resort on the south coast of England. Based on the exploits of Deacon (William) Brodie, a respectable Edinburgh cabinet-maker by day and leader of a gang of thieves by night, the novella was an acknowledgement of Stevenson's obsession with dual personality (as a comfortably well-off young man, he used to dress in rags, hoping to be arrested for vagrancy). The tale is a culmination of his life-long fascination with the concept of sin and evil, prompted, no doubt, by his unhappy relationship with Calvinism, which he had renounced at an early age.

It was conceived in a nightmare, possibly under the influence of laudanum. When his wife woke him from his slumbers, Stevenson was angry. 'I was dreaming a fine bogey tale,' he told her. After writing 30,000 words of a first draft, Stevenson and his wife had more cross words and he threw the manuscript in the fire. He then sat down to rewrite it, and finished the entire second draft of 64,000 words in just six days. A much-needed success, in its first six months it sold 40,000 copies in Britain and guaranteed the author's literary immortality.

After Stevenson's death on the South Sea island of Samoa (which he had made his home in the hope of improving his health), his friend, the author Henry James was horrified, writing to the critic Edmund Gosse: 'Of what can we think or utter or dream, save of this ghastly extinction of the beloved RLS?'

MUST READ *Dr Jekyll and Mr Hyde*
READ ON Wilkie Collins, James Hogg, **Edgar Allan Poe**

Bram Stoker

1847—1912
The man who lifted the lid on The Count's coffin

Abraham Stoker was a sickly child who didn't walk upright till he was seven; as he put it: 'All my early recollection is of being carried in people's arms and of being laid down somewhere or other.' Educated at Trinity College, Dublin he studied law and science and wrote theatre reviews for the *Dublin Mail*. His review of *Hamlet* caught the leading actor's eye and after meeting Henry Irving, Stoker agreed to follow him to London and co-manage the Royal Lyceum Theatre. He remained at Irving's beck and call for the next 28 years.

Although he had written and published short stories and had published a novel, *The Snake's Pass*, in 1890, it was not until 1897 that Stoker achieved literary immortality when he produced *Dracula*, the ultimate vampire novel.

Having recently celebrated its hundreth birthday, *Dracula* shows no signs of flagging. It has been translated into 44 languages and countless film adaptations have been made, although the best is undoubtedly F W Murnau's 1922 classic *Nosferatu*, itself the subject of a vicious legal battle between the director and Stoker's widow. It is the only one of Stoker's 18 books to have made any impact, although some are memorable, particularly *The Lair of the*

< 267 >

White Worm (1911), his final novel. Filmed in 1989 by Ken Russell, this book's rather heavy-handed symbolism, is gossamer thin compared to Russell's bludgeoning treatment.

Said by Stoker's son Noel to have 'originated in a nightmarish dream after eating too much dressed crab', *Dracula* was not just a brilliant Gothic horror story (there are many predecessors: Sheridan Le Fanu's 'Carmilla', 1872; John Polidori's *The Vampyre*, 1819; Mary Shelley's *Frankenstein*, 1818), but a melting pot of Victorian fears and taboos. Sexual deviations, symbolic or otherwise, including necrophilia, incest, seduction, group sex and rape, run riot throughout. Almost certainly it was also about Stoker's relationship with Irving. In his diary, sounding uncannily like Jonathan Harker's reaction to Count Dracula, Stoker writes of Irving's hypnotic charisma: 'So great was the magnetism of his genius, so profound was the sense of his dominancy that I sat spellbound.' Perhaps for Stoker the novel was also a form of revenge on the man who had held him in thrall for so long.

MUST READ *Dracula, Lair of the White Worm*
READ ON George Du Maurier, **Sheridan Le Fanu**, John Polidori

< 268 >

Robert Stone

1937–
Stoned States: drugs and corruption in post–Vietnam America

Stone was raised on the West Side of Manhattan, and worked for the *New York Daily News* while he attended New York City College. He also attended Stanford College in California, where he met and befriended Ken Kesey and became a convert to the latter's drug-fuelled alternative lifestyle.

Stone lived in New Orleans in the early sixties, and his first novel, *A Hall of Mirrors* (1967), was set there. Featuring a powerful hallucination passage, it was filmed in 1970 as *WUSA*, starring Paul Newman.

In 1971, Stone went to Vietnam as a journalist and reported on the war for numerous papers. His second novel, *Dog Soldiers* (1974), used the conflict as a bleak backdrop to a story of an ex-Marine smuggling heroin across the Mexican border to California. It won the National Book Award in 1975, and was filmed in 1978 as *Who'll Stop the Rain?* (the title came from a Creedence Clearwater Revival song), starring Nick Nolte and Tuesday Weld, with Stone co-scripting. Universally praised, the book was Stone's biggest success, with the writer A Alvarez claiming it to be 'a spare and unrelievedly black story...It can be read as a Conrad-like fable about Vietnam's legacy of corruption to America, or simply as a Ross Macdonald-styled thriller. Either way, it is exceptionally powerful stuff.'

By the time of his third novel, *A Flag for Sunrise* (1981), Stone had moved on to a new trouble spot, Central America, and the US's dubious involvement there. Set during a revolution and armed with the, by now, customary drug references, it was an unsettling book that reflected balefully on America's increasingly murderous political machinations. At the novel's conclusion, in a deeply ironic observation, a protagonist notes: 'A man has nothing to fear...who understands history.'

Stone has also written a novel, *Children of Light* (1986), about the decadence of the Hollywood film industry. It is a love story of two drug-ravaged spirits set around the filming of Kate Chopin's *The Awakening* down in Mexico. His latest work, *Damascus Gate* (1998), set in the hotspot of Jerusalem, is about a man's search for faith set within a thrilling terrorist plot. Many of Stone's characters are looking hopelessly for some kind of redemption in a godless world. Like Tom Wolfe, Stone combines his journalistic experience with inside knowledge of the counterculture, to produce stunning fiction.

MUST READ *Dog Soldiers, A Flag for Sunrise*
READ ON **Joan Didion, Ken Kesey, Terry Southern, Tom Wolfe**

S IS FOR SLACKER
5 novels about loafers old and new

GENERATION X
Douglas Coupland
smart kids going nowhere fast

THREE MEN IN A BOAT
Jerome K Jerome
Victorian clerks going nowhere slow

OUR TOWN
Jeff Gomez
smalltown, Southern slackerdom with a band called Bottlecap

RIGHT HO, JEEVES
P G Wodehouse
lazy living narrated by Bertie Wooster of the Drones club

THE COLOUR OF MEMORY
Geoff Dyer
bohemian laziness in post-riot, pre-buppie Brixton

< 269 >

D M Thomas

1935–
Freud–inspired novelist of the erotic

Donald Mitchell Thomas was raised mostly in Australia, but returned to England in his teens and was educated at New College, Oxford. As well as teaching, he wrote verse, and between 1973 and 1983 produced several volumes of poetry, including *Love and Other Deaths* (1975), a title that virtually sums up his entire oeuvre.

His first novel, *The Flute Player*, appeared in 1979. It pays homage to Russian artists threatened by totalitarian forces (during his National Service he had learnt Russian and later translated verse by Pushkin and Akhmatova), as well as being highly erotic.

His third novel, *The White Hotel* (1981) was acclaimed as a masterpiece and nominated for the Booker Prize. Graham Greene praised it, claiming: 'There is no novel to my knowledge which resembles this in technique or ideas. It stands alone.' The American novelist John Updike called it 'astonishing…A forthright sensuality mixed with a fine historical feeling for the nightmare moments in modern history, a dreamlike and quickness.' A combination of case history (Sigmund Freud is a character in the novel and Thomas claimed that his case histories were 'masterly works of literature'), love story, and retelling of the Holocaust, it was translated into 20 languages. However, its mix of sex and death and the brutal fate of its female protagonist (raped with a bayonet after climbing from a death-pit) is viewed in other quarters as deeply misogynistic and exploitative of the Holocaust.

Thomas also depicted Freud in his 1994 novel *Eating Pavlova*, which incorporated fragments of his diaries and letters to form a kaleidoscopic picture of the psychoanalyst, now an exile from the Nazis and living (or actually, dying) in Hampstead with his daughter Anna. In between these two books Thomas wrote his 'Russian Nights' sequence: five novels detailing political and cultural (and erotic) life in Eastern Europe after the war.

MUST READ *The White Hotel*
READ ON Georges Bataille, Sigmund Freud, **Milan Kundera**, D H Lawrence

Jim Thompson

1906–1977
The dimestore Dostoevsky

For an author who wrote about insanity, incest and obsessive desires, the central figures in the Jim Thompson story (which really reads like a Jim Thompson story!), were inevitably his parents – more specifically, his father, James Thompson. Sheriff of Andarko, Oklahoma, James foiled jail breaks and arrested horse

< 270 >

thieves. He was also a chronic gambler, and in 1907 was dismissed for misappropriating funds worth $5,000. Avoiding arrest, he fled to Mexico. For the next 14 years he drifted in and out of various occupations, dragging his family with him, until in 1921 he suffered a breakdown. He died in an institution 20 years later. In Thompson's 1942 novel, *Now and on Earth*, protagonist Jim Dillon's father dies in an asylum, killing himself by eating the stuffing from his mattress, a fate Thompson often claimed for his own father.

Thompson held a series of jobs to provide for his family: bellhop, oil-pipe layer, journalist, bootlegger, teacher. In 1936, he became head of the Oklahoma Writer's Project and joined the Communist Party. He also wrote 23 novels or novellas, each one autobiographical to some degree, each one placed in what William Burroughs called: 'a space between, in popular songs and Grade B movies, giving away the basic American rottenness'. Hollywood sniffed him out and in 1956 he co-wrote *Killer's Kiss* with the young Stanley Kubrick, going on to co-write *Paths of Glory*, Kubrick's brilliant anti-war film. Kubrick later acclaimed Thompson's *The Killer Inside Me* (1952), to be 'probably the most chilling and believable first-person account of a criminally warped mind I have ever encountered'.

Thompson knew that he wasn't destined for big success, at least not in his lifetime. Before he died, with none of his work available in America, he told his wife to protect his manuscripts and copyrights. 'Just you wait, I'll become famous after I'm dead about ten years.' He was about right. In 1990 *The Grifters*, the first of five film adaptations of his work, received four Oscar nominations; gradually, all his books were republished.

Possibly the weirdest artist ever to grace the pulp genre, Thompson once said: 'There are 32 ways to write a story, and I've used every one, but there is only one plot – things are not what they seem.' In his stories nothing is certain – not even the narrative, and any sense of stability can only be temporary. In a sadistic world of barflies, grifters and cheap hotels, Thompson exposes primitive and unpalatable impulses in his characters and, by implication, in all human beings. This is a moral wasteland without a safe place from which to view it. That's why critic Geoffrey O'Brien dubbed him the 'dimestore Dostoevsky'.

MUST READ *After Dark My Sweet, The Getaway, The Killer inside Me, Pop. 1280*
READ ON **Fyodor Dostoevsky, David Goodis, Horace McCoy**

T IS FOR TINSELTOWN

15 novels set amid the cold dark heart
of Hollywood

THE DAY OF THE LOCUST Nathanael West

WHAT MAKES SAMMY RUN? Budd Schulberg

THE LAST TYCOON F Scott Fitzgerald

THE PLAYER Michael Tolkin

THE LOVED ONES Evelyn Waugh

THEY SHOOT HORSES DON'T THEY?
Horace McCoy

THE BLACK DAHLIA James Ellroy

LA CONFIDENTIAL James Ellroy

LITTLE SISTER Raymond Chandler

THE SLIDE AREA Gavin Lambert

TRUE CONFESSIONS John Gregory Dunne

PLAY IT AS IT LAYS Joan Didion

AFTER MANY A SUMMER Aldous Huxley

FLICKER Theodore Roszak

I WAKE UP SCREAMING Steve Fisher

< 272 >

Hunter S Thompson

1939–
Drug–fuelled antihero of New
Journalism

Thompson's childhood friend was one Duke Rice, like him a sports fanatic, whose surname he borrowed for one of his alter egos: Raoul Duke (later caricatured in Garry Trudeau's 'Doonesbury' newspaper strip as just 'Duke'). As a teenager, Thompson became the natural leader of more friends who would join him in his forays into drunken vandalism and skirmishes with the law.

When he was 15 his father, an insurance salesman, suffered a fatal heart attack. As Rice put it: 'His dad was a nice and quiet man who kept him on the straight and narrow the best he could. When he died there was no one to do that. His life got turned upside down from that point on.' Eleven days before graduation, Thompson was arrested with some friends at the scene of a robbery and, though innocent, was sentenced to 60 days in the Louisville Children's Centre. He served 30 days and then enlisted in the air force, where he worked as sports editor on the *Command Courier*, his airbase's paper, until he was discharged.

Thompson worked in New York as a copy boy for *Time* magazine and wrote for provincial newspapers until he became sports editor for *Sportivo*, a Puerto Rican paper. He also wrote for the *San Juan Star*, edited by William Kennedy, future author of *Ironweed*. (Kennedy first of all turned him down, and Thompson wrote promising to 'jam a bronze plaque far into your small intestine' – the first salvo in a colourful correspondence). When not writing, he was chewing coca leaves, smoking 'the best grass in the world', and eating peyote.

Back in America, he wrote for the *National Observer* and did a piece on the Hell's Angels for *Nation* magazine that aroused considerable interest. It formed the basis for his first book, *Hell's Angels* (1967), which sold 40,000 copies in hardback, with paperback sales exceeding 2,000,000.

Thompson's next, and greatest success was *Fear and Loathing in Las Vegas* (1971), an extravagant account of his experiences at a political convention in the city of sleaze, accompanied by Oscar Zeta Acosta, a 250 lb Chicago attorney and enough drugs to pulverise the best minds of Harvard and Yale combined. Praised by Tom Wolfe as 'a scorching, sensation', the book was filmed (badly) in 1980, starring Bill Murray as Thompson, and once again in 1998 by Terry Gilliam, this time starring Johnny Depp as Thompson.

Although he continued to write some excellent pieces, primarily for *Rolling Stone* magazine, self-parody was starting to creep into Thompson's work. Rampant drug abuse was robbing his writing of its original spark, and on several occasions Thompson failed to deliver (notably on the occasion of the Ali–Foreman fight in Zaire, which cost the magazine $25,000).

The Great Shark Hunt, a collection of his best pieces, was probably proof that his finest work lay behind him – and at its conclusion, Thompson put 'RIP' and the date after his name. He now lives in fashionable Aspen and continues to write (he's said to be working on a novel called *Polo is My Life*), although his more recent work, such as *Better than Sex* (1995) looks increasingly eccentric. The late 90s also saw the publication of his first volume of letters *The Proud Highway* and a long lost novel *The Rum Diary*.

In putting himself at the the centre of his own stories, Thompson was merely following the example set by Tom Wolfe and other New Journalists. His unique contribution was to put himself in awkward and dangerous situations and then record the spectacular results; in this respect Thompson is godfather to a whole generation of prankster reporters. The gonzo method was inaugurated with Thompson's piece on the 1970 Kentucky Derby. In commenting on it afterwards he wrote: 'Objectivity is impossible in journalism.' Less than 30 years later this is the new orthodoxy among journalists.

MUST READ *Fear and Loathing in Las Vegas, The Great Shark Hunt*
READ ON P J O'Rourke, **Ken Kesey, Tom Wolfe**

< 273 >

Newton Thornburg

1930–
The man who dreamt the end of the American Dream

Born in Harvey, Illinois, Newton Thornburg took a degree in fine arts at the University of Iowa, then odd-jobbed his way around New York and California before coming back home in 1958 to join the family business (paper-goods wholesaling) in Chicago. Six years later he went into advertising and became creative director for agencies in Milwaukee, St Louis and California. By the mid-seventies Thornburg was writing novels and film scripts full time, with a little bit of cattle ranching on the side.

Thornburg's debut was *Gentleman Born* (1967). *Knockover* (1969) was a solid but unremarkable story about a bank robbery. *To Die in California* (1973) was trendy and topical (Hal Wallis bought the film rights). But in 1976 Thornburg moved up several gears with *Cutter and Bone* (1976), the tale of two Vietnam veterans (one a good-looking gigolo; the other bitter and twisted, and crippled by a war wound), who embark on a last mission to expose one of the fat cats of corporate America. There is no better fictional summation of the atmosphere of post-Vietnam, post-Watergate disillusion that was pervasive at the time. The *New York Times* recommended *Cutter and Bone* as 'a classy big

< 274 >

league act…the best novel of its kind for 10 years'. With the title changed to *Cutter's Way* (1981), Thornburg's book was successfully filmed by the Czech-born director Ivan Passer, with Jeff Bridges and John Heard in the starring roles.

In the late seventies and early eighties, Thornburg retreated to a rural setting for his novels *Black Argus* (1978) and *Beautiful Kate* (1980). In between these two, he produced the post-apocalyptic *Valhalla* (1980), twice optioned for the cinema but never made into a film, although it prefigures the mood of the highy influential *Mad Max* series. *Dreamland* (1983) takes a wry look at the underbelly of the American Dream.

MUST READ *Cutter and Bone*
READ ON **David Goodis**, Arthur Miller,
Hunter S Thompson

John Kennedy Toole

1937–1969
A confederacy of publishers

Born in new Orleans, Toole was educated at Tulane University, New York, where he received a Masters degree in English. He then taught at Hunter College and at the University of South Louisiana. His formidable reputation is based almost entirely on the strength of one novel and the bizarre and tragic story of its eventual, posthumous publication.

A Confederacy of Dunces, a hilarious, picaresque romp, wasn't published until 1980, and even then, it was largely due to the efforts of another New Orleans writer, Walker Percy. The following year, it won the Pulitzer Prize and was justly acclaimed as a classic. Toole wrote the novel in the early sixties and shopped it around a number of publishers. After more than a dozen rejections, he gave up and, in a state of despondency, killed himself. Ten years later, his mother showed the manuscript to Percy, who offered his services as an agent. Excerpts appeared in the *New Orleans Review* in 1979, and the book was finally published by the Louisiana State University Press in 1980. In his brief introduction to the book, Percy writes eloquently of his delight in reading the battered manuscript and of his shock and sadness at discovering its author's demise. *The Neon Bible* (1989), another posthumously published work, was a fictional account of Toole's childhood in the rural South. Witty and moving, it was written during the author's teens.

With such an extraordinary publishing history, it is easy to overlook the novel itself. Its protagonist, Ignatius J Reilly, is a brilliant comic creation: fat, flatulent, intellectual, full of scorn for the middle-class emptiness of American life. Scribbling down his thoughts on his ubiquitous Big Chief writing tablets, Reilly provides a hilariously pessimistic monologue, while around him the richly comic plot unfolds.

MUST READ *A Confederacy of Dunces*
READ ON *Herzog* by Saul Bellow, Walker Percy, Gargantua and Pantagruel by Rabelais

Alexander Trocchi
1925–1984
The cosmonaut of inner space

Born to a Scottish mother and an Italian father, Trocchi was raised in Glasgow and went to Glasgow University. After graduation he was awarded a travelling scholarship, whereby he decamped to Europe with his wife and daughter in tow. Settling in Paris, Trocchi rapidly became king of the Left Bank, with various expatriate Americans under his spell, including Terry Southern, Richard Seaver, George Plimpton, and Jane Lougee, a wealthy young woman who became his mistress and bankrolled his magazine *Merlin*, an alternative *Paris Review*. He met Maurice Girodias, publisher of the infamous Olympia Press, who commissioned him to write erotica. Under the name Frances Lengel, Trocchi churned out numerous pornographic books, including the now classic *Helen and Desire* (1954) and a 'dirty' version of his own novel *Young Adam* (1954). Trocchi and his friends also published Samuel

< 275 >

T

Alexander Trocchi

Beckett's *Watt* and *Molloy*, and Jean Genet's *Thief's Journal* in English for the first time. Despite his busy schedule, Trocchi found time to become a hopeless drug addict, virtually writing porn for heroin.

In 1956, after the collapse of *Merlin*, Trocchi moved to New York and lived on a barge, writing his second novel, *Cain's Book* (1960), an autobiographical work describing his life on the boat and his addiction. Edited by his old friend Richard Seaver for the Grove

Press, the book was well received and praised by the likes of Norman Mailer: 'It is different from other books, it is true, it has art, it is brave.'

For most of his contemporaries, the truth was that the heroin was taking its toll on Trocchi, who never published another book, and that not only his writing was suffering. He married his second wife Lyn Hicks in 1957, and within a year she was also an addict, prostituting herself to earn their drug money. Faced with arrest for supplying narcotics to a minor, Trocchi fled to Canada, where he met poet and potential songwriter Leonard Cohen ('his skin was grey. We'd never seen skin quite that shade of grey'), who helped Trocchi return to Britain.

Often compared with William Burroughs, the only thing they really had in common was heroin, as Burroughs admitted: 'Well, I was on heroin too…he used to help me shoot up. See, my veins had gone in my arms. Old Alex could find a vein in a mummy…He was an individual…They don't make 'em like that any more.'

MUST READ *Cain's Book, Young Adam*
READ ON **Paul Bowles, William Burroughs, Irvine Welsh**

Dalton Trumbo

1905—1976
Screenwriter and anti-war novelist

Born in Montrose in the Midwestern state of Colorado, Dalton Trumbo moved to the West Coast where he attended the University of California in Los Angeles before becoming a movie scriptwriter, magazine feature writer (*Saturday Evening Post, McCall's, Playboy*, the *Nation*) and novelist. His film scripts include *A Man to Remember, Kitty Foyle, A Guy Named Joe, Thirty Seconds over Tokyo, Spartacus, Exodus, Lonely are the Brave*, and *The Brave One*, which won an Oscar in 1957. Trumbo's novel *The Remarkable Andrew* was made into a film, but he is best known as the author of *Johnny Got His Gun* (1939), a novel of war which the book reviewer in the *New York Herald Tribune* described as 'a shocking and violent experience …the toughest assignment I have ever had'.

Joe, the protagonist of *Johnny Got His Gun*, is a soldier of the First World War whose body has been destroyed in battle. Without arms or legs or face or sight or hearing, by some perverse miracle he has been left alive in the hell of his own solitude. Trumbo's novel follows his thoughts, feelings and memories as he lies helpless in a hospital bed. The passage where Joe realises the extent of his disfigurement lives up to the *Washington Post's* description of 'a terrifying book, of an extreme emotional intensity':

'The hole began at the base of his throat just below where his jaw should be and went upward in a widening circle. He could feel his skin creeping around the rim of the circle. The hole was getting bigger and bigger. It widened out almost to the base of his ears if he had any and then narrowed again. It ended somewhere above the top of what used to be his nose.

'The hole went too high to have any eyes in it. He was blind.

'It was funny how calm he was. He was quiet just like a storekeeper taking spring inventory and saying to himself I see I have no eyes better put that down in the order book. He had no legs and no arms and no eyes and no ears and no nose and no mouth and no tongue. What a hell of a dream. It must be a dream. Of course sweet god it's a dream. He'd have to wake up or he'd go nuts. Nobody could live like that. A person in that condition would be dead and he wasn't dead so he wasn't in that condition. Just dreaming.

'But it wasn't a dream.'

Where other writers might have shattered their sentences into unintelligible fragments, Trumbo maintains a lucid tone; and his use of stream of consciousness is all the more effective for being only occasional. Indeed the disciplined character of Trumbo's writing only adds to its power and resonance.

Johnny Got His Gun was published after the start of the Second World War but before the Japanese attack on Pearl Harbor and the entry

T

of the USA into the war. Initially a 'rally point for the left', after the USA declared war on Japan it became a cause célèbre among peace groups and extreme right-wingers. Trumbo was happy to see *Johnny* stay out of print for the duration, on the grounds that it might be used to obstruct the war effort. He even reported some of the book's wartime fans to the FBI, but the federal investigators who visited him seemed more interested in the author himself than in the names he had given them.

In 1959, when the Korean War too was safely over, *Johnny Got His Gun* was republished. The *New York Times* described it as an 'underground' classic, and it may well have had an influence on the emerging generation of Beats, peaceniks and protest singers. Trumbo's final sentence ('You plan the wars you masters of men plan the wars and point and we will point the gun'), seems to prefigure the lyrics to 'Masters of War' by Bob Dylan; and the character of Joe might even be regarded as the antecedent of Pete Townshend's *Tommy*.

Trumbo was one of the Hollywood Ten (scriptwriters and Hollywood players who were arrested for contempt of Congress i.e. being Communist). Formerly Hollywood's highest paid scribbler ($75,000 a script), he wrote under pseudonyms after being blacklisted.

MUST READ *Johnny Got His Gun*
READ ON Wilfred Owen, Erich Maria Remarque, Arnold Zweig

< 278 >

T IS FOR TRANSFORMATIONS
5 novels in which characters turn into something else

DR JEKYLL AND MR HYDE
R L Stevenson
no more Mr Nice Guy

THE BREAST
Philip Roth
man makes a tit of himself

METAMORPHOSIS
Franz Kafka
beetling about

A DOG'S HEAD
Jean Dutourd
it's a dog's life

GREAT APES
Will Self
primate of all fiction

Boris Vian

1920—1959
Alfred Jarry meets Chet Baker

Educated at home in Ville D'Avray and then at the Lycée Hoche in Versailles, Vian developed rheumatic fever aged 12 and missed much of his schooling. Later, he contracted typhoid, and both ailments severely weakened his heart.

At 17 he learnt trumpet after seeing Duke Ellington play, and gigged with a jazz orchestra in Paris. In 1958, he and the director Louis Malle persuaded Miles Davis to play the music for Malle's film *Lift to the Scaffold*. Vian's weak heart forced him to abandon trumpet, and he became a singer, writing hundreds of songs, including 'Le Déserteur', about the Algerian War, which sold thousands of records before being banned – Vian's first, but not last, taste of censorship.

In 1946 he wrote his most famous novel, *Froth on the Daydream*, featuring among others, a character who is obsessed with collecting works by his favourite author, one Jean Sol Partre (or Jean Pulse Heartre, depending on the translation). Sartre himself admired the book, and author Raymond Queneau called it 'the most poignant romance of modern time'. In America, the 1968 translation was called *Mood Indigo*, after Duke Ellington's famous composition.

Vian translated many American hard-boiled novels, including works by Raymond Chandler, James M Cain, and Nelson Algren. Asked by an editor if he knew any similar American writers he could publish, he soon produced the manuscript of a crime novel called *I Shall Spit on Your Graves*, by 'Vernon Sullivan'.

The novel received rave reviews, with French critics comparing 'Sullivan' to Faulkner and Hemingway. In 1948, a copy of it was found in the hotel room of a murder victim. Sales of the book and its sequels rocketed, but Vian was dragged into court, and, having admitted authorship, fined 100,000 francs. The book was banned in 1949, but not before Vian had published his English translation.

While attending a screening of the film adaptation, he died of a heart attack. Louis Malle was sure that the poorly made film had finished Vian: 'I've always thought that Boris died of shame from having seen what they'd done to his book. Like anything else, the cinema can kill.'

MUST READ *Froth on the Daydream, Heartsnatcher*
READ ON **Raymond Chandler, Alfred Jarry, Nathanael West**

< 279 >

V IS FOR VAMPIRE
10 tales with a lust for blood

DRACULA
Bram Stoker
the great classic of Victorian sexual
repression

THE VAMPIRE CHRONICLES
Anne Rice
existential ennui and angst among the
undead

LOST SOULS
Poppy Z Brite
drug—crazed white trash vampires on
the road to New Orleans

THE HUNGER
Whitley Strieber
blood lust in modern Manhattan, filmed
with David Bowie

THE VAMPYRE
John Polidori
the first modern vampire tale, from
friend of Shelley and Byron

I, VAMPIRE
Michael Romkey
were Hitler, Jack the Ripper and Mozart
all vampires?

SALEM'S LOT
Stephen King
vampires terrorise a small New England
town

CARMILLA
Sheridan Le Fanu
female vampire classic from the master
of Victorian Gothic horror

LOVE IN VEIN
Poppy Z Brite ed.
contemporary vampire erotica
collection

THE VAMPIRE TAPESTRY
Suzy McKee Charnas
Dr Weyland; anthropology professor and
1000—year—old vampire

< 280 >

Gore Vidal

1925–
The radical patrician

Gore Vidal's father was a teacher at West Point Military Academy. As a boy, Vidal was close to his grandfather, the distinguished senator Thomas Gore. During the Second World War he joined the armed forces, drawing on these experiences in his shipboard novel *Williwaw* (1946). At 21, Vidal seemed well placed for a successful literary career, but after the acclaim prompted by his debut, the novels he published during the next decade were poorly received, particularly *The City and the Pillar* (1948), which told the story of a young man's homosexual awakenings, indicating that the author's own inclinations lay in the same direction. *The Judgement of Paris* (1953), about a young man travelling with the jet-set and wondering how to satisfy his own part-cynical, part-romantic outlook, is fairly well thought of today but was not so well received when it was published.

Vidal stopped writing for a while and went to work in television (he still pops up occasionally as an on-screen intellectual; along with the right-winger William Buckley he was one of the commentators on the disturbances surrounding the 1968 Democratic Convention in Chicago which culminated in a police riot (the two of them swapped comments about Vidal's homosexuality and Buckley's alleged crypto-Fascism).

In 1960 he ran for Congress. Between 1970 and 1972 he was co-chairman of the left-leaning People's Party. In the Democratic primary in California in 1982 (to select the candidate to stand for election in the Senate), he came second out of a field of nine, polling half a million votes.

Meanwhile, Vidal had been climbing back up the literary ladder. His recovery began with *Julian* (1964), written in the form of a journal by the eponymous Roman emperor. *Myra Breckenridge* (1968) and *Myron* (1974) were camp cartoons which fitted in with the excessive appetites of the late sixties and seventies. On a more serious level, Vidal completed a series of three novels which investigated political power and the exercise of it: *Washington DC* (1967), *Burr* (1973) and *1876* (1976). He was to return to these themes in *Lincoln* (1984), a carefully reconstructed account of the life of the US president, and *Empire* (1987), a fictional but factually detailed examination of the birth of the USA as an international power. While Vidal's old rival Norman Mailer was largely silent during the Reagan years, Vidal published a collection of opinion pieces, *Armageddon: essays* (1987), in which he articulated his love–hate relationship with dumbed-down America.

Vidal writes about political power as if it belongs to him. His critics point out that he has never managed to get elected.

MUST READ *Myra Breckenridge, Washington DC*
READ ON **Norman Mailer**, Arthur Miller,

V

Kurt Vonnegut Jr

1922–
Where (Groucho) Marxist tendencies
meet Kafka

Kurt Vonnegut grew up in Indianopolis and studied biochemistry at Chicago's Cornell University. During the Second World War he fought in Europe until captured by the German army. As a POW, he witnessed the bombing of the medieval city of Dresden by the RAF. This experience inspired Vonnegut's most famous novel, *Slaughterhouse Five, or the Children's Crusade* (1969). The barbarity of total war, and the discrediting of the ideological and economic systems that produce it, are a staple element in Vonnegut's work.

A few years after he returned from the Western Front, Vonnegut began to submit stories to magazines. His first published work was 'Report on the Barnhouse Effect', which appeared in the prestigious *Collier's* magazine in 1950. A few of Vonnegut's stories were published in sci-fi magazines, and his constant concern for the effects of technology on humanity has led some critics to pigeon-hole him as a sci-fi writer; but Vonnegut himself has always resisted this categorisation.

Vonnegut's first novel was *Player Piano* (1952), a tale of black humour in which the functions of human beings are gradually taken over by machines. In 1959 he published *The Sirens of Titan*, which features a character for

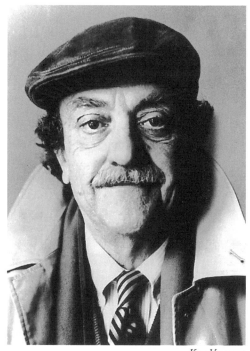

Kurt Vonnegut

whom the events of history take place simultaneously – a notion that some critics have described as 'an extratemporal viewpoint' while others have dubbed it 'simultaneity'. This was a recurring theme in the pop culture of the sixties, and Vonnegut returned to it himself in *Slaughterhouse Five*, which follows a character of childlike simplicity called Billy Pilgrim who survives the Dresden firestorm and learns to live in only the pleasant, life-enhancing moments of a simultaneous existence.

< 282 >

The absurdity of the human condition is another of Vonnegut's themes. In *Cat's Cradle* (1963) he sets up a battle of ideas between the destructive rationality of Western science, and the self-deluding mythology of the turn towards mysticism that was just then beginning to take hold among young people in the USA and Europe. Faced with two unsatisfactory options, Vonnegut seems to conclude that there's no particular place for the intelligent individual to go.

Graham Greene praised Vonnegut as 'one of the best living American writers'. His ability to combine laughter and sorrow is widely revered. But when throughout the seventies Vonnegut continued mining his seam of sardonic humour, some critics accused him of recycling essentially the same fuel. In 1990 he showed a return to form with the publication of *Hocus Pocus*, a novel 'of Swiftian satire and gonzo wit' set in the chaos of American society following the defeat of Uncle Sam in Vietnam.

Whereas most satirists take aim at a particular target, Vonnegut's barbs are not usually directed at a specific villain: there is no identifiable culprit responsible for the ills of the world. Either misfortune comes about by chance, or it is part of our common nature to screw things up. In this respect, Vonnegut is characteristic of the postwar generation which was the first to give up on traditional politics, and whose radicalism often took the form of a pranksterish piss-take of the entire human condition, warts and all. File him alongside *Mad* magazine, the Sex Pistols and hip cartoonist Robert Crumb.

For ten years Vonnegut struggled with a new novel called *Timequake*. Then in 1996, he gave up on it. Instead of throwing it away, however, he published this failed work alongside fragments of autobiography. One reviewer described the result as 'the ramblings of a conspicuously humane man'.

MUST READ *Player Piano, Sirens of Titan, Slaughterhouse Five*
READ ON **Philip K Dick, Joseph Heller**

V IS FOR VERBOTEN
5 novels which were initially banned on publication

LOLITA
Vladimir Nabokov

NAKED LUNCH
William S Burroughs

LADY CHATTERLEY'S LOVER
D H Lawrence

LAST EXIT TO BROOKLYN
Hubert Selby, Jr

CANDY
Terry Southern

V

a reader's guide

< 283 >

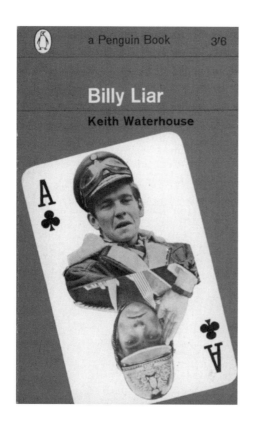

a Penguin Book   3/6

Billy Liar

Keith Waterhouse

Keith Waterhouse

1929–
The truth about not-so-Swinging Britain

Born in the Yorkshire city of Leeds, Keith Waterhouse came to prominence in 1959 with *Billy Liar*, a matter-of-fact novel about a whim-sical lad who works in an undertaker's but cannot stop fantasising about the life of glamour and adventure which he would love to be leading. In collaboration with Willis Hall, Waterhouse turned the book into a highly successful stage play (1960); in 1963 he wrote the script for the John Schlesinger film of *Billy Liar*, starring a gauche Tom Courtenay as Billy and the young Julie Christie as the love interest. By this time the gap between Billy's fantasy life and the drabness of his day-to-day existence had itself become a pertinent metaphor for the discrepancy between the quasi-mythology of an emerging Swinging London and the mundane character of real life in provincial cities that remained as conservative as they were windswept.

Waterhouse continued to write novels (*Jubb*, 1963; *Office Life*, 1978) depicting characters besieged by the merciless forces of modern life, and he carried on writing and adapting plays with Willis Hall. He also produced an apparently never-ending stream of newspaper columns, and turned the life story of the legendary Soho drinker and writer Jeffrey Bernard into a hit play of the late eighties, *Jeffrey Barnard is Unwell*. (The title is taken from the line that used to appear in the *Spectator* when the magazine's best-loved columnist was too drunk to write his piece.) But none of these has matched the combination of Northern grit and youthful lyricism which made *Billy Liar* such a success.

MUST READ *Billy Liar*
READ ON John Braine, Shelagh Delaney, David Lodge, **Alan Sillitoe**

Denton Welch

1915—1948
The aesthetics of pain

Like Mervyn Peake and J G Ballard, Maurice Denton Welch was born in China. He was sent to public school (i.e. a private school, Repton) in England, which he disliked; his first book, *Maiden Voyage* (1943), is a largely autobiographical account of a young man making his escape from the straitlaced world of cricket and chapel. Welch tended towards the Wildean tradition of the aesthete, with homoerotic tendencies to match, and his *In Youth is Pleasure* (1945) combines adolescent sexuality, angst and aestheticism in equal parts. All Welch's writing contains a note of frustration, which may well derive from his own incapacity. While an art student at Goldsmiths College in 1935, he was seriously injured in a car accident. He never fully recovered, and the progressive effects of his injuries resulted in his death in 1948 at the age of 33.

Welch's account of his accident and its prolonged aftermath, *A Voice Through a Cloud* (1950), was published after his death. In many ways it prefigures the 'illiterati' of the nineties –

the growing number of books about debilitating illness written by those who have experienced it, such as *Patient* (1995) by Ben Watt of Everything But The Girl. Except that although Welch told the tale, his life was snuffed out before it was published in full, which makes the over-ripe sensuality of his autobiographical fiction all the more heady and arresting. Welch's *Journals* (1984) are equally poignant for the same reason.

MUST READ *In Youth is Pleasure, Maiden Voyage*
READ ON **Paul Bowles**, Adam Mars-Jones, **Oscar Wilde**, Ben Watt

Irvine Welsh

1955?—
Poet laureate of the chemical generation

Irvine Welsh has kept mum about his family background, but it is common knowledge that he was born in the mid-fifties and grew up in Muirhouse, a council-housing development on the outskirts of Leith, near Edinburgh. Welsh made it to London just in time to be on the punk scene, but by the early eighties he had become more financially oriented. Moving into the property market, Welsh anticipated the boom in house prices and seems to have done fairly well out of it himself. But then he went

Irvine Welsh

for behaving like co-operative human beings in a society dominated by the narrow individualism associated with Margaret Thatcher and successive Tory governments.

Trainspotting offers a darkly humorous picaresque take on the lowlife drug culture of East Coast housing estates like Muirhouse, written largely in the local vernacular. It contains many descriptions of degradation without being degrading itself, and it set Welsh on the road to recognition as the literary voice of a generation. Stage and film versions swiftly appeared. Welsh's second novel, *Marabou Stork Nightmare* (1995) features ex-raver and former football hooligan Ray Strang, who lies motionless in a coma while his mind tracks back to all the abuse he has taken and dished out during his violent life.

Launched in a fashionable nightclub, *Ecstasy* (1997), a collection of three tales, sold 100,000 copies in three weeks. The first story follows a Thalidomide victim and her lover in their vendetta against the marketing director of the drug. 'Lorraine Goes to Livingstone' features a TV personality with a Somerset accent and a penchant for necrophilia in a relationship with an obese Romantic novelist who suffers a stroke and undergoes treatment from two nurses whose only concern is the next gig by drum'n'bass man Goldie. In 'The Undefeated', Welsh returns to the format of the first-person monologue to tell the story of Heather, a suburban housewife who leaves home and husband

back to Muirhouse to work in the local authority housing department while writing short pieces, which were published by Kevin Williamson and his Edinburgh imprint Rebel Inc. Some of them later reappeared in the novel *Trainspotting* (1993) and a collection of short stories entitled *The Acid House* (1994).

Welsh has said that his work is a fictionalised version of the impact of drugs such as Ecstasy on British society, and he maintains that 'Ecky-culture' provided one of the few avenues

< 286 >

for the rave scene.

His latest offering, *Filth* (1998), is the hilarious story of Bruce Robertson, a corrupt and sadistic Edinburgh policeman and a detestable, rancid bigot of a man who has a love of eighties heavy metal and problems with a murder case and a tapeworm.

It remains unclear whether Welsh has ever used heroin himself, but his descriptions of heroin use are generally regarded as accurate by those who do. His reputation rests, however, not so much on factual accuracy (although this helps), as on his ability to mix and match voices and genres in a manner that he himself has compared to 'mixing' on the part of DJs. Behind all the high jinks, his novels and stories usually feature a strong sense of tightening guilt and the inevitable judgement of past acts (a Scots literary tradition that stretches back to Stevenson and James Hogg): dead babies, rape, murder. In fact, in one of the *Acid House* stories, 'The Granton Star Cause', God himself appears to do a little judging.

Welsh's success has brought in its wake a whole genre of imitative fiction, as hungry publishers have grown wise to a new non-traditional readership out there (virtually uncovered by the Welsh phenomenon) who want not Aga-sagas but street-sharp tales of sex, drugs and rock'n' roll.

MUST READ *Filth, Trainspotting*
READ ON **William Burroughs**, Maxim Gorky, Hunter S Thompson, Oor Wullie, **Alexander Trocchi**

Nathanael West

1903–1940
Grotesques of the dreamers

Born Nathanael von Wallenstein Weinstein to prosperous Jewish parents, from the first West set about creating his own legend, and anglicising his name was part of that process. At Brown University in New York, he befriended writer and humorist S J Perelman (who later married West's sister), and started writing and drawing cartoons. As his cousin Nathan Wallenstein also attended Brown, West took to borrowing his work and presenting it as his own. He almost didn't graduate at all, on account of failing a crucial course in modern drama. West indulged in a little dramatics of his own and, in tearful contrition, convinced a gullible professor to upgrade his marks.

After spending a couple of years in Paris, where he wrote his first novel, *The Dream Life of Balso Snell* (1931), West returned to New York, where he mananaged (badly by all accounts) a small hotel, the Sutton, owned by his family. As well as providing free board for struggling friends like Dashiell Hammett, the job also gave West ample opportunity to observe the strange collection of misfits and

Nathanael West

its dope dealers, extras, gangsters, whores, and has-beens. All would end up in West's final masterpiece, *The Day of the Locust* (1939). It is probably the seminal California novel, a mercilessly dark comic tale of a lust for fame and success amid Hollywood's trash. The story ends in an apocalyptic mob riot outside a Hollywood première, as a star feeding-frenzy runs out of control.

West's novels are grotesque with a bleakly pessimistic view of the human condition. He caricatured America's sad and lonely dreamers (in a land of false dreams) as automata in a spiritual desert that is always teetering on the brink of panic. He was fascinated by what he called 'the secret inner life of the masses', where the power of unfulfilled desire generated by the American Dream always threatens to turn into malignant violence. Edmund Wilson appraised his damning novels as 'more finished and complete as works of art than almost anything else produced by his generation'. A friend and fellow writer, Wells Root, described West the man as 'like a large, amiable lion wandering around with a thorn in his paw. Most of the time it didn't hurt…But when he sat down to write, the paw that picked up the pen was the one with the thorn in it.'

drifters who congregated in the hotel's drugstore. Some of these would appear in West's novel *Miss Lonelyhearts* (1933), the story of an agony columnist who takes a little too much interest in his correspondents and develops a Christ complex, a brilliant allegory of America as it struggled through the Depression.

West spent the rest of his days in Hollywood, writing B-movie screenplays for small studios and immersing himself in the unglamorous underworld of Tinseltown, with

West's life ultimately ended as tragically as his fictions. Recently married, and with better-paid script work coming in, West was happy and successful. Then, returning from a trip to Mexico with his wife Eileen, he crashed his car

< 288 >

after ignoring a stop sign and killed them both. This was just one day after the death of his friend F Scott Fitzgerald.

MUST READ *The Day of the Locust, Miss Lonelyhearts*
READ ON **Joan Didion**, Steve Fisher, F Scott Fitzgerald, **Aldous Huxley**, **Gavin Lambert**, S J Perelman, **Budd Schulberg**

Oscar Wilde

1854–1900
The Wilde One

Novelist, essayist, playwright and wit, Oscar Fingal O'Flahertie Wills Wilde was born in Dublin to unconventional parents (his mother Speranza warded off creditors by reciting Aeschylus). At Trinity College, Dublin, Wilde won prizes for his Greek and a scholarship to Magdalen College, Oxford, where he shocked the pious dons with his irreverent attitude towards religion and attracted the unwelcome attention of the college hearties, who jeered at his eccentric clothes and sneered at his collection of china. But when they came to 'rag' his room, Wilde-the-aesthete threw the biggest athlete down the stairs and invited the rest of them in to drink 'a bottle of excellent brandy'. Installed in London, he declared that 'to get into Society nowadays one has either to feed people or shock people – that is all'. Wilde opted for the latter, and was soon renowned for his unique combination of charm and provocation.

To support his wife and two children, Wilde edited *Woman's World* magazine. But he began to tire of family life, even when enlivened by trips to Paris and a long-standing feud with the artist Whistler. In July 1891 Wilde met Lord Alfred Douglas ('Bosie') – not just a pretty face but an athlete and a poet too, who was to become both the love of his life ('Bosie …lies like a hyacinth on the sofa, and I worship him', Wilde wrote to a friend) and his downfall. Hounded by Lord Alfred's father, Wilde brought an unsuccessful libel action against 'the screaming, scarlet Marquess' [of Queensberry] and soon found himself on trial for 'unnatural practices'. Convicted and sentenced to two years' hard labour, Wilde emerged from prison a broken man. Exiled in Paris, he eked out an existence in hotel rooms – sometimes under an assumed name – until he died on 30 November 1900.

Wilde's comic plays, such as *Lady Windermere's Fan* (1892) and *The Importance of Being Earnest* (1895), are inventive but ultimately lightweight. The sensual *Salome* (1894; revived in the eighties in a memorable slow-motion version by Steven Berkoff) is more adventurous (so much so that the Victorian Lord Chamberlain refused permission for it to be staged in Britain), while the long poem *The*

Ballad of Reading Gaol (1898) and the essay *De Profundis* (1905; published posthumously) reflect the deeper – if harrowing – experience that Wilde underwent in prison. But the work for which he is most revered is *The Picture of Dorian Gray* (1890), the story of a beautiful young man whose face remains flawless while his portrait is pitted by the ravages of time and the debilitating effects of a degenerate lifestyle. *Dorian Gray* was influenced by the writings of the art historian Walter Pater, and by Huysmans's novel of aestheticism, *A Rebours* (1884), but more than either of these, it is Wilde's novel that has exerted the greatest influence on successive generations of beautiful young men.

With actor–novelist–broadcaster Stephen Fry in the starring role, a biopic simply entitled *Oscar* was released to great acclaim in 1997. The irony is that the very acceptance of Wilde's homosexuality has robbed him of the rebel status that he formerly enjoyed. The mainstreaming of Wilde, at a time when British cabinet ministers can be out as well as gay, even raises a question mark over his continuing cult status.

MUST READ *The Ballad of Reading Gaol, Lord Arthur Savile's Crime and Other Stories, The Picture of Dorian Gray*
READ ON **Jean Cocteau, André Gide, J K Huysmans, John Rechy**

Charles Willeford
1920–1987
Maestro of the Miami psychopath

Charles Willeford, a veteran of 20 years' army service, tank commander turned novelist, was in his sixties when *Miami Blues* (1984; his publishers were hoping to capitalise on the popularity of the Don Johnson TV series *Miami Vice*) finally brought him the success he deserved for his black comedy crime novels. By this time Willeford had developed an extremely cantankerous persona: fellow novelist James Hall used to invite him to address creative writing classes in Miami and recalls Willeford being 'extraordinarily insulting', winding up the students 'like a radio talk-show host'. In private, however, Willeford was much less confrontational.

The protagonist of Willeford's Miami novels is Hoke Moseley, homicide detective and professional slob (played by Fred Ward in the 1990 film of *Miami Blues* directed by George Armitage). His psychopathic killers (Freddy 'Junior' Frenger in *Miami Blues,* Troy Louden in *Sideswipe*, 1987) are equally engaging. Louden even defines himself, disarmingly, as a psychopath: 'I'm a professional criminal, what the shrinks call a criminal psychopath. What it means is, I know the difference between right and wrong and all that, but I don't give a shit.'

Before settling on Miami as his manor,

Willeford used southern California as the location for *The Woman Chaser* (1960). He also wrote a volume of non-fiction about soldiering, *Something about a Soldier* (1986); and a novel, *The Cockfighter* (1972), which does not fit into the detective mould. It follows the fortunes of Frank Mansfield, described by publishers Black Lizard as 'a single-minded man whose pursuit of the Cockfighter of the Year medal takes him into the seamy underbelly of Southern life'. Willeford always used an authorial voice that resembled Ernest Hemingway's, but *The Cockfighter* is the clearest demonstration of his debt to the master-artist of rampant masculinity. This goes to make Willeford's writing particularly dubious in the eyes of the political correctness police, and all the better for it.

MUST READ *The Cockfighter, Miami Blues*
READ ON Ernest Hemingway, **Carl Hiaasen**, **Elmore Leonard**, Ross MacDonald

John A Williams

1925–
The writer who cried I am

John A Williams was already 35 when his first novel, *The Angry Ones*, was published by Ace Books in 1960. Born out of Williams's experience as the publicity man for the Comet vanity press in New York, *The Angry Ones* was turned down by most of the prestigious publishing houses on the Eastern seaboard; even Ace Books, who published it as a pulp paperback, insisted on changing the title (Williams wanted it to be called *One for New York*). Williams's reputation grew with the publication of *Night Song* (1961) and *Sissie* (1963), but the novel that really made his name was *The Man who Cried I Am* (1967), the tale of two black writers, Max and Harry, who have to fight twice as hard to get half as far as their white counterparts.

Williams's subsequent work includes *This is My Country Too* (1965), a non-fiction account of a journey across America; *The Most Native of Sons* (1970), a biography of fellow black novelist Richard Wright; and a book for young people, *Africa: her history, lands and people* (1962). As a journalist, Williams has worked for *Newsweek*, *Holiday* and National Educational Television. At one time he was the editor of *Amistad*, a biennial publication dedicated to black literature, history and culture which takes its name from the slave-ship rebellion that also inspired Steven Spielberg's eponymous film.

MUST READ *The Angry Ones/One for New York, The Man who Cried I Am*
READ ON James Baldwin, Ralph Ellison, **Chester Himes, Richard Wright**

W IS FOR WAR (AND ITS AFTERMATH)

10 embattled novels

JOHNNY GOT HIS GUN
Dalton Trumbo
a limbless soldier's life in post—war
purgatory

THE THINGS THEY CARRIED
Tim O'Brien
the Hell of Nam echoes on in men's minds

CATCH 22
Joseph Heller
no way out from the crazy world of war

UNDER FIRE
Henri Barbusse
war, suffering and the self—alienation
of Man

DESPATCHES
Michael Herr
stoned rock'n'roll trip through Vietnam

ALL QUIET ON THE WESTERN FRONT
Erich Maria Remarque
war's first protest novel

SLAUGHTERHOUSE FIVE
Kurt Vonnegut
sad comedy set around the Dresden
firestorm

THE SUN ALSO RISES
Ernest Hemingway
a post—war world that's lost its balls

THE NAKED AND THE DEAD
Norman Mailer
fuggin' hell in the Pacific

IN A LONELY PLACE
Dorothy Hughes
demobbed flyer turns psycho—killer in
40s LA

< 292 >

Colin Wilson

1931–
The outsider briefly at the centre of
the in–crowd

Married with a young son, Colin Wilson was
employed in a variety of menial jobs (in a tax
office, a plastics factory, and so on) in Leicester
(his home town) and London before he hit the
literary jackpot with the publication of *The
Outsider* (a study of alienated geniuses in modern culture) by Victor Gollancz in 1956. With
his mop of hair, polo necks and oversized
glasses, Wilson was perfect press fodder. Dubbed
'the coffee-bar philosopher' and 'Britain's existentialist genius', his looks and attitude were
widely imitated (see Malcolm Bradbury's first
novel, *Eating People is Wrong*, 1959). But the
backlash was not long in coming. Wilson's second book, *Religion and the Rebel* (1957), was
met with widespread hostility, not least for its
apparent elitism. Scurrilous press coverage of
Wilson's relationship with his estranged wife
(she had returned to Leicester before the publication of *The Outsider*), and of a threatened
horse-whipping from the father of his girlfriend, who had discovered pornographic fantasies in the diaries he kept, prompted Wilson
to leave London and retire to Cornwall. He has
lived there ever since, writing prolifically and
making frequent forays into the outside world
to research and promote his numerous books.

Apart from the largely autobiographical
Adrift in Soho (1961), which describes the
period in which Wilson made his entry into literary London, most of his novels are psychological thrillers heavily laced with sex and death.
His first novel, *Ritual in the Dark* (1960) is a
case in point, as are *The Mind Parasites* (1967)
and the *Janus Murder Case* (1984). Wilson's fiction is written in a straightforward style: some
would say it is so straightforward as to be formulaic. His non-fiction, however, is highly
complex and esoteric. Since the sixties Wilson
has poured out a stream of books on murder,
UFOs and just about everything in between.
Taken as a whole, his work seems to be striving
to find a way of reconciling human spirituality
with the workaday world that we have created.
But Wilson has remained strenuously outside
any recognised method of analysis or school of
thought; while this has helped him to preserve
his intellectual independence, it also means that
he is liable to go off at a tangent at any moment.
The resulting mix is both frustrating and occasionally illuminating.

Wilson's innumerable books on true crime
and psychic phenomena reveal his skills as (to
quote Iain Sinclair), 'a paste and scissors man'.

MUST READ *Adrift in Soho, The Mind Parasites,
The Outsider, Ritual in the Dark*
READ ON **John Fowles**, John Osborne, **Derek
Raymond**

W IS FOR WILD YOUNG THINGS
15 novels about juvenile delinquents

THE OUTSIDERS by S E Hinton
growing up on the edge in Middle America

RULE OF THE BONE by Russell Banks
growing up lost in slacker culture

BLACKBOARD JUNGLE by Evan Hunter
50s urban classroom terrorists

THE TIGER AMONG US by Leigh Brackett
revenge of the vigilante

DREADFUL SUMMIT by Stanley Ellin
talks like a kid, kills like a man

THE WANDERERS by Richard Price
60s Bronx gang warfare·

TOMBOY by Hal Ellson
girl gang pulp classic

THE BAD SEED by William March
underage sweet Miss serial—killer

LORD OF THE FLIES by William Golding
the beastliness of schoolboys

THE MIDWICH CUCKOOS by John Wyndham
children are aliens underneath

LES ENFANTS TERRIBLES by Jean Cocteau
wild and free without parental authority

THE CEMENT GARDEN by Ian McEwan
the seeds of incest

HUCKLEBERRY FINN by Mark Twain
the original untamed youngster on
the run

CATCHER IN THE RYE by J D Salinger
Holden's rebellion against the phoneys

NET OF JEWELS by Ellen Gilchrist
tales of an amphetamine—fuelled rich
Southern Miss

Jeanette Winterson

1959–
The lioness of lesbianism

Jeanette Winterson's biological parents are unknown to her; she says she feels no urge to find out who they are. At the age of six weeks she was adopted by the couple who furnished her name, Winterson. Her adoptive father worked in a television factory. Jeanette grew up in a terraced house in Accrington, Lancashire, but her upbringing was not quite run-of-the-mill. The Wintersons were Elim Pentecostalists, a sect which holds that every single word in the Bible is absolutely true. 'Their God', Winterson later explained, 'is very literal – Jimmy Swaggart's God, a television evangelist's God, whose theology never deviates from the Bible and has little intellectual content.' She concluded: 'God was so tattooed on me that I can't but believe in him.'

Elim Pentecostalism is not a religion that takes kindly to lesbianism, and when Winterson, at 16, was found in bed with a female fish-filleter, she was denounced by the sect. She left home, supported herself (undertaker's assistant, a stint in an ice-cream parlour) through A levels at a nearby technical college, and refused to accept that Oxford University had rejected her. Winterson says she told the dons 'You must let me in,' and they found her a place to read English at St Catherine's College.

After graduating with a middling mark, she took a series of jobs in London: editorial assistant for Brilliance Books, a few weeks as a stockbroker, odd-jobber for Pandora Press, which published her first book. Around this time she also had sex for payment (not for money: she was paid in Le Creuset saucepans). Through literary agent Pat Kavanagh, who also became her lover, Winterson eventually found a quiet place in which to work and write – the shed at the bottom of crime novelist Ruth Rendell's garden. Half-a-dozen mostly well-received books later, she has a 'hovel' of her own, in the field behind the house in Gloucestershire that she shares with the feminist academic and broadcaster Peggy Reynolds. Winterson also owns a property in the recently revamped district of Spitalfields in east London. In 1992 she informed readers of the *Guardian*: 'Unless I take to gambling in Las Vegas, it's very unlikely I'll be poor again.' Winterson is intensely proud of having made it to the centre stage of literary life, all the way from a background that she herself regards as both culturally and materially deprived.

In the eighties, Winterson was prolific. Her juvenilia are the comic novel *Boating for Beginners* (1985; secondhand copies now fetch a hundred pounds) and a fitness manual, *Fit for the Future* (1986). The novel that made her name is *Oranges Are Not the Only Fruit* (1985; subsequently televised), which Winterson has insisted is not autobiographical but which most reviewers interpreted as a thinly veiled account of her own formative years. It won the Whitbread Award for a first novel.

The protagonist of *The Passion* (1987) is a bisexual, web-footed daughter of a 19th-century Venetian gondolier; it was awarded the John Llewellyn Rhys Prize. *Sexing the Cherry* (1989), another novel of lesbian love, won the E M Forster Award. The explicitly erotic *Written on the Body* (1992) features a narrator whose gender is 'ambiguous' (but without a penis), and was widely assumed to be a disguised account of Winterson's own amorous adventures. In 1995 Winterson published a collection of essays (*Art Objects: essays on ecstasy and effrontery*). *Gut Symmetries* (1997), a love triangle involving two women and a man, set on board the *QE2* passenger liner, was the first Winterson novel to receive a host of unfavourable reviews. In 1998 she completed a collection of short stories and worked on a film script of *The Passion* for the production company Miramax.

Winterson has been criticised for writing almost exclusively about her own milieu. 'Her true understanding of the human heart is confined to passionate love between women – spirited, beautiful women at that,' complained one reviewer. Her extraordinary self-confidence has also prompted criticism. When asked to name the living writer she liked best, Winterson replied: 'No one working in the English language now comes close to my exuberance, my passion and fidelity to words.' Modest she

< 296 >

ain't; but her supporters – and they are legion – maintain she has the talent to back up her arrogance. Joan Bakewell believes that even when she makes a 'mess of a book' (*Gut Symmetries*), Winterson is still 'scintillating…a real writer'. On the other hand the novelist and critic Allan Massie felt it was 'sad that she should bury her talent beneath a froth of pretentious verbiage'. He also compared her to Hemingway in that 'in the past few years she has become more famous for what she is, and is taken to represent, than for what she writes'. But in Winterson's case, perhaps the 'froth' and the 'talent' are inseparable.

MUST READ *Oranges Are Not the Only Fruit, The Passion, Sexing The Cherry*
READ ON **Kathy Acker, Radclyffe Hall**, Virginia Woolf

Thomas Wolfe

1900—1938
Epic autobiographer or editor's nightmare?

Wolfe was born in Asheville, North Carolina, into a large family. His father was an alcoholic stonecutter who sculpted gravestones for a living; his mother ran a boarding house. He was educated at the University of Northern Carolina and at Harvard. He moved to New

York where he taught and wrote several minor plays which were seen by Aline Bernstein, a stage designer and actress, who soon embarked on a tempestuous affair with the young writer and encouraged him to complete his first novel, *Look Homeward, Angel* (1929), published just six days before the Wall Street Crash started the Depression.

As with his next book, *Of Time and the River* (1935), it was autobiographical and based on his early days in the South: 'All serious work is autobiographical…The book was written in simpleness and nakedness of soul…It is a book made out of my life, and represents my vision of my life to my twentieth year.'

The books were far from simple in form, however, and consisted of vast manuscripts, which Scribners editor Maxwell Perkins (the editorial genius behind F Scott Fitzgerald and Ernest Hemingway) honed into shape, virtually co-writing them. (In Wolfe's posthumous novel, *You Can't Go Home Again*, author George Webber declares: 'I've got too much material …It keeps backing up on me until sometimes I wonder what in the name of God I'm going to do with it all.') This unwieldy process and the resultant relationship with Perkins was described in Wolfe's 1936 book, *Story of a Novel*.

Although he died of influenza in 1938, Wolfe left behind numerous manuscripts, which were fashioned by editor Edward C Aswell into two last novels: *The Web and the Rock* (1939), and the classic *You Can't Go Home Again* (1940). The latter describes the outrage of his Asheville neighbours as they began to recognise themselves in his fiction.

Some see his work as unstructured and repetitious, while others feel it has an incantory, stream-of-consciousness power. Its gargantuan autobiographical desire to passionately embrace all life makes him in some senses a progenitor of the Beats and of Kerouac in particular.

MUST READ *Look Homeward, Angel*
READ ON Theodore Dreiser, F Scott Fitzgerald, **Jack Kerouac**, John O'Hara

Tom Wolfe

1931–

From New Journalism darling to Balzac on Viagra

Wolfe was educated at Washington and Lee Universities and also at Yale, where he received a PhD in American studies. Moving to New York in 1962, he wrote for the *Washington Post* and the *New York Herald Tribune*.

His first collection, The *Kandy-Kolored Tangerine-Flake Streamline Baby* appeared in 1965, and along with Truman Capote's *In Cold Blood*, published the same year, heralded the arrival of the 'New Journalism', a style which, in keeping with the times, blurred the lines between reality and fiction.

< 297 >

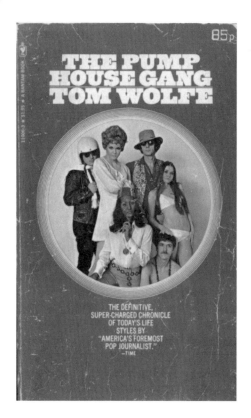

In his introduction, Wolfe explained how the eponymous article had originally been commissioned by *Esquire* magazine as a standard piece of reportage. But try as he might, Wolfe found that he could not write about Young America and its customised culture in an old-fashioned way. He virtually abandoned the piece, and started typing a memo to *Esquire* editor Byron Dobell explaining why. Hours later,

< 298 >

Wolfe was still writing. Dobell ran the memo as a major feature – and New Journalism was born.

His next book, *The Electric Kool-Aid Acid Test* (1968), was a blow-by-blow account of Ken Kesey and the Merry Pranksters, an LSD-fuelled commune-on-wheels in California in the mid-sixties. Wolfe, who even at his most flamboyant, was essentially a serious writer, saw Kesey's psychedelic Shangri-La for what it was: 'It gradually began to dawn on me that this was a religious group, a religion in its primary phrase…a religion based in large part on LSD.' (Wolfe's take on the whole phenomenon may have been influenced by the fact that he actually took the drug, for research reasons: 'It scared the hell out of me. It was like tying yourself to a railroad track to see how big the train is. It was pretty big. I would never do it again.')

Wolfe continued to write about the counterculture, but became even more critical of its radical postures. In 1979, he published *The Right Stuff*, a dazzling exposé of the deification of astronauts, and of test pilot Chuck Yeager in particular. It was filmed in 1983 starring Sam Shepard, ex-drummer from The Band, Levon Helm and, in a cameo role as a bartender, Chuck Yeager himself.

Wolfe's debut novel *The Bonfire of the Vanities* (1988) is a take on Thackeray's *Vanity Fair* set in New York during the yuppified eighties. It was accompanied by a declaration from Wolfe to the effect that writers should stop writing about writing and get out there as writer/reporters (in the manner of Zola and Dickens) and tell it like it is. Although Wolfe's own novel is more cartoon than naturalism, it certainly gets the flavour of a Big Apple split into ethnic fragments. His big follow-up, *A Man in Full* (1998) – ten years in the making, set amid Atlanta city politics, continues the grand stylistic sweep of his debut and was described by one reviewer as 'the sort of thing Balzac would be dishing up if he had made it into the Viagra era.'

MUST READ *The Bonfire of the Vanities, The Electric Kool-Aid Acid Test, The Right Stuff*
READ ON **Truman Capote, E L Doctorow,**

Tobias Wolff

1945–
Dirty realist and compulsive liar

Born in Birmingham, Alabama, Tobias Wolff was raised with his elder brother (and also author-to-be) Geoffrey, following their father, the self-styled Arthur Wolff III, all over America as he drifted in and out of work with a number of aircraft companies, each one taken in by his phony qualifications from good universities – Yale, even the Sorbonne (where he had apparently studied aeronautics, despite them having no department in that subject).

The family split up when Wolff was ten. He stayed with his mother; Geoffrey went to Seattle with their father, whose outrageously fictitious CV had been swallowed by Boeing, who had offered him a job. Wolff's life for the next eight years was chronicled in his brilliant memoir *This Boy's Life* (1989), in which Tobias soon picks up his father's gift for the tall tale. Dwight, his mother's second husband, who beats both mother and son, is eventually arrested for attempting to strangle his wife: 'By the time I got home Dwight had been arrested. He was standing outside with my mother and two cops, staring at the ground, the lights of the cruiser flashing across his face.' Geoffrey's side of the family adventure is brilliantly told in his book about their father, *Duke of Deception* (1979).

In 1964 Wolff joined the army and became a paratrooper, serving in Vietnam until 1968. He drew heavily on his experiences for his novella *The Barracks Thief* (1984) and his memoirs *In Pharoah's Army* (1994).

When he was discharged, Wolff resumed his education at Oxford and Stanford universities, and started writing stories. Since then he has published three collections. His stories are often overshadowed by his autobiographical works, but they are modern gems, tautly crafted, in the mould of Raymond Carver and Richard Ford.

MUST READ *The Barracks Thief, This Boy's Life*

< 299 >

READ ON **Raymond Carver**, Richard Ford, Geoffrey Wolff

Cornell Woolrich

1903—1968
Hard—boiled poet of grim fate

Woolrich's parents separated when he was a child, and he went to live with his father in Mexico. He was taken, aged eight, to see *Madame Butterfly*, his first experience of glamour and tragedy, and he realised that, like the opera's heroine, he too would die, leaving him with an overriding sense of doom. As he said in his autobiography: 'I had that trapped feeling, like some…insect…inside a downturned glass, and it tries to climb up the sides, and it can't, and it can't, and it can't.'

He returned to New York and enrolled at Columbia, where he took classes in journalism and novel writing. His friends considered him shy and utterly dominated by his mother. He started writing when an infected heel left him bedridden for six weeks; he finished a first draft of a novel, which was published in 1926 as *Cover Charge*. (The protagonist, in love with two women much older than himself, was left alone, in a cheap hotel room, with both women dead, contemplating suicide: 'I hate the world. Everything comes in it so clean and goes out so dirty.')

His second novel was bought by Hollywood and Woolrich went out to write the script. During this time, he was married, but the marriage, never consummated, was annulled and he returned home to his mother. He started writing suspense stories and selling them to the pulps. (He also wrote under the names William Irish and George Hopley.) Soon he was writing crime novels, including what the French called his *série noire* (black series): *The Bride Wore Black* (1940), *The Black Curtain* (1941), *Black Alibi* (1942), *The Black Angel* (1943), *The Black Path of Fear* (1944), *Rendezvous in Black* (1948). Many of these were filmed or adapted for radio, the most famous being Hitchcock's *Rear Window*, starring James Stewart and Grace Kelly. His fine plotting made him perfect for Hollywood; Raymond Chandler thought him 'the best idea man' in the business. However, Woolrich has been criticised for the frequently heavy-handed melodrama of his prose, which comes a pale second next to the streetwise naturalism of a Hammett. Woolrich's characters are invariably innocent victims, impotent in the face of bizarre and malevolent twists of fate – situations that reflected Woolrich's own doomed view of the human condition.

Woolrich wrote little after 1948, the start of his mother's lengthy illness. She died in 1957, and his output grew more sporadic. By then he was diabetic and an alcoholic, living out of hotel rooms, starting stories he never finished. He developed gangrene in his leg, which was left unchecked until his leg had to be amputated. When he died of a stroke he left two unfinished novels, an autobiography and scores of titles for stories not even started, including the prophetic *First You Dream, Then You Die*.

Woolrich had come a long way, from an infected heel to an amputated leg, and he had left behind a dark, dark legacy.

MUST READ The *Série Noir* novels
READ ON Lawrence Block, **James M Cain,**
Edgar Allan Poe

Richard Wright

1908–1960
Native son who lived in exile

Born on a plantation in Natchez, Mississippi, Richard Nathaniel Wright was the eldest son of an illiterate sharecropper and a schoolteacher. He spent much of his early life moving around Mississippi and Arkansas because of his mother's constant state of ill health and his father's eternal search for work. Although forced to leave school to find work, Wright rejoined later and did well. His spare-time jobs enabled Wright to buy schoolbooks, pulp magazines, and dime novels, all of which he read avidly.

He moved to Chicago and joined the John Reed Club, a literary organisation funded by the Communist Party, which he also joined. He wrote poems, and stories for *New Masses* and similar left-wing publications. All of this formed the basis for his finest novel, *Native Son*, published in 1940 to massive acclaim. It sold 215,000 copies in three weeks, was made into a play (directed by Orson Welles) and eventually a film, with Wright not only scripting it, but acting in it also. It was the uncompromising tale of Bigger Thomas, a black man growing up in the Chicago slums who accidently kills a wealthy white woman.

Wright moved to Paris, where he was feted. Like other black American writers he adopted it as his spiritual home and a sanctuary from the institutionalised racism back in the USA. An autobiographical novel, *Black Boy*, was published in 1945 to rave reviews, but was denounced as obscene by the senator of Mississipi, despite (or perhaps because of) being a bestseller. Wright helped the 20-year-old James Baldwin to win a prestigious literary fellowship, and Baldwin repaid him four years later by criticising the tactics of *Native Son* in his career-launching essay 'Everybody's Protest Novel'.

Influenced in Paris by Sartre and Camus, Wright produced an existential novel, *The Outsider* (1953), which sold relatively poorly. Ill health, financial troubles and political strife (he was worried about being deported by the French, while the US government and the FBI were investigating his communist beliefs), all took their toll, and Wright died in 1960 of a heart attack while being treated for intestinal pains.

When Wright wrote *Native Son*, he knew he was producing an entirely radical work, something America had never seen before. His first book, *Uncle Tom's Children* (1938), had been 'a book that even bankers' daughters could read and feel good about'. He realised that his next work would be powerful, without sentiment. He would ensure that 'no one would weep over it; that it would be so hard and deep that they would have to face it without the consolation of tears'. Like all classics, the book took on a life of its own, independent of the author. 'There are meanings in my books of which I was not aware until they literally spilled out upon the paper.'

MUST READ *Black Boy, Native Son*
READ ON James Baldwin, **Albert Camus**, Ralph Ellison, Langston Hughes, **Chester Himes**, Donald Goines

W   IS FOR WEIRD SEX
5 novels of the perverse

NAKED LUNCH
William S Burroughs
sex, shitting and strangulation

JUSTINE
Marquis De Sade
sex, pain and philosophy

VENUS IN FURS
Leopold von Sacher Masoch
sex, self-inflicted pain and philosophy

GUIDE
Dennis Cooper
sex, pain and a maternal porn director

THE STORY OF THE EYE
Georges Bataille
the agony and the ecstasy – sex, death and surrealism

< 302 >

Rudolph Wurlitzer

1938–
Hollywood maverick

Apparently the great-grandson of the man who founded the famous music company (although he claimed that his grandfather made the money, his father spent it, and he was left with nothing), little is known of Wurlitzer's early days other than that he was born in Texas, a situation he maintains through his enigmatic aloofness.

His first novel, *Nog*, appeared in 1969 and was published in Britain as *The Octopus*, a surreal and apocalyptic tale, as was *Flats* (1970), a nightmarish story set in the marshlands west of the ruins of an unidentified city, narrated by a protagonist of unknown and inconstant identity. Novelist Thomas Pynchon praised both the book and its author: 'Very important in an evolutionary way, showing us directions we could be moving in. Rudolph Wurlitzer is really, really good.'

Wurlitzer's 1972 novel *Quake*, set in California, was similar to Nathanael West's writing, in that the earthquake was merely an agent to start the crumbling of society's fragile structure.

For most of the seventies Wurlitzer worked in Hollywood, writing screenplays. His 1971 play *2 Lane Blacktop* was filmed by maverick producer Monte Hellman (executive producer of *Reservoir Dogs*), starring Warren Oates with singer James Taylor and Beach Boy (and Charles Manson fan) Dennis Wilson. In 1973 he wrote the screenplay for Sam Peckinpah's revisionist Western *Pat Garrett and Billy the Kid*, starring Kris Kristofferson and Bob Dylan (perhaps because of his background, he liked having singers in his films).

Slow Fade (1984), was the story of Wesley Hardin, director of 37 films, a 'man who cornered the market in Westerns', now in his declining years, oblivious to the fact that 'everybody says he should check into the puzzle factory'. It was a brilliant look at the tenuous gap between reality and celluloid, and was obviously influenced by his years in the Hollywood marketplace. The journalist and novelist Michael Herr said of it: '*Slow Fade* comes out of the space between real life and the movies and closes it up for good. A great book: beautiful, funny, and dangerous.'

MUST READ *Quake*
READ ON David Llewellyn Burdett, **Robert Stone, Nathanael West**